Language and Verbal Art Revisited

Language and Verbal Art Revisited

Linguistic approaches to the study of literature

Edited by
Donna R. Miller and
Monica Turci

LONDON   OAKVILLE

Published by
Equinox Publishing Ltd.
UK: Unit 6, The Village, 101 Amies Street, London, SW11 2JW
USA: DBBC, 28 Main Street, Oakville, CT 06779
www.equinoxpub.com

First published 2007
© 2007, Donna R. Miller, Monica Turci and contributors

British Library Cataloguing-in-Publication Data
A catalogue record for this book is available from the British Library.

ISBN 9781845530945 (Hardback)

Library of Congress Cataloging-in-Publication Data
Language and verbal art revisited : linguistic approaches to the study of literature / edited by Donna R. Miller and Monica Turci.
    p. cm.
  Includes bibliographical references and index.
  ISBN 1-84553-094-2 (hb)
1. Philology, Modern. I. Miller, D. R. (Donna R.) II. Turci, Monica.
PB41.L362006
410--dc22
               2006000055

Typeset by Catchline, Milton Keynes (www.catchline.com)
Printed and bound in Great Britain and the USA.

Contents

List of contributors

Jean-Michel Adam is from the University of Lausanne
Mirella Agorni is from the Catholic University of the Sacred Heart of Milan
Anne Betten is from the University of Salzburg
David Butt is from Macquarie University, Sydney
Ruqaiya Hasan is from Macquarie University, Sydney
Ute Heidmann is from the University of Lausanne
Bill Louw is from the University of Zimbabwe
Donna R. Miller is from the University of Bologna
María José Rodrigo Mora is from the University of Bologna
Sandro M. Moraldo is from the University of Bologna
Carol Taylor Torsello is from the University of Padua
Monica Turci is from the University of Bologna

Acknowledgements

The editors and publishers wish to thank the following for permission to use copyright material:

Marina Warner, for her personal and enthusiastic consent to reproduce the extract from her (1993) *The Mermaids in the Basement*. London: Chatto and Windus.

Feridun Zaimoğlu, for having eagerly given us complete freedom to cite from any of the following works:

> (1995) *Kanak Sprak. 24 Mißtöne vom Rande der Gesellschaft*. Hamburg: Rotbuch.

> (1997) *Abschaum. Die wahre Geschichte von Ertan Ongun*. Hamburg: Rotbuch.

> (1998) *Koppstoff. Kanaka Sprak vom Rande der Gesellschaft*. Hamburg: Rotbuch.

> (2000) *Liebesmale, scharlachrot*. Hamburg: Rotbuch.

> (2001) *Kopf und Kragen. Kanak-Kultur-Kompendium*. Frankfurt am Main: S. Fischer.

Edwin Thumboo, for willingly giving his personal permission to cite his poem 'Steel', which was privately published in his 1956 volume, *Rib of Earth* (Singapore).

Faber and Faber Ltd., for their kind permission to reproduce the following poems by Wallace Stevens, taken from *The Collected Poems of Wallace Stevens* (1955):

> 'Thirteen Ways of Looking at a Blackbird', 'Metaphors of a Magnifico', 'Tea at the Palaz of Hoon', 'Tattoo', 'The Load of Sugar-Cane', 'Late Hymn from the Myrrh Mountain', 'Dry Loaf', 'Men Made Out of Words'.

Used by permission of Alfred A. Knopf, a division of Random House, Inc.:

> 'Thirteen Ways of Looking at a Blackbird', copyright 1923 and renewed 1951 by Wallace Stevens, 'Metaphors of a Magnifico', 'Tea at the Palaz of Hoon', 'Tattoo', 'The Load of Sugar-Cane', 'Late Hymn from the Myrrh-Mountain', 'Dry Loaf', 'Men Made Out of Words', from THE COLLECTED POEMS OF WALLACE STEVENS by Wallace Stevens, copyright 1954 by Wallace Stevens and renewed 1982 by Holly Stevens.

Harper Collins Publishers, for their kind permission to reproduce the poem 'Fixed Ideas' by Kenneth Slessor, taken from *Kenneth Slessor. Selected Poems* (1988).

Every effort has been made to trace all the relevant copyright holders, but if any have been inadvertently overlooked, the publishers will be pleased to make the necessary arrangement at the first opportunity.

Introduction

Donna R. Miller and Monica Turci

1 Linguistic approaches to the study of literature: a look at how we got here and at how we're positioned

What we'd like to do in this introduction to the volume is to, firstly, give a general schematic overview which very briefly traces some of the major approaches to literature that have played a role in bringing us to where we are today regarding the linguistic analysis of verbal art. At the same time, we will make clear where we stand on the disputes surrounding that approach and argue the case for such analysis as a socio-cultural practice, or a special brand of 'stylistics'.[1] Here we also raise issues with no pretence at adequately defining their contours or resolving their problematics. Nor, despite the influence of much past and present work on the linguistic approach to verbal art, is it our intention in this short introduction to minutely map out the development of any one movement and its proponents. In the second place, we want to talk a bit about what our contributors do, the literature they do it to, and the models they do it with. We also hope to show some ways in which the essays in this volume make an original contribution to this field of research.

Notwithstanding this premise, some small space should, we feel, be given to certain milestones on the path to the linguistic analysis of literature. The Formalists are among these, not least because of fact that they are cited and made use of, or at the very least seriously reckoned with, by stylisticians even today. They are, indeed, generally seen as being precursors in applying a modern linguistic analysis to the literature text.[2]

It's been over 80 years since, in the 1920s, a small group of Soviet critics, Shklovsky, Mukarovsky, and Jakobson (the latter afterwards in the Prague Linguistic Circle) among them, initiated what has been defined as an only '[…] superficially purely aesthetic approach to literature […]' (Lemon and Reis, 1965: xv). Their work has in fact conditioned much of the way in which literature has been seen, studied and spoken about throughout the twentieth century. Another Soviet critic, Bakhtin, might also be mentioned: a social theorist working in the 1930s, whose writings were rediscovered in the 1970s and immediately and enthusiastically appropriated by both linguists and literary critics alike. It is to his credit that he, unlike the Formalists, placed at the centre of his work the socially-based, diverse nature of, firstly, voices (what he called *heterophony*), then, of languages (*heteroglossia*), and finally, of discursive types (*heterology*) (Todorov, 1984: 56). His work on dialogism was also a seminal early version of an equally popular critical theory among both linguists and literary critics: intertextuality, despite what can be critiqued as his insufficient attention to the relations between text and context (cf. Hasan, 1992). But more particularly, many of the textual devices these scholars theorised have played, and still play, a role of paramount importance in the theory and analysis of the use of language in verbal art. These include, for instance: (1) Shklovsky's (1917 [1965]) notion of *defamiliarisation*, or 'making strange' and 'new' again what has been de-lexicalised, i.e. become so habitual that its inherent meaning has been lost; (2) Mukarovsky's (1932 [1964]) *foregrounding* and *de-automatisation*, the first of which refers to a contrast between a textual 'background' and more prominent patterns which emerge as fundamental to articulating a text's deepest meanings; the second of which is a question of the lack of the correspondences typically obtaining between context and text that literature displays; and (3) Jakobson's *poetic function*, and what he defined as its empirical evidence, *grammatical parallelism* (1960, 1966, 1968), consisting in a reiteration of elements of grammar, from the phoneme and morpheme to all higher ranks of syntactic construction, a repetition whose ultimate significance is seen as being the contemporaneous semantic parallelism these construe.

The Formalists and neo-Formalists acquired the reputation, however, in both literary and even some linguistic circles, of simply limiting the scope of stylistic inquiry *too* much. They were not the only ones doing this of course. The New Critics, whose hey day was in the 1940s and 1950s, also separated their analyses from history, sociology and philosophy, avoiding discussions of anything but the analysis of the structure of the text. The theory of such 'close reading' was further popularised in the work of the best known of these critics, F. R. Leavis.[3]

In the meantime, linguistics itself, as Fowler (1981: 13–14) relates, was making steps forward that had an influence on stylistics as well. The terminology of American Structuralism, rooted in the work of Sapir and Bloomfield in the 1920s and 1930s (e.g Sapir, 1921; Bloomfield, 1933), was what was used in the earliest stylistic descriptions in the 1950s. Then came Chomsky's revolutionary *Syntactic Structures* (1957), and his subsequent work, which, in our opinion, muddied the critical waters even more, by circumscribing the field of inquiry still further, despite his criticism of the American Structuralists for the limitations of their model as an instrument of analysis. His Transformational Generative Grammar (TG) became a new tool for stylisticians and gave rise to a generative stylistics, enthusiastically embraced by many, including Fowler himself (1981), Kress and Hodge (1979), and many doctoral students in their dissertations during the 1960s and 1970s. However, as Fowler himself had to admit, TG doesn't explain variation in structure; nor does it concern itself with the functions of language or relate linguistic structure to social context, all of which adds up to a startling deficiency in an instrument for linguistic criticism, as Functionalists were quick to point out. These were basically neo-Firthians (see Firth, 1957 [1968]) who embraced Malinowski's theory of 'context of situation' and 'context of culture' (1923).[4] The social semiotic perspective is an essential development in this same neo-Firthian tradition (see Hasan, this volume). However, its roots are, interestingly, actually in the work of the Russian Formalists and Prague Linguistic Circle.

But whatever the descriptive-analytical framework proposed, in a real sense a re-discovery was taking place. As Fowler (1971: 9) notes, the history of 'linguistic' approaches to literature can be said to be a very long one: from Sanskrit Indian grammarians' attempts to preserve the language of the Vedic religious texts, through the philological scholarship which in the nineteenth century, he notes, was directly influenced by the contemporary rediscovery of those same grammarians. Jakobson too laments that even:

> The ancient and medieval theory of poetry had an inkling of poetic grammar and was prone to discriminate between lexical tropes and grammatical figures (*figurae verborum*), but these sound rudiments were later lost. (Jakobson, 1968: 602)

In any case, as the century went on, linguistic criticism, of whatever persuasion, seemed fated to set itself up in competition with the literary criticism. As Fowler notes, 'It is only in this century [the twentieth] that linguistics and literary studies have lost their *inter*dependence' (1971: 9, our emphasis), a rather surprising announcement in a way, as one tends to see the late twentieth century at least as the site of an at times impassioned *agon* for pre-eminence between linguistic stylistics on one hand, and, on the other, a myriad variety of lit-crit angles which contend with, but are basically tolerant of, each other. And this was, and continues to be, the case. After all, it was one thing to smile on linguistic attention to texts in 'dead' languages, and quite another to concede equal dignity to a linguistic approach to thriving modern and contemporary literature. Still, in an effort to resist unfairness, we might ponder what de Beaugrande wrote in 1993:

> It would be unjustified to attribute this divergence to mere feelings of mutual rivalry, insecurity or mistrust. Instead, the two domains [linguistic and literary criticism] have differed so fundamentally in their traditional conceptions and directions that immediate interaction has been difficult on purely logistic grounds. (de Beaugrande, website version: 1)

However, conceding such logistic grounds, and the intrinsic difficulties for even peaceful coexistence they create, will not close the gap. This was, indeed, the global import of the famous Fowler-Bateson controversy, played out in the pages of *Essays in Criticism* during the 1960s: never the two viewpoints could meet (reprinted in Fowler, 1971). Notwithstanding, there is to our minds no cause for renouncing the legitimate challenge contained in the claim that '[…] in verbal art the role of language is central. Here language is not as clothing to the body; it IS the body' (Hasan, 1985: 91, our emphasis). The declaration immediately, if provocatively, delineates the terms of the struggle and the strategic position of the linguist. The main message of this volume is, precisely, this. In addition, any true 'appraisal' of the meanings of the literature text must *always* address that language with reference to the text's specific 'context of creation', and of culture (Hasan, 1985: 101ff.). This is the second, equally essential message of the volume. To rephrase the title of Fowler's volume (1981), literature *is* social discourse.

Though this last assertion may be accepted by most scholars who see their work as the study of literature, the linguistic perspective is still neither generally established nor a welcome one in the main. But perhaps we should ask ourselves more precisely what, for us, a 'linguistic', or 'stylistic' approach to literature consists in, and why is it felt to pose such a threat to other critical approaches of verbal art? The answer may partially lie in the modifier of the expression just used: *verbal* art. The attention of the language scholar focuses primarily on the raw material of the text, its language, or better the specific functions of its language, without which s/he firmly believes it would not be literature. Of course, many non-linguistic scholars would be the first to deny that they did *not* concern themselves with language. They might even be convinced that they are telling the truth. But they should be invited to meditate on the following unmistakeable assertion of the paramount role of linguistic analysis for verbal art:

> [..] it may be said that stylistics is concerned solely with verbal art as art, not as history, cultural evidence, philosophy or catalyst of change; even though a study of any of the angles mentioned above will always lead to a greater understanding of the work *in toto*, its understanding as *art* requires the techniques of stylistics. (Hasan, 1975: 60, our emphasis)

The statement may seem confrontational, at least to those scholars who eschew stylistics and yet feel they are indeed addressing literature as artistic expression. However, together with this inflexible defence of linguistic stylistics, it seems to us that the need for an interdisciplinary dialogue is equally being admitted, if one is to move towards a thorough understanding of the text in its historical, cultural, philosophical and even revolutionary character. It seems that we've come, in a way, full circle. The Formalists, who advocated the divorce of literature from politics, did so in the service of the interests of a language-based approach. Today, however, a language-based approach that is genuinely interested in the functions of language has to bring the political, the social, and all these imply, back in.

Hasan's voice is not an isolated one of course. Many other scholars, albeit working from different perspectives to which they carefully hold, have also raised their voices in language-based appeals. The volume edited by Fabb et al. (1987) on the *Linguistics of Writing* is a good example of such polyphony. In this collection, the proceedings of a conference that confronted the mid-1980s state of the language-literature art in a socio-political context, Hasan's own argumentative piece, 'Directions from structuralism' (Hasan, 1987), rubs shoulders with those of scholars such as the like-minded Halliday, applied linguist Widdowson, stylistician Banfield, literary critic Fish, but also of Marxist cultural theorists like Williams and Jameson. The contributions to the present volume, however, are more consistent in their belief that the methods of linguistic analysis are entirely appropriate in the literature domain.

The controversy over the nature of verbal art, how it is to be studied, but also how it is to be taught, and thus institutionalised, is a heated one still today without a doubt and shows no sign of cooling down. At least as far as linguistic vs. non-linguistic approaches goes, this is probably as it still must be, as there isn't much room for 'compromise'. This is not to abandon all hope for some way to identify and explore areas of common interest, in an attempt to foster cooperation rather than conflict among diverse schools of thought. Such indeed was the admirable aim of the Journal of the Poetics and Linguistics Association (PALA), *Language and Literature*, when it first started publication back in 1992. But although it succeeded in offering a site for papers doing linguistic criticism and stylistic analysis and acting as a forum for the open discussion of the many issues involved in these fields, the lit crits stayed away. The time would seem to be not yet ripe. Yet, despite this, somehow, sometimes, and in some places, teachers and researchers do manage to negotiate not a few interdisciplinary hurdles.

2 The authors and their papers: a look at what they do, what they do it to, and how they do it

The editors of, and contributors to, this volume all firmly underwrite Hasan's opinion on linguistics being *the* proper tool for studying literature as art. At the same time, however, they have diverse provenances, culturally and as scholars: a virtue in our opinion, which has made for the richness of their papers and of the volume as a whole.

The authors had come together for a symposium in Bologna, Italy in September 2004 to share their work and exchange views. The debate at the end of that two-day conference was a lively and fruitful one. One of the questions addressed was indeed, though hardly new, still fundamental: What *is* literature, and why/how is it somehow 'different' from other text-types? Contrasting, but not for that wholly incompatible, opinions ranged from: literature is whatever a culture considers literature to be vs. literature is text whose meanings successfully, and lastingly, articulate a generalisation on the nature of social existence. It was also noted that such a generalisation might be exactly what a specific culture values in, and institutionalises as, its literature, as well as the fact that many belief and value systems have been, are and will continue to be cross-cultural, if not universal. In any case, as the following quote brings home, the question continues to be a thorny one: '[…] the paradox of 'poetic' language [is] that there is no such thing […] but we can all recognize it when we see it' (Halliday, 1982: 134).

For all that, the participants also had to admit the problem of defining the language in literature as distinct from language in other text types, something further complicated by the co-existence of all sorts of languages and genres in verbal art itself. This was generally recognised, but one strong opinion was that, rather than concentrate on the kinds of language or even genres possible in language in literature, or even on the 'virtual universe' this creates, what needs to be engaged with is *how* the text articulates that universe and the events within that universe, and how it makes these *act* as a manifestation of, if you will, some profound 'philosophical' proposition.

Another question, not unlinked to the preceding one, regarded the idea of context and its importance for the literature text, which no voice denied. What emerged were various, but again not irreconcilable, ways of defining 'context'. All apparently agreed that the literature text had two orders of context: that from which it came, its 'real' context of creation (call it a Malinowskian 'context of situation' and/or 'culture', or a 'pragmatic' one),[5] and that which it created, as fiction. It was rightfully stressed, however, that context in verbal art has a primacy that may not be quite as apparent in the linguistic criticism of other text types. In short, all language arises out of a context (and Halliday and

Hasan, 1980, was cited on this particular point), but the feeling was that there is a special need for coherent forms of contextual involvement on the part of the linguistic critic of the literature text.

Finally, the act of reading was rightly and readily acknowledged to involve its own complex problematics. Some participants clearly felt that space needed to be given to readers' responses and their negotiation with the meanings of the text; others felt that there were 'better' ways of reading, ones that could be articulated and made 'public', externalised. In any case, as Butt judiciously puts it (this volume): '[…] we interpret by informed and artful inference – by reading off the choices that must have gone into making the text'. This means, however, that readers must be trained to do this. Better ways might also include attempts to put aside one's own subjective cultural paradigm and intuitive reactions, to be able to better enter into the work, across temporal but also cultural distance, as the author understood it. Such an endeavour would make one a 'model reader' in Eco's terms (1979), or a 'super-receiver', in Bakhtin's (in Todorov, 1984: 110). The editors are among those who believe in such 'better' ways.

In a diachronic perspective, we see this volume as following in the tradition of the collections which came out of the 1958 'Conference on Style', held in Indiana (Sebeok, 1960) and the 1986 Glasgow conference on the 'Linguistics of Writing' (Fabb et al., 1987). As these did, for their times, it would access the current state of the art and even point to the future directions which that art might take in the twenty-first century. However, unlike these, on the whole the contributions address the epistemological and ontological questions rather more implicitly, as the volume's primary concern is to offer illustrations of current possibilities for application. Practice, however, is never seen as being separable from theory.

Focusing on a wide range of world literatures and literary genres, the authors often boldly cross what are still institutionally rigid boundaries between disciplines. This we see as a positive aspect of the volume. Indeed, one of the book's principle aspirations is to provide a variety of applications of theoretical and methodological approaches, all firmly rooted, however, in specific contexts of culture, a belief in the importance of which the contributors all share, as we've said. This means that the papers all espouse a context-rooted linguistic approach to the literature text as primary, albeit working within various linguistic frameworks. Their tools for analysis explicitly interweave stylistics with descriptive-analytical models such as: Systemic Functional Linguistics in a social semiotic perspective (Hasan; Miller; Butt; Turci; Taylor Torsello); pragmatics (Betten; Moraldo), comparative textual discourse analysis (Agorni; Heidmann and Adam); corpus linguistics (Turci; Taylor Torsello; Louw), but also gender (Heidmann and Adam; Betten) and translation studies (Heidmann and Adam; Agorni), as well as the history of ideas (Butt and Rodrigo Mora in particular). The end result is a variety of 'stylistics', if you will, including the functional, pragmatic, comparative, corpus-based or driven, gender and translation types. Also addressed are pedagogical issues (Hasan; Agorni) and philosophical-critical ones, such as the very nature of language and meaning (Hasan; Butt; Rodrigo Mora). No paper eschews sociological and/or anthropological concerns.

Concerning their linguistics, there is a shared focus on micro-structure, as well as an equally important concern with macro-structure and the extra-linguistic plane. Centripetally, the papers analyse elements of morphology, of lexicogrammar, or lexis and syntax, as you will (e.g. transitivity, clause expansion and projection, personal pronouns and vocatives, grammatical parallelism, thematic structure, etc.) and the semantics of these (e.g. respectively, experiential and logical representation, interpersonal status and power relations, meaning reiteration, method of meaning development, etc.). And, on the extra-linguistic level, they also move, centrifugally, to links with different levels of context, but also with intertext. This we will broadly define as what accounts for the way any text is produced and consumed, i.e. as the types of connections which, within a given discourse community, are made, or not made, between the text(s) construing them and the set of texts to which it/they may be said, both synchronically and diachronically, to belong (Lemke, 1995). As Halliday puts it: 'What can be meant, at any moment in the discourse, is very much the product of history; of what could be meant, and what has been meant, before' (1992: 33). In the case of authors dealing with translation (Heidmann and Adam; Agorni), this can be explicitly seen in an intriguing, if intricate, dialogue between texts across linguistic, temporal and thus cultural distance.

In doing this, nothing is taken for granted; a good amount of demystification of, and challenge to, conventional, widely-held theories concerning single time-honoured authors and/or traditions is tendered. Linguistic *and* extra-linguistic analysis leads to, among other consequences:

a) recontextualisations and reinterpretations being offered – e.g. by Turci – positioning Conrad's *Heart of Darkness* as an Imperial Victorian representation of Africa;

b) subtle distinctions being revealed – e.g. by Hasan, regarding the semiotic construal of balance and imbalance as value in Elizabethan society; by Moraldo, between German and Turkish, on one hand, and the ethnolect, *kanak sprak*, on the other; by Rodrigo Mora, in the often divergent meta-textual reflections of the Spanish poets of the 1950s, and by Agorni, between the 'contrastive' and 'comparative' translation methods, *or*

c)   distinctions being conflated – e.g. by Heidmann and Adam, in the comparative and textual approaches, and by Butt, in the psychological-social nature of language and 'thought experiments' in science;

d)   the ostensibly 'marginal' being raised to its 'proper' significance – e.g. the import of the nine-word collocational window, by Louw; the framing function of projection in the literature text, by Taylor Torsello; the phenomenon of grammatical parallelism in Lawrence, by Miller, or the device of fragmentation in Streeruwitz, by Betten, and, again by Moraldo, the ethnolect *kanak sprak*'s role in the construction of immigrant identity.

The texts that are addressed by the papers include the canonical: e.g. The Gospel of Saint John, Shakespeare's *As You Like It*, Perrault's *Histoires et contes du temps passé*, Angela Carter's translations of these, Anglo-American-Australian (more or less) Modernist poets (D. H. Lawrence, Pound, Stevens and Slessor), and novelists (Conrad, Orwell and Woolf), the Spanish poets of the *Generación del '50*, Thomas Bernhard and Marina Warner. The less canonical is also represented, however: Austrians Jelinek and Streeruwitz, Turkish-German Feridun Zaimoğlu, Singaporean Edwin Thumboo and, less exotic and certainly more popular, J. K. Rowling's *Harry Potter* books.

On the whole, the papers have been arranged in a chronological order as far as the texts they deal with go: beginning with Shakespeare, moving on to the Modernists and proceeding to later twentieth century writers. Conveniently, this organisation has also allowed juxtaposing and overlapping papers with like linguistic approaches: SFL-*ers* Hasan, Miller, Butt, Turci and Taylor Torsello; corpus analyses by, again, Turci, Taylor Torsello, and then Louw; comparative translation studies by Heidmann and Adam and Agorni, and the essentially pragmatic approaches of Betten and Moraldo. The article by Hasan comes in first position, not only to award her pride of place, but also due to its providing essential theoretical and methodological background for the Systemic analyses which follow it. Rodrigo Mora's paper has been positioned last, owing to its historical and meta-poetic nature. Her contribution focuses attention on the history of the ideas on language that made up the heterogeneous explicit 'poetics' of the Generation of Spanish poets of the 1950s.

In closing this brief introduction, the editors would voice the conviction that the authors' own discursive practices will be largely accessible to both specialists and students specialising in the field of stylistics. At the same time, we also hope that these papers will provide our readers with original and stimulating ideas. We end by once more drawing attention to the all-important, and always thorny question of interpretation and bias, or the culturally and socially-rooted, ideological nature of readers' (and analysts'!) subjective responses to texts. But bias we can only be aware, and beware, of, and, of course, declare.

Notes

1   That there are various sub-categories of stylistics, influenced by diverse theoretical and methodological angles, is the working premise of the recent volume of collected papers edited by Weber (1996). With reference to his categorical distinctions, we can say that this volume offers illustrations of the following types: functionalist, pragmatic, critical, feminist and pedagogical, with some overlap. In addition, however, the volume includes examples of what we'd call corpus-assisted, and even driven, stylistics, as well as comparative stylistics. It should also be immediately said that, despite undeniable divergences in thought and practice over the years among those flying the various banners, we are using the terms: 'stylistics', 'linguistic stylistics'; 'linguistic criticism', 'linguistic analysis of verbal art' and the 'linguistic approach to literature' in a quasi-synonymous way.

2   The expression is Hasan's (1985: 90–91), and linked to her view that the term 'literary' language is misguided, the wrong way to look at things. She suggests in fact that we need to look, not at the language *of* literature, but at that *in* literature, by which she means that we should investigate the 'functions of language in literature'. As her paper in this volume reiterates, the elements of language do not have any artistic value, in and of themselves, inherently, *per se*. It is rather the special role they play, their articulating function *in* the literature text, that makes them art.

3   For more on the similarities between the approaches of Formalism and New Criticism, see the Introduction to Lemon and Reis (1965: ix–xvii).

4   The Malinowskian concept of context was incorporated, first into Firthian linguistics and then by Firth's 'successor', M. A. K. Halliday, into Systemic Functional Linguistics (SFL) (cf. Halliday and Hasan, 1980).

5   Context in the 'pragmatic' view is not too far removed from Malinowski's concept, although this extra-linguistic level is not formally integrated into a model of the process of text creation, or a text-realisatory cycle (i.e. Context → Meaning → Wording) in the same way as in the SFL model.

References

Bloomfield, L. (1933) *Language*. New York: Henry Holt & Co.

Chomsky, N. (1957) *Syntactic Structures*. The Hague: Mouton.

De Beaugrande, R. (1993) Closing the gap between linguistic and literary study: discourse analysis and literary theory. *Journal of Advanced Composition* 13.

2: 423–448. Retrieved from http://www.beaugrande.com/listofworks.htm on September 29, 2005.

Eco, U. (1979) *The Role of the Reader*. Bloomington, Indiana: Indiana University Press.

Fabb, N., Attridge, D., Durant, A. and MacCabe, C. (eds) (1987) *The Linguistics of Writing. Arguments between Language and Literature*. Manchester: Manchester University Press.

Firth, J. R. (1957 [1968]) *Selected Papers of J. R. Firth, 1952–1959*. Edited by F. R. Palmer. Bloomington and London: Indiana University Press.

Fowler, R. (1971) *The Languages of Literature. From Linguistic Contributions to Criticism*. London: Routledge and Kegan Paul.

Fowler, R. (1981) *Literature as Social Discourse. The Practice of Linguistic Criticism*. London: Batford.

Halliday, M. A. K. (1982) The de-automatization of grammar: from Priestly's 'An Inspector Calls'. In J. Anderson (ed.) *Language Form and Linguistic Variation* 132–158. Amsterdam and Philadelphia: John Benjamins.

Halliday, M. A. K. (1992) The history of a sentence: an essay in social semiotics. In V. Fortunati (ed.) *Bologna, la cultura italiana e le letterature straniere moderne*. Proceedings of the International Conference of the same title held during the 9th centenary celebrations of the University of Bologna, October 17–22, 1988, Volume 3: 29–45. Ravenna: Longo Editore.

Halliday, M. A. K. and Hasan, R. (1980) *Text and Context*. Sophia Linguistica VI: 4–15. Tokyo: Sophia University.

Hasan, R. (1975) The place of stylistics in the study of verbal art. In H. Ringbom (ed.) *Style and Text. Studies Presented to Nils Erik Envist* 49–62. Stockholm: Skriptor.

Hasan, R. (1985) *Language, Linguistics and Verbal Art*. Geelong, Vic: Deakin University Press.

Hasan, R. (1987) Directions from structuralism. In N. Fabb, D. Attridge, A. Durant and C. MacCabe (eds) *The Linguistics of Writing. Arguments between Language and Literature* 103–122. Manchester: Manchester University Press.

Hasan, R. (1992) Speech genre, semiotic mediation and the development of higher mental functions. *Language Sciences* 1. 4: 489–528.

Jakobson, R. (1960) Closing statement: linguistics and poetics. In T. A. Sebeok (ed.) *Style in Language* 350–377. Cambridge, Mass: MIT Press.

Jakobson, R. (1966) Grammatical parallelism and its Russian facet. *Language* 42. 2: 399–429.

Jakobson, R. (1968) Poetry of grammar and grammar of poetry. *Lingua* 21: 597–609.

Kress, G. and Hodge, R. (1979) *Language and Ideology*. London: Routledge and Kegan Paul.

Lemke, J. L. (1995) Intertextuality and text semantics. In P. Fries and
    M. Gregory (eds) *Discourse in Society*: *Systemic Functional Perspectives*
    85–114. Norwood, NJ: Ablex.
Lemon, L. T. and Reis, M. J. (eds and trans.) (1965) *Russian Formalist
    Criticism*: *Four Essays*. Lincoln, Nebraska: University of Nebraska Press.
Malinowski, B. (1923) The problem of meaning in primitive languages, supple-
    ment 1. In C. K. Ogden and I. A. Richards (eds) *The Meaning of Meaning*
    451–510. London: Kegan Paul.
Mukarovsky, J. (1932 [1964]) Standard language and poetic language. In P.
    Garvin (ed. and trans.) *A Prague School Reader on Esthetics, Literary
    Structure, and Style* 17–30. Washington, DC: Georgetown University Press.
Sapir, E. (1921) *Language. An Introduction to the Study of Speech*. New York:
    Harcourt Brace.
Sebeok, T. A. (ed.) (1960) *Style in Language*. Cambridge, Mass: MIT Press.
Shklovsky, V. (1917 [1965]) Art as technique. In L. T. Lemon and M. J. Reis
    (eds and trans.) *Russian Formalist Criticism*: *Four Essays* 3–24. Lincoln,
    Nebraska: University of Nebraska Press.
Todorov, T. (1984) *Mikhail Bakhtin*: *The Dialogical Principle*. W. Godzich
    (trans.). Minnesota: University of Minnesota Press.
Weber, J. J. (ed.) (1996) *The Stylistics Reader. From Roman Jakobson to the
    Present*. London: Arnold.

1 Private pleasure, public discourse: reflections on engaging with literature

Ruqaiya Hasan

Macquarie University, Sydney

Editors' Introduction

Ruqaiya Hasan is among the first language scholars to have dealt with the topic of this volume, starting back in the 1960s with her PhD thesis. Her complete works are currently being published by Equinox.

Hasan's paper has been deliberately positioned first in the volume, as it intimately addresses the most vital theoretical and methodological issues concerning the book's general topic, and does this in such a way that the paper also serves as an essential background to the Systemic Functional Linguistics (SFL)-based contributions which follow, but not solely. She begins with underlining the complexity of the nature of the activity of engaging with literature, admitting that the multiplicity of resources that supports the creation of a literary artifact also implies that there will necessarily be many different ways of doing this. She doesn't deny that the practice of creating literature, as with most valued cultural practices, has a 'past' to reckon with. Nor does she overlook the fact that writers, as practicing agents, have always been socially positioned, ideological beings, in the same way as their readers are, or that the originality, impact, and contribution of the literary artifact to a community's evolving consciousness are socio-historically determined. This, she acknowledges, is all true. Notwithstanding, she insists on the centrality of language in the study of literature, and would shed new light on the subject: a social semiotic light, one that would question many long-standing, taken for granted attitudes towards this activity of 'doing lit'.

The social semiotic perspective that Hasan puts forward here is rooted in SFL, the linguistic model, she argues, which is best capable of globally assigning an appropriate place to the essential features of the language of verbal art that must be probed. This is closely linked with her premise that doing literature is far more than a question of deriving subjective private pleasure from it, gratifying as that may be. What's needed, if the study of literature is to be a deserving discipline in its own right, is public, externalisable, discourse, based on the analysis of the *intrinsic* characteristics of the text in context: its lexicogrammatical form and the semantic value this instantiates. Only such explicit analysis can provide a satisfying account of what verbal art is.

The model of literature analysis she suggests was first presented and illustrated in Hasan (1985). It is based on two, overlapping semiotic systems, the first order system being that of language and the second, the higher order, that of verbal art. Appropriating the notion of the *foregrounding* of meaning from Mukarovsky, she proposes that it is through patterns of foregrounding that the literature text's deepest abstract meanings on the nature of human existence, or its *theme*, is *symbolically articulated*. The theme, in brief, can only be properly 'appraised' by re-interpreting the first order meanings that have been consistently (in terms of consistent meaning and meaning-location) foregrounded. 'What makes verbal art *art*', she says, 'is th[is] feature of double articulation'. The analytical model is illustrated by the means of the foregrounding of theme in Shakespeare's *As You Like It*, where the value of equilibrium, and the dire consequences of its overturning, can be seen to be construed in and by features such as the use of personal pronouns, as well as questions and commands.

The questions her paper addresses are thus essential ones: why insist that language is primary? What kind of reading is at issue? And what does the language of a piece of verbal art have to do with the reader's ways of meaning? Her essential claim, in brief, is that a creation in literature is valued culturally as art; that the art in the literary artifact is, by definition, *verbal* art, and that this is realised in the language that is the raw material of the work. For Hasan, the production of literature is not simply a management of a particular mode of discourse; it is above all the creation of a universe which stands in as complex a relation to the writer's world as it does to the reader's: these two socially positioned semiotically active beings. And the relation between the two is symbiotic, and elemental. On the one hand, as she puts it:

> The challenge for the creator of verbal art is that the symbolically articulated theme has to be capable of striking a chord in the reader across substantial distances in time and space, even though the roots of theme lie in the artist's own social existence, and even though theme is refracted through the artist's own ideological stance.

That is so, if the verbal art is to last and be remembered. With reference to the reader, however, there is an additional fundamental point that Hasan makes regarding what is required of him/her. This is the issue of pedagogy, of the teaching of *how to read* literature as a phenomenon of *languaging in a particular way*. If the academic discipline is to have any sense, and dignity, rather than being aimed at the imitation or reproduction of the teacher's, or authoritative literary critic's, reactions to and extrinsic evaluations of literature, as it most commonly is, it should be about *enabling* the student, across cultural distance, to 'speak the author's language'. As she puts it, 'The author can only be read with the socio-semiotic capabilities the reader is able to bring to the task'.

---

1   Introduction

That the arts are somehow good for us is a common idea, but explaining what is meant by 'good' or 'us' or even 'art', is a tricky business.

(Morrison, 'A lesson with the art master', 2005: 26)

Most people are familiar with the activity of engaging with literature; so the expression seems pretty straightforward until one happens to ask: What exactly is the nature of this activity? The answer is far from straightforward. To begin with, literature is read in a multiplicity of ways, and the reasons given for engaging in this activity have varied both diachronically and synchronically, as has the very interpretation of the word 'literature', which is quite obviously ambiguous in many ways. As if this wasn't complex enough, there also exists a wealth of literature on literature dating back from the various ancient civilisations to today's post-post-Modernist fragmented world. Ambitious as it may seem, in this chapter I propose to visit many of these issues, though briefly. My aim in doing this is not to offer the kind of critique that Bernstein once described as a 'strategy of disposal', whereby everything that has ever been said with respect to some problem may be shown by some commentator to be entirely pointless. Rather, I would like to throw a new light on many of our taken for granted attitudes regarding literature by bringing them face to face with arguments from the social semiotic approach to language. So the question I am asking is: what would some of these repeatedly described 'facts' about literature look like when seen through the eyes of language as social semiotic? The rationale for taking language as integral to the enquiry is not simply that literature is expressed and accessed as language: this fact, though important, is not specific to literature alone; it applies to *all* texts, irrespective of their context of discourse and the variety they instantiate. What justifies the assigning of a central position to language in the study of literature is the fact that those properties of literature that permit its identification as literature are *created by languaging in a particular way*. Literature is a kind of art; it differs from other arts by being *verbal* art; i.e. the 'art' in verbal art is essentially crafted with language.

I should hasten to add that the term *verbal art* is used here simply as a descriptive label for the language variety we call 'literature': as a label it can be applied to any instance wherein art is brought into being by a particular way of languaging (see Section 3 for discussion), irrespective of whether or not the instance is highly valued in the community. The concept of *valued text* is complex. In the first place, literature texts are not the only ones that are valued in a community; but secondly, and more importantly, value does not inhere entirely in the instance being valued, which is not to claim that the attributes of the instance are irrelevant to the evaluation, but simply to say that value is a relation between a valuer as a socially situated being and the valued object as an instance of some specific kind of social practice in some community. If the evaluating reader is positioned as a social subject, then the valued instance is positioned as an element of cultural capital. It is to address the question of *value/valuation* that the perspective *must* be that of language as *social* semiotic, i.e. an approach to language that takes *the social* as seriously in the study of literature as it does the semiotic. And it is to account for the property of *art* that the perspective *must* be that of language as social *semiotic*, i.e. an approach to language that takes the *potential of language for meaning* as seriously as it does the social. An adequate theory for modelling literature must account both for the fact that it is a form of human activity in societies and, as such, subject to evaluation, and that the activity has a specific character which distinguishes it from other activities which are just semiotic or just artistic. The nature of literature can never be specified either as *just discourse* or as *just art*: as a variety, it is discourse fused with art.

2 Engaging with literature

I begin by briefly examining two possible reasons for engaging with literature – reasons chosen primarily because they appear far apart in terms of the
demands they make on readers of literature – the first is reading literature
for 'private pleasure', and the second, reading it as a recognised discipline
within the framework of official pedagogy, which necessarily involves 'public
discourse' since whatever has to be taught or shown to have been learned has
to be 'externalisable'.

The first reason has the privilege of being a constant over the ages: everywhere and always in literature on literature, some members of the society have
associated it with pleasure – with positive reaction, or 'appreciation' (Hasan,
1985). Simple as this observation is, it is surrounded by a tangled net of assumptions. There is the basic assumption that evaluation is a subjective phenomenon;
not far behind is also an assumption that whatever is subjective inheres in the
individual, which in its turn is accompanied by the belief that 'individual-ness'
is given by nature: one is said to be born with the blueprint of some given
personality type, and it is this which is supposed to determine the nature of
one's reaction to some phenomenon.[1] In this perspective, one reads literature
and reacts to it, in the last analysis, only as one's 'nature' demands! Failing
to give enough time and care to deconstructing the 'logic' of long accepted
beliefs, we are often persuaded to ascribe to nature what nature alone could
never produce, and the tangle of assumptions just described is a case in point.
There are certainly cases, especially in the early stages of human life, when
the act of evaluation could justifiably be said to be rooted in sensory reaction;
for example, the goodness of some substance that tastes 'good' to the baby's
tongue, or her body's spontaneous response to some rhythm. However, even
such simple sensory reactions get modified with different cultural experiences
– one person becomes the lover of classical music, another, the admirer of rap
rhythm! Modern research finds overwhelmingly that our mental dispositions,
which are the moving force behind most of our seemingly free and voluntary
acts, are produced socio-genetically. It seems highly probable that taste in
literature is created by the weaving of 'nurture into nature [*which is done, RH*],
with the most powerful magic – speech' (Firth, 1957: 185), i.e. language used
in everyday life, including encounters with verbal art and participation in its
appreciation with other community members (Hasan, 1985).

I have pursued these issues rather closely in the hope that even so brief a
deconstruction might foreground certain fundamental facts. It is obvious that
the process of experiencing is private and pertains to the experiencing subject,
but the person doing the experiencing is a *social* subject. And, by definition,
social subjects are not socio-culturally innocent: from their infancy, they have

been brought into the circle of their meaning group, an inclusion made possible through semiotic interactions throughout life. What passes in the various interactions is the mediation of meanings significant for the living of one's life, and it is these meaningful experiences which fashion the social subjects' mental dispositions, shaping their taste and their 'individuality' (Firth, 1957; Bernstein, 2000; Halliday, 1973, 2004a). The identity of the social subject is shaped, the habits of mind are formed, and a personality is created *in* and *by* familiar, everyday experiences. As the neurologist, Susan Greenfield (1997: 156), puts it: '[…] experiences we have never had can play no part in framing our personality'. It follows that, although the actual act of experiencing is private, our judgments about those experiences and the significance we assign to them are, at their very source, socially nuanced. Our value systems are, thus, essentially social artifacts. The principles underlying the evaluation of literature, as of other text types/instances, could not be an exception to this generalisation. The socio-historical genesis of value systems is one reason why 'tastes' in literature have varied both synchronically and diachronically: the same creators of literature have risen and fallen in the market of taste; the same instances have been revered and ignored by the 'same' community over time.

What makes a judgment subjective is not that it is 'given' by nature, or that it is the manifestation of a mythical 'authentic self' not contaminated by the social: rather, the subjectivity of judgment lies in its not having been subjected to analysis – perhaps because there does not exist an argued theoretical framework, or because in quotidian, non-specialist contexts we leave many things unanalysed, allowing their bases to remain unarticulated. Whatever the case, judgments will remain subjective so long as they remain unanalysed. Being unanalysed, their basis may not be clear, even to the experiencing subject. So while in reading for private pleasure, it may be possible to employ epithets to describe the qualities of such judgments, i.e. to express one's personal *appreciation* of a particular instance of verbal art, it is not possible to explain what such appreciation is based on, much less to generalise about what constitutes verbal art, or where the foundations of evaluation lie. Clearly, such lack of analysis poses no serious problem in reading for private pleasure, which often ends up as a species of 'self-communion'. But the situation is obviously different in engaging with literature for the second reason, i.e. as a recognised discipline within the framework of official pedagogy: this demands 'public discourse' from both the teacher and the learner. But, does this demand really make a critical difference?

Not necessarily, since the demand for public discourse may be met in at least two different ways. Firstly, one may simply describe one's appreciation of some instance of verbal art or verbal artist. To make such judgments public, all one would need is the language resources for expressing one's beliefs, judgments, personal reactions etc., such as those described, for example, by Martin's 'Appraisal theory' (Martin and Rose, 2003). In such public discourse on verbal art, since the bases of reactions have not been analysed, one has not moved away from subjective judgment. I believe it is fair to assume that the teaching of literature as a discipline needs to go beyond the retailing and recycling of personal reactions, that it should concerns itself with making clear the basis of one's claims about (some instance of) literature. To do this, public discourse will have to move beyond the simple assertion of appreciation and evaluation. The need for explicit analysis will arise, posing questions such as: what is one studying when one studies 'literature'; what, if any, are the critical attributes that justify treating some discourse as an instance of literature; what are the ways of reading literature that might show explicitly how such attributes have been construed; how is some instance of literature positioned with regard to these attributes; and why is the instance valued in the community the way it is. In pursuing issues of this kind, one will have to go beyond subjective appreciation, from appraisal in Appraisal theory's sense of the word to what *I* meant when I used the term 'appraisal' with regard to the study of literature (Hasan, 1985).[2]

I believe that throughout the various stages of official pedagogy a good deal of the 'teaching' of literature has adopted precisely the first strategy: if the teaching of 'elocution' used to be about teaching people 'received pronunciation'; the teaching of literature has typically continued to be about teaching people 'received evaluation' (Hasan, 1964; Lukin, 2002). Milton is *in*, Milton is *out*: authority T. S. Eliot; Tennyson is passé: no 'respectable' critic talks any more about him; ancient critical authority elevated Shakespeare to literary canon: follow the critics of late 1970s, early 1980s, in defying that canon – in other words, replace ancient authority with the new regime of 'lit-crit'! The principle underlying such teaching is 'doxic', not analytic. This is not to say that the evaluations of the 'acknowledged authorities' are, *ipso facto*, untenable or irrelevant; they may or may not be. The worry is that there is simply no efficient way of knowing, since often the bases of judgment are not made explicit and neither are the comments presented in the context of a model of literature by reference to which their value could be assessed. It follows that ideas about the defining attributes of literature remain unclear, as do the bases of reaction and evaluation. 'Doing literature' becomes a refined art in repeating the 'master readers' without appearing to repeat, which calls for clever verbal camouflage. Obviously such teaching is far from enabling; in fact, it is primarily reproductive. While pedagogy of any kind, official or local, continues to have a reproductive bias, and while reproduction appears to be an important and unavoidable part of any pedagogy, very little reflection is needed to realise that a *reproductive and doxic intuitive* approach is a recipe for fundamentalist fervour. I am not implying that nothing new happens in the teaching of literature in official pedagogy; of course it does. We now recognise many more varieties of literature with 'politically correct' labels, such as feminist, ethnic, colonial, post-colonial etc. literature(s), and many schools of 'empowering' criticism. But in moments of lucidity, we might perhaps rightly refer to all this 'progress' as *the more things change, the more they stay the same.*

From this point of view, a potted summary of the progress and preoccupations of lit-crit through the ages makes fascinating reading. No matter what the critical theory, one or more of the following three traits will be noticed in all:

i)   The defining attribute(s) of literature, with few exceptions, are shown to be extrinsic: from *catharsis* to moral elevation, from holding a mirror to society to making the familiar 'strange', from aesthetic gratification to tingle down the spine, from eternal truth to social therapy, from 'sublimation' to the expression of the repressed, and so on.

ii) The language *of* literature, alias *style*, is identified by such epithets as poetic, creative, 'ungrammatical', expressive, evaluative, etc., and these qualities are treated as specific to literature. Tropes and figures of speech are analysed purely on the basis of their meaning, and often offered as the heuristic criteria for literature-ness, but it is seldom made clear what part they play in the overall design of some instance of literature, let alone relating them to what constitutes 'art' in literature. Style is seen as an element of literature, but it is treated as if it exists apart from the structure of a literature text. The analogue in other cases of textual analysis might be an absurd claim, namely that, if a particular text has 'grammatical metaphor',[3] then it must belong to the scientific variety. Using this logic much bureaucratic 'officialese' would be 'science' – as, indeed, much of *belles-lettres* 'is' literature.

iii) Sundry sub-varieties of literature – genres – and the parts/stages that make them up, i.e. their form (or schematic structure) are labelled; e.g. novel, novella, short story; lyric, sonnet, elegy; drama; beginning, middle and end; climax, denouement, and so on.[4] Little or no indication is given of how the elements of structure/stages/segments – call them what you will – are realised, either by reference to the patterning of language forms or by their semantics.

The first set of factors is about 'what literature does; why it is good for us': in this sense the factors invoke pragmatic criteria, which rest on its supposed benefits. The second and third are about what literature is like in itself, i.e.

what kind of language is used in literature and how some variety of literature text is made up: it thus concerns its intrinsic properties, the nature of language in literature, the formal structures of its sub-varieties/genres. Missing from this list is an overall model that can characterise the nature of the category 'literature' in general. Thus, by default, the properties that make literature verbal art get confounded either with the qualities of isolated language patterns (as in ii) – the conflation of *belles-lettres* with literature as an art form calls for more reflection than it has ever received in the critical canon – or they get confounded with questions concerning generic form or mode (as in iii), witness the discussion still current about the superiority of 'poetry' over prose, of blank verse over rhyming couplets, of *stream of consciousness* over realism, and so on. The evaluation of literature typically appeals to some of these considerations as if they were proven 'indicators' of the variety 'literature'. While none of these factors is irrelevant to engaging with literature, none on its own or even in combination is powerful enough to reveal the essential characteristics of verbal art: to achieve this, we need a model that assigns these features an appropriate place in the over all explanatory strategy – and this need is urgent if studying literature as a discipline is to be a meaningful concept. So, what might a model of literature look like in the perspective of language as social semiotic?

3 Modelling literature: a social semiotic perspective

The social semiotic perspective is not new: it actually predates the 1960s' *structural stylistics*, one offshoot of which was *generative stylistics*: the former typically counted lexicogrammatical patterns without unduly worrying about the *nature* of literature, the latter suggested that it was a set of sentences char-acterised by ungrammaticality.[5] All three approaches to the study of literature – social semiotic, structural and generative stylistics – were ultimately inspired by Saussurean linguistics; the latter two highlighted formal-structural aspects of its framework, while the former emphasised its social and semiotic nature. An initial approach to a social semiotic perspective was made early last cen-tury by the Russian neo-Formalists, and equally vigorously by the scholars of the Prague Linguistic Circle, who, using their social functional approach to interpret Saussure's semiological theory, developed accounts of what they called the 'aesthetic function' of language (for some discussion, see Lukin and Webster, 2005). The best known Prague School scholar, Mukarovsky (1977, 1978), came nearest to enunciating an over all framework for the study of literature. However, this group's work did not become available to most English speakers until mid-1960s, when Garvin's 'little book' (1964) first offered a glimpse into Prague School aesthetics. To this day, their work remains a rich resource for understanding crucial issues in the study of literature. The model of literature I present below is in many respects similar to theirs.[6] However, I would suggest that it has a tighter syntax than Mukarovsky's and it uses a social semiotic model of language based on Halliday's Systemic Functional Linguistics (SFL).

Unlike many other linguistic models, SFL theory treats Saussure's *langue* and *parole* not as mutually irreconcilable, but as two complementary and inherent aspects of language, engaged in a dialectic whereby the system of language supports and makes interpretable the instances of language use, while the process of language creates and renews the language system. The model, thus, attends to the description of both aspects as equally important in the study of language. Obviously, language use is inherently social, and so interest in language use entails interest in social context as well as in the metafunctions of language (Halliday, 1973; Hasan, in press).[7] Insofar as literature texts are instances of language, the basic resources for their production and reception are provided by the same system of language which we use in the production and reception of texts in other domains, such as physics, history, philosophy, everyday conversation etc.; and the contribution of these latter varieties to renewing the system of language is just as critical as that of literature. It follows that in the study of literature, SFL's modelling of language in use, known as 'register theory', is of particular interest. Simplifying greatly, register theory provides a framework for identifying specific categories of language use, allowing instances to be seen in relation to each other. It thus becomes possible to view certain instances as pertaining to this or that kind of language use, each kind representing a language variety, which is what a 'register' is. Every instance of language use occurs in the context of some social situation. The recognition criteria for assigning instances to specific categories of a register variety rely on both the features of the category's relevant social context and the features of the language which are typical of that category.

In this perspective, literature too can be seen as a kind of language use: it too occurs in some social context; it is communally seen as a particular kind of use of language; and, as in many other varieties/registers, the variety-label refers to 'a family of sub-varieties', comprising in this case such specific genres as novel, novella, drama, lyric, sonnet, and so on. The question naturally arises: on what basis are these various 'genres' to be put under the rubric of 'literature'?; e.g., what have a sonnet and a novel got in common?; how is a play like a lyric? It is no use saying 'literature is that which the community regards as literature', since this is equally true of the other varieties. However, the latter do permit the setting up of recognition criteria by reference to their context and language patterns. It is reasonable to think that an examination of the role of language and context in literature might also yield useful results.

Review of discourse on literature reveals that the identifying properties of the variety have been predominantly sought at the level of language patterns. There can be no quarrel with claims about the importance of language patterns; after all, they are important in the recognition of other language varieties too. However, in the case of literature, what is usually said about the 'diagnostic' features of language leads to problems rather than to clarification: language patterns, such as ungrammaticality, ambiguity, metaphor, simile, imagery, alliteration, assonance etc., are mentioned as important, which they may well be, but when it comes to identifying what part they play in the make up of the text, no satisfying account emerges. In a non-literature variety, it is relatively easy to demonstrate the realisational connections from features of the social context in which an instance is embedded, right through to wordings: certain patterns of language – their meaning and grammar – can be shown to be activated by certain features of the variety's relevant social context (Halliday and Hasan, 1985). In literature, turning to the context-language connection opens up yet another complex set of issues (Hasan, 1996: 49–54). Thus attempts to model literature reveal fault lines of complexities in the exploration of both its semiotic and its social foundations.

To manage this complexity, I have suggested (Hasan, 1971, 1985) a tri-stratal model of verbal art analogous somewhat to the SFL stratal model of the inner structure of language, which too is a complex phenomenon (Matthiessen, 2005). The basis for suggesting a stratal organisation of verbal art rests on the observation that, as a variety of social semiotic practice, both the production and reception of verbal art almost always represent a specific kind of meaning exchange (see discussion in Section 3.1). The construal of meaning calls for the recognition of distinct orders of abstraction. The strata postulated in the modelling of verbal art allow us to show how the artist's message is 'orchestrated'. By the same token, it becomes easier to assign functional roles to both language *and* to society, both of which are crucially implicated in the production and reception of verbal art. Accordingly, we postulate that verbal art has a level of meaning organisation called *theme* (Hasan, 1971). Theme is the deepest level of meaning in verbal art: meanings which concern the human condition (again, see Section 3.1 below). But this deepest meaning is not declared to the reader directly by the author. Rather, it is inferred on the basis of the foregrounded patterns of relations between events, characters and experiences that are presented in any instance of verbal art, certain aspects of which are, as it were, foregrounded as crucial. I have referred to this level of foregrounding as *symbolic articulation*. The configuration of events, relations and experiences at the level of symbolic articulation form part of the 'grammar' of verbal art;

the meanings construed by this grammar contribute to the realisation of some elements of the theme of the work. The foregrounding is where the most crucial work of verbal art is done, and here language plays an important role. Symbolic articulation is brought about by patterns of the author's language selection. Such patterned use of language occurs at the level referred to as *verbalisation*,[8] i.e. the act of producing linguistic structures which bear meaning(s) by virtue of being semiotic constructs. The reader's initial contact with an instance of verbal art is at the level of verbalisation, where the author uses the already existing and sometimes especially created resources of natural language for construing meanings. As a meaning potential, the use of natural language is obviously for mediating meanings for the living of life in society, both in *mundane* and *exotic* spheres of human life. This is the fact which justifies the claim that the evolution of language and society is governed by a co-genetic logic, whereby each maintains and renews the other through time. Artifacts pertaining to verbal art are thus inherently socio-semiotic because, in every stage of their being, the social semiotic system of language is an active player, not least because both the producer and the reader of literature are socially positioned, and possess a consciousness that is semiotically shaped. Space limitations do not permit a detailed account of the reach of this model; an indicative discussion follows.

3.1 Theme and symbolic articulation in verbal art

Theme is *the* message of an instance of verbal art: if, as a reader, one failed to 'get it', then the work has not been read so as to facilitate engagement in public discourse on verbal art; if, as a serious student of verbal art, one cannot engage in discourse on how the theme was symbolically articulated via verbalisation, then one's assessment of the work will fall way below the standard required for teaching literature as an academic discipline. This does not necessarily mean that theme is what initially engages the reader; however, theme is what stays in the reader's consciousness long after the pleasure of encountering the 'artistic turn' of phrases has dissipated itself. Even the most assiduous student of verbal art cannot retain the actual patterning of language patterns at the verbalisation level of specific works; but if the ideological message of the work has spoken to the reader, who him/herself is obviously not ideologically innocent, then the theme impression will last. Having analysed the symbolic articulation of the theme in Shakespeare's *As You Like It*, one is not likely to forget the various guiding forces of equilibrium in human action, reflection and locution which keep the material and social world sweetly rotating in peaceful harmony. Frost's *The Road Not Taken*, read with an understanding of its deepest message, will leave an impression of the theme, viz., the immutability of human choice, made lightly because through the thick curtain of the present it appeared less than momentous; the realisation comes too late that the lightly made choice 'has made all the difference'. Les Murray's *Widower in the Country* poignantly points to its theme concerning the essence of humanity: to be human, to be an individual, you need to be with others; what makes human existence sane, what protects it from nightmarish chimera, is an other's company (Hasan, 1985).

The subject matter of theme concerns some aspect of the human condition, a sense of what the flesh is heir to, what irks the spirit, what seems risible, what profound, what is subject to change, what immutable. And this sense is created in the artist by the experience of the ordinary patterns of living in the society in which the artist is both player and observer, acted upon and acting. Thus the foundations of (the elements of) theme lie in 'local knowledge', the gateway to which is thrown open by the experience of being, sensing, saying and acting with others in ways that are 'natural' to one's community: it is in participating and attending to such experiences that the artist develops a sense of the material social conditions of human existence which are at once enabling and constraining to the free play of human action and imagination. From this point of view, verbal art offers the best re-contextualisation[9] of the kind of knowledge that is based on the experience of everyday life as it is lived unselfconsciously by the members of some community. It is in this sense that verbal art is 'truer' than history: its truth is akin to hypotheses based in a deep understanding of the experience of being human.

As indicated earlier, the social impinges on verbal art in multiple ways, both in its creation and its reception, but perhaps the most critical part it plays is in shaping the ideological orientations of those who write and of those who read literature. It is this ideological orientation that guides the artist's selections of certain elements of local knowledge as significant enough for his artistic endeavour, and it is also what guides the reader in determining what is 'really' worth reading. The character of an artist's themes is thus ideologically refracted, and no reading is free of ideological orientation. In the nature of things, the actual experience of any one person is finite and largely shaped by the exigencies of their life. The challenge for the creator of verbal art is that the symbolically articulated theme has to be capable of striking a chord in the reader across substantial distances in time and space, even though the roots of theme lie in the artist's own social existence, and even though theme is refracted through the artist's own ideological stance. The distances in time and space translate themselves into ideological and semiotic differences: between the work of verbal art and the ultimate inference of its theme lies the receivers' ideological stance, as well as their understanding of the meaning making resources of the language in which they encounter the text. Success in meeting the challenge of theme construal becomes a condition for a work to be remembered by distant communities. In fact, over centuries of producing and receiving instances of verbal art, humanity has clearly displayed a predilection for valuing only those instances whose themes are symbolically articulated as the distillation of a deep perception of the human condition that speaks to readers so that, notwithstanding large cultural distances, they declare: *yes, indeed I recognise this condition*. Critics and philosophers have sometimes claimed that verbal art has a 'spiritual' function (see, for discussion, Carey, 2005); that it humanises; that its effect on the reader is cathartic; or that it offers solutions for cultural dilemmas (Butt, 1996). If so, this is something accomplished by the artistic enunciation of theme, and it is worth adding that literature can perform these functions *only* to the extent that the reader is able and willing to be 'ennobled', 'cleansed' or 'cured', and *only* to the extent that the author's ideology 'speaks' to the reader's ideological stance. For, I repeat, both the author and the reader are equally socially positioned.[10] The author can only be read with the socio-semiotic capabilities the reader is able to bring to the task. The reader has to be able to 'speak the author's language' in more than one sense of the expression. Hence, my insistence that engaging with verbal art as an academic field ought to be about creating and enhancing this capability, not about inculcating the learners into the opinions of the acknowledged masters.

In talking of theme, a question naturally arises: do authors 'consciously and knowingly' choose the theme of a work? In one sense raising this question is very much like asking: do you know what meanings you are about to construe by the wordings you are about to utter? It would be as foolish to answer with an unqualified 'yes' as with an unqualified 'no': obviously speakers *must* have *some* sense of the intended meaning; they don't just open their mouth and utter something at random in the hope that what is uttered will make some sense to the listener. Nor would writers keep editing their discourse, as they are known to do. But this knowledge of what one meant to mean when one started saying *must* also be a developing process: in all likelihood, the meaning becomes more 'visible' as one continues 'talking'. And there grows a sense of: *here is what I really meant to say!* Some of us are better and quicker in getting to this point, some, slower. Successful producers of verbal art must belong to the former category, but even here there must be variation. There is evidence that authors have varied in pinpointing (or at least 'naming') their theme: Elizabeth Gaskell (1855 [1995]) wanted to call her famous work *Margaret Hale*; the publishers suggested *North and South* as capturing better the concerns, i.e. the theme, of her novel. Trollope (1875 [1982])[11] began writing a novel apparently to be called *Lady Carbury*, but recognised before its completion that he was really writing *The Way We Live Now* – a savage attack on 'business ethos' which destroys humanity; a theme which would not speak readily to the glorified captains of our present day 'corporate culture'. Arnold Bennett, on the other hand, knew what the theme of *The Old Wives' Tale* was going to be, even before he began to write his famous novel (Carey, 1992: 152–182). The fact is that authors' intentions are not always recorded. But even if recorded, they do not have to be accepted as gospel. The author is the *producer* of verbal art; to be able to argue the artistic qualities of his work, he also needs to be a particular kind of *receiver* of art. And this calls for a special kind of expertise: an expertise that might be lacking not only in the artist but also in most of the self-appointed authorities on literature.

Any author can claim that, in creating a text, they have created an instance of verbal art; any reader having read some text can claim to have encountered therein verbal art. If all such claims were to be taken as assigning the said text to the category of verbal art, then we would have to grant that the *teaching* of verbal art as an academic discipline is simply a pretence. The social semiotic model of verbal art suggests that such claims should *not* be accepted without debate, no matter how high a position the claimant has in the world of verbal art. To be taken seriously, claims about themes – indeed about any aspect of litera-ture – need to be examined. But examined how? This is where a consideration of the level of symbolic articulation becomes crucial. If symbolic articulation is the grammar that construes the meaning configuration called theme, then any claims about theme have to be argued by analysing that grammar, i.e. by showing that the structuring of foregrounding indeed supports the reading of the postulated theme. It is neither the author's intention nor some authorised opinion that we need to seek or follow; what we need to establish is what Mukarovsky (1977) called the *artistic intention* of an instance of verbal art. This can be done by examining the *consistency of foregrounding* (Hasan, 1985). Foregrounding may be said to be consistent under two conditions: semantically, i.e. in terms of the meaning to which it points, and structurally, in terms of the work's structure, i.e. being consistently located – as it were, 'congregating' – at some significant point of the work. Theme is not what it pleases you or me to claim:[12] theme is what the patterns of foregrounding support, just as the lexicogrammar of a clause supports its meaning construal. But what exactly is meant by foregrounding and where do these patterns of symbolic articulation come from?

3.2 Symbolic articulation and verbalisation in verbal art

Symbolic articulation is itself construed by verbalisation, i.e. the act of using language at both the conscious and unselfconscious levels (see Note 9). As argued earlier, when using language, we have some sense of relevant mean-ings; we also have a fairly reliable perception of the sounds (and graphs) encountered by the body as it acts by way of saying. What remains entirely invisible, however, is the wording, i.e. the lexicogrammatical patterns we have had to produce in order for the meaning to be construed. We grow up from infancy to adolescence to adulthood, acquiring the grammar of the language current in our communities: the act of meaning becomes 'second nature' to us, but this does not mean that we also acquire the *ability to analyse* that grammar without which our acts of meaning would not come about. In order to be able to see the wording-meaning nexus, the principles of what Halliday (2002) calls *grammatics* have to be deliberately learned as part of the discipline of functional linguistics. This deliberately acquired ability to deconstruct lexicogrammar is essential to understanding how meanings are construed. There exists an analogous relationship between theme, the deep meaning of verbal art, and symbolic articulation, which acts as its grammar; in Butt's (1988) terms, symbolic articulation is the 'implicate order' underlying verbal art. The knowledge needed to deconstruct this hidden grammar is what allows us to see the work's artistic intention. And the construer of this hidden grammar is located at the level of verbalisation.

In engaging with literature, two distinct processes are relevant to the level of verbalisation. One is the ordinary process of interpretation that occurs in all language use: simply getting the meaning of what is being worded. This process is familiar to us by virtue of the fact that we are speakers of some language; in it the mediation of meaning typically appears 'natural' and non-problematic. Thus, for most speakers of English, a poem such as Murray's *Widower in the Country* presents little or no problem; it can be easily paraphrased or summarised. In summarising or paraphrasing, reliance is placed mainly on the meanings, not on the 'invisible' element of lexicogrammatical patterning. We can think of this process as the *first order of meaning in verbal art* – a basic 'naturalised' form of interpretation; and for many purposes of language use it suffices. For example, this is precisely the level of interpretation we would bring to reading history, chronicles, and many other varieties. This also happens to be the level reached in the reading of literature for private pleasure. Further, when traditional lit-crit describes the plot of a work, presents character portrayals, or accounts of relationships between characters, it uses precisely this kind of 'intuitive' understanding of meanings. But stopping simply with this first order process would mean that one 'reading' of theme would be as valid as any other. Arguments cannot be presented in support of some specific postulated theme without engaging in the second kind of process. This is where the special expertise comes in.

The second kind of process goes beyond the basic ability to interpret one's language, as it were, intuitively. It extends to:

(a) the ability to *reinterpret* the first order meanings of events, relations and reflections at a more abstract level, inferring from them some more abstract and general meaning.

(b) The ability to consciously analyse the lexicogrammatical form of language, establishing their semantic value, given the context and co-text of their use. Analysis of this kind enables one to see more clearly what patterns occurred with what semantic value at what point in the work's structure. The consistency of foregrounding is determined by such analysis, and it works in cooperation with the process described in (a) (for an example, see Hasan, 1985: Chapter 2, on Murray's *Widower in the Country*).

In what follows, I take as an example the theme of *As You Like It* as described above (Section 3.1). I will focus on what passes between the two cousins, Rosalind, daughter of the exiled Duke Sr. and Celia, daughter of Duke Frederick who has usurped his elder brother's throne:

- Act I opens the play with a universe in disequilibrium; in the last Scene of the Act, chaos becomes more chaotic. Life in and around the court is irrationally unfair; resentment, unhappiness, suspicion, intrigue abound around the two pair of brothers: Duke Frederick has usurped his elder brother's rights; among Frederick's courtiers, Oliver, who is Orlando's elder brother, is scheming against Orlando's life. These are two parallel events at two distinct social levels of the characters' world, each contributing in its way to disequilibrium through a disruption of normal, balanced relationships between relatives, friends and acquaintances.

- Acts II and III are mostly set in the green of the forest of Arden where the exiled Duke Sr. leads a carefree life with some faithful courtiers; his daughter Rosalind, his niece, Celia, arrive there in disguise; Orlando, whose life is under threat from his brother, as well as from Duke Frederick, also arrives in the forest. Practically every tree in the forest begins to bear witness to his declaration of love for Rosalind, who is now disguised as a young gentleman. Life in the green presents a contrast to life in and around the court – carefree, admiring nature, and absorbed in love – an idyllic existence, far removed from 'normal' life, presenting a state of another kind of lack of balance.

- Act IV ends with the start of equilibrium-creating moves: Oliver repents and promises fair treatment for his brother who has, despite Oliver's cruelty, saved his life; wooing pairs move towards consummation.

- Act V ends the play with a return to equilibrium: injustice and unfairness are repaired; seekers are granted their wish: daughter finds father;

> lovers find love; brothers find brothers who had been lost through greed and malice; dukes find their duchy, and the repentant find the healing touch of nature.

This interpretation of the restoration of order and equilibrium is inferred from the first order meanings alone. But what would clinch the theme's symbolic articulation, if it were questioned, is the consistency of foregrounding in *As You Like It*. The structurally significant location for consistent foregrounding of the initial lack of balance is clearly in Act I. In Acts II and III, which present a contrast to the court ('society' vs. 'nature') the earlier form of imbalance is reversed, producing yet another form of imbalance. If the first stage is one of terror, fear and conspiracy, the second is like being in the land of lotus eaters: the first *cannot* be endured; the second, in the nature of things, *will not* endure. Finally, Acts IV and V return the situation to an equilibrium which avoids both forms of excess, allowing life to resume a stable existence. To see symbolic articulation at work, we examine the foregrounding of wordings which concern the developing pattern of Celia and Rosalind's mutual relationship. This relationship metaphorically follows the same stages as discussed above with respects to the inferred meaning of the events in the various Acts of the play. Here I briefly examine their use of *thou/you* to refer to each other (Table 1.1), the frequency of questions they ask each other (Table 1.2) and the frequency of commands they issue (Table 1.3) as consistently foregrounded indicators of their changing relationship.

Table 1.1 shows that in Act I Celia uses *thou* more than twice as often as she uses *you* (29 vs. 12) to refer to Rosalind, whereas Rosalind uses *thou* for Celia only once: in fact, altogether in Act I, Celia refers to Rosalind 5 times as often (C→R = 41 vs. R→C =8). The situation changes dramatically when, in disguise, they find themselves in the forest and under changed circumstances with the arrival of Orlando. For Celia the over-all frequency of address forms is halved by contrast with the initial stage; for Rosalind, it is more than two and a half times higher than in the initial stage. And (speaking facetiously) her use of *thou* is now 10 times greater than before!

	Celia → Rosalind		Rosalind → Celia	
	Thou	You	Thou	You
In the court	29	12	1	7
In the green	4	17	10	11

Table 1.1: Contrasting imbalance in Celia and Rosalind's use of 'thou' and 'you'

These tendencies are again repeated in Table 1.2 with reference to questions. Compared to Rosalind, Celia is very much more outgoing in the initial stage, and more successful at getting her cousin to engage in conversation. But once again, in the Forest of Arden, the reverse situation obtains: here Rosalind is far more importunate, more in need of her cousin's communications than Celia is.

	Celia → Rosalind	Rosalind → Celia
In the court	17	10
In the green	7	30

Table 1.2: Contrasting imbalance in Celia and Rosalind's asking of QUESTIONS

Table 1.3 presents the same pattern, this time with regard to commands, requests (i.e. using language to get the other to do something).

	Celia's commands ...	Rosalind's commands ...
In the court	27	4
In the green	5	16

Table 1.3: Contrasting imbalance in Celia and Rosalind's issuing of COMMANDS

How are these patterns relevant to changing or maintaining human relationship? Simplifying somewhat, one might offer a general interpretation of *thou* here as a form used to express intimacy, closeness, and dependence (for some discussion, see McIntosh, 1966). The three indicators whose foregrounding is discussed above are alike in one respect: each is a semiotic device for engaging an other in interaction. They are thus instances of semantically consistent foregrounding which also display structural consistency. Tables 1.1, 1.2 and 1.3 demonstrate a reversal of the patterns of interaction: if in the initial stage it is Celia who shows greater keenness to engage her cousin in conversation and a greater dependence on her communication, then in the second stage it is Rosalind who goes overboard in these same respects. Lack of balance characterises their relationship in both stages. Ironically, in both stages, it is the stronger party that displays greater dependence: Celia as the Duke's daughter in the initial stage has a superior status to her cousin, who is the daughter of an exiled uncle, and in the second stage, Rosalind in disguise, as a male sibling and the protector of Celia, would be seen as stronger than her protégé. True that their circumstances have changed; their needs have changed; but this is immaterial to the argument because the social material conditions of human beings do affect their patterns of interaction, changing the relationship and their conditions of co-existence. In the play there are also other indicators showing consistency of foregrounding: for example, in Act I, Scene 3, Rosalind's sudden infatuation with Orlando amazes Celia. Not quite believing in this love-at-first-sight phenomenon, she wants to 'talk in good earnest' to Rosalind, asking: 'Is it possible, on such a sudden, you should fall into so strong a liking for old Sir Rowland's youngest son?' (I. 3: 24–26). When in Act IV, Scene 3, this love-at-first-sight smites Celia and Oliver, Orlando is heard asking a very similar question: 'Is't possible that on so little acquaintance you should like her? That but seeing you should love her? And loving, woo? And wooing, she should grant? [...]' (IV. 3: 1–3). Further, the one who brings the news of Duke Frederick's conversion is not the *eldest* brother Oliver, not the *youngest*, Orlando, but the *middle* brother, Jacques de Boys: first mentioned early in Act I, Scene 1, he appears in person only once in the last Scene of the last Act just before the Epilogue. Being the middle brother cannot be described as some kind of standard symbolism; but here, within the context of the play's structure, it can be given such significance, only because the patterns of foregrounding sensitise us to this possibility. In fact, none of the language patterns discussed above instantiate tropes, metaphors, similes; none have anything to do with imagery: what they *do* do, however, is to guide our interpretation of the play's theme. I am not implying that the patterns of what is typically identified as 'artistic language' are inherently irrelevant to the creation of verbal art. The claim is simply that they do not become relevant by virtue of their status as some kind of figure of speech, as a 'methodological tool of artistic convention' for the creation of art. In order to be seen as relevant, they have to contribute to the working of the text as an instance of verbal art. In principle, it is possible for tropes and figures of speech to be consistently foregrounded. If and when this happens, it should be quite easy to show their role in the creation of verbal art.

4   Concluding remarks

It remains to be added that the art in verbal art is not centred primarily in the ideational *content* of theme: after all, if we want to understand labour relations in the early industrial world, we do not seek out Elizabeth Gaskell's *North and South*. To counter present day ravages of corporate culture, we do not go to Trollope's *The Way We Live Now*, nor do we read *As You Like It* as a recipe for restoring 'sane' human relations so the world may resume its state of equilibrium. Other disciplines exist which have developed better ways and means of bringing these and other such phenomena to our attention. If literature engages our attention and emotion, it is because of the art that has gone into the construal of theme, because of both what is said and how it is 'said' as described above (see Sections 3.1–3.2 above). Another way of saying the same thing is to draw attention to the feature I have called *double articulation*: it is this feature that makes verbal art *art*. The three level modelling of verbal art enables us to discuss how this is achieved. Let me add a few words on the concept of double articulation.

Going back to the consistency of foregrounding discussed above (Section 3.2), we note that at the level of verbalisation questions have some meaning as questions, commands as commands, assertions have some meaning as assertions, and so on. Each of these meanings is specific, in that each question has some unique meaning, each order is different in some way from the others, each assertion concerns some specific belief, some unique reflection or observation, and so on. These specific meanings make a contribution to the over all meaning of the work: this is the first level of meaning 'articulation', which can form the basis for any paraphrase or summary of what has been read; these are the meanings I referred to earlier as *first order meanings*. A double articulation of meaning occurs when such patterns of wordings-meanings create another order of patterns by virtue of sharing some characteristic that allows the reader-interpreter-analyst to group them together – recall for example, the grouping of thou/you, of questions and of commands in *As You Like It*. All of these devices were said to be semantically consistent: each is a semiotic device for engaging another in discourse. Consistent foregrounding plays a crucial part in doing the second, higher level of 'reading', allowing, or more precisely, guiding, the inference of something which is more abstract, in the sense that it is less specific, and by the same token, has a wider embrace, applying across a larger number of classes. In inferring this meaning, we are no longer at the level of paraphrase: Celia said this and Rosalind said that. Rather, we are now at the level of symbolic articulation: we infer something abstract: human relations are askew; all's not right with the world. In making such higher level inferences, the consistency of foregrounding plays a crucial and guiding role. Double articulation is what, in Gaskell's *North and South* for example, transforms Margaret Hale's story and that of those she lived and interacted with into an observation on labour-capitalist relations, seen with the eye of human accountability: the first order meaning becomes an extended metaphor for a truth that is more general than the specific events, the localised deliberations, and the situated reactions of specific (groups of) characters in the novel. The essence of double articulation lies in the 'transformation' of the first order meaning into the inferred theme, by the working of patterns of foregrounding: it is the patterns of foregrounding that, if you like, furnish the evidence for the claim that the theme of a work is such and such. In this sense, double articulation is a critical attribute of literature: we learn lessons from human life, we make inferences in other varieties of language use, but it is only in verbal art that the nub of the message – its theme – is 'symbolically articulated' via the consistent patterns of linguistic foregrounding. To reiterate, foregrounding is the 'implicate order' of verbal art, and it acts as the grammar which construes the thematic significance of the work.

Traditionally the study of literature has been preoccupied with 'eccentricity' in the name of novelty, uniqueness and creativity, which have been taken to be the hallmark of art, and whose nature has been, for the most part, seriously 'misrecognised' (see discussion in Section 2). In this search for artistic uniqueness, the category of verbal art itself has 'disappeared' except in name; only sub-varieties and their instances remain. Thus we 'teach' Elizabethan literature, romantic poets, colonial literatures, each represented by a number of instances, without a viable hypothesis about the very basis on which they are brought together as verbal art. The social semiotic model of literature reinstates verbal art as the focal concern of the discipline of literature, treating it as a variety of language use, with its own specific dynamics, its own mode of art construal. Instead of mystifying the nature of verbal art, it offers a framework for its study, which frees the reader from unquestioningly following the opinions of 'authorities'; what is more, it provides a mode of analysis that is open to scrutiny, so that evidence for the competing claims can be compared. In this sense, the model is enabling. It provides a vocabulary for discussing problems related to the discipline of literature and highlights important questions, many of which have never been asked. Let me close this chapter by identifying three issues which are seldom discussed in the study of literature, but each of which is highly relevant for understanding significant aspects of literature.

First, take the issue of *reading literature across spatial-temporal distances*. The social semiotic model 'translates' spatial-temporal distance into semiotic-social distance: other places, other times have other designs for living, other languages for construing meaning, and so most probably different reservoirs of meanings, with different orientations to them. Since, as argued above, both social structure and language system play a crucial role in the creation as well as the reception of verbal art, reading an instance across such a gulf is in principle a somewhat different kind of activity than reading contemporary instances. If it is difficult for us to read Chaucer as Chaucer's contemporaries might have read him, then it is also difficult for us to read *Doctor Zhivago* as a Russian would read it, whether we read it in translation or as foreign speakers of Russian. The same argument applies to sub-cultural distances: the social semiotic model identifies ideology as active both in creating and reading literature and we know that ideologies are linked to social positioning of subjects. These observations have significant implications both for the teaching of literature – who are we teaching? What have they brought to the task? – and for the translation of instances of verbal art: how much of the artistic construal has been preserved in translation? How much of the first order meaning? How much of the patterns of foregrounding?

A *second*, and closely related, issue is that of *context*. To the best of my knowledge, Malinowski was the first to point out that, in story telling, two distinct orders of context operate: a primary context, that of telling the story: who is telling the story to whom and why; and a secondary context which is construed by the language of the 'storying' text. When the first order meaning is derived from the language of a literature text, in that process of interpretation the reader is also construing the context relevant to the story itself – what action is going on, what relations obtain between the participants, and how are they placed in contact with each other. To a certain extent, the double context feature may be said to apply to all 'displaced' texts, i.e. texts that are not produced in a face-to-face communication, as happens in literate societies. And in all cases, from the point of view of the Receiver, the primary context is critical for success in the construal of the first order meaning. So what is the difference between a displaced verbal art text and a non-art text? How is reading Chaucer's *Astrolabe* different from reading his *Canterbury Tales*? The social semiotic model suggests the major difference lies in two features: ideology and double articulation. Only the latter Chaucer text calls for attention to these features, not the *Astrolabe*, an excellent example of early scientific writing. By implication, this highlights the importance of the artist's social background, thus indicating the significance of knowledge about the 'author's milieu' in engaging with literature as an academic discipline. In considering how the work is received by the reader, the evaluation of an instance of verbal art is not independent of the distance between the author's and the reader's milieu.

A *third* issue is the difference between *popular and high literature*. This distinction is clearly based on 'who likes to read what', and given the connotations of 'popular' and 'high' in this context, it is as much a classification of the reader as of what is read: popular literature is read by the 'non-elite' – for which read 'non-rich'– high literature by those who belong to the higher echelons of the society. However, in discourse on art, the 'democratic' view typically taken is that all art is alike in that it is considered to be art by some one in the community to whom it has given pleasure and satisfaction of the kind that comes in engaging with art (see, for discussion, Carey, 2005). Since the social semiotic approach to verbal art insists on identifying the specific attribute of verbal art, its take on this distinction is likely to be different. Taking theme construal as the critical criterion, the model would suggest that, by comparison with 'high' literature, theme construal in popular literature would be found to be less elaborate; the first order meanings would be more centre-stage. A further observation is relevant at this point: in many cases, instances of verbal art may be read pretty much as popular literature, with only the first order meanings engaging the attention of the reader, or the same instances may be read as 'high' literature, when one goes on to explore the basis of its art. Narratives (whether dramatised or not) are particularly amenable to this dual mode of engagement; by contrast, lyrics, sonnets and elegies are not. The ideological message of Mills and Boon (Thwaite, 1983) is not any less amenable to analysis than Jane Austen or George Eliot. It is interesting to ask: is there a way of identifying the character of theme in such a way as to state categorically its non-appeal to the non-elite? From his first publication to the most recent, I have found Salman Rushdie not too rewarding. Does this say something about me as a reader, or about Rushdie as an artist? Does the answer have to be either this or that? And what is the basis of that answer? Trite as these questions might appear, they are at the heart of any discussion of verbal art as a discipline. The social semiotic model goes some way in addressing such issues.

Notes

1   Sometimes, though, it is also maintained that the quality of appreciation depends on the reader being 'cultured' in appropriate ways, a belief that can neither be rejected as entirely irrelevant, nor accepted without challenging the baggage of assumptions it carries without clear articulation.

2   I used the word 'appraisal' in Hasan, 1985 (see, e.g., Chapter 1). In recent years, however, it has been used by Martin (e.g. Martin and Rose, 2003), but with a sense that is rather different. Thus Martin and Rose (2003: 16) describe 'Appraisal' as follows:

> 'Appraisal is concerned with evaluation: the kind of attitudes that are negotiated in a text, the strength of the feelings involved and the ways in which values are sourced and readers aligned. Appraisals are interpersonal kinds of meanings, which realize variation in the tenor of social interactions enacted in a text.'

Compare this with Hasan (1985: 27):

> 'At this stage [*when one is enquiring into the basis of one's response to verbal art*, RH], it is no longer simply a question of receiving with pleasure, of understanding and enjoying the meanings of the text; it is more a question of being able to state clearly the nature of one's response, and to examine explicitly the bases for it. At this stage, then, appreciation must give way to appraisal; the private must be made public; the internalized must be overtly 'externalizable' *– it should be possible to talk coherently about the bases of one's preference and evaluation*'. (emphasis added)

What Appraisal in Appraisal theory does is to offer a framework for the *linguistic* analysis of the wordings that realise attitudes and values; thus the focus of the description is the construal of interpersonal meanings, and despite the claim about describing 'the ways in which values are sourced' I have seen nothing in Appraisal theory that 'talks coherently about the bases of one's preference and evaluation'. My use of the term appraisal concerns not simply how verbal art is realised, but rather with how one explains 'the basis of one's preference and evaluation of some instance' – in other words, not how attitudes and values are referred to in language but what is the basis of the value one attaches to an instance of verbal art, which naturally entails also a framework for the analysis of art in verbal art. This will involve attention to interpersonal meanings but will always need to go beyond it.

3   For the definition of the term 'grammatical metaphor' see Halliday (2004b); Halliday and Martin (1993).

4   Neither Firth (1957) nor Halliday (e.g. in Halliday, McIntosh and Strevens, 1964), used the term 'genre' for language varieties, because the term, familiar through literary criticism, celebrated 'poetic convention' rather than relation to context of language use. It was Bakhtin (e.g. 1986) who, *without* sufficient linguistic analysis of the relations of text and context (cf. Hasan, 1992) extended the term to language varieties other than literature, referring to them as 'speech genres'.

5   For lack of space, no further comments on these two schools of stylistics will be offered. Chatman (1971) presents examples of both approaches. I take this opportunity to distance myself from that interpretation of 'linguistic stylistics' which demands that the literature text be treated as autonomous: a literature text cannot be any more autonomous than language, which only evolves in and with society.

6   It is always difficult to trace the origin of an idea. The model I present here owes much to my doctoral research (1964), which is where many of the ideas were 'honed'. The thesis was submitted just before Garvin became available. The account presented since the early 1970s has, I hope, benefited from my reading of Prague School linguists, but my framework was constructed in the early-mid 1960s, when I lectured on 'stylistics' at University College London. My greatest debt is to M. A. K. Halliday, whose social semiotic modelling of language enabled the emergence of these ideas.

7   The concept *metafunction* in SFL differs crucially from that in Prague School Linguistics, in how it relates to both language and social context. The terms used in describing aspects of language in this chapter are derived from SFL. For some discussion of SFL modelling of language, see Hasan, Matthiessen and Webster (in press).

8   Choice of terminology is fraught with problems. In choosing 'verbalisation', I wished to emphasise the active aspect of language use, which, in the case of verbal art, includes both the unselfconscious use of much of language but

certainly also some deliberate choice in elements of wording, as most evident from the practice of editing.

9   It is often claimed that local knowledge is qualitatively different from special-ised knowledge structures (Muller, Davies and Morais, 2004): it is not theorised and there is no site dedicated to its re-contextualisation (Bernstein, 2000). With the approach to the study of literature being introduced here, we might be able to show that this is not the case: local knowledge could be re-contextualised in a social semiotic study of literature.

10   On ideology in relation to social positioning, see Bernstein (2000).

11   Gaskell's *North and South* was first serialised in Dicken's *Household Words* between 1854–1855, Trollope's *The Way We Live Now* first appeared in 1875. However, here I have referred to the date of the editions which provide the infor-mation about the authors' awareness of the theme: Gaskell (1995) and Trollope (1982). For details of these latter publications, see references.

12   Carey (2005: 20) says '[…] meanings are not things inherent in objects'. I agree: meanings are not *things*; and they do not inhere in *objects*. I would however suggest that meanings are *semiotic construals* and they do inhere in *semiotic objects*. To the fashionably arrogant claim that meanings reside in the reader, one must respond by asking: why do you use language then, if it is just 'sound and fury, signifying nothing'?

References

Bakhtin, M. M. (1986) The problem of speech genres. In C. Emerson and M. Holquist (eds) V. W. McGee (trans.) *Speech Genres & Other Late Essays* 60–106. Austin: University of Texas Press.

Bernstein, B. (2000) *Pedagogy, Social Control and Identity: Theory, Research, Critique*. London: Taylor and Francis.

Butt, D. (1988) Randomness, order and the latent patterning of text. In D. Birch and M. O'Toole (eds) *Functions of Style* 74–97. London: Pinter.

Butt, D. (1996) Literature, culture and the classroom: the aesthetic function in our information era. In J. E. James (ed.) *The Language-Culture Connection*. Anthology Series 37, 86–106. Singapore: SEMEO Regional Language Centre.

Carey, J. (1992) *The Intellectuals and the Masses*. London: Faber & Faber.

Carey, J. (2005) *What Good are the Arts?* London: Faber & Faber.

Chatman, S. (ed.) (1971) *Literary Style: A Symposium*. London: Oxford University Press.

Firth, J. R. (1957) *Papers in Linguistics 1934–1951*. London: Oxford University Press.

Garvin, P. L. (ed. and trans.) (1964) *A Prague School Reader on Esthetics, Literary Structure, and Style*. Washington, DC: Georgetown University Press.

Gaskell, E. (1855 [1995]) *North and South*. London: Penguin Books.

Greenfield, S. (1997) *The Human Brain: A Guided Tour*. London: HarperCollins.

Halliday, M. A. K. (1973) The functional basis of language. In *Explorations in the Functions of Language* 22–47. London: Arnold.

Halliday, M. A. K. (2002) On grammar and grammatics. In *On Grammar: The Collected Works of M. A. K. Halliday* Volume 1: 384–417. J. W. Webster (ed.). London: Continuum.

Halliday, M. A. K. (2004a) *The Language of Early Childhood: The Collected Works of M. A. K. Halliday* Volume 4. J. W. Webster (ed.). London: Continuum.

Halliday, M. A. K. (2004b) *The Language of Science: The Collected Works of M. A. K. Halliday* Volume 5. J. W. Webster (ed.). London: Continuum.

Halliday, M. A. K., McIntosh, A. and Strevens, P. (1964) *The Linguistic Sciences and Language Teaching*. London: Longmans.

Halliday, M. A. K. and Hasan, R. (1985) *Language, Text and Context: Aspects of Language in a Social Semiotic Perspective*. Geelong, Vic: Deakin University Press.

Halliday, M. A. K. and Martin, J. R. (1993) *Writing Science: Literacy and Discursive Power*. London: The Falmer Press.

Hasan, R. (1964) A linguistic analysis of contrasting features in the style of two contemporary English prose writers. Unpublished PhD thesis. Edinburgh: University of Edinburgh.

Hasan, R. (1971) Rime and reason in literature. In S. Chatman (ed.) 299–329.

Hasan, R. (1985) *Linguistics, Language and Verbal Art*. Geelong, Vic: Deakin University Press.

Hasan, R. (1992) Speech genre, semiotic mediation and the development of higher mental functions. *Language Sciences* 1. 4: 489–528.

Hasan, R. (1996) On teaching literature across cultural distances. In J. E. James (ed.) *The Language-Culture Connection*. Anthology Series 37, 34–63. Singapore: SEMEO Regional Language Centre.

Hasan, R. (in press) Language and society in a systemic functional perspective. In R. Hasan, C.M.I.M. Matthiessen, and J. Webster, (eds) *Continuing Discourse on Language: A Functional Perspective* Volume 1: 55–80. London: Equinox.

Hasan, R., Matthiessen, C. M. I. M. and Webster, J. (eds) (in press) *Continuing Discourse on Language: A Functional Perspective* Volumes 1 & 2. London: Equinox.

Lukin, A. (2002) Examining poetry: a corpus based enquiry into literary criticism. Unpublished PhD thesis. Sydney: Macquarie University.

Martin, J. R. and Rose, D. (2003) *Working with Discourse: Meaning beyond the Clause*. London: Continuum.

Matthiessen, C. M. I. M. (in press) The 'architecture' of language according to a systemic functional theory. In R. Hasan, C.M.I.M. Matthiessen, and J. Webster, (eds) *Continuing Discourse on Language: A Functional Perspective* Volume 2. London: Equinox.

McIntosh, A. (1966) 'As You Like It': A grammatical clue to character. In A.
     McIntosh and M. A. K. Halliday (eds) *Patterns of Language: Papers in
     General, Descriptive and Applied Linguistics* 70–82. London: Longmans.
Morrison, B. (2005) A lesson with the art master: Review of *What Good are the
     Arts?* by J. Carey. *Guardian Weekly*, June 24–30: 26.
Mukarovsky, J. (1977) *The Word and Verbal Art: Selected Essays by
     J. Mukarovsky*. J. Burbank and P. Steiner (eds and trans.). London: Yale
     University Press.
Mukarovsky, J. (1978) *Structure, Sign, and Function: Selected Essays by Jan
     Mukarovsky*. J. Burbank and P. Steiner (eds and trans.). London: Yale
     University Press.
Muller, J., Davies, B. and Morais, A. (eds) (2004) *Reading Bernstein,
     Researching Bernstein*. London: Routledge Falmer.
Shakespeare, W. (1623 [1975]) A. Latham (ed.) *As You Like It*. The Arden
     Shakespeare series. London: Methuen & Co.
Thwaite, A. (1983) Sexism in three Mills and Boon romances. Unpublished
     BA (Hons.) dissertation. Sydney: University of Sydney, Department of
     Linguistics.
Trollope, A. (1875 [1982]) *The Way We Live Now*. Oxford: Oxford University
     Press.
Webster, J. J. and Lukin, A. (in press) SFL and the study of literature. In R.
     Hasan, C.M.I.M. Matthiessen, and J. Webster, (eds) *Continuing Discourse
     on Language: A Functional Perspective* Vol. 1. London: Equinox.

2 Construing the 'primitive' primitively: grammatical parallelism as patterning and positioning strategy in D. H. Lawrence

Donna R. Miller

University of Bologna

Editors' Introduction

Donna R. Miller's research focuses, in a Systemic Functional Linguistics (SFL) perspective, on text and discourse analysis (often corpus-assisted) and ESP: political, deliberative, juridical and literary varieties principally. In this paper, she investigates the hypnotic rhythmic quality of the style of D. H. Lawrence, beginning with the description/explanation which Lawrence himself had offered:

> In point of style, fault is often found with the continual, slightly modified repetition. The only answer is that it is natural to the author; and that every natural crisis in emotion or passion or understanding come from this pulsing, frictional to-and-fro, which works up to culmination. (1930: 276)

The basic assumption of Miller's paper is that the chief linguistic resource through which Lawrence constructs his style is grammatical parallelism, an originally 'formalist' discovery (Jakobson, 1960, 1966, 1968), which she would use as a 'functional' investigative tool. She posits that the phenomenon is essentially a device for re-enacting a presumably primitive way of meaning, or oral-based thought, which she links up to Ong's repertoire of the 'psychodynamics of orality' (Ong, 1982: Chapter 1). Her starting point, however, is Jakobson's hypothesis that the ultimate importance of this marked textual reiteration of (phonological, morphological, lexical and syntactic) form is in its ability to call forth a corresponding recurrence of 'sense', so that grammatical parallelism, following up on Hopkins' 1865 insight, is also, and at the same time, semantic parallelism. From there she links up to the phenomenon's ostensible textual function and to findings concerning the 'surfeit' of cohesive harmony that it can be said to confer on a text (Martin, 1992: 386). Thus, she argues, if one can assume that textual cohesion is *not* the primary purpose of the (over)use of the resource in Lawrence, but can also suppose that such an excessive use is presumably 'motivated', i.e. *does* realise meanings, the question seems to become: unto what experiential and interpersonal meanings in Lawrence is this markedly exploited surfeit of '[…] gorgeous grammatical tropes and figures' (Jakobson, 1960: 375), or 'syntactic imagery' (Halliday, 1973: 121)?

Miller, however, sees meaning as inseparable from context, no matter how de-automatised the former may be, or how unpredictable the latter. Thus her investigation draws on Malinowskian (1923) and Firthian (1957 [1968]) situational and cultural context as well, something Jakobson did not do. Her aim is to identify the functions of this patterning and positioning feature with reference to both the fictional context Lawrence's poetry creates, and the 'real' context of creation it's rooted in, especially Lawrence's obsession with writing and re-writing his vision of the intrinsically dual nature of both the individual and creation itself, a *Mysterium tremendum et fascinans*. To this end, she also deals briefly with Lawrence as contra-textual Modernist, as well as with his reflections on 'the seething poetry of the incarnate now': what he most wanted to produce. Grammatical parallelism, she suggests, was the means he employed for its production.

Miller's study is carried out on a very small, though diachronically 'representative', corpus of Lawrence's poems. Though the corpus is in electronic form, her analysis here is manual, and qualitative. Parallelism is explored as a means of consistent, significant and motivated meaning-patterning, or foregrounding, or 'symbolic articulation', of the poems' deepest meanings, or what Hasan calls 'theme' (Hasan, 1985, this volume). At the same time, and not unrelatedly, parallelism is also examined from the point of view of its function as resource for aligning speaker/hearer positioning (White, 2003a and 2003b), in an attempt to get at what is treated by Lawrence as being *at stake*. But the phenomenon is also, and ultimately, queried as a means of enacting Shklovosky's (1977: 35) claim that 'Art is a way of experiencing *the making* of a thing'. In short, in Lawrence, parallelism would seem to be construing experience as process, as a process of 'flux'. As she notes, this 'primitive' way of meaning might also be usefully compared to the medium of 'spoken-ness'. As Halliday has convincingly argued, the 'choreographic' complexity of the spoken mode lends it

> [...] the power to intuit, to make indefinitely many connections in different directions at once, to explore (by tolerating them) contradictions, to represent experience as fluid and indeterminate. (1987: 148–149)

From this it should be clear that the author also posits that *Literature [i]s Social Practice* (Fowler, 1981).

---

1   Introduction

> It is by blood that we are [...], that we live and move and have our being. In the blood, knowing and being, or feeling, are one and undivided: no serpent or apple has caused a split. (Lawrence, 1930: 505)

That the style of D. H. Lawrence tends to either bore or enthuse his readers is certainly no secret. That it is its hypnotic rhythmic quality that elicits such contradictory reactions is equally well-known (cf. Balbert, 1974). E. M. Forster, giving voice to a positive, minority, critical opinion, called Lawrence '[...] the only living novelist in whom the song predominates, who has the rapt bardic quality [...]' (1927 [1962]: 130). For the majority, however, that 'song' smacks strongly of self-indulgence. In his unpublished Foreword to *Women in Love*, Lawrence describes his style and offers a justification of sorts for it, one which implicitly ties his 'form' to what might be seen as his artistic aim, in terms of 'content', or better, of representation:

> In point of style, fault is often found with the continual, slightly modified repetition. The only answer is that it is natural to the author; and that every natural crisis in emotion or passion or understanding come from this pulsing, frictional to-and-fro, which works up to culmination. (1936: 276)

As is presupposed in the above quote, this 'natural crisis', or 'culmination', is Lawrence's concern. The opaqueness of the above description-justification is perhaps only fully comprehensible in terms of Lawrence's 'pseudo-philosophy' (1922 [1960/ rpt.1974]: 57), or 'two-fold way', which is fraught with combativeness, but also inconsistency. The *means* to this culmination, or 'consummation', is pulsive, *pro*pulsive, and at the same time also jarring, conflictual. The 'way' may be construed as a primeval and creative, if antagonistic, 'flux' between the two ways, the two extremes of what Lawrence sees as the intrinsically dual nature of both the individual and creation itself, call them mental-spiritual and phallic consciousness, Not-Self and Self, mind and body, knowledge and feeling, light and dark, Lamb and Lion (see Appendix and Miller, 1989a and 1989b); his dyads are myriad.

A basic assumption of this paper is that the chief linguistic resource through which Lawrence construes this fluid, but strained-to-ultimate-breaking-point, relationship between these two ways is grammatical parallelism (Jakobson 1960, 1966, 1968, hereafter GP). The paper posits that a detailed linguistic analysis engages with, and leads us to, an understanding of this characteristic of Lawrence's art in a more fruitful way than other, albeit valid and insightful, critical approaches alone have, or can (Miller, 1989b, 2000). This does not imply that the Lawrencian socio-cultural context, and intertext(s), are neglected, for also assumed is that *Literature [i]s Social Practice* (Fowler, 1981), that, i.e. Lawrence's grammatical patternings are always a way of dynamically positioning himself, as both man and writer, socio-culturally. Therefore, the 'context of creation' (Hasan, 1985: 101–102) of Lawrence's art, in terms of the world view articulated in and by that art, is also a fundamental aspect of this study.

2   More on parallelism

Gutwinski, in his 1976 study of *Cohesion in Literary Texts*, declines to count GP as a cohesive device in and of itself '[…] because too little is known about it to make any count of this feature meaningful' (1976: 97n). Granting the still notable lack of studies on the phenomenon, this paper's point of departure is Jakobson (1960: 358ff.), who sees this marked reiteration at the syntagmatic level of (phonological, morphological, syntactic and lexical) form as '[…] the empirical criterion of the poetic function'. The ultimate significance of grammatical reiteration, however, is its capacity to call forth a corresponding recurrence of 'sense', so that GP, according to Jakobson, following up on Hopkins' 1865 insight, is seen to construe also, and at the same time, semantic parallelism.

This is a vital hypothesis, one that brings the narrow Formalist concern with syntactic patternings to the level of meaning. It would appear to work well with the finding that the role of parallelism as structural cohesive device in realising what Halliday (1978) calls 'textual' meanings typically works in a way that goes considerably beyond what is warranted, cohesively. As Martin (1992: 386) puts it:

> Grammatical parallelism [...] is exploited rhetorically in contexts where strictly speaking it is not needed to realise the meaning at hand. The result is a 'surfeit' of cohesive harmony [...]

So that it becomes superfluous, annuls its own textual function and illustrates the (typically literary) process of *de-automatisation* (Halliday, 1982), '[...] whereby a particular linguistic stratum makes meaning which is not predicted by its context' (Martin, 1992: 386). But surely that cannot be the whole story. What *else* can the result be said to be? What *more* can this rhetorical exploitation be seen to be unto?

Jakobson also makes clear that, although the poetic function cannot '[...] be arbitrarily confined to the domain of poetry' (1960: 359), in the other varieties of text the phenomenon is typically enacted in (among them, mnemonic texts, advertising, medieval law and Sanskrit theses!), it works '[...] without, however, assigning to this function the coercing, the determining role it carries in poetry' (1960: 359). The very saturation of Lawrence's texts with the device appears to be proof of such a 'coercing [and] determining role'. Thus, if one assumes that cohesion is *not* the primary purpose of the (over)use of the resource, but that such an excessive use of GP is presumably 'motivated', i.e. *has been chosen for the purpose of instantiating meanings*, the question seems to become: unto what experiential and interpersonal semantics in Lawrence's work can such a markedly exploited surfeit of these '[...] gorgeous grammatical tropes and figures' (Jakobson, 1960: 375), or 'syntactic imagery' (Halliday, 1973: 121) be said to be?[1] But, as a systemicist, i.e. a linguist working with the Systemic Functional Linguistic (SFL) model, which sees context as being largely determinant of meaning, I would of necessity link the phenomenon of GP to the level of Malinowskian (1923) and Firthian (1957 [1968]) situational and cultural context as well. I will be making what was a seminal Formalist approach fully Functional, something Jakobson did not quite do.

Parallelism is also still frequently seen as a survivor of a primitive, tongue-tied way of meaning that preceded, and was superseded by, the written word (cf. Ong, 1967, 1982). Lawrence's poetry is, I suggest, firmly located in the oral tradition, though his is obviously not a 'primary' orality, i.e. not the 'real thing', but rather a re-presentation of a pristine, pre-literate consciousness, a re-construal of the evanescent, magic potency of words and sounds. Admittedly, the re-creation is only as accurate as Lawrence's own hyper-literacy will allow (Ong, 1982: Chapter 1). I will be coming back to the 'oral' characteristics of Lawrence's poetry below. For now, I will, with Jakobson, merely say, 'Let us insist on the strikingness of these devices' (1968: 603).

3   On the corpus and plan

This study is carried out on only a very small part of a diachronically and ideologically, or thematically, 'representative', electronic text collection of Lawrence's poems that I have created. As many other poems might have been chosen in support of my aims here, the final selection has been made according to personal predilection. Though the texts are machine-readable and inter-rogate-able, analysis here is strictly manual, and the investigation qualitative. Unlike Louw's paper (this volume), my concern is not with the revelations of the 9-word collocational window in the corpus (or the fact that Jakobson could not be aware of its power). Rather it is with the semantic prosodies that GP can be seen to be weaving throughout each single text.

The study would interweave linguistic analysis with a constant concern with the context of the texts' creation. The 'primitive' in Lawrence is regarded as conceptual basis of his thinking and writing and this is set against the background of Modernism, to explore the extent to which Lawrence mis-fits. His own ideas on the kind of poetry he had to write, and the ways in which those notions connect by way of GP with Ong's decidedly related 'psychodynamic' features of orality (1982) are also set forth.

GP is then explored, in a social semiotic (see Hasan, this volume) /SFL perspective, as a vital strategy for construing the primitive in three poems: as the essential means of the consistent, significant and motivated meaning-patterning, or 'foregrounding' (Mukarovsky, 1932 [1964]), or 'symbolic articulation' of the poems' deepest meanings, i.e. their theme (Hasan, 1985; this volume). In addition, GP is also cursorily considered as resource for aligning speaker/hearer positioning, from the perspective of recent developments in Engagement theory (White, 2003a and 2003b), to get at what is treated as being *at stake*. Finally, the phenomenon of GP is ultimately queried as a means of enacting Shklovosky's claim that 'Art is a way of experiencing the making of a thing' (in Sher, s.a.).[2] In short, in Lawrence, parallelism would, I suggest, construe experience as *process*, as a process of 'flux'. Indeed, this 'primitive', 'tongue-tied' way of meaning might also usefully be compared to the medium of 'spoken-ness'. As Halliday has convincingly argued, the spoken mode is far from being inferior to its written counterpart; its 'choreographic' complexity actually lends it:

> [...] the power to intuit, to make indefinitely many connections in different directions at once, to explore (by tolerating them) contradictions, to represent experience as fluid and indeterminate. (1987: 148–149)

Such, I propose, is the function of language that Lawrence would exploit and enact, and thus preserve, and propagate. As he himself put it in his essay 'Art and Morality':

> What art has got to do, and will go on doing, is to reveal things in their different relationships [...] the relation [...] between the various elements in the creative flux. (1925: 524–525)

4   Mysterium tremendum et fascinans

And now for a few more words on what Lawrence called his 'pseudo-philosophy', what he distinguished from his novels and poems, or his 'pure passionate experience', but what is essentially inextricable from that articulated experience. Thus I am dealing with Lawrence's world view, one vital variable of the context of creation of his verbal art. This corresponds to the assumptions that the writing construes, and these speak, albeit chiefly contra-textually in his case, of the culture Lawrence was part of.

4.1 Lawrence and Modernism

What follows is a very schematic rundown of Lawrence's position vis-à-vis the prevailing artistic and cultural movement of his time: Modernism, and in particular, the German variant he came into contact with through his German wife, Frieda, i.e. Expressionism. But firstly, an important caveat: as already said, it is impossible to represent Lawrence's thought as a systematic, unwavering absolute, as it was ruled by the same capriciousness and love of contradiction that imbued every aspect of his life. It is thus useless to try to categorise his primitivism as either Hobbesian 'hard' or Rousseau-esque 'soft' (Lovejoy and Boas, 1935). By turns, he saw positive aspects of what to most are the brutish and nasty qualities of the primitive, came dangerously close to embracing its violent brutality, but then came down on the side of its inarticulate and benign warmth and 'tenderness' (Miller, 1989a).

How Lawrence 'fits' into the movement is primarily in terms of his critical sense of the dislocation of the individual in the face of the modern, industrial world. He saw wo(man) as being cut off from society, or better, society as no longer being fertile ground for the human, or capable of nurturing meaningful beliefs, values, roles, i.e. identities. He too reacted against the rise of industrialism, the break up of community, perceived as having led to the new and ultimately sterile values of efficiency, productivity, profitability, to a utilitarian worship of the great bourgeois machine and the progress it promised. But here the fit ends. Lawrence aimed to go beyond mere repudiation and put something in the place of this mechanistic modern order and his attempt was fuelled by Vitalism, a primitivist urge for an elemental, 'natural' being, an authentic ethos of life and living. He incessantly shunned meek acceptance of what was and insisted on the possibility of transformation and a new beginning.

Lawrence has in fact never been acknowledged a 'Modernist' writer. He's just too *serious* about his art, and intrusively present IN it (Ingram, 1990: 16ff.). He never 'plays' with technique, for the sake of technique alone. Language in Lawrence is manipulated, not playfully, but *prophetically*. At one point, for him the very act of writing was a, indeed *the*, way of 'doing', of going *forward*, of giving utterance, of '[…] break[ing] through […] deliberately, in knowledge […]' (1920 [1960]: 178–79), i.e. his way of realising the '*Not*-Self'. As he writes about the process of '[…] going back': Yes, we have '[…] to gather up again the savage mysteries. But this doesn't mean going back on ourselves' (1923 [1964]: 138). And yet, his repugnance for and refusal of modern society ultimately meant doing just that: renouncing the struggle for the two-fold way, and embracing but one path, that of the 'Self'. Ideally he had aimed at reconciling the two, but in due course he concedes that they've become, irrevocably, 'daggers drawn' (Brewster and Brewster, 1934: 166). At that point, he comes down on the side of the primitive, and takes arms against all that he comes to connote with 'the machine'.

Abandoning the move *forward*, he opts for limiting that break-through in knowledge to the past and the primitive: a primeval desire for an encounter with the cosmic, the symbolic, the ritualistic, the sacred: a yearning after *Mysterium tremendum et fascinans*, awe in the face of the creative mystery (Otto, 1973: 53ff.). But far from renouncing the urge to utterance, this move backward entails a shift towards becoming the speaker of the unspeakable. For Lawrence, this primitive knowledge is a question of '[…] feeling, wordless, and utterly previous to words […] the primeval, honourable beasts of our being […]' (s.a.: 759). And the rhetoric of celebration of such unutterable knowledge is, in Lawrence, its imitation, or better, its enactment: a 'passionate form', as Sipple (1980: 134) calls it, which, I am arguing, is construed in large part through parallelism.

4.2 'The seething poetry of the incarnate now'

Such is the kind of poetry Lawrence would write. But first, we need to go back a step.

Lawrence, in 'Hymns in a man's life' (1928a: 597), testifies to the powerful influence of '[…] the hymns which I learned as a child, and never forgot'. These hymns, or more precisely, their 'undimmed wonder', stayed with him, he says, never ceasing to exert their deep and poignant sway.

> 'Son of my soul, thou Saviour dear,/It is not night if Thou be near.' [...] it did
> not mean to me any Christian dogma or any salvation. Just the words, 'Sun
> of my soul, Thou Saviour dear' penetrated me with wonder and the mystery
> of twilight. (1928a: 599)

So it was his early religious training that first taught Lawrence to feel, in
rhythms. And it was indeed his re-creation of such rhythms that caused the
editor of his early poems, Edward Marsh, to both extol his imperfect writing as having a '[...] great and rather strange power and beauty' (Hassall,
1959: 193–194) and at the same time decry, together with most of Lawrence's
Modernist contemporaries, his waywardness and scorn of technical formalities
as being different and strange, clearly undisciplined, and therefore defective,
but, somehow, despite all this, special. Turning his back on his brief experience
as Georgian poet and leaving Marsh behind, Lawrence detailed for the latter
his still embryonic theory:

> I think I read my poetry more by length than by stress – [more] as a matter
> of movements in space than footsteps hitting the earth [...] I think more of
> a bird with broad wings flying and lapsing through the air, than anything,
> when I think of metre [...] It all depends on the *pause* – the natural pause,
> the natural *lingering* of the voice according to the feeling – it is the hidden
> *emotional* pattern that makes poetry, not the obvious form. (1913, in Zytaruk
> and Boulton, 1981: 102–104)

Pace Lawrence, it is my contention that this emotional pattern is retrievable
precisely *because* it has been made visible in the grammatical patterning, i.e.
the 'obvious form', of his poems. As Jakobson also had to say about the com-
mensurable patterning of the poetic function, 'Only in poetry with its regular
reiteration of equivalent units is the time of the speech flow experienced, as
it is – to cite another semiotic pattern – with musical time' (1960: 358). In
Lawrence's case, the fugue comes to mind.

In a typically Lawrentian two-fold manner, he developed a theory of two
basic kinds of poetry. In his 'Poetry of the Present', he tells us that the first of
these is traditional. This he calls 'The poetry of the beginning and the poetry
of the end' (1919: 181–186), and clarifies that it is not involved with enacting
change, but with looking calmly at what has been and what is to come. But
such poetry is finished, whole, 'complete and consummate'. The second kind
is the '[...] poetry of that which is at hand: the immediate present'. Such poetry
is not meant to be perfect, consummate or finished: 'The strands are all flying,
quivering, intermingling into the web'. And, though Lawrence appreciates the
'exquisite form: the perfect symmetry' (1919: 182) of the former, by now it
should be easy to identify which he thinks is best:

> The seething poetry of the incarnate Now is supreme, beyond even the everlasting gems of the before and after [...] there must be the rapid momentaneous association of things which meet and pass, on the forever incalculable journey of creation: everything left with its own rapid, fluid relationship with the rest of things. (1919: 183)

What Lawrence is hypothesising is a poetry that is as life and human beings, in his estimation, should be: nakedly alive, urgent and insurgent, unstable, unfixed, boldly shedding the old and donning the new, or vice-versa, as 'the logic of the soul' dictates (1915b [1961]: 36). All quite like what:

> [...] Gerard Manley Hopkins called *haeccitas*, the *thisness* of things, the phenomenon of the here-and-now, the flesh you can pinch and that feels pain, the base and raw material of life. (Warner, 2005: 16, my emphasis)

All a bit hazardous, and frightening as well: the product of a 'demon' that Lawrence with time comes to know and respect and be less haunted by, or so he says (1928b: 849–852). But it was actually even earlier on, in 1915, that Lawrence had theorised the act of writing as a mysterious, almost metaphysical, process, something the writer, as the instrument of 'some greater inhuman will' (Clark, 1969: 29), is neither completely in control of nor thoroughly understands (Miller, 1989a: 35–49). Moreover, 'It does not want to get anywhere. It just takes place' (1919: 185). This kind of verse must clearly be 'free', bird-like. GP, I submit, is what gives it its wings.

It is also a poetry with its roots firmly located in the oral tradition, as I suggested above. Indeed, I believe the characteristics of oral based thought, or the 'psychodynamics of orality', as outlined by Ong (1982: Chapter 2), read extraordinarily like a compendium of a psychodynamics of Lawrentian verse. Without drawing explicit connections, which, given what has been said thus far, I think my reader may trace for him/herself, I present these here below with a minimum of explanation only.

The 'psychodynamics of orality' can be said to be:

- heavily rhythmic, with balanced patterns in repetitions or antitheses, alliterations and assonances etc.;
- additive, rather than subordinative (e.g. marked by an excessive use of biblical 'And');
- aggregative, rather than analytic (i.e. marked by crystallised clusters of often heavily modified, parallel terms, phrases and clauses, helping, according to Ong, to keep thought intact: 'As Lévi-Strauss has well put it [...] "the savage [i.e. oral] mind totalizes"' (cited in Ong, 1982: 39);

- redundant, or 'copious'. Since the oral utterance vanishes as soon as it is uttered, repetition, exact or 'slightly modified', keeps speaker and hearer together, so that neither gets lost;
- conservative, or traditionalist, in the sense that much energy is invested in asserting, over and over again, the wisdom which has been learned only arduously, over time. Lawrence's own practice of reassertion is notorious;
- close to the human lifeworld: having no elaborate, written, analytical categories, oral culture must conceptualise and verbalise knowledge with close reference to the immediate and the familiar. For Lawrence, of course, this is a deliberate choice rather than a requirement;
- agonistically toned. As Ong puts it (1982: 44): '[Writing] separates the knower from the known […] orality situates knowledge within a context of struggle'. Lawrence says, 'It is the joy forever, the agony forever and above all, the fight forever' (1924: 743);
- empathetic and participatory, rather than objectively distanced. Narrator, narrated and audience are made to fuse, and *communality* thus dominates, rather than either subjectivity or objectivity;
- situational rather than abstract. This links up to orality's closeness to both the human lifeworld and communal role system. Bernstein's class-based 'restricted' and 'elaborated' coding orientations (1971 [1974]) could indeed, as Ong suggests (1982: 106) be relabelled, without undue distortion, 'oral-based' and 'text-based'.

So the proposal is that Lawrence's poetry can be seen to partake of these psychodynamics of orality. If the suggestion is a valid one, then it is odd, one might object, that the tools of a presumably text-bound critical movement such as Russian Formalism should be made use of to examine the construal of secondary *orality* in a poet. Perhaps, though Jakobson himself examined the device in, for example, the travel songs of the Kola Lapps and Russian sung and narrated folk stories (1968: 601–602). And, if it is true that Mukarovsky, Shklovsky, Jakobson, and Co., made much of poetry as foregrounded language within the written closure of the poem, they also made much of the process of the poem's *making*, and of its making what were stale and hackneyed ways of saying new, or 'strange'. I am certainly not claiming that Lawrence's poetry is not *written*, but I contend that an important part of the defamiliarising function in his poetry is its painstaking process of authentication of the primacy of the oral, and that a strikingly oral-like GP is the foremost means of its making. But now to a select analysis of the construal of Lawrence's rhetoric of celebration, realised in and by the 'passionate form' of his poetry of the moment.[3] No pretence at being able to detach the poetic voice from Lawrence's own will be made.

5   Construing the primitive primitively

5.1 Bei Hennef (We have come through! 1917)[4]

Bei Hennef

1   The little river twittering in the twilight,
2   The wan, wondering look of the pale sky,
3   This is almost bliss.

4   And everything shut up and gone to sleep,
5   All the troubles and anxieties and pain
6   Gone under the twilight.
7   Only the twilight now, and the soft 'Sh!' of the river
8   That will last for ever.

9   And at last I know my love for you is here;
10   I can see it all, it is whole like the twilight,
11   It is large, so large, I could not see it before,
12   Because of the little lights and flickers and interruptions,
13   Troubles, anxieties and pains.

14   You are the call and I am the answer,
15   You are the wish, and I the fulfilment,
16   You are the night, and I the day.
17   What else? It is perfect enough.
18   It is perfectly complete,
19   You and I,
20   What more – ?

21   Strange, how we suffer in spite of this!

One of Lawrence's first poems to be written in free, unrhymed, but largely parallel form is 'Bei Hennef'. Sound reiteration is the first level of GP that is noticeable, as Ingram (1990: 145) remarks. Take the /tw/ of 'twittering [...] twilight', the /wa:/ of 'wan, wandering', but also the third line's dense /s/ and /z/ phonemes, where the pivotal mood adjunct of degree, 'almost', is first made explicit, setting up the pattern of not-quite-right feeling in the poem.[5] The first two lines are also 'almost' parallel in their nominal group (henceforth NG), experiential structure: Specific Deictic + Epithet + Thing + qualifying defining relative in line 1, and Specific Deictic + Epithet + Epithet + Thing + Qualifier in line 2: two NGs seemingly striving to be complete independent clauses, but made, instead, to wait to resolve themselves in anaphoric 'This' in the (finally) complete clause in line 3.

In the second stanza, more reiteration is at work, not just cohesively, but again experientially: in line 4, the Attributes of 'everything', 'shut up and gone to sleep'; line 5's extended NGs (A *and* B *and* C), and in line 6, their Attribute, 'Gone under the twilight', the second instance of 'gone', and of 'twilight'. A dark and dormant peace results, also because all this is brought back, ambiguously, by the textual Theme 'And' to 'bliss', but again in incompleteness. There is no finite verb at all in this second stanza, a finding I'll come back to below. The grammar continues to tell us that completeness is but an illusion.

Again, no finite appears to anchor this mere, dual, timeless 'Existent', whose existence, it is said, will have no end: 'the twilight now, and the soft 'Sh!' of the river'. At the same time, however, this river, which you can hear (sh-ushing?), is a telling instance of what Hopkins called *haeccitas*: the *thisness* of things. An eternal immediateness, if you will.

In the third stanza, at last we get three complete clauses. The end-focus of the stanza's first line (9) is 'here', and what is 'here' is perceived, and perceived as being good. Again there is lexical repetition: 'last' for the second time, now nominal; 'twilight' for the third time; 'see' and 'large'. The reiterations, however, seem to prolong the perception just a bit *too* much, enough to get to the causal clause in lines 12 and 13: 'Because of the little lights and flickers and interruptions,/ Troubles, anxieties and pains', whose extended NGs re-propose not only the structure of the second stanza's 'All the troubles and anxieties and pain', but its very lexis as well. The rhythms function in opposite ways, however. Those in the second stanza lulled, while these, at least in some measure due to their reiteration, pinch up an ache. This is also due to the prominent semantic location of the repetition: as Ingram too has noted (1990: 147). At the very moment of being able to perceive his complete love, the poet recalls what made him *in*capable of seeing it before. The foregrounded modality (because markedly scarce overall) of the 'can' of capacity in line 10 is, in fact, immediately followed in line 11 by a reminder of what, 'before', he 'could *not* see'.

A radical structural change comes about in the fourth stanza. In lines 14, 15 and 16, we have three almost-perfectly parallel, complete and coordinated relational clauses, one following the other, with identical subjects ('I'/'you') and explicit, or ellipted, verbs ('am'/'are'). The Values assigned to the Things being Identified are in each case typically strong collocates, the Identifying elements moving from the field of language ('call'/'answer'), to that of the sensual and/or spiritual ('desire'/fulfilment'), to the natural, cosmic rhythms of 'night' and 'day'. But then the defining cycle stops; it stops short, and just short of incoherence:

> What else? It is perfect enough.
> It is perfectly complete,
> You and I,
> What more – ?

The symmetrically located interrogatives are, significantly and foregroundedly, two. They are also parallel structures: Wh- + adverbial group of degree. In the first, the poetic voice seems to, ingenuously enough, demand information (from himself? From 'you'?) as to what else 'I' and 'you' can be said to be. But the following declarative's first instance of 'perfect', with modifier 'enough', betrays anxiety, and belies the second instance's adverbial function ('perfectly') of 'complete'. In line 19, the reiterated, but now isolated, 'You and I', after the preceding expanded definitions of what they are, seem again to be searching for something further to define them, but the search ends in another aborted clause: 'What more – ?' Any attempt to read these inarticulate lines as genuinely and confidently affirming the lover's fulfilment is cruelly thwarted by the last stanza's single, albeit now complete and conversational, exclamative clause, significantly located as the concluding line of the poem, and thus also foregrounded:

> Strange, how we suffer in spite of this!

As Ingram (1990: 149) so aptly comments: 'The source of the poet's potential happiness is also the source of his dissatisfaction [...]'. And I believe we have seen how the grammar of the poem has enacted just 'this'.

The parallelisms in the poem are also, fittingly, those of *absence*. I have already remarked the incomplete clauses, devoid of finites, and thus Mood-less. In this way, not only is time written out of the poem (cf. Butt on this aspect of the ending of *Sons and Lovers* in this volume), but the poem's interpersonal communicative function is continuously thwarted. Even logically, the clauses, as we've seen, are incomplete. Topical Themes are identifiable only if seen as being realised implicitly, i.e. only if we see the key third line's 'This' as functioning, both anaphorically and cataphorically, as the node of a reference chain which is also an implicit, long, and complex Theme. But even if we do, the poem's method of development is decidedly erratic, as inconsistent as the poet's perception of his love.

Post-analysis, one might recall that the ideal Lawrentian relationship is also superlatively rapid, fluid, momentaneous, a fleeting meeting that then retreats to singleness, to come together again. Similarities of such a process with those 'little lights and flickers and interruptions' might be noted. Permanent union, lasting 'for ever', is in fact anathema to his creed. Yet the human *will* ache for a less short-lived two-in-one; hence, perhaps, those recurring 'troubles and anxieties and pain'. One might also remember that, for Lawrence, and again very ideally, each individual needed to be 'fulfilled' in the opposite ways in him/herself, *before* searching out the 'other'. Otherwise, their meeting was doomed to failure. So, one's being but an imperfectly realised half of the whole could not work, was inadequate, not at all 'perfect enough'. His belief demanded there be something 'else', something 'more'.

Which brings me to the Engagement mechanisms at work in the poem: the Speaker's complete clauses are prevalently monoglossic: unarguable, bare assertions of what *is*. As we have seen, however, the confidence ostensibly communicated is vulnerable to an extreme. The foregrounded interrogatives, 'What else? […] What more?', may be functioning as resources for actively Entertaining dialogic alternatives, or better, additions, to the clearly imperfect completeness being thematically articulated, and even, perhaps, dialogically embraced. But, as we've seen, though they act to conjure up the possibility of perfection, such perfect perfection is ultimately articulated as being beyond reach. Paradoxically, 'strange[ly]', this 'perfect enough', 'despite' itself, gives way to 'suffer[ing]'. Lawrence had also written: 'Love is not a goal; it is only a travelling' (1918: 152).

5.2 Underneath (Pansies, 1929)

Underneath

1   Below what we think we are
2   we are something else,
3   we are almost anything.

4   Below the grass and trees
5   And streets and houses and even seas
6   is rock; and below the rock, the rock
7   is we know not what,
8   the hot wild core of the earth, heavier than we can even imagine.

9   Pivotal core of the soul, heavier than iron
10   so ponderously central;
11   heavier and hotter than anything known;
12   and also alone. –
13   And yet
14   reeling with connection
15   spinning with the heaviness of balance
16   and flowing invisibly, gasping
17   towards the breathing stars and the central of all sunninesses.

18   The earth leans its weight on the sun, and the sun on the sun of suns.
19   Back and forth goes the balance and the electric breath.

20   The soul of man also leans in the unconscious inclination we call
     religion
21   Towards the sun of suns, and back and forth goes the breath
22   Of incipient energetic life.

23   Out of the soul's middle to the middle-most sun, way off, or in every
     atom.

The second poem I offer as evidence of how GP primitively construes Lawrence's 'primitive' thought, is 'Underneath', one of the few longer and less lapidary *Pansies*. The poem construes life, not as rational knowledge and thought would have it, but according to intuitively grasped, inhuman, inanimate, if often personified, things in motion. Its lexicogrammar and symbolic articulation instantiate this.

The human 'we', in fact, is immediately and thoroughly de-legitimated as Senser, or Attributor. 'What we think we are' is not the whole story and 'we know not what' that whole story is ('something else', '*almost* anything', where once again we have that key degree adjunct at work). 'We' cannot even imagine how heavy 'The hot wild core of the earth' is. There is even something indefinite implied about the name 'we' attribute to 'The soul of man['s…] unconscious inclination': 'religion'. There is, indeed, also some doubt as to whether the Speaker is including himself at all or in part in this 'we'.

It is the largely abstract, elemental Things that are the protagonists of the poem. These are set against those unmodified and rather hum-drum single Things that are amassed as though immaterial through extension in lines 4 and 5: 'the grass *and* trees *and* streets *and* houses *and* even seas'. Underneath, or far above these, the central characters are realised in a contrastingly extended NG structure: the X of the Y (Specific Deictic + Thing + Qualifier), seven times more or less exactly reiterated:

> 'The hot wild core of the earth'
> 'Pivotal core of the soul'
> 'the heaviness of balance'
> 'the central of all sunniness'
> 'the sun of suns' (twice)
> 'the breath of incipient energetic life'

These inanimate, ambiguous Things are certainly more stimulating, if (or perhaps even *because*) highly indeterminate. In the second stanza of the poem, they participate grammatically in reiterated relational identifying Processes: X = Y, notably with circumstances of Location as participant: 'Below the grass and' etc. etc. IS [...] 'The hot wild core of the earth' etc. That relational Processes should be typical of the Lawrencian text is, of course, unsurprising; he is obsessed with describing and defining. But here this function is frustrated by unknowns. Below X is rock (lines 4–6), but below that twice-reiterated rock 'is we know not what' (line 7), something that gets immediately 'disambiguated' in line 8, however, but by the thoroughly indeterminate 'hot wild core of the earth, heavier then we can even imagine'.

In stanza three, this latter NG then participates as implicit Actor in structurally parallel and physically (in the sense of the science of physics as well) powerful, even feral, material Processes, many with the persistently reiterated /ŋ/ sound, in the participle of the present, of the *Now*, so common in Lawrence: 'Reeling [...] Spinning [...] flowing [...] gasping'. It is significant that this third stanza is also foregrounded in terms of mood structure. The finite verbs are ellipted and, with them, polarity and concrete temporality. Further, the Subjects are for the most part suppressed, or suspended, to return in the fourth stanza, together with finites, in a simple, generalising present tense of the way things *are*, e.g. the twice each reiterated 'leans' and 'goes'.

Prepositions and prepositional phrases as circumstances are rampant, and relevant, those of Location in particular. They move from static presence 'below' (thrice repeated), to dynamic motion, with 'towards' ('twice'), 'on' (twice), and 'out of', doing their part, along with the enjambments, to accelerate the pace. Circumstances also function, symmetrically, as marked Topical Theme of the clause, or head word of the line, in the beginning of the poem (lines 1, 4, and within 6), and at the end (17, 19, 21 and 23). The concern with what is 'below X' can be topically linked to Lawrence's way of the Self, the anti-rational, dark, pagan, primitive mysteries of the blood, and death. But the 'towards', and the twice repeated 'back and forth' and 'Out of the soul's middle to the sun's middle [...]', take us back to a concern with otherness, and life. A certain confusion enters in if the reader 'knows' the sun's connection to the sensual in other works of Lawrence, but in 1922 Lawrence *was* still trying to reconcile his two ways. To better understand the 'ideas' that the poem gives voice to, the section entitled 'cosmological' of *Fantasia of the Unconscious* (1922 [1960/ rpt.1974]: 183) is the place to go. There we are told that:

> [...] the sun is the great sympathetic centre of our inanimate universe [...] is the soul of the inanimate universe [...] To the sun fly the vibrations or the molecules in the great sympathy-mode of death, and in the sun they are renewed, they turn again as the great gift back again from the sympathetic death-centre towards life, towards the living.

Undoubtedly the poem is 'clearer', in terms of its didactic message, after that rather exasperating instruction, a lesson which the predominant and portentous monoglossic character of the poem corroborates. But perhaps something vital is lost. Although it may seem strange to ask, given my avowal of the role of the author's world view in interpretation, I will: is one so much poorer for the cognitively *un*informed experience? Surely one need not sniff out every recorded intertextual clue to the Lawrentian dogma being 'intentionally' propagated in his text. Now, what I'm suggesting is not at all a reading for mere 'private pleasure' (see Hasan, this volume). Yet if, *after* analysis, one can also 'go with the flow' that has been disclosed, as it were (but *not* as it was for some belonging to an earlier, more 'spontaneous' 1960s' counter-culture that, selectively and un-analytically, took Lawrence up), one should also be able to delight in the meanings made by those intrinsic 'gorgeous grammatical tropes and figures' which, summarised, include:

- the paratactically linked NGs: the A *and* the B *and* the C … vs.
- the more expanded X of the Ys;
- the parallel relational Processes: X = Ys;
- the phoneme /ŋ/, and the /h/s and /r/s of 'heavier' and again 'heavier' and then 'hotter';
- the circumstances: 'below', 'towards', 'on', back and forth', 'out of', and so on.

Once we have inferred, that is, on the basis of analysis of the poem's articulated patterns, that a mysterious two-fold way of existence in motion is indeed the poem's theme, to allow ourselves to move with and be moved by what has been shown to be its grammatically instantiated 'pulsing, frictional to-and-fro' is only proper, a fair return, I'd say.[6]

5.3 Lonely, Lonesome, Lonely – O! (More Pansies, in Last Poems, 1932)

Lonely, Lonesome, Lonely – O!

1   When I hear somebody complain of being lonely
2   Or, in American, lonesome
3   I really wonder and wonder what they mean.

4   Do they mean they are a great deal alone?

5   But what is lovelier than to be alone?
6   Escaping the petrol fumes of human conversation
7   And the exhaust-smell of people
8   And be alone!

9	Be alone, and feel the trees silently growing.
10	Be alone, and see the moonlight outside, white and busy and silent.
11	Be quite alone, and feel the living cosmos softly rocking
12	Soothing and restoring and healing.

13	Soothed, restored and healed
14	When I am alone with the silent great cosmos
15	And there is no grating of people with their presences gnawing
16	At the stillness in the air.

There is something light-hearted and even playful about this poem, certainly after 'Underneath' at least! The title itself is mischievous in its reiterated quasi-synonymous NGs. Its message is quite serious, of course, but its Speaker keeps within a simple, accessible lexis, and the 'living cosmos' comes out decidedly less baffling and forbidding as a result.

The parallelism of Processes in the poem is again significant. Once more the predominant semantic direction of these is relational: being 'alone'. Nine times some form of the verb 'to be' is explicit. Four of these are the bare infinitive and correspond to 4 of the 7 imperatives of the poem. This is the foregrounded mood, what I will call, despite their coercive form, rhetorical 'suggestions', rather than commands. They are suggestions by the poem's 'I' to those who would 'complain of being lonely', which pleasingly lack the exasperating urgency that this mood, in Lawrence, can often communicate.

Material Processes feature significantly too. These are seven in all, and all are in the *–ing* non-finite of a perpetual atemporality, construing the unending nature of the Processes. Apart from 'escaping', in line 6, throughout the third stanza these represent the life of inanimate, but personified as benevolent, Things: 'trees silently growing', but especially that 'living cosmos' as munificent and compassionate Actor: 'softly rocking', 'soothing', 'restoring', 'healing'. These last three are then immediately quasi-reiterated in their *–ed* form and made to function as Attributes of the Speaker. In textually-created opposition to the foregoing, both lexically and phonologically, there is the onomatopoeically *dis*pleasing human activity of 'gnawing', but also of 'grating', though the latter a nominalisation here.

The Process-types that contrast with these are: (1) the mental, five in all, the two twice-repeated ('wonder' and 'feel'), and (2), the verbal ('complain' and twice-reiterated 'mean', i.e. in the sense of 'want to say'). All have explicit, or potential, animate participants as Subject. These foregrounded Processes set up one of the vital tensions in the poem: the inconceivable complaining of the 'other' of what, to the 'I', is supreme: being alone! And the two significantly located, contiguous rhetorical questions in lines 4 and 5, together with the initial counter-expectational 'But' of the second one, reinforce the unimaginable nature of the complaint.

The other tension, which works together with the first to articulate the poem's theme, is instantiated in and by the grammatical participants. Besides animate 'I', 'someone' and 'they', the participants in the poem are, on the one hand, all those inanimate, but personified, aggregate Things the reader is invited to perceive: the natural, hushed, potent and pleasurable, and, on the other, what solitude 'escapes': the nauseating products of industrial progress, 'petrol fumes' and 'exhaust-smell', NGs that in lines 6 and 7, through their Qualifiers, are coupled grammatically, if uncommonly, to 'people' and their 'human conversation'.

The alliteration and assonance of the /s/ and /r/ in particular emphasise the semantic likeness, and unlikeness, between many of the material Processes, and elsewhere, as within the semantically synonymous lexical string: 'stillness', 'silent' (in some form, 3 times) and 'softly'. In spite of the reasonable reservations one may have regarding 'sound symbolism', Lawrence's constant penchant for a quasi-perceptible sinuous, sensual /s/ is difficult to discount. Temporally, the setting is anywhere; spatially, it is *every*where. In striking contrast to 'Underneath', the poem is devoid of any location whatsoever, apart from 'outside', and that which is denoted, and connoted, by the 'cosmos', great, silent, and living.

The Speaker, monoglossically, or through rhetorical imperatives and interrogatives which function to Contract his meanings, clearly takes his stand on the side of the way of the natural, the instinctive, the speechless. Towards that silent and solitary way of being, in relation with the cosmos, he stands serenely reverent, awed, while towards the human he is inflexibly intolerant and harsh in his critique. There are no half-way measures to his tribute, or condemnation, typically, for Lawrence was not a half-way man. He is always the preacher, telling us what he knows better than we do, calling for us to believe and behave as he does, but here, because not exasperated, the conative message does not 'grate'. It is a delightful hymn to the wordless crafted in words, 'a raid on the inarticulate', if you will.

6   In closing

This paper has attempted to argue for, and illustrate, the fundamental role that the strategy of GP has in the linguistic construal of the themes, or the deepest meanings, that D. H. Lawrence's poetry articulates. I have proposed, firstly, that such meanings are rooted in the essentially 'primitive' path of Lawrence's initial 'two-fold way', that of the Self rather than the Not-Self, the frontrunner in their long and often fierce struggle for Lawrence's ultimate commitment.

In brief, the primal blood consciousness is the keystone of those meanings. In the second place, I have argued that GP can be seen to be the primary tool for 'primitively' enacting them, by means of that 'pulsing, frictional to-and-fro' that the writer knew characterised his writing, and of which he was proud, protective, and defensive.

But here in closing, I would come back to that *Mysterium tremendum et fascinans* I touched upon above. That Lawrence saw his writing as doing more, being more, than a (however technically successful) construal of a secondary orality needs to be emphasised. For him GP was definitely *unto* some higher function, as even the 'pulsing, frictional to-and-fro' quote I opened with makes clear. From his earliest poetry writing years, he hypothesised being in contact with, being in fact an 'impersonal instrument' of, that 'greater inhuman will' cited above (Clark, 1969: 29). In his review of the anthology, *Georgian Poetry 1911–1912*, Lawrence explicitly delineates the arcane 'revealing' function that he invested in his writing. The notion in itself is metaphysical, but also primordial: a sort of uncanny overturning of the Word Made Flesh, the *Logos* incarnate, in which the very ink of the artist's pen, blending as it were with the blood of the writer, bequeaths Revelation:

> Now the warmth of the blood is in everything, quick, healthy, passionate blood. I look at my hands as I write, and I know they are mine, with red blood running its way, sleuthing out Truth and pursuing it to eternity, and I am full of awe for this flesh and blood that holds this pen. Everything that ever was thought and ever will be thought lies in this body of mine [...] This [...] impersonal flesh and blood, greater than me, which I am proud to belong to [...]. (1913: 306)

'Homo sum'! (1924: passim), indeed. The passage also illustrates once again how unfeasible it is to classify Lawrence as Modernist writer. As I noted above (see Section 4.1), he is prophetic, rather than playful. I now add that the primitive is traditionally seen as having the gift of prophecy, and, perhaps an even more pertinent observation, that the 'gift' of the shaman is to remember on behalf of his or her people. What Lawrence puts forth in the above quote is not simply (and, one might note, more suitably) the writer as inter-, or contra-textual voice of his cultural context, his discourse community. Rather, it is a kind of transcendental function of human language, with the Divine as its guiding principle, or, to put it another way, with the writer as encoder of ontologically pre- existing, immanent referents – which is also further evidence of how frustrating Lawrence can be to the practical-, but above all social semiotically-minded! Exasperating he is, but also path-etic, etymologically intended.

As the third poem I analysed above illustrated, Lawrence had little time for 'the petrol fumes of human conversation'. I conclude by recalling that the ultimate grand challenge for this indefatigable writer was actually to give utterance to the *un*utterable:

> In the very darkest continent of the body there is God. And from Him issue the first dark rays of our feeling, *wordless, and utterly previous to words*: the innermost rays, the first messengers, the primeval, honourable beasts of our being, whose voice echoes wordless and forever wordless down the dark avenues of the soul, but *full of potent speech*. Our own inner meaning. (s.a.: 759, my emphasis)

Of course, both passages quoted above are clearly heaving with the parallelism which has been the focus of this paper: a further demonstration, I suggest, of my thesis that such parallelism is the main device that Lawrence employs in his concrete struggle for bespeaking the unknown, and for enacting that struggle in his art – or, as Shklovsky put it: '[…] experiencing the making of a thing'. Although the data offered in this paper are unquestionably scant, I would hope that the hypothesis has been at any rate plausibly argued and illustrated. I would also hope that I've managed to render some service to a writer who I consider as exciting as he is exacting, and a bit to his admiring readers as well. To speak in Hasan's terms (this volume), Lawrence's 'perception of the human condition' speaks to me-as-reader; his themes often succeed in striking in me a chord that prompts the declaration: '*yes, indeed I recognise this condition*' – which means of course that the writer and this reader must share, to some degree in any case, their ideological stance.

Notes

1   Reference here is to the tripartite division of semantic metafunctions, or meanings, modelled by Systemic Functional (or Hallidayan) Linguistics (Halliday, 1994). As a lengthy delineation of this and other aspects of the model, and its metalanguage, is beyond the confines of this paper, a basic shared background needs to be presumed. The same is true of Engagement theory, though the use that is made of it is limited and straightforward enough to follow without undue difficulty. These too-brief remarks on GP will need to suffice as well.

2   The wording of the 1917 quote offered here is the literal, and to me preferable, translation given by another translator of Shklovsky: Benjamin Sher, in his fascinating online piece (see http://www.websher.net/srl/tran.html), entitled 'Nature vs. art: a note on translating Shklovsky', where he convincingly argues that neither his own 1990 version ('Art is a means of experiencing the process of creativity'), nor the Lemon and Reis translation ('Art is a way of experiencing the artfulness of an object', 1965: 12), are satisfactorily close to the Russian original, which fits my requirements perfectly.

3   In Lawrence, admittedly, there is also a rhetoric of ridicule, of invective, of railing against the collapse of civilisation, as Lawrence wanted it to be, which I am deliberately overlooking for my purposes here.

4   In parentheses, the original volume in which the poem appeared and its date of publication is provided.

5   What go by the names of sound symbolism, linguistic iconism, and phonosemantics, are hardly exact sciences, and yet studies into these interrelated subjects are fascinating and perhaps even revealing and reliable to some extent. Margaret Magnus' research (1999) deals with the relationship between the sounds of a word and its meaning, how to discover these meanings, and what this may signify for our understanding of language, symbolism, and human consciousness in general. See her website too for much more on this subject.

6   Many of my own findings on 'Underneath' can be usefully compared to those of Butt concerning the closing vision of *Sons and Lovers* (this volume). Butt also proposes that as early as that 1913 novel, Lawrence anticipated '[…] a universe that scientists were yet to comprehend'. Perhaps. I believe, however, that it's hazardous to ignore the quite peculiar nature of the cosmology that Lawrence was developing, and which is widely seen as being *pseudo*-scientific, much as his philosophy, according to his own admission, recall, was also '*pseudo*-philosophical' (Preface to 1922 [1960/ rpt.1974]). That much said, it is indubitable, and obvious in this poem as well, that the scientific theories of his times fascinated Lawrence. My point is that he made his own very personal use of them, as he did of all knowledge that he acquired, and that what he may have achieved *ante-litteram* might well have been realised *in spite of* himself. That this should be so is, of course, neither unfeasible nor particularly extraordinary. As Butt also reminds us, language is not a passive, referential tool for a preexisting subjectivity.

References

Balbert, P. (1974) *D. H. Lawrence and the Psychology of Rhythm*: *The Meaning of Form in 'The Rainbow'*. The Hague: Mouton.

Bernstein, B. (1971 [1974]) *Class, Codes and Control*: *Volume 1*: *Theoretical Studies towards a Sociology of Language*, 2nd edition. London: Routledge & Kegan Paul.

Brewster, E. and Brewster, A. (1934) *Reminiscences and Correspondences*. London: Secker.

Clark, C. (ed.) (1969) *D. H. Lawrence*: *'The Rainbow' and 'Women in Love'*: *A Casebook*. London: Macmillan.

Firth, J. L. (1957 [1968]) Enthnographic analysis and language. In F. R. Palmer (ed.) *Selected Papers of J. R. Firth, 1952–1959*. Bloomington, Indiana and London: Indiana University Press.

Forster, E. M. (1927 [1962]) *Aspects of the Novel*. Harmondsworth: Penguin Books.

Fowler, R. (1981) *Literature as Social Discourse: The Practice of Linguistic Criticism*. London: Batsford.

Gutwinski, W. (1976) *Cohesion in Literary Texts*. The Hague: Mouton.

Halliday, M. A. K. (1973) Linguistic function and literary style. An inquiry into the language of William Golding's *The Inheritors*. In *Explorations in the Functions of Language* 103–143. London: Edward Arnold.

Halliday, M. A. K. (1978) *Language as Social Semiotic. The Social Interpretation of Language and Meaning*. London: Arnold.

Halliday, M. A. K. (1982) The de-automatization of grammar: from Priestley's 'An Inspector Calls'. In J. Anderson (ed.) *Language Form and Linguistic Variation* 132–158. Amsterdam: John Benjamins.

Halliday, M. A. K. (1987) Language and the order of nature. In N. Fabb, D. Attridge, A. Durant and C. MacCabe (eds) *The Linguistics of Writing: Arguments between Language and Literature* 135–154. Manchester: Manchester University Press.

Halliday, M. A. K. (1994) *An Introduction to Functional Grammar*, 2nd edition. London: Arnold.

Hasan, R. (1985) *Language, Linguistics and Verbal Art*. Geelong, Vic: Deakin University Press.

Hassall, C. (1959) *A Biography of Edward Marsh*. New York: Harcourt, Brace & Co..

Ingram, A. (1990) *The Language of D. H. Lawrence*. London: Macmillan.

Jakobson, R. (1960) Closing statement: linguistics and poetics. In T. A. Sebeok (ed.) *Style in Language* 350–377. Cambridge, Massachusetts: MIT Press.

Jakobson, R. (1966) Grammatical parallelism and its Russian facet. *Language* 42. 2: 399–429.

Jakobson, R. (1968) Poetry of grammar and grammar of poetry. *Lingua* 21: 597–609.

Lawrence, D. H. (1913) Review of E. Marsh (ed.) *Georgian Poetry 1911–1912*. London: The Poetry Bookshop. In E. McDonald (ed.) *Phoenix: The Posthumous Papers of D. H. Lawrence* 304–307. New York: Viking Compass.

Lawrence, D. H. (1915a) The crown. In W. Roberts and H. T. Moore (eds) *Phoenix II* 364–415. New York: Viking Compass.

Lawrence, D. H. (1915b [1961]) *The Rainbow*. New York: Viking Compass.

Lawrence, D. H. (1918) Love. In E. McDonald (ed.) *Phoenix: The Posthumous Papers of D. H. Lawrence* 151–156. New York: Viking Compass.

Lawrence, D. H. (1919) Poetry of the present (Introduction to the American edition of *New Poems*). In V. de Sola Pinto and W. Roberts (eds) *The Complete Poems of D. H. Lawrence* 181–186. London: Heinemann; London: Penguin.

Lawrence, D. H. (1920 [1960]) *Women in Love*. New York: Viking.

Lawrence, D. H. (1922 [1960/ rpt.1974]) *Fantasia of the Unconscious*. [version published together with *Psychoanalysis of the Unconscious* in 1960/ rpt.1974 by New York: Viking].

Lawrence, D. H. (1923 [1964]) *Studies in Classic America Literature*. New York: Viking Compass.

Lawrence, D. H. (1924) Climbing down Pisgah. In E. McDonald (ed.) *Phoenix: The Posthumous Papers of D. H. Lawrence* 740–744. New York: Viking Compass.

Lawrence, D. H. (1925) Art and morality. In E. McDonald (ed.) *Phoenix: The Posthumous Papers of D. H. Lawrence* 521–526. New York: Viking Compass.

Lawrence, D. H. (1928a) Hymns in a man's life. In W. Roberts and H. T. Moore (eds) *Phoenix II* 597–601. New York: Viking Compass.

Lawrence, D. H. (1928b) Foreword to *Collected Poems*. In V. de Sola Pinto and W. Roberts (eds) *The Complete Poems of D. H. Lawrence* 849–852. London: Heinemann; London: Penguin.

Lawrence, D. H. (1930) Apropos of *Lady Chatterley's Lover*. In W. Roberts and H. T. Moore (eds) *Phoenix II* 487–515. New York: Viking Compass.

Lawrence, D. H. (1932) The study of Thomas Hardy. In E. McDonald (ed.) *Phoenix: The Posthumous Papers of D. H. Lawrence* 398–516. New York: Viking Compass.

Lawrence, D. H. (1936) Foreword to *Women in Love*. In W. Roberts and H. T. Moore (eds) *Phoenix II* 275–276. New York: Viking Compass.

Lawrence, D. H. (s.a.) The novel and the feelings. In E. McDonald (ed.) *Phoenix: The Posthumous Papers of D. H. Lawrence* 755–760. New York: Viking Compass.

Lemon, L. T. and Reis, M. J. (eds and trans.) (1965) *Russian Formalist Criticism: Four Essays*. Lincoln, Nebraska: University of Nebraska Press.

Lovejoy, A. O. and Boas, G. (1935) *Primitivism and Related Ideas in Antiquity* (with supplementary essays by W. F. Albright and P. E. Dumont). Baltimore, Maryland and London: Johns Hopkins University Press.

Magnus, M. (1999) *Gods of the Word: Archetypes in the Consonants*. Kirksville, Missouri: Truman State University Press.

Magnus, M. *Margo's Magical Letter Page*. Retrieved on August 24, 2005, from http://www.conknet.com/~mmagnus/

Malinowski, B. (1923) The problem of meaning in primitive languages, supplement 1. In C. K. Ogden and I. A. Richards (eds) *The Meaning of Meaning* 451–510. London: Kegan Paul.

Martin, J. R. (1992) *English Text: System and Structure*. Amsterdam and Philadelphia: Benjamins.

McDonald, E. (ed.) (1936 [1974]) *Phoenix: The Posthumous Papers of D. H. Lawrence*. New York: Viking Compass.

Miller, D. R. (1989a) *L'etica della narrazione: moralità e scrittura in D. H. Lawrence*. Abano Terme: Piovan Editore.

Miller, D. R. (1989b) 'This pulsing, frictional to-and-fro': The function(s) of lexico-grammatical reiteration in D. H. Lawrence. *Lingua e Stile* 24. 3: 467–483.

Miller, D. R. (2000) A linguistic approach to the teaching of Lawrence's 'verbal art' to non-native speakers. *DHLR* (D. H. Lawrence Review) 29. 3: 53–69.

Mukarovsky, J. (1932 [1964]) Standard language and poetic language. In P. L. Garvin (ed. and trans.) *A Prague School Reader on Esthetics, Literary Structure, and Style*. Washington, DC: Georgetown University Press.

Ong, W. (1967) *The Presence of the Word*. New Haven: Yale University Press.

Ong, W. (1982) *Orality and Literacy: The Technologizing of the Word*. London and New York: Methuen.

Otto, R. (1973) *The Idea of the Holy*. London: Oxford University Press.

Roberts, W. and Moore, H. T. (eds) (1959 [1971]) *Phoenix II*. New York: Viking Compass.

Sher, B. (s.a.) Nature vs. art: a note on translating Shklovsky, retrieved on August 24, 2005 from http://www.websher.net/srl/tran.html

Shklovsky, V. (1917 [1965]) Art as technique. In L. T. Lemon and M. J. Reis (eds and trans.) *Russian Formalist Criticism: Four Essays* 3–24. Lincoln, Nebraska: University of Nebraska Press.

Shklovsky, V. (1925/29 [1990]) *Theory of Prose*. B. Sher (ed. and trans.). USA: Dalkey Archive.

Sipple, J. B. (1980) *Passionate Form: Life Process as Artistic Paradigm in the Writings of D. H. Lawrence*. PhD thesis. Ann Arbor, Michigan and London: University Microfilms International.

Sola Pinto, V. de and Roberts, W. (eds) (1964 [1993]) *The Complete Poems of D. H. Lawrence*. London: Heinemann; London: Penguin.

Warner M. (2005) Angels and engines: apocalypse and its aftermath, from George W. Bush to Philip Pullman. *TLS* no. 5382/3. August 19 and 26: 14–17.

White, P. R. R. (2003a) Beyond modality and hedging: a dialogic view of the language of intersubjective stance. In S. Sarangi and J. Wilson (eds) *Text* 23. 2: 259–284.

White, P. R. R. (2003b) Appraisal – the language of evaluation and stance. In C. Bulcaen (ed.) *The Handbook of Pragmatics Online*. Benjamins: Amsterdam. Retrieved on August 20, 2005 from http://www.benjamins. com/online/hop/

Zytaruk, G. and Bolton, J. T (eds) (1981) *The Letters of D. H. Lawrence. Volume 2: 1913–16*. Cambridge: Cambridge University Press.

Appendix

D. H. Lawrence's 'Two-fold' way or, 'Existence in the Flux of Time' or, 'Being as Duality'

KEY: the numbers refer to the relative source pages in the following works:

   *   *The Study of Thomas Hardy* (1932)

   ** *The Crown* (1915a)

   ****Fantasia of the Unconscious* (1922 [1960/ rpt.1974])

PRINCIPLE of 'NOT-SELF'		PRINCIPLE of 'SELF'
Mental-Spiritual Consciousness	**THE THIRD THINGS OR, LINKS**	**Phallic Consciousness**
446		
Time		Eternality
Registers Relationship		occupied in self-feeling
451 Multiplicity/Diversity		Oneness
455 Knowledge	The Holy Ghost	Feeling
Love	or Holy Spirit	The Law
	(373, 389, 396,	
476 God the Son	*403, 404, 412)*	God the Father
Spirit		Flesh
Service of some idea		Full life in the body
	The Rainbow	
	373	
481 Doing		Being
484 Utterance	The Crown	Gratification: Sensual
487 Public Good	*373*	Enjoyment: Sensual
501/509 Consciousness		Instinct/ Feelings
	The Iris	
513		
Brain		Body
Light	The Song	Darkness

**

PRINCIPLE of 'NOT-SELF'	THE THIRD THINGS	PRINCIPLE of 'SELF'
365 Unicorn	The Foam of Waves	Lion
369 Chastity/ Virginity/ Purity	*375*	Beast(iality)
369/370 St. Francis/ Shelley	The Timeless Flame	David/ Solomon
368 End	The Absolute	Beginning/ Source
373 Day	Timelessness	Night
373/74 Dove	*375/376*	Eagle
374 Bright, Ultimate Spiritual	Consummation	Dark, Original Flame
Flame	Flowering	
377/78 Way of the Spirit	*387*	Way of the Blood
380 The Meek/ Love	Blossoming	Power
Lamb	*393*	Lion
404 Creation	The God-Quick	Destruction
	411	
407 Unselfish/ democratic		Aristocratic/ Lordly
Spiritual/humble	The Flux	Sensuous
	The Kingdom	
409 Christian Attitude	of Heaven	Pagan Eternity
	in Timelessness	
411 Submitting	*413*	Conquering

***

PRINCIPLE of 'NOT-SELF'		PRINCIPLE of 'SELF'
187 Principle of Fire		Soul of Water
188 Sun Pole or Principle		Moon Pole or Principle

3 Thought experiments in verbal art: examples from Modernism

David Butt

Macquarie University, Sydney

Editor's Introduction

David Butt is Associate Professor in Linguistics at Macquarie University in Sydney and the Director of the Centre for Language in Social Life, whose research ranges from the field of stylistics to natural language processing. His current research concentrates on critical information in contexts of surgical care, multi-stratal modelling of service encounters, the grammar of discourses of war and the development of intelligent language-based systems.

In this article, Butt offers a linguistic analysis of a selection of Modernist literature texts that is based on the assumption that there are several 'complementarities' between science and verbal art. This assumption is challenging in that it contradicts common place statements made at various points in time by scientists and, most notably, by writers such as Blake and W. B. Yeats, who held that science is antagonistic to literature and the literary imagination. Butt is all too aware of such traditions of thought and he is successful in convincing the reader of the validity of his position. He does so by linking the work of Saussure, the father of modern linguistics, with that of Einstein, the father of a new era of physics. As Butt rightly argues, Saussure and Einstein engaged in similar epistemological projects, the former introducing the principle of relativity of the sign system, and the latter the principle of relativity of time and space.

After establishing this premise, the first part of the article clearly sets the specific context of such 'complementarities', which in science involve the hypothetical 'thought experiment'. 'Thought experiments' are defined by Butt as constituting an extension of a 'Philosophy of "As-If"' which focuses on, amongst other things, the way in which hypotheses are formulated. He proposes that the texts of modern poems enact similar linguistic 'thought experiments', that is to say, that they can be read as negotiations of a system of possible choices by which the poet construes his or her own, and also the reader's, thought experiments. The article is concerned with the investigation of concerns and philosophical positions that in the modern period are debated both in literature and science, such as logical languages, solipsism, phenomenology, and the representation of objects in the external world and in time and space. These discussions are aptly illustrated through analysis of Wallace Stevens's poems, but also of D. H. Lawrence's final section of *Sons and Lovers*, as well as the work of Australian Modernist poet, Kenneth Slessor.

A preliminary version of the paper was presented at the Australian Science Communicators' Conference which took place in Sydney in 2001. It is an original interdisciplinary contribution to the fields of linguistics, science, literature and philosophy, and offers its readers a particularly innovative insight into the poetry of Wallace Stevens, one that literary critics have typically confined themselves to merely noting, but have never properly or fully pursued.

---

1   Investigating human experience through symbols

All our enquiries into human experience exhibit certain affinities. One source of such affinities is the fact that our enquiries must be, at various stages, turned into *symbols*. All enquiry trades in symbols, and symbols have their own characteristics and, perhaps, even their own 'laws'.

We might venture that much of what counts as enquiry is the result of just 'moving symbols around', so to speak; that is, of bringing symbolic forms into new relationships, relationships which are better *motivated* by (well, usually) relations with other symbols – or at least better motivated by other symbols and their grounding in 'chunks' of experience.

Now, if the 'chunk' of experience happens to be experimental observations, we find we are being carried along in the metaphors and the symbolic imperatives of a science. If the chunk of experience is more evanescent, more reliant on the intervention of an individuated point of view, we are being drawn into the vortex of artistic imagination – let us say, the artistic imagination in verbal art. For in linguistic *art* we have the greatest possible reliance on a psycho-social 'material': we must take stock of the fact that grammar and words in verbal art (unlike the stone or paint of plastic arts) already, as the basic material of the art form, have an intricate symbolic existence, an existence shared in the living and work of both artists and scientists.

And it is this intricate symbolic network of meanings which is further extended as it is put to work in verbal art. How things change when the 'mute' material, the basic stuff of art, is neither mute nor basic! Language is a paradoxi-cal 'order' in our experience: it is only psychological because it is first social, and only social through being psychological. This is only one of the inescapable complementarities that were first stated clearly by Saussure in 1906, around the same year in which Einstein began to change what was legitimate as ways of regarding our physical universe. Saussure's *Course in General Linguistics* (1915 [1959]) introduced us to the inescapable relativity of sign systems just as Einstein was removing the concepts of absolute time and space.

Poets and writers have often found ingenious ways to investigate this com-plementarity of the psycho-social: that is, without knowing about Saussure's revolution. Unfortunately, unlike the Einsteinian and Quantum revolutions, much of the debate about language even today is conducted as if the epistemo-logical problems concerning language can be disregarded, as if language were a passive, referential tool for a preexisting subjectivity. Here I will consider those poets and writers who, I argue, have found that their methods of enquiry are analogous to those of thought experiments. To do so, I will first explain what I mean by this term, and what kind of complexity these writers have achieved. In the following analyses, my aim is also to demonstrate how we, as interpreters, can manage the complex evidence offered to us in textual creativity. It is necessary, in this comparison, to regard language as an equal partner in any epistemological project. In other words, the poet's language is itself a participating subject, not a mirror of private, Cartesian reflections. And this may be the deepest level of the poet's meaning, the deepest consequence of the poem's organisation, in a number of poems which are considered below.

2   Thought experiments

Bohr's résumé of the debates with Einstein (see Bohr's contribution to the 'Library of living philosophers' volume on Einstein, reprinted in Bohr, 1958: 32–66), along with more recent general accounts (e.g. Gribbin, 1998), guide the discussion on the characteristics and use of thought experiments which follows. Bohr summarised the role of the latter experiments thus:

The contemplation of such more or less practical arrangements and their more or less fictitious use proved most instructive in directing attention to essential features of the problems. (1958: 50)

Crucial points for Bohr included the facts:

1 that the measuring instruments and the 'whole experimental arrangement' were part of a total system and, as such, were not distinct from the 'objects' being investigated;

2 that 'we are beyond the reach of pictorial visualisation'; and,

3 that the Einstein, Podolsky, Rosen objections to quantum theory (as expressed by the 'EPR' experiment, after the initials of the three scientists: see Gribbin, 1998: 126–127; 22–24) actually hung upon an 'essential ambiguity', i.e. an issue of meaning: namely, that the authors' 'criterion of reality' did not apply to the problems at issue.

Thought experiments might be characterised, then, by:

1 the difficult, philosophically ambivalent nature of the problems they address (often with an epistemological/'how we come by knowledge at all' slant on the phenomena);

2 the 'impossible' arrangements and impracticable methods by which they are structured;

3 the shifts of scale that they often demand; and

4 their typically 'heuristic' status (following from 1–3) – in the traditional terminology of grammarians, they are irrealis rather than realis (unactualised rather than actual).

Because they are unactualised, or only hypothetical, thought experiments constitute a recent extension of a 'Philosophy of "As-If"', as explored by Hans Vaihinger (1925). It is not as if they are totally unlike the tools employed in previous centuries in science and philosophy. They are simply one of the kinds of 'useful fiction' by which humans interpret the world. The affinities with other kinds of useful fiction, however, are not always obvious. But points, parallel lines, the whole contraption of calculus (with its 'limit' and 'ingenious fallacies' for subdividing process or change (Kline, 1953 [1990]: 266ff.) all exemplify the way human thinking can utilise a fallacious, artificial or contradictory picture in order to quantify, model, or interpret a complex process in practical terms. For instance, calculus quantifies change by treating it as increasingly smaller slices of a static, not changing, picture (hence Newton's name for calculus: 'fluxions').

Given the charges of nonsense made against calculus when it was first introduced by Newton and Leibniz (in fact, Newton aptly called his a theory of 'fluxions', or units of change), it is ironic that Newton's teacher, Barrow, referred to poetry as 'ingenious nonsense' (Kline, 1953: 315). Bishop Berkeley's *The Analyst* (1734) created the greatest havoc, in lampooning concepts like infinitesimals ('the ghost of departed quantities') and instantaneous velocities. Berkeley claimed that such contradictions present mysteries beyond any of those in the Bible (e.g. Struik, 1986: 333–338).

Charges of 'willful nonsense' also characterised critics' responses to some of the poetry written in the milieu of twentieth century innovations. When poets responded to the scientific attack on common sense, whether in physics, in epistemology, in language or in logic, they found many aesthetic traditions provided fortuitous methods for strange ways of knowing the world. But such methods no longer had to be set up in opposition to science, not at least in the way that Blake (1757–1827) fumed against all whom he deemed to be opposed to the imagination – e.g. the early Greek philosopher of atomic theory, Democritus, and Newton – and the way that W. B. Yeats (1865–1939) kept up a war on science, Modernism, and Rationalism. In fact, the 'danger' was that science was usurping the artist's mantle of paradox, of metaphoric creativity, and of romantic imagination.

This was indeed a time for the scientific endorsement of aesthetic methods, which involved:

- shifting points of view;
- quirky scales of phenomena;
- a lack of any absolute boundary between the object and its observing subject;
- alternative 'universes' each with its own internal coherence;
- non-Euclidean space; and
- complementarity and inclusion vs. contradiction and exclusion.

Even Wordsworth, who studied some geometry at Cambridge, is strangely in step with this way of construing experience. Despite his protestations against science, Wordsworth articulates (for example, in 'Tintern Abbey') a complex relational theory of patterns amidst the flux of human experience, a relational perspective not unlike that of the leading philosopher/mathematician A. N. Whitehead (Durrant, 1970: 27–31; Nugroho, 1999: 28–53).

3   Texts as layers of choice

After this brief digression on thought experiments, I will now return to my initial premise on the intricate symbolic characteristics of the basic material of the art form. In order to track a psycho-social material, we need to view all textual construction as the exercise of choice amongst a number of available ways to mean. So, to evaluate the thought experiments of poets, we need to ask ourselves about the choices by which the poets have led our thoughts in negotiating the poem. Certain choices are controlled by the poet, even though these may be liable to change due to our variable 'take' on the value of any choice (or system of choices). Inevitably, choices reflect changing relations between us and the social and authorial contexts of the poem's origin. Still, in all, we interpret by informed and artful inference – by reading off the choices that must have gone into making the text.

A guiding question can be: what effect is gained by choosing to do this rather than that? And, hence, the semantic effect rather than the psychological intent is at issue. More technically, the question can be subdivided into:

1   How are the choices organised as an unfolding process in reader's time?

2   How do certain choices accumulate and dominate, either by creating a consistency in the text or, sometimes more apparent, by breaking a pattern or consistency?

3   Have the choices in meaning changed over time, or are they changed across cultures, between the context of the poet and that of the reader?

You may have been worried by my claim that art was more reliant on point of view – that is, more reliant than science. In the twentieth century, point of view (undergoing refinement in various forms of novel and short story genres) entered science as a theoretical necessity rather than as a subjective embarrassment, in the form of Einstein's relativity and Bohr's complementarity. As Bohr said in a presentation to anthropologists (1938 [1958]), the role of the physicist had become like that of the observer in a different culture – inevitably a factor which can perturb the system under investigation. When I first read this and related matters as a student, it struck me that science had taken on the relational character that I had been 'naturalised' into through the study of literature and language. This is to say, that there were context-dependent potentials only, i.e. possibilities of interaction in which any 'piece' could take on a dramatically shifting function or value, depending on its new relations vis-à-vis all the other pieces. Following de Saussure's account of sign systems (1906–1913; again see Saussure, 1915 [1959]), linguistics is an ideal illustration of why we need 'complexity theory': what does it mean to live and think in relational terms, in a genuinely 'relational universe'? Proposing answers to this question is a challenge to the imagination, whatever your training.

One of the tools of the imagination has been the thought experiment. Einstein again comes to mind, with the EPR experiment (mentioned above). This heuristic device or conceptual model was later modified by the American physicist, David Bohm, and further developed by Bell, so that, by 1982, what was previously only a *thought* experiment became an actual experiment (see Gribbin, 1998, especially on the Aspect experiment: 22–24). The crucial point here is that imaginative fictions – in the present case, 'thought experiments' – may not only figure in arguments, but can also lead, as experiments do, to empirical findings. From this, it is reasonable to ask how poetry, as another form of abstract engineering, can have a bearing on the material order of human lives.

In a life that spanned precisely the same years as Einstein's, 1879–1955, a very different titan of symbolic forms and of heuristic experiments set out his own theories of a relational universe. The experiments of the poet, Wallace Stevens, were first brought together in an early volume, *Harmonium* – a title with a clear scientific and artistic pedigree. His major project, i.e. creating a 'new text of the world', was more explicit in other individual poems: 'Connoisseur of Chaos' (1942) and 'Notes towards a Supreme Fiction' (1947). This latter poem, which is somewhat like a poet's calculus for metaphor, or a contribution to the then-current fashion for a 'theory of everything', had three sections: 'It Must Be Abstract'; 'It Must Change'; and 'It Must Give Pleasure'.

While trained in philosophy at Harvard before his lifetime as a lawyer for (and vice president of) the Hartford Insurance Company, Stevens had little direct knowledge of the scientific ferment of the twentieth century. Ultimately, however, he came to regard the physicist Max Planck as the quintessential hero of the imagination (1957: 201). Furthermore, through various secondary sources, Stevens came to the philosophic questions of modern science in a way which influenced the structures and idiom of his Modernism. Curiously, this influence has not been sufficiently emphasised by his critics.[2] In what follows, I will try to give you a sense of the structures and strategies relevant to the idea of poetry as 'thought experiments'.

The character of Stevens's experiment changes, even jumps around, fortuitously. Many of us would have come across anthologised pieces, say, from 'Thirteen Ways of Looking at a Blackbird' (1923): thirteen vignettes, beginning with Japanese models, each of which isolates one dimension of the complexity we experience as phenomena.

> Among twenty snowy mountains
> The only moving thing
> Was the eye of the blackbird.
>
> (Wallace Stevens, 1955: 92)

My main aim is to show how the poems depend on precise relations in the language: the value of the texts is in their difficult-to-paraphrase relations between the grammar, the textual sequencing, which, to some degree, controls the reader's reception and interpretations, and the cultural background, which is the source of the particular values behind each symbolic move.

4   On logical languages

Many critics between World Wars I and II were baffled by Stevens's Modernist experiments. For instance, one critic referred to his poem 'Metaphors of a Magnifico' (1923) as 'willful nonsense' (Winters, 1943 [1972]: 133).

	T	**Metaphors of a Magnifico**
A	I	Twenty men crossing a bridge,
	II	Into a village,
	III	Are twenty men crossing twenty bridges,
	IV	Into twenty villages,
	V	Or one man
	VI	Crossing a single bridge into a village.
B	VII	This is old song
	VIII	That will not declare itself …
C	IX	Twenty men crossing a bridge,
	X	Into a village,
	XI	Are
	XII	Twenty men crossing a bridge
	XIII	Into a village.
D	XIV	That will not declare itself
	XV	Yet is certain as meaning …
E	XVI	The boots of the men clump
	XVII	On the boards of the bridge.
	XVIII	The first white wall of the village
	XIX	Rises through fruit-trees.
F	XX	Of what was it I was thinking?
G	XXI	So the meaning escapes.
H	XXII	The first white wall of the village …
	XXIII	The fruit-trees. …

(Wallace Stevens, 1955: 19)

Even a modicum of systematic work on the grammar, however, immediately rewards the reader. Verbal equations of slightly different grades of redundancy are set off against brief remarks about the verbal equations (axioms A and C lead to metacomments B and D; language on language, if you like). These systematic contrasts are represented diagrammatically in Figure 3.1. A third kind of language organisation enters the poem at the sound of the boots on the bridge. This is the language of perceptual report, concerning the here and now (so, deictic language (E): from the Greek word for 'pointing', i.e. to an immediate context). The poet places us in the moment; we must be moving towards the 'first white wall of the village' for it to be rising. So too there is a shift of point of view obtained by the movement to synecdoches (parts standing for wholes, as in 'boots' for 'men', and 'boards' for 'bridge').

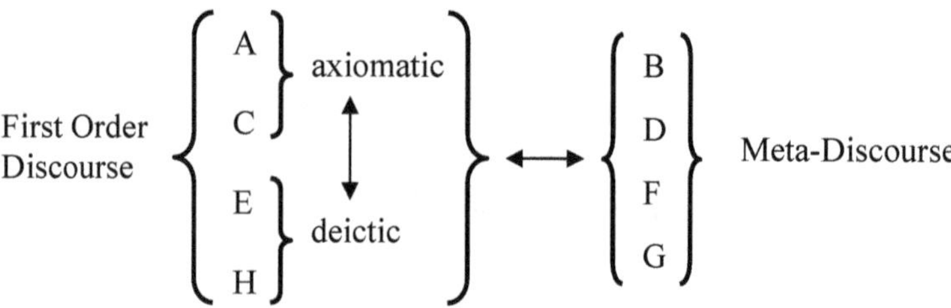

Figure 3.1: Two systematic contrasts in Wallace Stevens's 'Metaphors of a Magnifico'

Compare this to the torturous debates of that period which circled around distinctions between actual descriptions of the world (in an object language), axioms that are necessarily true (as in logical languages), the oddities of metalanguage (i.e. language describing language), the value of redundancy (in which all mathematical statements appeared to resolve themselves), and the extent of what is 'sayable' (the limits of language). These issues fuelled the traffic of debate surrounding Wittgenstein's *Tractatus Logico-philosophicus* (1918); Russell and Whitehead's *Principia Mathematica* (1910–1913); the Vienna Circle logicians; and Logical Positivism (which held to the credo that meaningfulness was contingent upon verifiability) (see Glock, 1997). Much of the ferment grew up as a response to the ambiguous character of natural languages in statements of 'truth' in relation to science. A shared philosophical project was that we should have a symbolic tool that does not mislead us into false assumptions about what is, or is not, the case. Hence Russell's philosophical concern regarding our power to make assertions like 'the King of France is bald', when there was no king of France! (as discussed in Watling, 1970: 65–67).

The poet has found a weird conjunction of many of the issues in these evanescent 'fragments' of reflection (F, G, H). Yes, language has its axiomatic and logical functions, but redundancy of reference is never quite redundant in meaning; and through shared meanings – e.g. we can be with the troops on a bridge to a village – we have the constructive, participatory power of language extending the imagination. You can enter the moment like one can enter the village. In this village, along with a suggestion of menace, there can be 'a king of France' (contrary to Russell's referential exorcisms), and behold, yes, as a matter of *meaning*, if not of 'fact,' he may be 'bald'!

5   On solipsism

Let us move to solipsism, a problem that was variously described as the 'scandal' of Western philosophy, in that it showed that philosophers had not yet established an unimpeachable basis for believing in any world external to human consciousness. Again, Russell had settled on the likelihood that there was probably no case one could bring to push a solipsist out of his or her denial of the existence of such an external world (Hacker, 1972: 187). So too Wittgenstein used the problem as the 'test case' for progress in his project in semantics, namely his drive to clarify the role of language in mediating our knowledge of experience (Hacker, 1972: 185–251). Around 1915, Stevens produced this poem which was labeled 'solipsist'.

Tea at the Palaz of Hoon (1923)

I	Not less because in purple I descended
II	The western day through what you called
III	The loneliest air, not less was I myself.
IV	What was the ointment sprinkled on my beard?
V	What were the hymns that buzzed beside my ears?
VI	What was the sea whose tide swept through me there?
VII	Out of my mind the golden ointment rained,
VIII	And my ears made the blowing hymns they heard.
IX	I was myself the compass of that sea:
X	I was the world in which I walked, and what I saw
XI	Or heard or felt came not but from myself;
XII	And there I found myself more truly and more strange.

(Wallace Stevens, 1955: 65)

'Tea at the Palaz of Hoon' illustrates the fact that, as with any experiment, it is the method that determines the meaning of the experiment, particularly when, by meaning, we include 'cultural significance'. The subject matter of the poem includes exotic suggestions: magnifico, palace, purple, perfumed beard (motifs which are constantly in evidence across Stevens's oeuvre).

More crucial to a discussion of method in the textual organisation is the significance of a potentate: a magnifico can create by edict; his world is his whim, his fiat, or his imagination. The usefulness of the metaphor may be confirmed by the fact that Wittgenstein also used an oriental despot in one of his 'hypotheticals', or thought experiments (Hacker, 1972:195). The analogy with the solipsist, whose world comes 'not but from myself', seems direct enough. But that is not how the poem is *made*. And my claim is that the meaning is in the *mode of making*.

First of all, the highly marked opening lines: the unusual, labyrinthine qualifications which precede the main clause ('Not less was I myself', in line III), immediately challenge the reader, leaving interpretation unsettled. Let us call this 'strangeness by hypotaxis' (the subordination of one clause to another) and also strangeness by what the speaker offers you as a starting point or point of departure for the poem (i.e. what Stevens makes 'thematic').

Secondly, the poet is addressing someone (perhaps himself).

Thirdly, all the verbs of sensing are not parts of major clauses; they are embedded structures (structures within structures) and in that sense they are locked away from a dominating role in the texture. The grammar of 'It was x' – a verbal equation – dominates the mere qualifiers like 'that I heard'. This has the effect of emphasising the relation of identification over and above the processes of seeing, hearing, feeling.

Fourth, the bundling up of information about the senses (the embedding) is even stronger in the '[[what I saw || or heard || or felt]] came not but from myself'. The bracketed material has been treated as a 'job lot' in the clause: i.e. all of it has been made to stand as the Subject to the one verb 'came'.

Fifth, the final clause involves a zeugma: a figure of speech noted by the classical Greek rhetoricians as yoking or binding, i.e. one structure has to serve two or more other structures. Of note here, more precisely, is the fact that we have an incomplete, semantic zeugma: 'I found myself more truly and more strange'. The 'more truly' and 'more strange' are not semantically and grammatically equivalent, though they have been placed after 'found' in a way in which you may typically expect to see equivalence. The 'more truly' is an adverbial group, which functions grammatically as a circumstance that describes the Manner, and the degree of the act of finding; whereas 'more strange' is part of what was found – the Range[3] of the act of finding, which, if rendered without ellipsis, might be something like 'I found myself to be more strange'.

Sixth, the verb 'found' produces two categories of phenomena: 1) material discoveries, and now, more commonly, 2) mental realisations, though this is a situation that is reflected even in key passages of the Old English poem 'Beowulf', which is approximately 1000 years old. The issues around 'found' are related to those highlighted by Ryle and Wittgenstein later, in the 1940s, concerning verbs like 'see', and other systematically misleading expressions. These philosophers of ordinary language argued that we are all ensnared by our grammar into false beliefs about our experience (see Passmore, 1968). Their demonstrations were often in the form of analogies and thought experiments.

What can we conclude about the six observations on the making of 'Tea at the Palaz of Hoon'? Critics since the early twentieth century have assumed this poem to be a straightforward exercise in solipsism, but in fact its grammar creates a weird contradiction in the very act of articulating the doctrine of the solipsist. As argued by Wittgenstein, much later, there is an inherent contradiction in expressing solipsism in language, in that language can *never* be a private affair; there can never be a private language, even if you try to create codes to exclude some people (Hacker, 1972: 201). The poet's construction brings out – by the various strategic choices I have mentioned – this semantic dissonance, which was later to be made more explicit in the slow build up of exempla by the philosopher.

6   On seeing

Let us modify the order of abstraction, down from Stevens's experiments with symbolic representation, to a more direct phenomenology, namely his quizzing of all sights and sounds. In relation to this focus in his poetry, I will restrict myself to just one dimension of two texts, and one that is typically *not* taken up by critics as being crucial to Stevens's meaning-making.

The two poems below were written about 1915; they are of equal length (in lines), and deal with acts of observation: with imagery and directionality in the process of seeing. Among many precise linguistic arrangements in 'Tattoo' (1923), the image of the spider of light comes to us as a result of a slow accumulation, an aggregate of paratactic clauses, piece by piece. In 'The Load of Sugar-Cane' (1923), the observation begins *as if* the same aggregation will take place. We come to the image of 'the going of the gladeboat' three times, each time extending the description slightly up to the middle line or axis of the poem. There the word 'Turning' makes the shift in the poet's trope, or figure of speech ('trope' means 'turn', i.e. a 'turn' in the meaning). From that point, the text moves more and more deeply into an embedding of an embedding of an embedding (six in all). The comparisons ('like …', 'as …') appear to take us further from the initial observation. But, in a moment of paradoxical circularity of reading, we are returned to the first line, through the final word, 'boatman' – a reference to the boatman of the 'glade-boat' in line I.

The effect is subtly enhanced by the greater action being more a feature of the deeper degrees of embedding and metaphor: the further we appear to be from the initial observation, the stronger becomes our sense of something happening: the grammar becomes subtly more realis, less irrealis.

Tattoo

I	The light is like a spider.
II	It crawls over the water.
III	It crawls over the edges of the snow.
IV	It crawls under your eyelids
V	And it spreads its webs there –
VI	Its two webs.
VII	The webs of your eyes
VIII	Are fastened
IX	To the flesh and bones of you
X	As to rafters or grass.
XI	There are filaments of your eyes
XII	On the surface of the water
XIII	And in the edges of the snow.

(Wallace Stevens, 1955: 81)

The Load of Sugar-Cane

I	The going of the glade-boat
II	Is like water flowing;
III	Like water flowing
IV	Through the green saw grass;
V	Under the rainbows;
VI	Under the rainbows
VII	That are like birds,
VIII	Turning, bedizened,
IX	While the wind still whistles
X	As kildeer do,
XI	When they rise
XII	At the red turban
XIII	Of the boatman.

(Wallace Stevens, 1955: 12)

In the two poems, we find the 'incremental', or the 'slow-creep', model of perceptual experience ('Tattoo') pitted against the 'unity discovered' model (with 'The Load of Sugar-Cane' involving a dramatic, retrospective reading). The two poems work as exempla of issues that go back to Democritus and Empedocles and their theories of perception: in 'Tattoo', the implication is of eidola (simulacra) exchanged between the world and the eye.[4]

7   An external world

In 'Late Hymn from the Myrrh-Mountain' (1947), change is examined beneath the constellations of a starry twilight or evening.

Late Hymn from the Myrrh-Mountain

I	Unsnack your snood, madanna, for the stars
II	Are shining on all brows of Neversink.
III	Already the green bird of summer has flown
IV	Away. The night-flies acknowledge these planets,
V	Predestined to this night, this noise and the place
VI	Of summer. Tomorrow will look like today,
VII	Will appear like it. But it will be an appearance,
VIII	A shape left behind, with the wings spreading out,
IX	Brightly empowered with like colours, swarmingly,
X	But not quite molten, not quite the fluid thing,
XI	A little changed by tips of artifice, changed
XII	By the glints of sound from the grass. These are not
XIII	The early constellations, from which came the first
XIV	Illustrious intimations – uncertain love,
XV	The knowledge of being, sense without sense of time.
XVI	Take the diamonds from your hair and lay them down.
XVII	The deer-grass is thin. The timothy is brown.
XVIII	The shadow of an external world comes near.

(Wallace Stevens, 1955: 349–350)

The linguistic units become particularly complex around clause 9. The clause analysis is shown in Figure 3.2, and an analysis of the complexity of the alignments of clauses with sentences and lines, in Figure 3.3. The revisions and ellipses are part of a wider strategy in which the 'it' that is changing (and any other major *entity* in the poem) becomes increasingly vague and indeterminate, while the expression of *process* is increasingly emphatic (i.e. something *is* happening, but the participant in the process remains less and less identifiable).

Late Hymn from the Myrrh-Mountain

I	**A1** Unsnack your snood, madanna, ‖ **A2** for the stars
II	Are shining on all brows of Neversink. ‖‖
III	**B3** Already the green bird of summer has flown
IV	Away. ‖‖ **C4** The night-flies acknowledge these planets, ‖
V	**C5** Predestined to this night, this noise and the place
VI	Of summer. ‖‖ **D6** Tomorrow will look like today, ‖
VII	**D7** Will appear like it. ‖‖ **E8** But it will be an appearance, ‖
VIII	**E9** A shape [[**9.1** left behind, [[**9.1.1** with the wings spreading out,]]
IX	**9.2** Brightly empowered with like colours, ‖ **9.3** swarmingly, ‖
X	**9.4** But not quite molten, ‖ **9.5** not quite the fluid thing, ‖
XI	**9.6** A little changed by tips of artifice, ‖ **9.7** changed
XII	By the glints of sound from the grass.]] ‖‖ **F10** These are not
XIII	The early constellations, ‖ **F11** from which came the first
XIV	Illustrious intimations – ‖ **F12** uncertain love,
XV	The knowledge of being, sense without sense of time. ‖‖
XVI	**G13** Take the diamonds from your hair ‖ **G14** and lay them down. ‖‖
XVII	**H15** The deer-grass is thin. ‖‖ **I16** The timothy is brown. ‖‖
XVIII	**J17** The shadow of an external world comes near.

Note: lines are numbered with Roman numerals; clause complexes (sentences) are numbered with capital letters; clauses are numbered with Arabic numerals.

Figure 3.2: Clause analysis of Wallace Stevens's 'Late Hymn from the Myrrh-Mountain'

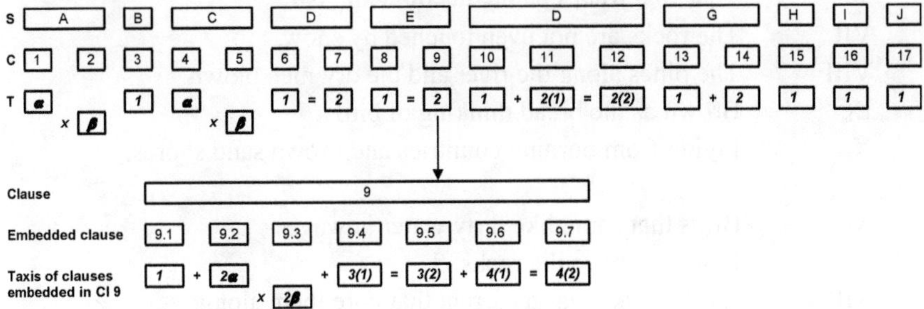

Figure 3.3: Taxis in Wallace Stevens's 'Late Hymn from the Myrrh-Mountain'

So, essentially, we read our way into a process-dominated, Whiteheadian world in which *the thing* is nothing more than 'the shadow of an external world'; but this indeterminacy is set against the 'here and now' of *event*, the 'comes near' of process.

Such a meaning is difficult to construct in English for, as Whitehead himself pointed out in *Process and Reality* (1929 [1978]: viii; 70), the pressure on a speaker to set up a Subject-Predicate structure dominates the operations of sentence meaning. Across the poem, however, Stevens has brought other relations into play, thereby toning down the control of the 'thingifying' Subject, and the Greek *onoma* ('name' or 'noun').

8　Tragic space = tragic time (QED)

In 'Dry Loaf' (1942), Stevens tests the possibilities of poetic deduction. Setting out from a verbal equation which functions like the QED structure of logic, the reader must negotiate a clausal vortex (including more 'strangeness by hypotaxis'), after which we are naturalised into accepting a deictic paradox, namely, the terms of the opening equation: 'It is equal to living in a tragic land to live in a tragic time'. In the 'reasoning', however, he gives a core role to emotional affinities and analogies, rather than to logical sequence and its typical claim: causation.

Dry Loaf

I	It is equal to living in a tragic land
II	To live in a tragic time.
III	Regard now the sloping, mountainous rocks
IV	And the river that batters its way over stones,
V	Regard the hovels of those that live in this land.

VI	That was what I painted behind the loaf,
VII	The rocks are not even touched by snow,
VIII	The pines along the river and the dry men blown
IX	Brown as the bread thinking of birds
X	Flying from burning countries and brown sand shores,
XI	Birds that came like dirty water in waves
XII	Flowing above the rocks, fl
XIII	As if the sky was a current that bore them along,
XIV	Spreading them as waves spread flat on the shore
XV	One after another washing the mountains bare.
XVI	It was battering of drums I heard
XVII	It was hunger, it was the hungry that cried
XVIII	And the waves, the waves were soldiers moving,
XIX	Marching and marching in a tragic time
XX	Below me, on the asphalt, under the trees.
XXI	It was soldiers went marching over the rocks
XXII	And still the birds came, came in watery flocks,
XXIII	Because it was spring and the birds had to come.
XXIV	No doubt that soldiers had to be marching
XXV	And that drums had to be rolling, rolling, rolling.

(Wallace Stevens, 1955: 199–200)

Readers with the motivation to follow up the subtle parallel structures of the poem should consider many aspects of analysis (see Butt, 1988, for a number of connections to linguistics and complexity theory). The one issue to which I have confined discussion can be seen in the diagram of analysed clauses (see Figure 3.4 for the clause analysis, and Figure 3.5 for an analysis of taxis in the first three sentences), beginning around the word 'thinking', and continuing in a virtual slide of analogies made upon analogies. This is indicated by the sloping, or unpacking, formula in the poem's description. This cascading of possibilities, beginning as it does in line IX's single non-finite verb 'thinking' (the traditional 'dangling participle'), contributes to a turning over of orders of reality: are we in the painting? or in one of the analogies? or in the 'street below'? We cannot settle the status of the phenomena because they are equal in the making of the text; they are equally available to the conscious mind, through language.

Dry Loaf

I	**A1** It is equal to [[**1.1** living in a tragic land]]
II	[[**1.2** To live in a tragic time]].
III	**B2** Regard now the sloping, mountainous rocks
IV	And the river [[**2.1** that batters its way over stones]], ||
V	**B3** Regard the hovels of those [[**3.1** that live in this land]].
VI	**C4** That was [[**4.1** what I painted behind the loaf]],
VII	The rocks [[**4.2** not even touched by snow]],
VIII	The pines along the river and the dry men [[**4.3** blown
IX	Brown as the bread]] || **C5** thinking of birds
X	[[**5.1** Flying from burning countries and brown sand shores]], ||
XI	**C6** Birds [[**6.1** that came like dirty water in waves ||
XII	**6.2** Flowing above the rocks, || **6.3** flowing over the sky, ||
XIII	**6.4** As if the sky was a current [[**6.4.1** that bore them along, ||
XIV	**6.4.2** Spreading them || **6.4.3** as waves spread flat on the shore ||
XV	**6.4.4** One after another washing the mountains bare]]]] . ||
XVI	**D7** It was battering of drums [[**7.1** I heard]] ||
XVII	**D8** It was hunger, || **D9** it was the hungry [[**9.1** that cried]] ||
XVIII	**D10** And the waves, the waves were soldiers [[**10.1** moving, ||
XIX	**10.2** Marching || **10.2** and marching in a tragic time
XX	Below me, on the asphalt, under the trees]] . ||
XXI	**E11** It was soldiers went [[**11.1** marching over the rocks]] ||
XXII	**E12** And still the birds came, || **E13** came in watery flocks, ||
XXIII	**E14** Because it was spring || **E15** and the birds had to come. ||
XXIV	**F16** No doubt [[**16.1** that soldiers had to be marching]] ||
XXV	**F17** And [[**17.1** that drums had to be rolling, rolling, rolling]] . ||

Figure 3.4: Clause analysis for Wallace Stevens's 'Dry Loaf'

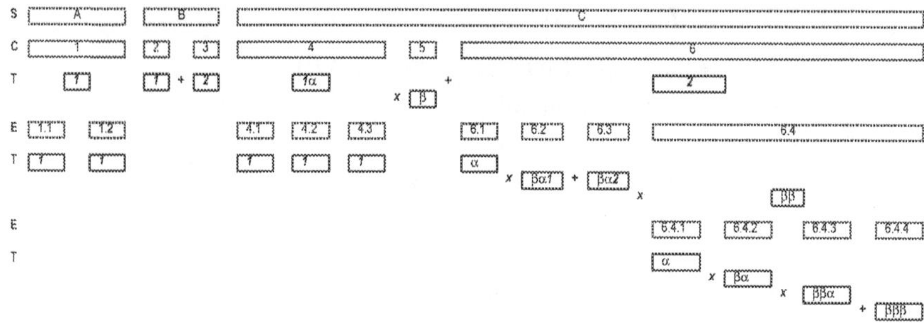

Note: s = sentence; c = clause; e = embedded clause; t = taxis

Figure 3.5: Taxis in the first three sentences of Wallace Stevens's 'Dry Loaf'

9 Entity vs. Process

Was Stevens the only poet conducting such mind enquiries, or thought experiments, in the contexts of living? And are such techniques special to poets, and unlikely in other genres, like the novel? My own answers to these questions are 'No', and 'No'. Seminal strategies of text construction can be isolated whenever you apply the appropriate linguistic, cultural, and, particularly, grammatical tools. Wordsworth can make nature sentient with its interrelations, its 'outscape' (Durrant, 1970: 45). So too, he renders human responses more complicated than is the case in the unrealistic separations of thought and emotion which have characterised much twentieth century psychology (I am considering again 'Tintern Abbey': see discussion and analysis in Nugroho, 1999).

The Australian Modernist Kenneth Slessor (1901–1971) demonstrates the *Thing/Process* bifurcation in our patterns of speaking with the poem 'Fixed Ideas'. The power of the demonstration derives from a lexicogrammatical contrast between an aggregate of arcane and odd entities (ideas and objects) and a brief excursus into a reality of verb-y nouns and noun-y verbs: 'glitters' and 'prickles', etc.

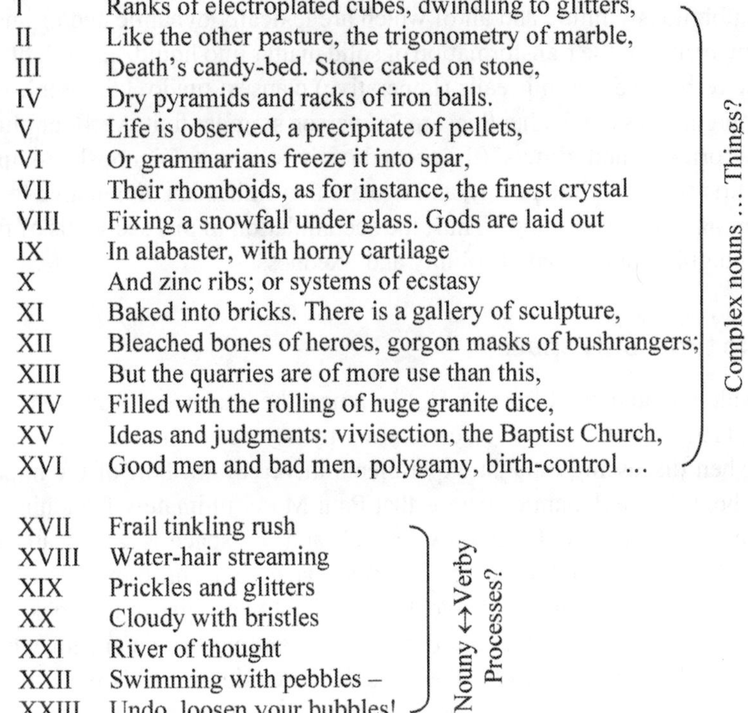

Fixed Ideas

I	Ranks of electroplated cubes, dwindling to glitters,
II	Like the other pasture, the trigonometry of marble,
III	Death's candy-bed. Stone caked on stone,
IV	Dry pyramids and racks of iron balls.
V	Life is observed, a precipitate of pellets,
VI	Or grammarians freeze it into spar,
VII	Their rhomboids, as for instance, the finest crystal
VIII	Fixing a snowfall under glass. Gods are laid out
IX	In alabaster, with horny cartilage
X	And zinc ribs; or systems of ecstasy
XI	Baked into bricks. There is a gallery of sculpture,
XII	Bleached bones of heroes, gorgon masks of bushrangers;
XIII	But the quarries are of more use than this,
XIV	Filled with the rolling of huge granite dice,
XV	Ideas and judgments: vivisection, the Baptist Church,
XVI	Good men and bad men, polygamy, birth-control …

XVII	Frail tinkling rush
XVIII	Water-hair streaming
XIX	Prickles and glitters
XX	Cloudy with bristles
XXI	River of thought
XXII	Swimming with pebbles –
XXIII	Undo, loosen your bubbles!

(Kenneth Slessor, 1924 [1972]: 146–147)

Figure 3.6: The Thing/Process division in our thinking, as illustrated by Slessor's 'Fixed Ideas'

The first part of the poem is largely an accumulation of nominal groups referring to rocks, death and geometric regularity – fixed things – and explicitly opposes thought to solid lumps of rock in 'the rolling of huge granite dice, ideas and judgments'. There are relatively few verbs in this section (ten in 118 words) and all of them are lexically 'static', i.e. they imply, rather than action, a lack of it ('dwindling') and/or a transformation from fluidity to solidity ('freeze', 'baked', 'caked'). Five of the verbs are clearly in independent clauses and are finite ('is observed', 'freeze', 'are laid out', '(there) is', '(the quarries) are') and five are non-finite (and probably embedded as post-modifiers in nominal groups); of the five non-finite verbs, three are perfective, realis ('caked', 'baked', 'filled'), adding to the ideology of substance in this section.

The second part of the poem, by contrast, is shorter, but 'verbier', and construes thought as flux and evanescence – explicitly so, in the nominal group 'river of thought'. There are six (possible) verbs in 21 words, none of which is unambiguously finite, and all of which are lexically dynamic and/or imply movement and/or the transformation of solid matter into liquid, air or light. Of the six verbs, two are in irrealis (imperative) clauses: 'undo, unloosen'; two are ambiguous as to whether they are 3rd person singular finite verbs or plural nouns: 'prickles and glitters' (the second of these is unambiguously nominal in the first section of the poem); and two are non-finites in continuative form: 'streaming' and 'swimming'. Thus, the accumulation in this section is of flux and ambiguity rather than of solidity and fixedness.

10 'No time, only space'

One widely read extract from D. H. Lawrence, the final scene from *Sons and Lovers* (1913 [1966]: 509–511), can show why we need to broaden the generic base when discussing thought experiments in verbal art. Part of the impact of the book is the dynamic cosmos that Paul Morel ultimately finds himself within: 'There was no Time, only Space', and the space is grammatically agentive. Space, indeed, becomes the most dynamic agent in the oppressive moments of Paul's thoughts of suicide in the final two pages of the book. The heavens are remarkably like the dynamic, expanding firmament for which Edwin Hubble later argued on the basis of the evidence of his telescope: a universe demonstrated to doubters (including Einstein!) only in 1929. *Sons and Lovers* was published in 1913. In his description, Lawrence instantiates what was to move (for scientists, and all of us) beyond the formal enquiries of cosmology: namely, a second 'Copernican' shift in our place in space and time. After Hubble, the cosmos is relentlessly expanding and we are growing smaller against its flow and intimidating entirety. The novel is noted for its awareness of Freud (viz. the title); it merits further consideration for its anticipation of a universe that scientists were yet to comprehend.

Lawrence finds a linguistic pattern by which our habitual experiences of time and space are gradually, incrementally, shifted, albeit in a way that is sub-liminal to anyone who cannot attend to the slowly changing grammatical 'tide'. The critical ensemble of effects is displayed in Appendix 1, and includes:

1   Humans become static and are replaced by verbless accumulations of spatial descriptions. For example, Paul himself (or parts of his body) tends to be the first participant (the 'do-er') of relational (stative) Processes (many of which are verbless, e.g. clauses 66a–68 and 77–79), or the first participant of relatively static and/or intransitive material Processes (as in

clauses 30–42). In relational clauses, Paul is equated with a lack of space (as in clause 30) and with almost (but not complete) nothingness (e.g. clauses 71, 77–79). The few times Paul is the do-er of a slightly more dynamic material Process, the dynamism is limited by the fact that the circumstances are very local (as in clauses 23 and 39); the few times he is the do-er in a transitive clause, the transitivity is attenuated by such features as modality and/or negative polarity (as in clauses 57 and 69), or by the fact that the clause is embedded (as in clause 35.2).

2   The Spatial circumstances become the Subject and Actor in the clauses (circumstantial meaning becomes the major participant in the messages, rather than the second order Adjunct to the message). Spatial entities are equated with each other (e.g. clauses 41–44) and act on each other (e.g. clauses 49, 74 and 75); they also act on Paul (clause 70) and other humans, and in relation to Paul and other humans as circumstances (e.g. clause 23).

Most of the emphatically dynamic verbs in the passage are in clauses with spatial entities rather than humans as do-er: 'spread' (clause 42); 'went reaching out' (clause 72); 'went spinning' (clause 74); 'holding' (clause 75).

3   There is one dynamic verb associated with a human Actor – 'hurrying' in clause 35.1 – but this dynamism is again countered by the fact that this clause is embedded and non-finite and associated with others as impersonal phenomena.

4   The selection of finiteness through tense is strategically avoided in key or main clauses, and then the whole verb disappears in the last few messages of this passage (clauses 77–79): 'So much and himself, infinitesimal, at the core a nothingness, and yet not nothing'. The narratorial voice draws attention to this 'backgrounding' of time and the foregrounding of space noted in points 1, 2 and 3 above: 'There was no Time, only Space' (clause 50).

5   The externalised narration shifts to intensifying, free, direct discourse (of both thought and speech).

The graphs presented in Appendix 2 set out samples of the instantial weight, grammatically and semantically scaled, for the final section (about 100 clauses) of the novel. Finiteness, agentive role, and the material orientation of processness are all coded on a 4-point scale, so that the highest values would indicate a finite clause in which Paul is an unambiguous Actor/Agent in a material Process. The graph displays (1) how Lawrence has naturalised us into a figure-ground reversal (with the star background moving to Agent) and (2) how Paul's grammatical profile reaches its nadir (i.e. an absence of grammatical force) as he is contemplating suicide (clauses 77–81).

11 Making strange

The way we construe experience is not given by perception or reference; it is under constant re-negotiation by the repeated choices of community and culture. But this kind of re-negotiation is difficult: one has to be able to sense the consequences, especially the limits, in the symbolic structures we currently use. As emphasised by the Russian critic Victor Shklovsky (1893–1984), the first device amongst the artist's tools is 'to make strange', to force us into noticing our own habitual patterns of representation. A poetic tradition is one mode of such 'estrangement', and of renegotiating our cultural contracts with experience (Shklovsky, 1925/29 [1990]: 5–6).

The fault lines and gaps in our symbolic 'architectures' can be the result of many different kinds of contradiction in the conventions of behaviour within a community. The contradiction may be a discrepancy between our avowals of morality and our actual behaviour (so often the theme of novels); it could be our understanding of change or mutability (so suited to the observations of lyric poetry); so too could it be a conundrum from the realm of physical science, such as the wave-particle duality of electrons, which not only challenged classical physics, but also contradicted the law of logic that states that something cannot be *A* and *not A* at the same time (Heisenberg, 1958: 180ff).

The Romantic poet, Shelley, was wrong to see poets alone as the 'legislators' of the future; the scientific imagination is a kind of 'parallel processing' in the culture. The thought experiment, whether of science or poetry, is focused on the fissures in our versions of the world and the anomalies in the way we experience such versions. As these heuristic devices are more widely understood, and the problems to which they are addressed are more visible, we can reflect with Wallace Stevens that:

> The whole race is a poet that writes down
> The eccentric propositions of its fate.
> (From 'Men Made Out of Words' (1947) Wallace Stevens, 1955: 355–356)

This improves on Shelley. It also summarises the scientific career of the linguist (and chemist) Benjamin Lee Whorf (1897–1941) who stressed the psychological and cultural construction we do through language (see Whorf, 1956). These lines seemed peculiarly apt when, it struck me, in the 1970s, that Stevens and Whorf must have both worked for different departments of the same Hartford Indemnity Insurance Company, and carried out their projects (the poet as Vice President and the linguist as chemical hazards assessor) with both idiosyncratic originality and institutional encouragement. When this 'coincidence' has been mentioned in American-based literature on Stevens (see, for example, Richardson, 1986: 25), the close relationship between their symbolic preoccupations has been noted but not pursued. Neither was the intellectual network from which they both drew (exemplified in the interdisciplinary principles of the journal *Main Currents of Modern Thought*, which Whorf co-edited before his death in 1941: see Margenau and Sellon, 1975). My point here is that we must think in terms of the semiotic landscape that poet and scientist shared. It should be no shock that these two interrogators of symbols turn up so closely on the co-ordinates of any sociosemiotic atlas for Modernism.

Greater attention to what we share when we share symbols could help us to bring about new models of our dynamic, relational universe. Whether it sets out from maths, metaphors, memes, or music, 'the new text of the world', the 'supreme fiction' of Stevens, or of a scientist, will have to come to terms with the complexity of language. It is a complexity in which things do not exist of themselves, but only as a function of the role played within the totality of other terms. Scientists, poets, and artists alike will have little trouble recognising the affinities between their own enquiries and the investigation of such complexity. The shared quest, or so it seems to me, is to live in this relational cosmos without manufacturing, without uttering, unproductive 'pictures' of it.

Appendix 1

Abbreviated analysis of transitivity and finiteness in the last two pages of
D.H. Lawrence's 'Sons and Lovers'

Cl #	Clause text	1	2	3
21	He shook hands	P	F	S
22	and left her at the door of her cousin's house.	P	F	S
23	When he turned away	P (L)	F	S
24	he felt	P	F	S
25	the last hold for him had gone.	(P)	F	S
26	The town << 27 >> stretched away over the bay of the railway,	S	F	D
27	as he sat upon the car	P (L)	F	S
28	a level fume of lights.		A	S
29	Beyond the town the country, little smouldering spots for more towns – the sea – the night – on and on!	S (S)	A	D
30	And he had no place in it!	P {-S}	F	S
31	Whatever spot he stood on,	P (L)	F	S
32	there he stood alone.	P (L)	F	S
33	From his breast, from his mouth, sprang the endless space,	S (P)	F	D
34	and it was there behind him, everywhere.	S (P, E)	F	D

35	The people [[35.1]] offered no obstruction to the void [[35.2]].	H (-S)	F	S
35.1	hurrying along the streets	H (L)	NF	D
35.2	in which he found himself	P{P}(-S)	F	S
36	They were small shadows	H	F	S
37	whose footsteps and voices could be heard,	{*H*}	F	S
38	but in each of them the same night, the same silence.	S (H)	A	S
39	He got off the car.	P (L)	F	S
40	In the country all was dead still.	(S) E	F	S
41	Little stars shone high up;	S (S)	F	D
42	little stars spread far away in the flood-waters,	S (S)	F	D
43	a firmament below.	S (S)	A	S
44	Everywhere the vastness and terror of the immense night	S (S)	A	D
45	which is roused	{S}	F	D
46	and stirred for a brief while by the day,	{S}	F	D
47	but which returns,	S	F	D
48	and will remain at last eternal,	S (T)	F	S
49	holding everything in its silence and its living gloom.	S {E}	NF	S
50	There was no Time, only Space.	-T, S	F	S
51	Who could say		F	S
52	his mother had lived	M	F	S
53	and did not live?	M	F –	S
54	She had been in one place,	M (S)	F	S
55	and was in another;	M (S)	F	S
56	that was all.		F	S
57	And his soul could not leave her,	*P* {M}	F –	D
58	wherever she was.	M (S)	F	S
59	Now she was gone abroad into the night,	M (S/T)	F	D
60	and he was with her still.	P (M)	F	S
61	They were together.	P,M {P,M}	F	S
62	But yet there was his body, his chest,	*P* (L)	F	S
63	that leaned against the stile,	*P* (L)	F	S
64	his hands on the wooden bar.	*P* (L)	A	S
65	They seemed something.	*P* {?}	F	S
66	Where was he? –	P {?}	F	S
66a	one tiny upright speck of flesh,	P {N}	A	S
67	less than an ear of wheat	P {N}	A	S
68	lost in the field.	P {N}	A	S
69	He could not bear it.	P {?}	F –	S
70	On every side the immense dark silence seemed pressing him, so tiny a spark, into extinction,	S {P}	F	D

71	and yet, almost nothing, he could not be extinct.	P {N}	F –	S
72	Night, << 73 >> went reaching out, beyond stars and sun.	S (S)	F	D
73	in which everything was lost,	E(S){N}	F	S
74	Stars and sun, a few bright grains, went spinning round for terror,	S	F	D
75	and holding each other in embrace,	S {S}	F	D
76	there in a darkness [[76.1 ǁ 76.2]].	S (S)	A	S
76.1	that outpassed them all,	S {S}	F	D
76.1	and left them tiny and daunted	S {N}	F	D
77	So much, and himself, infinitesimal,	P {N}	A	S
78	at the core a nothingness,	*P* {N}	A	S
79	and yet not nothing.	P {N}	A	S

Key to columns 1, 2 and 3

In column 1

P = Paul Morel, M = his mother, H = other humans, L = local space, S = general space/time/light/silence, T = time, E = everything, N = nothingness/extreme smallness; if these initials are in italics = part of, e.g. *P* = part of Paul Morel (his chest etc.); when these codes are in round braces, e.g. (P), they indicate that the element occurs in a Circumstance; when they occur in curly braces, e.g. {P}, they indicate the element is the 'done to' or 2nd participant rather than the 'do-er' or 1st participant of the Process.

In column 2

F = finite verb (– = negative polarity), NF = non-finite verb, A = the verb is absent.

In column 3

D = dynamic (the combination of Process & Circumstances in the clause suggests movement through space extending well beyond the 1st participant and/or affecting a 2nd participant), S = static (either there is no movement, e.g. the clause is relational, or the movement does not extend, or extend much, beyond the person or locale of the 1st participant).

See the text for a discussion of the analysis of this extract, as well as Miller (this volume) for not dissimilar findings in her analysis of Lawrence's poem 'Underneath'.

Appendix 2

The graphing of values for finiteness, process type and agentive role - highest 'realis' values approach 4.

Note the critical absence of grammatical force between clauses 77 and 80.

Clauses 26 - 50

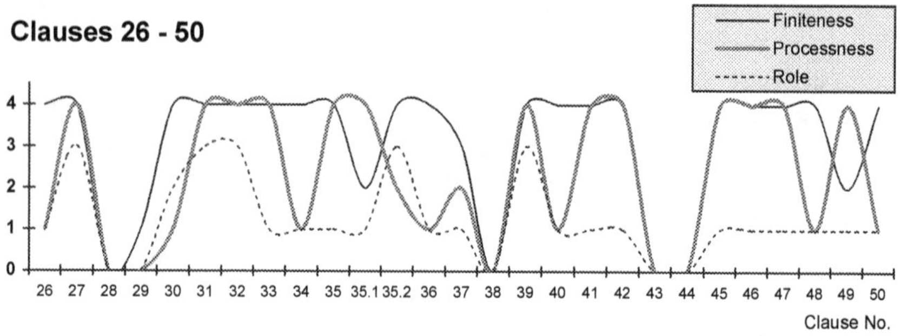

Clauses 76- 96

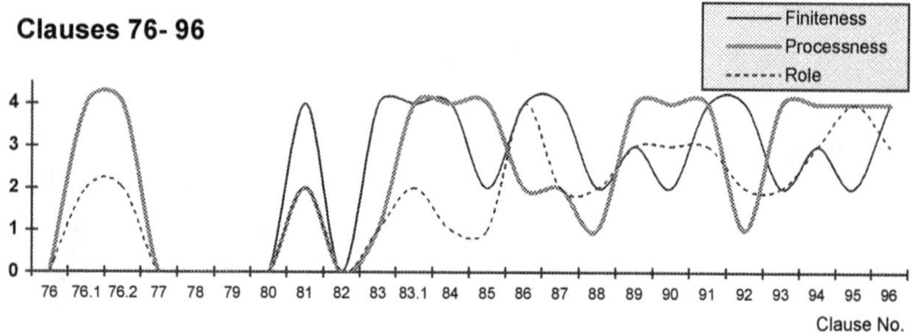

Notes

This paper was first presented to the Australian Science Communicators' Conference, which took place at the Powerhouse Museum in Sydney in 2001.

1   Note that the dates given in parentheses after the titles of Wallace Stevens's poems in this paper are the dates that the poems were first published in individual volumes, namely *Harmonium* (1923), *Parts of a World* (1942), and *Transport to Summer* (1947). These volumes, and several others, have been published together as *The Collected Poems of Wallace Stevens* (1955).

2   Curious, that is, given the leads that are explicit in Stevens's prose writing, and even in his letters; e.g. see the reference to de Broglie and the limits of symbols in Stevens, 1957: 196).

3   Terms such as Range and Actor are capitalised in this paper to indicate that they are labels for the functions of specific wordings in the analyses presented here.

4   Some early theorists of perception, including Democritus and Empedocles, proposed that vision worked as a kind of direct exchange, between the world and the brain, of tiny copies of the objects seen.

References

Bohr, N. (1938) *Natural Philosophy and Human Cultures*. Copenhagen: Comptes Rendus du Congrès International de Science, Anthropologie et Ethnologie. (Also published in *Nature* 143 [1939]: 268–272 and in Bohr, 1958.)

Bohr, N. (1958) *Atomic Physics and Human Knowledge*. New York: Science Editions, Inc.

Butt, D. (1988) Randomness, order and the latent patterning of text. In L. M. O'Toole and D. Birch (eds) *Functions of Style* 74–97. London and New York: Pinter.

Durrant, G. (1970) *Wordsworth and the Great System: A Study of Wordsworth's Poetic Universe*. Cambridge: Cambridge University Press.

Glock, H.-J. (1997) *A Wittgenstein Dictionary*. Oxford: Blackwell.

Gribbin, J. (1998) *Q is for Quantum: Particle Physics from A–Z*. London: Weidenfeld & Nicholson.

Hacker, P. M. S. (1972) *Insight and Illusion: Wittgenstein on Philosophy and the Metaphysics of Experience*. Oxford: Oxford University Press.

Heisenberg, W. (1958) *Physics and Philosophy: The Revolution in Modern Science*. New York: Harper & Row.

Kline, M. (1953 [1990]) *Mathematics in Western Culture*. London: Penguin.

Lawrence, D. H. (1913 [1966]) *Sons and Lovers*. Harmondsworth: Penguin.

Margenau, H. and Sellon, E. B. (eds) (1975) *Main Currents of Modern Thought. Retrospective Issue 1940–1975*, Volume 32. nos. 2–5. New York: Center for Integrative Education, and Ann Arbor, Michigan: Xerox University Microfilms.

Nugroho, H. (1999) Investigating Wordsworth: from lexicogrammar to cross cultural parallelism. Unpublished PhD thesis. Dept of Linguistics. Sydney, Macquarie University.

Passmore, J. (1968) *A Hundred Years of Philosophy*. Harmondsworth: Penguin.

Richardson, J. (1986) *Wallace Stevens A Biography: The Early Years, 1879–1923*. New York: Beech Tree Books.

Saussure, F. de (1915 [1959]) *Course in General Linguistics*. W. Baskin (trans.). New York: McGraw-Hill.

Shklovsky, V. (1925/29 [1990]) *Theory of Prose*. B. Sher (ed. and trans.). USA: Dalkey Archive.

Slessor, K. (1924 [1972]) Fixed ideas. In H. Heseltine (ed.). *The Penguin Book of Australian Verse*. Ringwood: Penguin.

Stevens, W. (1955) *The Collected Poems of Wallace Stevens*. London: Faber & Faber.

Stevens, W. (1957) *Opus Posthumous*. S. F. Morse (ed.). New York: Alfred A. Knopf.

Struik, D. J. (ed.) (1986) *A Source Book in Mathematics, 1200–1800*. Princeton: Princeton University Press.

Vaihinger, H. (1925) *The Philosophy of 'As if'. A System of the Theoretical, Practical and Religious Fictions of Mankind*. New York: Harcourt, Brace & Co.

Watling, J. (1970) *Betrand Russell*. Edinburgh: Oliver and Boyd.

Whitehead, A. N. (1929 [1978]) *Process and Reality*. Corrected edition. D. R. Griffin and D. W. Sherburne (eds). London: The Free Press.

Whorf, B. L. (1956) *Language, Thought, and Reality: Selected Writings of Benjamin Lee Whorf*. J. B. Carroll (ed.) Cambridge, Mass: MIT Press.

Winters, I. (1943 [1972]) Wallace Stevens, or the hedonist's progress. In I. Ehrenpreis (ed.) *Wallace Stevens: A Critical Anthology* 120–142. Harmondsworth: Penguin.

4 The meaning of 'dark*' in Joseph Conrad's *Heart of Darkness*

Monica Turci

Università di Bologna

Editors' Introduction

Monica Turci teaches at the Faculty of Modern Languages of the University of Bologna. She received her MA and PhD in English from the University of Kent at Canterbury (UK). Her research fields include Systemic Functional Linguistics (SFL), cultural studies and literary theory.

In this article, Turci makes a contribution to the still ongoing debate concerning the relation among Joseph Conrad's *Heart of Darkness*, representations of the African continent and the phenomenon of Imperialism. She does so through an analysis of the lemma dark*, and its diverse word forms, as it is reiterated throughout this novella. This is a crucial aspect of *Heart of Darkness*, as it is precisely this stylistic feature that has been pointed out as having played a decisive role in the construction of the well-known myth of 'dark Africa'. And yet, the word has rarely been examined with the tools of the linguist (a recent exception is Stubbs, 2005).

The central part of this article is divided into two stages: the first one performs a quantitative analysis of the lemma dark*. Making use of Wordsmith Tools (Scott, 1999), quantitative data are marshalled on the frequencies, collocation patterns and dispersion of dark* in the electronic corpus of the original version of this novella, which originally appeared in three instalments in the *Blackwood's Magazine* between 1899 and 1901. In the second stage, these patterns are qualitatively analysed in an SFL perspective (Halliday, 1994), according to an ascending rank scale: i.e. dark*, here, is considered in relation first to the group, then the clause and clause-complex, but also the co-text in which it works, with the aim of establishing the experiential meanings being realised in the environment of all occurrences.

The last part of this article argues that SFL analysis is not meant solely to aid the process of understanding the grammar of a text, but would connect that grammar to the meanings it realises within the situational and cultural context in which it is created. In line with this assumption, Turci closes her article by connecting the findings of her quantitative and qualitative textual analysis with the novella's extra-textual plane, in order to place Conrad's novella within the historical and cultural context in which it was written. She argues that, far from transcending this context, as has been argued, the reiterated patterns of the lemma dark* and the meanings they realise can be seen to re-propose the dominant cultural paradigm of the period in which *Heart of Darkness* was written, and, in particular, to work intertextually with the theories on degeneration that were current in the turn of the century fields of physics and anthropology in both Britain and continental Europe.

Turci would bring together the methodologies of both corpus linguistics (CL) and SFL in studying the literature text (cf. the introduction to Thompson and Hunston, 2006, for the complexities in so doing). In particular, she would show that a linguistic analysis can provide a new angle from which critics can look at too long established and widely accepted critical paradigms, in this case, a simple assimilation of the political meanings of Conrad's novella as a reflection of Modernism as imbricated in colonialism.

---

1   Introduction

In this paper I want to analyse the use of language in Joseph Conrad's seminal novella *Heart of Darkness* with reference to its linguistic representation of Africa. More particularly, I wish to contribute a linguistic and cultural perspective to the debate on *Heart of Darkness* and imperialism, which has divided critics with opposite views. The terms of the debates were spelled out during a lecture by Chinua Achebe on Conrad in 1974, during which he accused the writer of providing a racist and stereotypical view of Africa and the African people. Reactions then were mixed, as Achebe himself records in a later essay:

> [...] an elderly English professor had walked up to me and said: 'How dare
> you!' and stalked away. A few days later another English professor said to me:
> 'After hearing you the other night I now realize that I had never really read
> *Heart of Darkness* although I have taught it for years'. (1988: ix–x)

Notwithstanding the personal tone of the debate, which involves the first
African writer in English and a couple of English professors, the representation of Africa in *Heart of Darkness* has for decades been at the centre of
attention of scholars of modern literature and culture, post-colonialism,
critical theory and politics, mobilising discourses in different disciplines
which range from literary criticism to cultural studies, anthropology and
politics. The split opened up by Achebe is far from healing: if, on the one
hand, more and more post-colonial critics, amongst whom most notably
Edward Said (1993), have joined their voices with Achebe's,[1] on the other
hand, critics such as Michael Bell contend that a more inward understanding
of Modernism than that shown by Achebe and Said in their writing would
demonstrate that:

> [...] rather than modernism being reluctantly disturbed by an incipient late-
> colonial conscience, although that is part of it, modernism was itself the means
> for a diagnostic understanding of the colonial mentality. (1997: 149)

They way I intend to contribute to this debate is not by offering a solution, but
rather a critical perspective that has rarely been taken in relation to this novella.
As Michael Stubbs has noted '[...] despite extensive critical discussion, there
is surprisingly little work on the book's linguistic style' (2005:14). If scholars
and teachers have in fact been quick to note and praise the stylistic merits
of *Heart of Darkness* to the point that this novella is generally viewed as a
'masterpiece' of modern literature and is also the most commonly prescribed
reading in literature courses in American universities, little attention has been
paid to the analysis of the role that style plays in its representation of Africa.
Significant, for reasons that will become clearer in my following discussion, is
the use of the lemma dark*, the pattern of its reiteration and, as a consequence,
the meanings it construes.

Generally speaking, reiteration is regarded a significant feature of any
fictional discourse across different disciplines and critical approaches. As Hillis
Miller (1982) and Jacques Derrida (1988) have noted, any work of fiction is
a necessarily complex tissue of repetitions, iterations and differences, linked
in chains of relations and associations with other repetitions: there are repetitions making up the texture of the work, as well as repetitions determining
its multiple intertextual relations to what is outside it. More importantly,
linguistic patterns of repetition are significant not merely for style, but also

for the production of meanings, as Roman Jakobson reminds us.[2] Repetition, I submit, is also of central importance to CL, which, in the words of Stubbs, is based on the assumption that '[…] events that are frequent are significant' (2001: 29).

My attempt to show how the lemma dark* and its various word forms contribute to the debates on *Heart of Darkness* and imperialism involves four stages: the first one consists in an analysis of the ambiguous use of 'darkness' in the title; in the second part, I will consider the recurrence of the lemma dark* in order to isolate predominant patterns of repetition in both the whole novella and each of the three instalments.[3] The third stage is an analysis of the lexicogrammatical functions of the reiterations individuated in the previous stage. In the fourth, and final, stage, I will try to demonstrate that the findings of this linguistic analysis are not solely significant for an understanding of the text, but are the linguistic manifestation of historical and cultural issues that in an overt or covert way have shaped the relation between England and Africa not only in *Heart of Darkness*, but also in the late Victorian period, a vision that has perpetuated up to the present time.

2   On titling: collocation and context

Why start from the title? Though there is a simple answer to this question, in that the title seems to be the logical and obvious place to start from, here I will quote from Fisher's article on the matter, as it unpacks important issues which are often taken for granted. In the process of analysing the multi-faceted nature of names, Fisher concentrates on the particular case of titles:

> […] while titles are names, they are a good deal more than just names. They are not necessarily descriptions. […] They are names for a purpose, but not merely for the purpose of identification or designation […] The unique purpose of titles is hermeneutical: titles are names which function as guides to interpretation. […] Titles do *more* than identify, and in that lies their uniqueness. The title points and, in pointing, forces and limits the range of interpretations. […] Titles are names which have a sense; they call for responses. […] Not all artworks are titled. Not all artworks need to be titled. But when an artwork is titled, for better or for worse, a process of interpretation has inexorably begun. (1984: 288–298)

If titles, as Fisher has proposed, initiate the reader into a hermeneutical process, in the case of Conrad, *Heart of Darkness* introduces the reader into what appears right away to be a hermeneutical maze. The reason lies first and foremost in the fact that here 'darkness' collocates with 'heart'. It is just a felicitous coincidence that Louw in his article included in this book quotes a passage from Firth on collocation, where he says that 'One of the meanings of *night* is its collocability with *dark*' (this volume). Re-phrasing Firth's observation in relation to the title of Conrad's novella, we can say that typically 'darkness' does not define one of the meanings of 'heart', not one that is easily available to the reader. In the attempt to find clues for this hermeneutical enigma, critics have often turned their attention to the titles of literary works written at the same time as Conrad's and which are equally concerned with journeys to Africa. Most notably, they refer to Henry Morton Stanley's accounts of his travels to Africa, entitled *Through the Dark Continent* (1878) and *In Darkest Africa* (1890), which are cited as key references Conrad drew upon and with which his book is aligned (cf. Goonetilleke, 1995: 174–202). For those who have pointed to such relations, the 'heart of darkness' of Conrad's title is, like in Stanley's works, the African continent. According to this reasoning, the title of Conrad's novella goes through a process of re-lexicalisation whereby we do not consider the two words separately but as one metaphorical expression whose more congruent instantiation would be something like the titles of Stanley's novels. To do so would effectively mean equating Stanley's and Conrad's representations of Africa as a dark continent, which was already a cliché by the time Conrad was writing. Further, it would mean eliding the differences between the two works these titles identify: on the one hand, a documentary reportage, on the other, a work of fiction. Moreover, from a stylistic point of view, it would also mean eliding the differences between a congruent and metaphorical way of meaning, a solution that is far from satisfactory both from a hermeneutical and from a stylistic stance.

Here I want to adopt a different strategy: instead of inferring the meaning of the title of this novella from the literary context of sources, I intend to focus on a linguistic analysis, which will, then, provide the basis for a consideration of the cultural context of its creation.

3   A quantitative analysis of the lemma dark*

The first stage of this textual analysis is quantitative and involves the use of computer software to investigate significant micro-patterns of Conrad's use of language by means of a systematic analysis of the frequency and collocation patterns of particular words. Wordsmith Tools 3.0 (Scott, 1999) is used as an indexing tool for interrogating the electronic transcription of the text of the original version of *Heart of Darkness*, the one which appeared in three instalments in the *Blackwood's Magazine* between 1899 and 1901. While frequency cannot of course be simplistically equated with significance, there is a relation, even if indirect, between frequent vocabulary and content. As

Stubbs maintains, '[…] frequency lists are one essential starting point for a systematic textual analysis' (2005: 11). What follows are some global quantitative comments on this novella.

If we exclude grammatical words, the analysis shows that the lemma dark* in its different word forms is among those that occur most often: a total of 56 times, after 'Kurtz' 100 times and 'river' 65 times. More precisely, 'dark' recurs 24 times, 'darker' 3, 'darkly' 3, and 'darkness' 26 times. As far as the three instalments are concerned, the pattern of the distribution of such reiterations is showed separately in the following concordance tables:

```
1.    sea in vanishing flatness. The air was dark above Gravesend, and farther
2.    en on 'Change; captains, admirals, the dark "interlopers" of the Eastern
3.     Marlow suddenly, "has been one of the dark places of the earth." He was
4.   ong as the old earth keeps rolling! But darkness was here yesterday.
5.   haps. They were men enough to face the darkness. And perhaps he was
6.    is very proper for those who tackle a darkness. The conquest of the
7.   riously over. It had become a place of darkness. But there was in it one
8.   ght of these two, guarding the door of Darkness, knitting black wool as
9.   ess. The edge of a colossal jungle, so dark green as to be almost black,
10. clump of trees made a shady spot, where dark things seemed to stir feebly.
11.   and brass-wire set into the depths of darkness, and in return came a
12.  ough it had been a door opening into a darkness he had in his keeping.
13.  gain As I approached the glow from the dark I found myself at the back of
14.  m you know. …"  It had become so pitch dark that we listeners could
15.  the pilgrims sit up in their hovels. A dark figure obscured the lighted
```

Table 4.1: Concord search dark* in the first instalment

```
1.   ath,to the hidden evil, to the profound darkness of its heart. It was so s
2.   ted deeper and deeper into the heart of darkness. It was very quiet there.
3.   o posts; a heap of rubbish reposed in a dark corner, and by the door I pic
4.   e is not careful,' muttered the manager darkly. I observed with assumed i
5.   ach in daylight--not at dusk, or in the dark. This was sensible enough. E
6.   broad-chested black, severely draped in dark-blue fringed cloths, with fi
7.    pool of blood lay very still, gleaming dark-red under the wheel; his eyes
8.   w from the the heart of an impenetrable darkness. 'The other shoe went fl
9.   what he belonged to, how many powers of darkness claimed him for their ow
10.  ou are being assaulted by the powers of darkness. I take it, no fool ever
11. getting well away down the river before dark at all events, when I saw in
```

Table 4.2: Concord search dark* in the second instalment

```
1.   ng sky, appear to me so hopeless and so dark, so impenetrable to human
2.   s, were poured into the clearing by the dark-faced and pensive forest.
3.   ng, the eyes of that apparition shining darkly far in his bony head that
4.   es at a motionless crowd of men made of dark and glittering bronze. I saw
5.   etimes even a savage soul in the lonely darkness of its being?  Who can
6.    presence of victorious corruption, the darkness of an impenetrable night.
7.   bulging with cartridges, from the other (dark blue) peeped
8.   t of danger that seemed, in the starred darkness, real enough to make me
9.    to listen. The night was very clear: a dark blue space, sparkling with
10.  current ran swiftly out of the heart of darkness, bearing us down towards
11.   gnificent folds of eloquence the barren darkness of his heart. Oh, he stru
12.  s.it's a duty' "His was an impenetrable darkness. I looked at him as you
13.  le querulously, 'I am lying here in the dark waiting for death.' The light
14.  -and outside it was so beastly, beastly dark. I went no more near the
15.  netrate all the hearts that beat in the darkness. He had summed up--he had
16.  tude with the spectacled man. He became darkly menacing at last, and
17.  ances, of frightful realities; a shadow darker than the shadow of the
18.  g of a heart--the heart of a conquering darkness. It was a moment of
19.  piano stood massively in a corner, with dark gleams on the flat surfaces
20.  uffering. The room seemed to have grown darker, as if all the sad light of
21.  rrounded by an ashy halo from which the dark eyes looked out at me.
22.   every word spoken the room was growing darker, and only her forehead,
23.   no one no one to - to "I listened. The darkness deepened. I was not even
24.  from beyond the threshold of an eternal darkness. 'But you have heard him!
25.  hat shone with an unearthly glow in the darkness  , in the triumphant
26.  glow in the darkness, in the triumphant darkness from which I could not
27.  r of the infernal stream, the stream of darkness. She said suddenly  very
28.   not tell her. It would have been --too dark too dark altogether
29.   l her .It would have been too dark too dark altogether …" Marlow ceased
30.  lead also into the heart of an immense darkness.
```

Table 4.3: Concord search dark* in the third instalment

This quantitative data across the whole novella is hardly surprising. Indeed, it is rare to find a piece of criticism that does not comment on the significance of the recurrence of 'dark' and 'darkness', something that has also caught the imagination of fictional writers who have tried to 'tackle', so to speak, Conrad's 'darkness', in order to emulate or subvert it.[4] However, the terms of such discussions have often been imprecise, paying little attention to the specific details of Conrad's use of the lemma dark*, and conditioned, one could add, by an understanding of Conrad in terms of his alleged complicity with, or resistance to, colonial ideology, or, as I have already mentioned, in relation to a too obvious connection with sources, which explicitly convey an image of Africa as the 'dark continent'.

Rather than confirming such suspicions of this novella, a close analysis of Conrad's use of language problematises it. In fact, while the word list search reveals a consistent reiteration of the lemma dark*, it also reveals an almost complete absence of references to Africa, which is mentioned only once in the whole novella. The concordance analysis reinforces this finding by revealing that, nowhere in the text, does Africa appear as a collocate of dark*. Unlike Stanley's work, *Heart of Darkness* never explicitly refers to Africa as the 'dark continent'. Those familiar with criticism of Conrad's work could rightly argue, as they have [5], that *Heart of Darkness* is not about a journey into a real place. The Africa portrayed by Conrad is an abstract container, in the words of Achebe, a mere '[...] battlefield devoid of all recognizable humanity, into which the wandering European enters at his peril' (1988: 8). However, if this interpretation can perhaps explain the absence of explicit references to the African continent, it leaves unexplained other less explicit aspects of the reiterated use of dark*, which remains covertly, but powerfully, connected with this novella's representation of Africa and the African people.

4   A qualitative analysis

This analysis is organised through an ascending rank scale as described in SFL (cf. Halliday, 1994: 17–30). The lemma dark* and its lexicogrammatical functions will be considered with reference to each of the three instalments, in relation first to the clause and then to the clause-complex and, where deemed useful, the co- text. In this part of the analysis, I will concentrate my attention on the metaphorical or less congruent instantiations of the lemma dark* as opposed to the more literal ones, as showed in the table below. Such a distinction is at times difficult to maintain, as there are cases in which the lemma dark* can be interpreted both in a literal and in a metaphorical way (see for example the discussion that follows on the first and last instantiations of dark*).

	Instalment 1	Instalment 2	Instalment 3
more congruent	1[A], 9, 10[A], 13, 14, 15[A]	3, 5, 6, 7, 11	1[A], 4, 6[A], 7, 8, 9, 13, 14, 17[A], 19, 20, 21, 22, 23[A], 25[A], 26[A] 28, 29, 30[A]
less congruent	1[A], 2, 3, 4, 5, 6, 7, 8, 10[A], 11, 12, 15[A]	1, 2, 4, 8, 9, 10	1[A], 2, 3, 5, 6[A], 10, 11, 12, 15, 16, 17[A], 18, 23[A], 24, 25[A], 26[A], 27, 30[A]

[A]   indicates overlapping instances

Table 4.4: Comparisons of the more and less congruent realisations of dark* in the three instalments (the numbers refer to the concordance lines in the tables above)

The first instalment opens with an ambiguous use of the epithet 'dark', in that this can be understood both as part of a literal description and as anticipating and building up an atmosphere. In the co-text that follows, the epithet 'luminous', which describes the sky at the opposite side of Gravesend, seems to signal a literal use of this term. However, this also prepares the ground for later and more metaphorical co-occurrences of 'dark' and 'light' which, as we shall see, will recur at various and different stages in the novella. Concordances 2 to 6 in Table 4.1 above occur in the same text segment. They are used in a definitely metaphorical sense, and construe a homophoric reference with the Enlightenment discourse on civilisation which popularised a use of the epithet 'dark' to connote a place, or an attitude, which lacks the 'lights' of a rational and progressive community, society and State. However, this text fragment proposes the terms of this discussion only to disallow them, destroying in this way the above-mentioned opposition between 'dark' and 'light'. If, in fact, in four cases (concordances 3 through 6) dark* realises an attribute of England prior to civilisation, or functions as substitute for the latter, in one case, 'dark interlopers of the eastern trade' (concordance 2), 'dark' is an epithet defining those who are active participants in the 'civilising' mission. This contradiction is carried on in concordance 7: 'It had become a place of darkness', here the VG is a relational attributive process of transformation. The reasons for the change of the carrier 'it', that is to say the Congo region, into a place of darkness is what is identified as the civilising mission of the Belgian company. The attribution of 'darkness' to the Belgian company features very strongly in this instalment, and is carried on in concordance 8, where the door leading to the company offices is defined through the post-modifying PP 'of Darkness'. The reference to this real entrance, leading into a metaphorical darkness, is later on recalled in a clause in which the same transitivity structure is re-proposed but this time in a more metaphorical fashion. Thus, in concordance 12, reference is made to a metaphorical entrance: '[…] that smile of his [of the manager], as though it had been a door opening into a darkness […]'(1902 [1973]: 51). The manager, like other 'dark' figures (concordance 15) which populate the company premises are in a relation of meronymy to the latter and contribute to the representation of the company as a 'place of darkness'. Only on one occasion in this instalment is the Congo described as a place of darkness: it is 'the depths of darkness' (concordance 11) where '[…] a stream of manufactured goods, rubbishy cottons, beads, and brass wire […]' were sent and '[…] in return came a precious trickle of ivory' (1902 [1973]: 46). Similarly, here Africans are only once called 'dark things' (concordance 10). However, as soon as these are identified as human beings, they significantly, if ambiguously, lose the epithet of 'dark' and acquire that of 'black'.

In the second instalment, the lemma dark* remains within the same semantic universe as in the first one, referring to European or African people and places. In addition, however, we should also note cases in which generic circumstances of Location: Space referring to Africa are experientially connected to the actions, state or consciousness of Kurtz, who, in this instalment, is a mere spectre of Marlow's imagination.

More particularly, the connection of the lemma dark* with European people is realised firstly in concordance 4 in Table 4.2: 'darkly' is a circumstance of Manner describing the already negatively connoted mutterings of the manager of the company, and secondly in concordance 10: 'Of course you may be too much of a fool to go wrong – too dull even to know you are being assaulted by the powers of darkness' (1902 [1973]: 85). Here 'the powers of darkness' is a nominal group (henceforth, NG) functioning as Actor of Process 'assault', an action directed towards an impersonal 'you' which encompasses Marlow and the sailors and functions as the Goal of their assault. This analysis strongly links 'the powers of darkness' to European characters, but leaves them undefined. An analysis of the co-text is useful in this regard, despite not providing definite answers. The 'powers of darkness' I refer to here are mentioned earlier on in concordance 9, reporting a speech by Kurtz: '"My Intended, my ivory, my station, my river, my – " everything belonged to him [Kurtz]. […] The thing was to know what he belonged to, how many powers of darkness claimed him for their own' (1902 [1973]: 85). Here 'the powers of darkness' can be better identified with part of the African landscape, or what constitutes it: the ivory, the station and the river. But through a transitivity analysis we can take this further: 'claim', though typically a verbal Process, in this co-text, i.e., together with both 'belonged to' and 'for their own', can be seen to reinforce a possession. Here, 'how many powers of darkness' is Possessor and 'him' Possessed, linking Kurtz and 'the darkness', into a mutual relation of domination. Thus, the human Participant, Kurtz, who is typically the possessor at the start of the segment becomes, less typically, the one who is possessed.

This merging together of Kurtz with the 'darkness', which on the surface refers to a generic and indefinite African space, is sustained throughout this instalment. When, for example, in concordance 2, Marlow recounts: 'We penetrated deeper and deeper into the heart of darkness', 'heart of darkness' functions as the circumstance of Location: Space, towards which the steamboat is travelling, an abstract space, which is never defined in proper spatial terms. However, a hint as to where this space could be is given in the following textual fragment: 'For me', says Marlow, 'it [the steamboat] crawled towards Kurtz – exclusively' (1902 [1973]: 68). Here Kurtz functions as the circumstance of Location: Space which is Marlow's above-mentioned final destination, thus establishing a relation of identification between this character and the 'heart of darkness' towards which the steamboat crawls.

Further examples of the relation between Kurtz and an ambiguous African landscape occur again a few pages later. In the context of an attempt to describe Kurtz, we read:

> [...] of all his gifts the one that stood out pre-eminently [...] was his ability to talk, his words – the gift of expression, the bewildering, the illuminating, the most exalted and the most contemptible, the pulsating stream of light, or the deceitful flow from the heart of an impenetrable darkness. (1902 [1973]: 83; concordance 8)

Here 'from the heart of an impenetrable darkness' is Qualifier of the NG 'deceitful flow'. Semantically 'flow' evokes the waterway on which Marlow is travelling and functions as one of the synonymous Identifiers of Kurtz's noteworthy 'gift'. In this way, the text establishes a mutual relation of identification that links together Kurtz, the symbolical deceitful waters of the river Congo and 'the heart of an impenetrable darkness'.

Such an identification between Kurtz and a landscape enveloped in darkness continues and reaches its peak in the third and last instalment, the only one in which the character of Kurtz features. This also significantly contains the highest number of instances in which 'dark' and 'darkness' straightforwardly refer to a setting in order to describe it and/or to create a certain atmosphere. Instances of both literal and metaphorical instantiations of dark* attributed to or connected with the setting here include the African landscape, but also London, London interiors and Gravesend. Identifications between Kurtz and the landscape occur once again: for example in concordance 2 which describes the first appearance of this character. Here, 'dark-faced and pensive forest' functions as the Actor of metaphorical material Process 'poured out' whose Goal is Kurtz and some other people carrying him. In the same way the forest pours out Kurtz, the earth is impregnated with the corruption which he and the Belgian company perpetrate: 'I felt an intolerable weight oppressing my breast, the smell of the damp earth, the unseen presence of victorious corruption, the darkness of an impenetrable night [...]' (1902 [1973]: 103; concordance 6). Through this implicit expansion 'the darkness' is compounded with the corruption and the smell of the earth to form a single NG.

In some instances 'darkness' is straightforwardly referred to Kurtz, where it belongs to him as Carrier: 'his was an impenetrable darkness' (1902 [1973]: 111; concordance 12), or in concordance 15 where 'all the hearts that beat in the darkness' is the Phenomenon of Kurtz's stare. Kurtz is a catalyst of darkness even after his death; his vision is a 'shadow darker than the shadow of the night' (concordance 17) and strides into the house of Kurtz's Intended with a regular pace reminiscent of 'the beating of a heart –the heart of a conquering darkness' (concordance 18):

> The vision seemed to enter the house with me – the stretcher, the phantom-bearers, the wild crowd of obedient worshippers, the gloom of the forests, the glitter of the reach between the murky bends, the beat of the drum, regular and muffled like the beating of a heart – the heart of a conquering darkness. (1902 [1973]: 116)

The reminiscences of the last part of this instalment, which recall Kurtz's last days, are stylistically realised through a Grammatical Parallelism that comprises not merely reiterations of the lemma dark*, but also of already instantiated tropes. This is the case of:

- concordance 11: 'Kurtz discoursed. A voice! a voice! It rang deep to the very last. It survived his strength to hide in the magnificent folds of eloquence the barren darkness of its heart' (1902 [1973]:110); this, as in the already mentioned concordance 8 in Table 4.2, refers to Kurtz's voice, his eloquence, as one of the synonymous Identifiers of 'the darkness';
- concordance 24, where 'darkness' is postmodifying PP of 'threshold' semantically linked to the 'door of darkness' back in concordances 8 and 12 in Table 4.1;
- concordance 27, where 'the infernal stream of darkness' is postmodification of 'over the glitter' which is reminiscent of concordance 8 in Table 4.2, which linked together Kurtz, the waters of the river, and, in this case, also Kurtz's African mistress.

The novella ends with an example of Grammatical Parallelism which functions on many levels and connects with its beginning in a perfect circular fashion: 'The offing was barred by a black bank of clouds, and the tranquil waterway leading to the uttermost ends of the earth flowed sombre under an overcast sky – seemed to lead into the heart of an immense darkness' (1902 [1973]: 121; concordance 30). The Grammatical Parallelism is realised through the re-creation of the same circumstance of Location: Space, which opened Marlow's story. Both the beginning and the end, refer to 'darkness' seemingly through a minute description of the naturalistic setting, offering therefore a literal meaning. Moreover, like at the beginning, the reference to 'darkness' also has an evocative function: at the beginning of the novella 'The air was dark above Gravesend […]' (1902 [1973]: 27) introduces the darkness of England in the past; here, in the closing, the reference to darkness envelops all the landscape, both African and European, through the presence or the memory of Kurtz who has become indistinguishable from the latter.

Table 4.5 concludes and sums up the results of my qualitative analysis of metaphorical instantiations of the lemma dark* conducted on each of the three instalments separately. These results can be usefully and significantly commented in relation to the subject matter of the instalments.

	Instalment 1	Instalment 2	Instalment 3
European people (colonisers, people who are involved in the Belgian company and Kurtz's intended)	2, 12, 15	4, 10	16
African people	10*		
Kurtz and/or Kurtz character merging with African landscape		2, 8, 9	2[A], 3, 6, 11, 12, 15, 17, 18, 26[A]
Kurtz's African mistress			5[A]
European places, including the Company, and London's interiors	1, 3, 4, 5, 6, 8		23, 24, 25, 26[A], 30
Africa and the Congo	7 **, 11***	1	1, 2[A], 5[A], 10, 27

[A]   indicates overlapping instances
*   here not identified as human beings but as 'Things'
**   following action of Belgian company
*** circumstance of Location: Space in clause in which the Actor is the company's goods

Table 4.5: Summary of less congruent or more metaphorical references realised by dark* (the numbers refer to the concordance lines in the tables above)

The first instalment starts with Marlow on the boat Nellie at Gravesend and finishes at the point in which he reaches the central station of the Belgian company at the mouths of the Congo River. It is 14,525 words long and is set in England, Belgium and, only at the end, in Africa. Out of a total of 15 occurrences of the lemma dark*, only 3 refer to African people and the African setting, while 9 refer to European places and characters.

The second instalment describes the journey from the central station and ends at the inner station where Kurtz is. It is 12,284 words long and is entirely set in Africa. There are fewer instances of the lemma dark* than the first and third instalment, 11 altogether. Only one of these refers to the African landscape and none at all to African people, despite the fact that they are present at various points of the narration. By contrast, Kurtz does not appear in person, but in three instances his presence is evoked in connection with the African landscape. In three instances dark* refers to European characters.

The third instalment opens with the arrival at the inner station and Marlow's encounter with Kurtz and ends with Marlow's return to England via Belgium. Despite being the shortest instalment, 11,993 words long, it is the one which counts the highest instances of the lemma dark*, a total of 30 times. Of these, 10 refer to Kurtz in connection with the African landscape and his African mistress, 5 to the London setting, 5 to the African landscape and 1 to European characters. No instances of the lemma dark*, like in the previous instalment, refer to African people.

5   The context of culture: dark* and imperialism

Functional linguistics analysis is not meant solely to enact a process of understanding of the grammar of a text, but to connect that grammar to the meanings it realises within the cultural context in which it is created. As Miller has succinctly put it, 'a text is a fragment of the culture that produces it' (1993: 105). The results of the quantitative and qualitative analysis performed above have clearly shown that the lemma dark* and its word forms are used to connote negatively the main character Kurtz, European characters, mainly connected with the Belgian company and also the European and African landscape in connection with the figure, character or actions of Kurtz.

This should not lead us to conclude that Africa and the African people are merely overlooked in this novella, but, rather, that this is the linguistic manifestation of a certain attitude of the European in relation to Africa and the African people. The significant number of instances in which the character of Kurtz merges with the landscape is reminiscent of a formal technique employed in John Ruskin's commentary on Turner's painting *Slavers Throwing Overboard the Dead and the Dying: Typhon Coming On* (*The Slave Ship*).

In his commentary, Ruskin (1897) refers to the dismembered bodies of the jettisoned slaves indirectly and only in relation to the landscape. As I have noted elsewhere:

> In Ruskin's description the colour red co-mingles and conflates the light of the sunset with the blood of the slaves; the breast of the woman drowning exists only to dissolve in the waves, the hands of the slaves are mere shadows, an effect of the play of light and shade produced by the sunset over the agitated sea surface. (Turci, 2000: 103)

In Ruskin's description the bodies of the slaves merge and are submerged by Turner's sublime ocean. In *Heart of Darkness*, it is the African landscape that is absorbed in the figure of Kurtz losing, like Turner's slaves, its specificity, immediacy and material physicality in the midst of a transcendental and abstract 'darkness'.

In *Heart of Darkness*, the representation of Africa is not only scanty, but also constrained within what can be called a cultural episteme common in Europe at the turn of the last century. This has been defined by Rod Edmond as follows:

> [...] [the] idea of the inevitable extinction of humanity had acquired particular and urgent meanings during the second half of the nineteenth century, putting new life into the time-honoured idea of historical decline and becoming associated with contemporary scientific theories of degeneration. (Edmond, 2000: 39)

In the later Victorian period, theories of degeneration declared that the black man was at a low level of development and therefore doomed to extinction. The concomitant spread of the European empires played a central role in defining a specific form of degeneration caused by contact and intermarriage with primitive populations, a phenomenon that became better known as 'going native'. This would to some extent explain the fact that the lemma dark* is applied to those European characters who have come into contact with Africa, and, in particular, to Kurtz.

Degeneration, however, applies not only to those who come into contact with natives, but also to places. If, around 1850s, Charles Darwin declared that no species was exempt from the universal law of extinction, the following decade was to bring fears about the permanence of the universe itself. William Thompson's theory about the cooling of the sun was accepted from the 1860s until the discovery of radioactivity in the twentieth century. In the last instalment of *Heart of Darkness* the incipient darkness of the colonial outposts –the Congo region- as well as that of the imperial centres, London and Bruxelles, give voice to this form of degeneration, and represents a restatement of the cultural climate in which this novella was written, one that is firmly rooted in the English Victorian period.

6 Conclusion

By way of concluding, I would like to make some brief remarks on the relation between *Heart of Darkness* and imperialism. As anticipated, I do not wish to take a pro or anti view on this matter. I only wish to note two contrasting results that have emerged from my analysis. On the one hand, analysis has shown that the seemingly ambiguous and symbolic meanings of the lemma dark*, which have usually been treated as universal, are intimately connected to the cultural climate of the period in which this novella was written. Context must be considered. In this sense, *Heart of Darkness* is not merely a timeless 'masterpiece', but a late Victorian novella whose horizons are clearly limited by visions that were popular in that period.

On the other hand, analysis of the reiteration of the lemma dark* has shown the 'poetic' quality of this work, in the sense attributed by Jakobson to this term (1966: 399), and although verbal art is not the only type of text to display the poetic function, I believe that Conrad's work has already proved itself capable of being appreciated as art by ever-more distant communities, in time and space. In this sense, like other poetic works, *Heart of Darkness* transcends its own time.

In the context of a biographical inquiry, Edward Said writes:

> Conrad's tragic limitation is that even though he could see clearly that on one level imperialism was essentially pure dominance and land-grabbing, he could not then conclude that imperialism had to end so that 'natives' could then lead lives free from European domination. (Said, 1993: 34)

I would only add that, although the novella undoubtedly is a complex, subtle and poetic work, another of its tragic limitations is not to have been able to transcend the ideological limits of the degenerationist theories so pervasive in the European cultural climate of that time.

Notes

1   For studies which represents Conrad's politics as a critique of European Imperialism, see for example Fleishman (1967: 80–125). Also, in a similar fashion, Torgovnick's study (1990: 141–158) notes Conrad's critical attitude towards European imperialism, but also underlines the fact that such critique is limited to some nations: '*Heart of Darkness* tries very hard to distinguish between British and Belgian colonialism [...]' (144). Like other post-colonial critics, Torgovnick further comments that this 'novella can be read as an affirmation

of humanistic values, in ways that make us feel good about its treatment of Africa and the Africans' (143), thus connecting humanist issues with political ones. The terms of Torgovnick's discussion also resurfaced in a much heated debate broadcast by the BBC in 1989, during which Achebe argued that *Heart of Darkness*, contrary to other masterpieces of English literature, deprives the African people of language, and therefore of the very prerequisite for their humanity.

2   According to Jakobson:

> '[...] on every level of language the essence of poetic artifice consists in recurrent returns. Phonemic features and sequences, both morphological and lexical, syntactic and phraseological units, when occurring in metrically or strophically corresponding positions, are necessarily subject to the conscious or unconscious questions of whether, how far, and in what respect the positionally corresponding entities are mutually similar.' (1966: 399)

For a discussion of Grammatical Parallelism in the poetry of D. H. Lawrence, see Miller (this volume)

3   I use this term with the meaning of one of several parts of something published or broadcast at intervals.

4   Graham Greene's novels, *Journey without Maps* (1936) and *In Search of a Character: Two African Journals* (1961), and André Gide's *Voyage au Congo* (1926), are among the many novels inspired by Conrad's novella. Achebe's *Things Fall Apart* (1958) was declaredly written in order to attempt to subvert the vision of Africa in *Heart of Darkness*.

5   The list of critics taking this position would be far too long and could never be complete. Suffice it here to say that this position has been most strongly maintained by criticism inspired by psychoanalytical theories. See, for example, P. Kirschner (1968).

References

Achebe, C. (1958) *Things Fall Apart*. Oxford: Heinemann.

Achebe, C. (1988) *Hopes and Impediments. Selected Writings 1965–87*. London: Heinemann.

Bell, M. (1997) *Literature, Modernism and Myth: Belief and Responsibility in the Twentieth Century*. Cambridge: Cambridge University Press.

Conrad, J. (1899–1901) *Heart of Darkness*. Electronic version prepared by C. Kogut. Retrieved from http://gaslight.mtroyal.ca/darkmenu.htm on July 30, 2004.

Conrad, J. (1902 [1973]) *Heart of Darkness*. London: Penguin.

Derrida, J. (1988) *Limited Inc*. S. Weber and J. Mehlman (trans.). Evanston Ill: Northwestern University Press.

Edmond, R. (2000) Home and away: degeneration in imperialist and modernist discourse. In H. Booth and N. Rigby (eds) *Modernism and Empire* 39–63. Manchester: Manchester University Press.

Fisher, J. (1984) Entitling. *Critical Enquiry* 11: 286–298.

Fleishman, A. (1967) *Conrad's Politics. Community and Anarchy in the Fiction of Joseph Conrad.* Baltimore: The Johns Hopkins University Press.

Goonetilleke, D. C. R. A. (ed.) (1995) *Heart of Darkness.* Peterborough, Ontario: Broadview Press.

Halliday, M. A. K. (1994) *An Introduction to Functional Grammar,* 2nd edition. London: Arnold.

Jakobson, R. (1966) Grammatical parallelism and its Russian facet. *Language* 42. 2: 399–429.

Kirschner, P. (1968) *Joseph Conrad: A Psychologist as Artist.* Edinburgh: Oliver & Boyd.

Miller, D. R. (1993) The juridical text as cultural fragment: discourse communities and the (re)creation of truth. In P. Bayley and D. R. Miller (eds) *Texts and Contexts of the American Dream: A Social Semiotic Study of Political Language* 101–146. Bologna: Pitagora.

Miller, H. J. (1982) *Fiction and Repetition. Seven English Novels.* Oxford: Basil Blackwell.

Ruskin, J. (1897) *Modern Painters* Volume 1. London: George Allen.

Said, E. W. (1993) *Culture and Imperialism.* London: Vintage.

Scott, M. (1999) *Wordsmith Tools.* Version 3.0. Oxford: Oxford University Press.

Stubbs, M. (2001) *Words and Phrases: Corpus Studies of Lexical Semantics.* Oxford: Blackwell.

Stubbs, M. (2005) Conrad in the computer. *Language and Literature. Journal of the Poetics and Linguistics Association* 19. 1: 5–24.

Thompson, G. and Hunston, S. (2006) *System and Corpus: Exploring Connections.* London: Equinox.

Torgovnick, M. (1990) *Gone Primitive: Savage Intellects and Modern Lives.* Chicago: University of Chicago Press.

Turci, M. (2000) Resurfacing Turner's bodies. *Textus* XIII: 93–112.

5 Projection in literary and in non-literary texts

Carol Taylor Torsello

University of Padua

Editors' Introduction

Carol Taylor Torsello holds the Chair of English Linguistics at the University of Padua. Her highly varied research interests include: Systemic Functional Linguistics (SFL), corpus linguistics, language teaching and testing methodologies and e-learning. Her application of a linguistic approach to the study and teaching of literature began in the 1970s and, since then, she has brought her expertise in corpus linguistics to bear on this research. In this second corpus-based contribution to our volume, Taylor Torsello continues her studies of particular linguistic phenomena across literary and non-literary genres to highlight the specificities of each. Here the phenomenon that is probed in this comparative perspective is projection.

The article does not aim at presenting the various descriptions of this linguistic phenomenon which can be found in the literature, although the author's profound knowledge of these is clearly a resource which strengthens her approach and method. What she aims to do is to provide corpus evidence from some literary and non-literary texts, to show how, with what frequency, and in relation to which strategies of the authors, this linguistic device actually occurs. What she truly and admirably succeeds in doing is demonstrating how the frequency and the form of projections can function as an important discriminating factor across genres, across instances of the same variety by different authors, and even across diverse texts by the same author. The works of verbal art which have been hand-tagged for types of projection and related phenomena, and analysed, using Wordsmith Tools software, include: *Saint John's Gospel*, Virginia Woolf's *A Room of One's Own, Mrs. Dalloway* and *To the Lighthouse*, as well as J. K. Rowling's *Harry Potter and the Philosopher's Stone*.

As Taylor Torsello establishes immediately, projection, or report of speech and ideas, is a complex area of grammar. She investigates the phenomenon in relation to what SFL calls the logical metafunction, due to its construal of a particular type of semantic relationship between the messages in the projecting and projected clauses. The basic distinction between projection of speech and of thought is taken into account, while the instances of projection she focuses on include the two types described in SFL: paratactic and hypotactic projections. The position of the projecting clause in relation to the projected clause (coming before, in the middle, or afterwards) is also investigated, as is Subject-Verb in the projecting clause. But projection is complex as far as its multifunctionality is concerned too. Unlike the connection between clauses typically constructed by expansions, the link forged by projection is between a phenomenon (the act of speaking or thinking), and a metaphenomenon (*what* is said or thought). She also examines projection's role in interpersonal meaning-making, however, illustrating how it construes speaker stance in terms of commitment, control and authority. Neither does she overlook its role in making textual meanings, working as it can to frame narratives.

The conclusions Taylor Torsello comes to concern how the authors of the works of verbal art use projection within their artistic strategies. The lucid discussion of the resulting data is undoubtedly strengthened by rigorous comparisons with the data from the non-literary genres, including newspaper and magazine articles and economic and financial news releases from Internet. It seems that a good way to end this introduction to Taylor Torsello's work is with her own closing words:

> The results definitely confirm what Halliday (2004: 447) says about the significance of projection as a discourse variable: 'Since the amount and type of explicit projection is a significant discourse variable, it is important to show exactly where and in what form it occurs'.

This is precisely what she's scrupulously done.

1   Introduction

Projection, as it is called in Systemic Functional Grammar, or report of speech and ideas, is a complex area of grammar, one which Halliday (e.g. 1979: 77, 2004: 441–482) relates particularly to the logical metafunction, since it sets up a particular type of semantic relationship between the messages in the clauses involved in the clause complex it is realised in: a relationship between a phenomenon (the act of speaking or thinking), and a metaphenomenon (what is said or thought). It is also a powerful tool within the interpersonal mean-ing-making potentialities of language, with its role in providing or denying commitment, evidence and authoritativeness (Martin, 1988: 264; McGregor, 1990: 37–42; Taylor Torsello, 1996a: 161–166; Halliday, 2004: 626–627). It has been studied by linguists adhering to various linguistic schools (Coulmas, 1986; Longacre, 1985; Munro, 1982; Partee, 1973; Rosenbaum, 1967; Stockwell, 1977; Zwicky, 1971; Janssen and van der Wurff, 1996; Lucy, 1993; Thompson, 1994). It is not the purpose of this article to present and discuss the various descriptions of this linguistic phenomenon found in the literature. Rather, the purpose here is to provide corpus evidence of how, and with what frequency, this linguistic device actually occurs. The data presented will be related to how the authors of the works of verbal art considered use projection within their artistic strategies. The literary works considered are *Saint John's Gospel*, J. K. Rowling's *Harry Potter and the Philosopher's Stone*, and Virginia Woolf's *A Room of One's Own*, *Mrs. Dalloway* and *To the Lighthouse*.[1] In the course of this article, I will sometimes refer to these works respectively using the short references *Gospel*, *Potter*, *Room*, *Dalloway*, and *Lighthouse*. The discussion will be strengthened by comparisons with data from different, non-literary genres, including newspaper and magazine articles, and economic-financial news releases from Internet.

The corpus analyses that provide the data have been carried out either by myself or by undergraduate degree students under my supervision at the University of Padua (see references) in different periods, and using methods that were not always exactly the same.[2] This creates some difficulty in putting them together into a unified report on projection in different genres, which has meant that some of the materials have had to be reanalysed, and some com-parisons have not been possible. Nonetheless, a rather clear picture emerges, I believe, of how important a differentiating factor the frequency and the form of projections can be across genres, across works by different authors, and even across different works by the same author. There are genres where projec-tion plays almost no role: for example, a study of 1000 proverbs revealed the presence of only 10 projections, all hypotactic. Our studies of recipes and of instruction manuals, although focused on other phenomena (Alò, 2000; Barbato

Ferrisio, 2003), allowed us to notice that these two genres also make little use of projections. On the other hand, our study of front-page newspaper articles has brought to light the fundamental role of projections in this genre (Taylor Torsello, 1996b). The studies carried out on projection in literary works have not only confirmed the important role this phenomenon plays, but have also allowed us to make some interesting distinctions regarding its use by different authors, and, through the study of three works by Virginia Woolf, in different works by one author.

Projections can be verbal, projecting speech, with projecting verbs like *say*, *tell*, *announce* and *claim*, or mental, projecting thought, with projecting verbs like *think, believe, understand, hope* and *want*, and this basic difference will be taken into account. The phenomena studied include the projections which form clause complexes of the two types described in Halliday's grammar: paratactic projections (both direct report and the 'free' forms – 'free direct' and 'free indirect' as exemplified below) and hypotactic projections (indirect report of speech or thought, whether with a finite or a non-finite clause projected hypotactically by the projecting clause). Example 1 is a paratactic projection in which speech is quoted in a direct report. Example 2 is a hypotactic projection in which speech is reported in an indirect report.

(1)   'Aren't you drenched to the skin?' she had said. (*Lighthouse*: 11)

(2)   Dr. Holmes might say there was nothing the matter. (*Dalloway*: 24)

Example 3, containing a mental projection, corresponds to the type of para-tactic projection which Halliday (2004: 465) refers to as 'free indirect', which combines the paratactic structure of quote with the shift in time and person reference typical of report.[3]

(3)   Always, Mrs. Ramsay felt, one helped oneself out of solitude
       reluctantly by laying hold of some little odd or end, some sound, some
       sight. (*Lighthouse*: 71)

There is another 'free' form, which I will refer to as 'free direct', in which the structure is paratactic and there is no shift in time or person reference, but the typical punctuation of direct report, the set of inverted commas, is not used.[4] Example 4 shows (in the clause complex before the semicolon) an instance of free direct thought.

(4)   That girl, thought Mrs. Dempster (who saved crusts for the squirrels
       and often ate her lunch in Regent's Park), don't know a thing yet;
       and really it seemed to her better to be a little stout, a little slack, a little
       moderate in one's expectations. (*Dalloway*: 29)

Projections of speech and of thought often continue beyond the sentence level in texts. The projection-continuation sentences do not properly belong to the grammar of projection-type clause complexes, but rather create cohesion on the text level (Halliday, 2004: 447). It is clear that, from the semantic point of view, projection is involved, and the choice on the part of authors to continue projections beyond the sentence level is considered of interest in this study. Most often the projecting clause can be retrieved from a preceding sentence (see Example 5), but it can also be necessary to await a subsequent sentence in order to find a projecting clause, as in Example 6.

(5)   If Shakespeare had never existed, he asked, would the world have differed much from what it is to-day? Does the progress of civilisation depend upon great men? Is the lot of the average human being better now than in the time of the Pharaohs? (*Lighthouse*: 48)

(6)   But how did she know that those were Mary and Joseph? Did she think the same birds came to the same trees every night? he asked. (*Lighthouse*: 89)

Continuous discourse can also present cases of projections with no projecting clause, as in Example 7, where the final *and so on* – not part of the projected speech – indicates that the character, Mrs. Ramsay, is thinking about her own speech. I introduce the term 'floating' for these, calling Example 7 (excluding *and so on*) a floating free quote ('free' to indicate the lack of inverted commas).

(7)   Do you want stamps, do you want tobacco? Here's a book you might like and so on. (*Lighthouse*: 47)

Attention is also focused on the position of the projecting clause in relation to the projected clause – before, in the middle, or after, respectively, as in Examples 8, 9 and 10.

(8)   And she thought, standing there with her book open, here one could let whatever one thought expand like a leaf in water; and if it did well here, among the old gentlemen smoking and *The Times* crackling, then it was right. (*Lighthouse*: 205)

(9)   That, more or less, is how the story would run, I think, if a woman in Shakespeare's day had had Shakespeare's genius. (*Room*: 50)

(10) 'Herbert has it now,' she said. (*Dalloway*: 46)

The order in which the constituents Subject and Verb occur in the projecting clause is also focused on: Subject before Verb, as in Examples 1, 2, 3, 5, 6, 8, 9 and 10, as opposed to Verb before Subject, as in Example 4.

Projections can also be embedded, or rank-shifted down to group level within the clause (Halliday, 2004: 467–476), but this particular article will not focus on these structures. Nor will it focus on partial or on summarising reports, which are also at group level rather than clause or clause-complex level, as described by Thompson (1994: 17–18).

2   Front-page newspaper articles

The first quantitative study I carried out on projection was an analysis of front page articles taken from eight newspapers (four US and four British), with their continuations on inside pages (Taylor Torsello, 1996b).[5] This study already made it quite evident that, in this genre, projection is an extremely frequent phenomenon. In fact, roughly half (49%) of the sentences in the corpus had projection as the primary structure, with a difference between the British (60%) and the US (46%) papers. Paratactic projections were more frequent than the hypotactic ones, making up respectively 57% and 43% of the first-order projection clause-complexes, and were of the verbal type. Looking now more specifically at the two kinds of paratactic projection which occur in the corpus, we see that these divide up as 83% direct (with inverted commas) against 17% free direct (without inverted commas). A study of the position of the projecting clause in the direct report type of paratactic projections reveals that the most common position, accounting for 78%, is after the projected clause, with only 21% coming before it, and 1% in the middle. [6] If we look at the free direct reports, here too, in the majority of the cases (54%), the projecting clause comes after the projected one, while it comes before the projected clause in 9% of the cases and in the middle of it in 37% of the cases. For data on the two types of paratactic projections together, see Figure 5.4 in the Conclusions.

If we consider the order of the Subject and Verb in the projecting clauses that come after the projected ones in these two types of paratactic projections, we see the normal SV order is maintained 48% of the time and inverted 52% of the time when the report is direct (see Example 11), whereas, when the report is free direct (see Example 12), SV order is maintained 72% of the time and inverted 28%.

> (11) 'A lot of agreements are being signed to push the refugees back
>   east', said Daisy Dell, the representative of the UN High Commissioner
>   for Refugees in Prague. (Doors are closing on East European refugees,
>   *International Herald Tribune*, July 1, 1993)

(12) The Clinton administration has abandoned a plan to conduct nine
more underground nuclear tests and now favours no resumption of
testing unless another country tests first, officials said. (Nuclear tests
are dropped in shift by White House, *International Herald Tribune*,
July 1, 1993)

Example 11 shows something which is frequently found in end-position projecting clauses with VS structure: the Subject Head is followed by a qualifier,
in this case an apposition. The preference for SV order in free direct report
(see Example 12) may relate to the tendency to avoid a multiplicity of marked
options (lack of quote punctuation and marked word order), so as not to make
the message too opaque in this genre, whose primary rhetorical mode is
informative (Taylor Torsello, 2000).

The articles have a great number of sentences which are marked as quotes
through punctuation without having a projecting clause in the same sentence.
These sentences are continuations of a quote which begins in an earlier sentence
having a projecting clause (see Example 13).

(13) 'We're in the preliminary stages of the talks', he said. 'They would pay
expenses, but they say they've got problems with payments to ex-
cons. But that rule only seems to apply in some cases. They didn't
have any problem with paying Albert Speer'. (BBC planning train
robbers' reunion in Rio, *The Daily Telegraph*, June 30, 1993)

If we add the direct report sentences and these continuing quote sentences
together to get the total number of quote sentences, we see that the continuing
quotes with no projecting clause account for 43.2% of the total. Free direct
report, on the other hand, rarely continues across sentence boundaries, with
continuing sentences accounting for only 4.3% of the sum of these and their
continuations. This too may relate to an effort to reduce the opacity which
free report entails.

3   Economic-financial news articles on the Internet and in 'The Economist'

A corpus of 50 Internet articles devoted to economic and financial news (22,142
words) was analysed for, among other things, projection (Marcon, 2002).[7] The
corpus was made up of both simple, one-clause sentences and complex ones,
and the type of complexity was more often parataxis and hypotaxis of the
expansion type (603) than of the projection type (464). A few of the articles
contain no projection at all. In this corpus, hypotactic projections, or indirect
report, are much more frequent (64%) than paratactic projections (36%), made

up of direct report and free direct report. The predominance of hypotaxis over parataxis is a datum which differentiates this genre from the newspaper genre presented in Section 2 above. Where parataxis is used here, the wording to be quoted is almost always what is put first in the sentence, since 99% of the time the projected clause precedes the projecting one. This is true whether the parataxis is a direct report, as in Example 14, or free direct, as in Example 15. Free direct structures account for over half (51%) of the paratactic projections. This freer form is less binding to the author, as far as the use of his source's exact wording is concerned. Furthermore, in this corpus it is very often used when there is no mention of a precise person who has made the statement. Sometimes the authors commit themselves to direct report only for a part of what they quote, as in Example 16. With direct report, the precise name of the speaker is most often given, whereas, quite often in this corpus, the source cited is not a precise person but a firm (*Merrill Lynch & Co.*), a stock market (*S&P*), a written document (*the paper*), an institution (*the Labor Department*), or a category of people (*other analysts*), and in these cases indirect report or free direct report are preferred.

(14) 'Any time you have anything, a stock or a market like Nasdaq, go
     up as much as it has in the past six or seven weeks, people look at their
     portfolios and see which gains are warranted and which are piling on
     from all the excitement', said Mark Cunneen, who manages $ 2.3
     billion at J. & W. Seligman & Co. (US Stocks Fall; Nasdaq on Track
     for First Drop in Seven Days, by David Wells, www.Bloomberg.com,
     May 23, 2001)

(15) Initial claims for regular state unemployment benefits rose 18,000 to
     a seasonally adjusted 408,000 for the week ended April 21, from a
     revised 390,000 in the previous week, the Labor Department said.
     (US weekly jobless claims up 18,000 to 408,000, nasdaq.com, April
     26, 2001, Copyright 2001 AFX News Ltd.)

(16) The signal given by the FOMC so far is that 'we are not going to
     allow recession to take hold', he added. (Merrill Lynch's Frenkel
     says US economic slowdown hit bottom in Q4, www.nasdaq.com, June
     2001, Copyright 2001 AFX News Ltd.)

Continuation of the quote beyond the sentence level, giving sentences made up solely of a quote with no projecting clause, does occur in this corpus (43 cases).

A small corpus study carried out on ten articles from *The Economist* (Peraro, 2005) shows that in this printed channel of economic and financial information only 17% of the sentences contain projections. In this case too, they are mainly indirect (81%), but much more often free direct (15%) than direct

(4%). The predominance of indirect report helps to explain the predominance of the position of the projecting clause before the projected clause (79%) and the scarcity of Subject-Verb inversion in the projecting clauses (9%).

4 Magazine articles from 'Time' and 'Newsweek'

Another small corpus study carried out at the University of Padua focused on projection in eighteen articles from the two American magazines, *Time* and *Newsweek*, for a total of 31,788 words (Rossetto, 2003). In this corpus 598 projections were found (excluding embedded ones). Of these, 194 (32.4%) were canonical paratactic projections, of the direct report or free direct report type, while 135 (22.6%) were continuations of the quotes in following sentences without a projecting clause, and 62 (10.4%) were quotes with no true projecting clause, even in a preceding sentence (see Example 17). Indirect report (hypotactic structures) accounted for the remaining 207 cases (34.6%). Whereas the paratactic projections were all verbal, the hypotactic ones divided almost equally between verbal (52%) and mental (48%).

> (17) When the king finally emerges, on the verge of collapse, he reaches
>   under his loincloth, displays a bloodstained hand and announces the
>   ancestors' message – the same message he has received so many
>   times in the past: 'Prepare to go to war'. (Secrets of the Maya, by
>   Michael D. Lemonick, *Time*, September 8, 1993: 44)

As for the position of the projecting clause in relation to the projected clause, 78% precede the projected clause. This is always the case in hypotactic constructions, but the position varies for paratactic ones, where almost 60% come after, about 15% before and about 25% in the middle. In these paratactic projections, the order of the Subject and Verb in the projecting clause varies according to the position this has in relation to the projected clause. In the few cases (only 27) in which the projecting clause is before the projected one, the order SV is found 59% of the time, while, interestingly, the order VS is found 41% of the time, as in Example 18. This is 4% of the total of projecting clauses (paratactic and hypotactic) which come before the projected clause. When the projecting clause falls in the middle of the projected clause, VS order occurs 31% of the time, while SV predominates with 69%. In cases where the projecting clause is after the projected clause, it is the VS order that predominates with 63%, while SV has only 37%.

> (18) Says Demarest: 'They defeated the king of Dos Pilas and probably
>   dragged him back to Tamarindito to sacrifice him'. (Secrets of the
>   Maya, as above)

These magazine articles bring science, history, lives of famous people and topical interest stories into the lives of ordinary people. The projection not only serves to give the accounts authoritativeness (a function it has in journalistic style generally), but also to make the subjects involved more appealing to the general public by bringing in various people in a sort of dialogue.

5   The 'Gospel according to Saint John'

Now we turn our attention to a fundamental religious text which is also a great work of verbal art, the *Bible*, and specifically *The New Testament*. The Gospel is the expression of the Word, and it is not surprising to see that projection plays a very significant role in this text, as was made evident by a study carried out at the University of Padua on the *Gospel according to Saint John* (Scarso, 1998).[8] What immediately strikes one is the predominance of projection, with 81% of the sentences containing at least one projection, whether of the canonical clause-complex type with projecting clause and projected clause, of the continuation type, or of other types. The Word is being presented, and it is presented mainly through quotes, as only 20% of the projections are indirect report. Four whole chapters – 14, 15, 16 and 17 – are made up entirely of sentences with projections, which continue over sentence boundaries. In fact, though these chapters are made up 100% of projections in the semantic sense, the majority of the sentences have no projecting clause. Projecting clauses are present in 34.6% of the sentences in Chapter 14, in 0% in Chapter 15, in 15% in Chapter 16 and in 9.1% in Chapter 17. These are the chapters in which Jesus, aware of his coming death, leaves his spiritual heritage to the disciples, and the exact wording of this message is fundamental to the authorial purpose. Continuation of quotes across sentence boundaries is a characteristic of this text as a whole: 55% of the sentences that make up the corpus contribute to quoting sequences made up of more than one, and sometimes many, sentences. The projecting clause is usually in the first of these.

Paratactic projections are of the direct report type, marked by inverted commas, and these paratactic structures make up 70% of the projection clause complexes, as opposed to 30% that are hypotactic. Even the paratactic projections usually present the projecting clause before the projected clause (78%), as in Example 19, whereas only 7% have the projecting clause in the middle and 15% have it after the projected clause.

> (19) Jesus said, 'I came to this world to judge, so that the blind should see and those who see should become blind'. (Saint John, 9, 37)

In the few indirect report sentences and also in all the direct report sentences with the projecting clause before the projected clause, the order of the Subject and Verb in the projecting clause is always SV. When the projecting clause is in the middle, the Subject usually precedes the Verb (85%). When the projecting clause comes after the projected clause, the Verb always precedes the Subject. Since the main speaker is Jesus, this means that, as Subject, he is typically either at the beginning of the sentence, in Theme position, or at the end, where the focus of New information lies.

6   Rowling's 'Harry Potter and the Philosopher's Stone'

Now, a jump from the Gospel to the first of the best-selling Harry Potter stories by J. R. Rowling will let us see that here, too, projection plays a very important role in the author's strategies. A study carried out in Padua (Pegoraro, 2004) shows that 60% of the sentences of this text have some type of projection. The type of projection involved divides up as follows: projections forming clause complexes account for 58% of the total, while sentence-length quotes not containing a projecting clause account for 36%; the remaining 6% are projections which function below the clause level (embedded, partial or summarising, as described in Thompson, 1994: 17, 28–29, 100–102).

Direct report is by far the preferred type of projection clause complex, with 71%, while indirect report accounts for only 26%. The free variety of report (without inverted commas) is rarely used by this author (3%). The book, in fact, reads very much as a lively and intriguing dialogue among its fantastic characters, and the reading is made easier for the readers, who are often children, by the explicit graphic distinction between what is a quote and what is not. The direct report is practically always of the verbal type (99.9%) rather than mental. Indeed, the author tends to reserve indirect report for thoughts, since the breakdown for this structure is only 31% verbal against 69% mental. The very few cases of free direct report are also used for thought (93%) rather than speech (7%). It is interesting to look more closely at the verbs in the verbal projecting clauses. The default verbal Process *say* accounts for only 60% of the processes used for projecting speech. The other 40% include not only the more 'normal' verbal Processes like *tell*, *ask*, and *announce*, but also such colourful choices as *grumble, mumble, reel off, screech, scream, stammer, stutter, squeal, mutter, burst out, cry, shriek, splutter, stammer, wheedle, whisper, yell* and even verbs which are not usually verbal Processes like *breathe, choke, chortle, gasp, groan, laugh, moan, pant, puff, sigh, smile, sneer, sob, wheeze, whine, bark, bellow, boom, croak, explode, growl, grunt, hiss, howl, rumble, snap, snarl, spit, squawk, squeak, storm* and *thunder*. These choices allow us not only to follow the dialogue, but also to get the feel of its tone and atmosphere, of the whirl of activity that is involved, and of the extraordinary nature of the characters and events, as in Example 20.

(20) 'Get out of the way', snapped Ron, taking a wipe at Peeves – this was a big mistake.

STUDENTS OUT OF BED!' Peeves bellowed. 'STUDENTS OUT OF BED DOWN THE CHARMS CORRIDOR!' [...]

'This is it!' Ron moaned, as they pushed helplessly at the door. 'We're done for! This is the end!' [...] 'Oh, move over', Hermione snarled. She grabbed Harry's wand, tapped the lock and whispered, '*Alohomora*!' (*Potter*: 118–119)

Focusing on the paratactic projections (direct report and free direct report), we can observe that the projecting clause almost always comes after the projected clause (83%), and only rarely in the middle (9%), or before (8%). This choice allows Rowling to foreground the dialogue of her characters, leaving the role of the narrator in the background. In these structures we also find Subject-Verb inversion in the projecting clause. Out of all the projecting clauses, 34% have the Verb before the Subject (54% in the paratactic projections). Subject-Verb inversion occurs most often when the projecting clause comes after the projected one (91%), but also in a few cases when it is in the middle (9%), though never when before. The choice of putting the Subject after the Verb in the projecting clause after the quote allows Rowling to end the sentence by focusing on the name of the character, but also to elaborate on this name, adding extra information or description. The projecting clause in end position with Subject-Verb inversion is the preferred place for clausal or adverbial expansions relating to the character, his or her manner of speaking, or what is going on at the same time as the act of speaking, as in Examples 21 and 22.

(21) 'I think I know who that one's from', said Ron, going a bit pink and pointing to a very lumpy parcel. (*Potter*: 147)

(22) 'I want Fang', said Malfoy quickly, looking at Fang's long teeth. (*Potter*: 183)

These tails of narration at the end of the sentence in non-finite clauses allow the author to carry the narration forward in a very unobtrusive way (Chatman, 1978: 219).

7 Woolf's 'A Room of One's Own'

Virginia Woolf's *A Room of One's Own* was analysed in Padua for, among other things, projection (Bettio, 2000). This text is probably best classified as an essay, but not without difficulty, as it grew out of two lectures and contains long passages of fictional narration. Furthermore, the speaker is not simply and only the author, as Woolf openly assumes different voices at different points in the work (Rosenberg, 1995: 71–77). The sentences with projection in this work are only 29%, so by far fewer than those in either *Saint John's Gospel* or Rowling's first Harry Potter book. Typically the projection in clause complexes in this work is paratactic, the structure which accounts for 76%. This percentage of paratactic projections breaks down as follows: free direct (69%), direct (5%) and free indirect (2%). Hypotactic projections (indirect report) account for only 24%. In this work, it is thoughts which are most often projected (53%) rather than speech (47%). The preferred Subject of the projecting verb is 'I' (68%), and the projecting clause 'I thought' occurs 52 times. Projections often extend beyond sentence boundaries. In fact, 37% of the projections in the text are continuations in separate sentences containing no projecting clause. The preferred position of the projecting clause is in the middle of the projected clause (45%), followed by before it (31%), but the position after the projected clause is also rather frequent (24%). For the data on the position of the projecting clause just in the paratactic projections, see Figure 5.4 in the Conclusions.

Thought is the manner of development of this work. In it, Woolf unveils her own thought processes to the readers, in a sort of mental debate with them. Her means of doing this are those of a skilled writer of fiction as well as of criticism. The text begins with the internal conjunctive *But*:

> But, you may say, we asked you to speak about women and fiction
> – what has that got to do with a room of one's own? (*Room*: 5)

She writes (to justify herself for not offering a solution to the question of women and fiction):

> But in order to make some amends I am going to do what I can to show you how I arrived at this opinion about the room and the money. I am going to develop in your presence as fully and freely as I can the train of thought which led me to think this. (*Room*: 6)

Free direct report, with its lack of inverted commas, allows Woolf not to present her thoughts as though they had been captured and clearly defined, or put into words. Indeed, the lack of inverted commas leaves some ambiguity as to how the reader should interpret some of the sentences, and where the intonation of projection should start or stop. In Example 23, for example, it is very easy to get the reading of the first sentence wrong.

(23) But I should need to be a herd of elephants, I thought, and a wilderness of spiders, desperately referring to the animals that are reputed longest lived and most multitudinously eyed, to cope with all of this. I should

> need claws of steel and beak of brass even to penetrate the husk. How
> shall I ever find the grains of truth embedded in all this mass of paper?
> I asked myself, and in despair began running my eye up and down the
> long list of titles. (*Room*: 28)

Even maintaining free direct report, it would not have been difficult for Woolf
to give the reader a hand by putting *desperately referring to the animals that
are reputed longest lived and most multitudinously eyed* in brackets, to indicate
that it is not a part of the quote which it interrupts but an expansion of *I thought*.
It seems, then, that she wanted to leave her thoughts a bit fluid and unclear in
their boundaries.

By putting the projecting clause – typically *I thought* – in the middle of
the projected clause, Woolf hides it away, downtoning her own role as narrator
of her thoughts, and leaving the thoughts themselves in the foreground. This
middle position, between the Theme and the Rheme, is, as has been pointed
out by Hartnett (1995: 199), the position with 'the lowest information value'
– so much so that she calls it 'the pit'. Continuing the thoughts in sentences
without projecting clauses is also a way to avoid calling the readers' attention
to the role of the reporter of the thoughts, thus allowing it to remain fixed on
the thoughts themselves.

8   Woolf's 'Mrs. Dalloway'

Three studies carried out in Padua provide data on projection in the novel by
Virginia Woolf, *Mrs. Dalloway* (Petronio, 2004; Pesaresi, 2005; Zampiron,
2005). It was found that 73% of the sentences in the novel contain some sort
of projection. However, it must be said right away that this novel presented
difficulties which were not encountered in the other studies so far presented
here, since Woolf's narration moves, often imperceptibly and even in a single
sentence, from a narrating voice which is outside the characters, to one that
takes on, to some extent, the point of view of one character or another, and then
on to one that becomes the voice of the character in free mental projection.[9]
The passage in Example 24, where the narration takes us into the mind of
Septimus Smith, illustrates this.

> (24) Here he opened Shakespeare once more. That boy's business of the
>   intoxication of language – *Antony and Cleopatra* – had shrivelled
>   utterly. How Shakespeare loathed humanity – the putting on of clothes,
>   the getting of children, the sordidity of the mouth and the belly! This
>   was now revealed to Septimus; the message hidden in the beauty of
>   words. The secret signal which one generation passes, under disguise,
>   to the next is loathing, hatred, despair. Dante the same. Aeschylus

> (translated) the same. There Rezia sat at the table trimming hats. She
> trimmed hats for Mrs. Filmer's friends; she trimmed hats by the hour.
> She looked pale, mysterious, like a lily, drowned, under water, he
> thought. (*Mrs. Dalloway*: 97)

There is constantly difficulty in determining how far the scope of a projecting clause should extend. How far back should we understand the scope to
extend of the final 'he thought' in the passage in Example 24? Seen from the
other direction, it is very difficult to determine what to ascribe to the narrator
rather than to the character, as his thoughts. Should we ascribe to the narrator only 'Here he opened Shakespeare once more', 'This was now revealed
to Septimus', and the final 'he thought', which in the last sentence projects
Septimus's thought as free indirect report? Going beyond these bits, which are
obviously the narrator's, we could go all the way up to the projected clause in
the last sentence, which is, on the contrary, obviously Septimus's thought. It is
hard to know where the cutting line is in between, because of Woolf's way of
incorporating a character's point of view into the narrative voice to different
extents. The same difficulty in determining the scope of a projecting clause,
and the limits of the narrator's intervention, is evident already in the opening
passage of the novel, as Example 25 shows. Are the second, third, and fourth
sentences in this example part of what Mrs. Dalloway said, part of what Mrs.
Dalloway thought, or an explanation of the events provided by a narrator who
is assuming aspects of Mrs. Dalloway's point of view?

> (25) Mrs. Dalloway said she would buy the flowers herself. For Lucy
> had her work cut out for her. The doors would be taken off their hinges;
> Rumpelmayer's men were coming. And then, thought Clarissa
> Dalloway, what a morning – fresh as if issued to children on a beach.
> (*Mrs. Dalloway*: 3)

This difficulty makes the datum given above on the overall presence of projection in the novel a very subjective one, and not particularly reliable. The
comparative presence of the different types of projection found, however, is
more relevant.

'Free' report (free direct or free indirect) makes up 76% of the first-order
projections. Only 14% are direct report, and only 10% are indirect. It is, indeed,
this use of 'free' projections which allows Woolf to make the narrator's and the
characters' roles in the creation of the narrative less clear-cut, and to downtone
the authorial and the narrative control. These free reports are predominantly
mental projections (74%, as opposed to 26% verbal).[10] By using the 'free'
forms for thoughts, the author represents these thoughts as being less clearly
verbalised into wordings, more fluid and changeable, than they would have been

in direct report. She also manages to avoid delimiting them through punctuation, and therefore is able to realise the narrative game of flowing imperceptibly inside and outside of the characters' subjectivity. The use of indirect report for thoughts, on the other hand, keeps the thoughts under the control of the narrator, whose omniscience is foregrounded through this choice.

Projection in this novel is more often mental (61%) than verbal (39%). Direct report in this novel is almost always verbal (99.4%). The few indirect reports that occur are divided more equally between verbal, which predominates with 57%, and mental, with 43%. The type of projection that tips the balance toward mental Processes is the 'free' variety, where the split is 74% mental and 26% verbal.

The novel takes place on the day Clarissa Dalloway puts on a formal party. The various characters of the novel interact in conversations during the time covered by the novel, and other conversations are remembered. But even more than the spoken conversations, the novel reports the thoughts of the characters during that day. The conversations, and even more, the thoughts, continue beyond the sentence level. This is evident from the datum relating to the frequency of direct and free reports without a projecting clause in the same sentence: 60% of the total.

Data is available on the position of the projecting clause in the novel as a whole, but unfortunately without distinction between the types of projection clause-complexes. The projecting clause comes before the projected clause 31% of the time, in the middle 20%, and after 49%. The Subject comes before the Verb 86% of the time and the Verb before the Subject 14%. In the first half of the novel, the cases of Verb before Subject divide up as follows: 76.5% in projecting clauses that come after the projected one and 23.5% in projecting clauses that come in the middle of the projected one. There are no Subject-Verb inversions in projecting clauses which come before the projected one.

Often in this novel, as in *Harry Potter*, the combination end position of the projecting clause and Subject-Verb inversion are used to present the name of a character and expand on it with an adverb, a prepositional phrase or a non-finite clause.

9   Woolf's 'To the Lighthouse'

A study carried out in Padua on *To the Lighthouse* (Baretta, 2004) indicates that 43% of the sentences have projection. A difference is revealed between the three sections of the novel. The beginning section, 'The Window', has the greatest presence of sentences with projection, accounting for 51%. The middle section, 'Time Passes', is the one with the least projection, since this is found in only 21% of the sentences. The last section, 'The Lighthouse', has projection in 36% of the sentences. These data go with the difference in function between the sections. The long beginning section, 'The Window', is where all the characters are introduced, and their conversations and thoughts are reported, within a frame of presentation in the voice of the narrator. The middle section, 'Time Passes', is an amazing choral interlude in which the main characters are winds, little airs, and sliding lights, and the news of the death of the main character of the novel, Mrs. Ramsay, is given in square brackets. Towards the end of this section, two cleaning women appear to prepare the house for the return of some of its inhabitants. The final section, 'The Lighthouse' shows the characters interacting mainly in silence, without saying what they might have said. This is true both for Lily, who, after not giving Mr. Ramsay the sympathy he demands, stays on the lawn to paint, and for those who go to the lighthouse, most of whom are upset over the tyranny of Mr. Ramsay, who has made them go, and do not want to give in to jovial communication, with the result that Mr. Ramsay also reads his book in silence. Their thoughts are, however, amply reported within the frame of the narrating voice.

In *To the Lighthouse*, as in *Mrs. Dalloway*, analysis is not easy. We cannot count on being able to analyse a whole sentence in the same way. In Example 26 (from 'The Window'), we see how, from the narrator's voice presenting the subjectivity of Mrs. Ramsay's daughter Prue, we move into free indirect thought with Prue's question.

(26) And, from having been quite grown up, a moment before, talking with the others, she became a child again, and what they had been doing was a game, and would her mother sanction their game, or condemn it, she wondered. (*Lighthouse*: 126)

Even more strikingly, Example 27 (again from 'The Window') shows how, in a single sentence, what begins as the projection of Charles Tansley's thought, continues, within the cascade of hypotactic modifications of the projecting clause, with the projection of Lily's thought.

(27) What damned rot they talk, thought Charles Tansley, laying down his spoon precisely in the middle of his plate, which he had swept clean, as if, Lily thought (he sat opposite to her with his back to the window precisely in the middle of the view), he were determined to make sure of his meals. (*Lighthouse*: 93)

This example illustrates how the narration is built up through the interaction of the characters, even when this is presented as mental rather than verbal (see Rosenberg, 1995: 90). The unspoken dialogue is not only between characters, but also between the narrator (or a narrator) and a character. This can be seen in Example 28, where Mrs. Ramsay thinks one thing and, within the structure of the same clause complex, the narrator clarifies what she actually means.

> (28) She kept looking at Minta, shyly, yet curiously, so that Mrs. Ramsay looked from one to the other and said, speaking to Prue in her own mind, You will be as happy as she is one of these days: You will be much happier, she added, because you are my daughter, she meant; her own daughter must be happier than other people's daughters. (*Lighthouse*: 119)

Speech and thought presentation through projection are, as has been pointed out by Simpson (1993: 21–30), crucially tied up with the concept of point of view (see also Leaska, 1970: 539). The complexity of projection in *To the Lighthouse* is a part of the complexity of point of view in this novel. As Leaska (1970: 20–21) writes of this work:

> [...] determining the angle of narration requires special attention, because the sharp line between narrator and character, between one character and another, or between the author and narrator has dissolved. In this manifold stream-of-consciousness novel, there may be as many as four or five shifts of point of view within a single sentence; and precisely where the shift occurs is often not easy to determine. Moreover, there are occasional passages which are presented simultaneously from more than one point of view – that is, the passage may be shared simultaneously by two or more of the narrators; or the material may be presented in such a way as to make it impossible to distinguish between the omniscient narrator and the perceiving consciousness of a character.

Now let us look at the distribution of the different kinds of projection in the novel. The whole novel is analysed for four different kinds of projection: direct report, indirect report, free direct report and free indirect report. Since most of the previous sections did not distinguish between the two types of free report, let us review the difference between them in our use of the terms (see notes 3 and 4). Free direct report is the same as direct report but without inverted commas around the projected clause (see the projections of the thoughts of Tansley and of Lily in Example 27 above). Free indirect report is a type of report in which the projected clause is paratactically linked to the projecting clause, there is shift of deixis to the speaker's point of view, and sequence of tenses, but the reported clause retains the mood of the quoted clause (see Example 26). We also find examples of projected clauses enclosed in inverted commas, but with no projecting clause (what I call floating quotes, see Introduction), and of projected clauses without inverted commas, and with no projecting clause (what I call floating free quotes). Example 29 illustrates both types. The first two lines of the poem which Mrs. Ramsay hears are represented as floating free quotes, probably to render, through the lack of punctuation, Mrs. Ramsay's impression that they had been said by no one. The line that follows, as Mrs. Ramsay becomes more aware of the presence of a speaker, even though confused with her own voice, is represented as a floating quote. Floating quotes and floating free quotes are usually nested within passages in which the narrator assumes the point of view of a character, reporting that character's thoughts and impressions (see also Example 7 above).

> (29) Her husband spoke. He was repeating something and she knew it was poetry from the rhythm and the ring of exultation, and melancholy in his voice: Come out and climb the garden path, Luriana Lurilee. The China rose is all abloom and buzzing with the yellow bee. The words (she was looking at the window) sounded as if they were floating like flowers on water out there, cut off from them all, as if no one had said them, but they had come into existence of themselves. 'And all the lives we ever lived and all the lives to be are full of trees and changing leaves'. She did not know what they meant, but, like music, the words seemed to be spoken by her own voice, outside her self, saying quite easily and naturally what had been in her mind the whole evening while she said different things. (*Lighthouse*: 120)

These floating quotes and floating free quotes should be distinguished from the continuation of projections across sentence boundaries, where the projecting clause which is present in a preceding or subsequent sentence can be seen as extending its range to include the continuation sentence. Direct report, free direct report and free indirect report all continue across sentence boundaries in this novel (see Examples 5 and 6 above). Example 30 shows a continuation of free indirect report across sentence boundaries. One could add the projecting clause 'she wondered' at the end of the second sentence and it would become a second free indirect report.

> (30) He was really, Lily Briscoe thought, in spite of his eyes, the most uncharming human being she had ever met. Then why did she mind what he said? (*Lighthouse*: 94)

Relating each of the four types of projections with a projecting clause to the sum of all four, we see that indirect report accounts for the highest proportion of projections in the novel, with 35%, followed closely by free indirect report of speech or thought with 30%; then we have direct report with 20%, and finally free direct report with 15%. Floating quotes and floating free quotes make up just over 6% of the total number of central projections in the novel. Continuations of a projection beyond the sentence in which the projecting clause is found make up a little over 7% of the total of all kinds of projections found in the text. These divide up rather evenly between continuations of direct, free direct, and free indirect report.

If we look separately at the three sections in which Woolf divides this novel, we see that in the longest section, 'The Window', the most frequent kind of projection is indeed (as in the novel as a whole) indirect report (38%), but only in this section. In fact, both 'Time Passes' and 'The Lighthouse' have a greater frequency of free indirect (respectively, 57% as opposed to 18% and 32% as opposed to 29%). This difference fits into the description given above of 'The Window' as the section in which the characters are introduced and their conversations and thoughts are reported within a frame of presentation in the voice of the narrator. Also noticeable is the fact that in the final section, 'The Lighthouse', the percentage for free direct report is higher than that for the whole novel (22% as opposed to 15%). This section, with all its verbal silence, is the place where free direct report of the characters' thoughts prevails.

Throughout the whole novel, direct report is used almost exclusively for verbal projections (96%). Indirect report, on the other hand, is used predominately for mental projections (71%), although verbal projections in the form of indirect report are also frequent (29%). Free indirect report is used predominantly for mental projections (64%). Free direct report divides up almost equally between verbal (49%) and mental (51%) projections. The processes of the projecting clauses of the whole corpus divide up as follows: 46% verbal and 54% mental.

The study of *To the Lighthouse* also provides information on the position of the projecting clause. In direct report, the most frequent position of the projecting clause is after the projected one (52%), but it is also very often before the projected clause (35%), and less frequently in the middle (13%). In free direct report, the projecting clause comes after the projected one 40% of the time; 25% of the time the projecting clause is in the middle, and 35% of the time it is before the projected clause. Free indirect report presents the projecting clause before the projected one 4% of the time, and, after it, 56% of the time, while the projecting clause comes in the middle of the projected one 40% of the time. See Figure 5.4 in the Conclusions for the combined data on the position of the projecting clause in paratactic projections.

Subject-Verb inversion within the projecting clause was also studied. Only 8% of the projecting clauses in the novel have Subject-Verb inversion, so the further analysis that follows is based on extremely small numbers. When there is direct report, the Subject-Verb inversion corresponds most often with the position of the projecting clause after the projected one (76%), and also with that in the middle (24%), but never before. With free direct report, the VS order is also associated with the position after the projected clause (47%) and in the middle (53%), but never before. Free indirect discourse with Subject-Verb inversion in the projecting clause corresponds to the position of the projecting clause after the projected one more often than in the middle (respectively 62% and 38%), but never to the position before the projected clause. See also Figure 5.5 in the Conclusions for the overall data on each position. Projecting clauses coming after the projected clause and with Subject-Verb inversion are, in this subcorpus as in the others, the preferred environment for clausal, appositional, and adverbial elaborations of the projecting clause.

10 Conclusions

From the analyses presented above, it is clear that the genres presented all make considerable use of projection in their strategies. The extent of the presence of projection in them differs, however, as is evidenced by the data given for the percentage of sentences which contain some kind of projection. Figure 5.1 illustrates these data for *The Economist, A Room of One's Own, To the Lighthouse*, front-page newspaper articles, *Harry Potter and the Philosopher's Stone, Mrs. Dalloway*, and *The Gospel according to Saint John*.

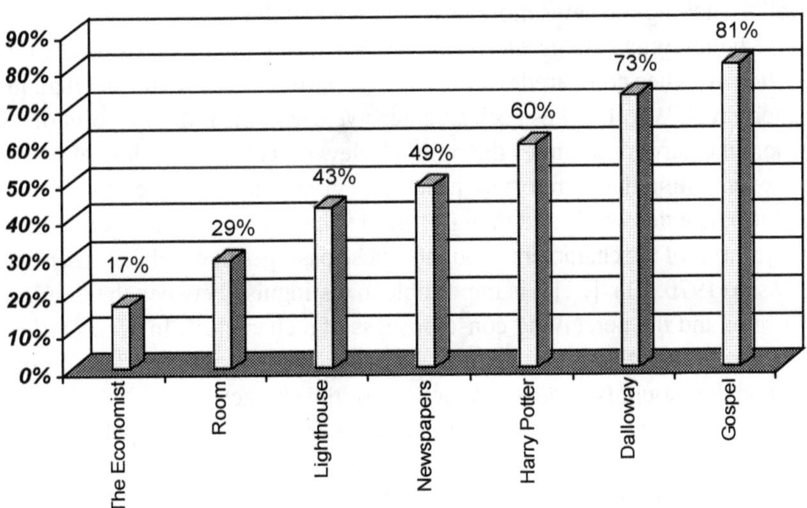

Figure 5.1: Percentage of sentences with projection

Both *The Economist* and the newspaper articles are examples of informative texts, but it would seem that the journalists of *The Economist* feel less need to filter the information through the words of others. Those who think of newspaper articles as just giving information will be surprised to see how prominent projection is in them, unless they consider that good journalism must be captivating reading, capable of involving the readers in the stories. This is particularly true of the daily paper, which is read quickly by a readership which, for the most part, picks and chooses from its contents. A magazine devoted to a particular interest area and bought by people because they share that interest will not have the same degree of pressure to captivate the audience and can concentrate more on the informing function.

The presence of projection in a text serves to make the discourse interactive and dynamic. If we simply consider *A Room of One's Own* as an essay, then it might surprise us that there is so much projection in it. To understand the use of projection in this work, we need to realise that Woolf wanted it to be dialogic, a sort of debate with her readers, as well as with herself. The fact that the author is so closely associated with both the narrating role and the main character role in *A Room of One's Own* can be seen as relating to the low proportion of projections. The Sayer or, more often, Senser (since thoughts are projected more often than locutions) in the projecting clause is most often 'I', whereas in the other texts the Subject in these clauses is in the third person. Projection of the words and thoughts of others also serves to background the role of the author or narrator, bringing other people to the foreground of attention. In news articles, reporting from sources takes some of the responsibility off the journalist, as well as making the news more authoritative and the story more enticing.

I believe that the greater proportion of projection that we find in *Mrs. Dalloway*, when compared with *To the Lighthouse*, is due to the fact that, in the latter novel, Woolf makes such an extensive use of the multiple point of view, where the narrator assumes the point of view of a character while at the same time remaining the narrator: in these cases grammatical projection is not used to introduce the words and thoughts of the characters. We thus get, instead of projections of the characters' thoughts, those passages in which, as described by Leaska (1970: 21) '[…] it is impossible to distinguish between the omniscient narrator and the perceiving consciousness of a character'. In *Mrs. Dalloway*, the use of projection is one of the ways in which the narrator tends to disappear behind the thoughts, words, and actions of the characters.

The greatest proportion of projection is found in the Gospel, which was written to record the words of Jesus for mankind. Saint John, more than any of the other authors, wants the words of Jesus to be foregrounded and his own narrating function to be backgrounded.

Figure 5.2 represents the relative proportion of paratactic projections (direct report, free direct report and free indirect report) and of hypotactic projections (indirect report) in *The Economist*, Internet economic and financial articles, *Time* and *Newsweek* articles, newspaper articles, *To the Lighthouse, Saint John's Gospel, Harry Potter and the Philosopher's Stone, A Room of One's Own*, and *Mrs. Dalloway*. Parataxis situates two (or more) ranking clauses on the same level, as equally important and at issue at the particular point in the

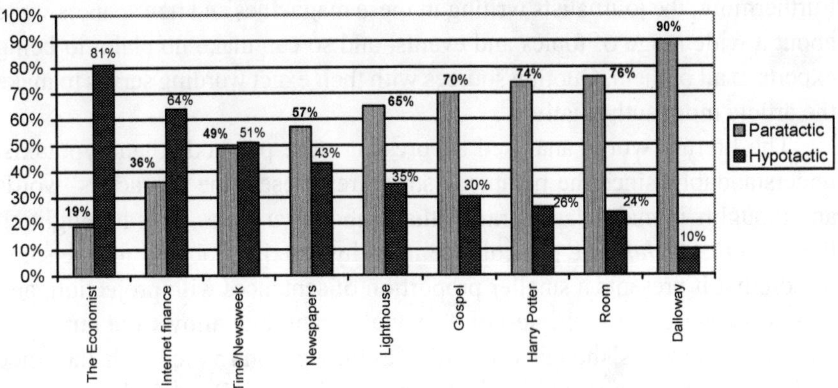

Figure 5.2: Paratactic and hypotactic projections

discourse, while hypotaxis subordinates one to another. In hypotactic projection, the projected clause is dependent on the projecting clause, it is put into a form which would not function independently in an exchange, and there is no claim that the wording corresponds to any wording actually pronounced. The function of hypotactic projection is to represent the sense or 'gist', rather than the wording (Halliday, 2004: 454). This is why hypotaxis is, in general, '[...] the typical pattern for representing a "thinking"' (Halliday, 2004: 452). We do not really know the wording of people's thoughts, although, of course, in fiction an omniscient narrator can present a character's thoughts as wordings, even in inverted commas. In hypotaxis, the speaker or writer of the sentence, or the narrator in the case of fiction, keeps control, using the third person for the Sayer or Senser in the projecting clause, and maintaining that same person in the projected clause. Temporal and spatial deictics in hypotactic projections preserve the orientation of the projecting clause, which is that of the speaker or writer or narrator, and the mood is also controlled through that perspective, as the mood of a whole hypotactic clause complex is given by the primary clause, which in projection is the projecting clause.

Articles in *The Economist* and economic and financial articles on the Internet are informative texts written by experts for people who have a particular interest in economics and finance and are looking for expert opinions. The job of the writer is, in both cases I believe, to select and summarise the information which will be most interesting and useful for the readers. When this involves reporting from sources, hypotactic projection is an appropriate way of doing it. The readers of *Time* and *Newsweek* are a more general selection of the public, as are those of front page articles in daily newspapers. The journalists, therefore, have to use more strategies to get and keep their attention, and the liveliness of the wording of various speakers can have this function.

Furthermore, the journalists writing in these magazines and newspapers write about a wide range of topics and events, and so can make no claim to being experts in all of them. Quoting sources with their exact wording serves to make the article more authoritative.

The literary works analysed all present more parataxis than hypotaxis, understandably, since the paratactic structures present the characters' words and thoughts in main clauses rather than subordinate ones, thus highlighting them. *To the Lighthouse* presents the most hypotaxis, probably for the same reason that it presents a smaller proportion of sentences with projection, and that is, because the multiple-point-of-view technique allows the author to introduce characters' thoughts and attitudes through, and mixed with, the voice of the narrator. The parataxis in the Gospel and in Harry Potter is direct report, with the inverted commas, and therefore the character's voice is made to be heard directly, as it were, throughout these works. Also, the reader is guided unmistakably in the interpretation of what part of the discourse is the wording of the characters and what is not. In the three works by Woolf, on the other hand, the percentage for parataxis is composed mainly of 'free' forms: *Lighthouse* – free indirect report 30%, free direct report 15%, direct report 20%; *Mrs. Dalloway* – 'free' report (free direct or free indirect) 76%, direct report only 14%; *A Room of One's Own* – free direct 69%, free indirect 2%, direct 5%. Since paratactic projection in any of its forms highlights the projected clause more than hypotaxis does, the data on parataxis tells us something about the relative foregrounding of the words and thoughts of the characters in these works. However, to get a clearer view of the function of the 'free' forms, we must go on to Figure 5.3 below.

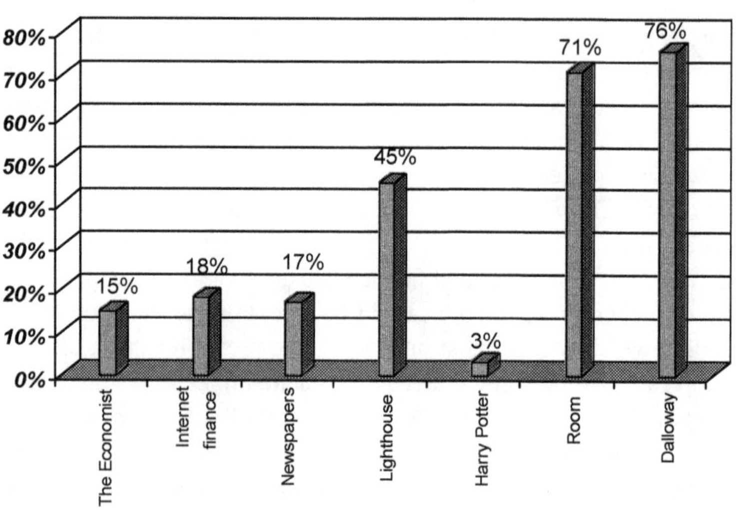

Figure 5.3: 'Free' report (free direct/free indirect)

Figure 5.3 represents the presence of the 'free' forms of paratactic projections (free direct and free indirect report) in *The Economist*, Internet economic and financial articles, newspaper articles, *To the Lighthouse, Harry Potter and the Philosopher's Stone, A Room of One's Own,* and *Mrs. Dalloway.* Both types of 'free' report avoid the use of inverted commas around the projected clause which characterises direct report. As said, this can be considered a way of downtoning narrative control, since the explicit use of the punctuation of quoting is a way of controlling what is quoted. Free indirect report, however, has one important characteristic which makes it similar to indirect report, which is that time and person reference are shifted away from that of the projected clause to correspond to that of the projecting clause, and therefore that of the speaker/writer/narrator. This means that, of the two, free indirect report reflects the greater narrator control, though less than with indirect report.[11] Both 'free' forms are paratactic, and therefore have the characteristic of giving the projected and the projecting clauses equal standing in the discourse. Therefore, there is no subordinator used to connect them, as there is in hypotaxis (typically *that*). What is projected maintains the status of an independent speech act, even in free indirect report (Halliday, 2004: 466), and therefore has its own mood. The independence of the two clauses makes it possible to sequence them in different ways. In free indirect report, the projecting clause is usually presented as a 'tail' after the projected clause, as in the final parts of Examples 6, 24 and 26 above (cf. Halliday, 2004: 466), but it can be put in the middle (see Examples 3 and 30 above), or even before, though in this position it is particularly hard to determine whether the characteristics of indirect report prevail, or if those of the paratactic structure do. Consider Example 8 above, where there is no subordinating *that*, and the spatial deictic *here* has the orientation of the Senser in the projected clause, but the tenses are sequenced according to the orientation set up by the writer/narrator in the projecting clause.

Figure 5.3 shows that the 'free' forms of projection are not just a characteristic of literary works. We find these (of the free direct variety) in all three informative text types represented, although with low percentages, ranging from 15%–18%. We also see that Rowling has avoided the 'free' option, in favour of direct report, which, with its inverted commas delimiting the characters' wording, facilitates the reading for her public. All three works by Woolf make considerable use of the 'free' paratactic options. These are the same works in which mental projections prevail over verbal ones, and the 'free' forms make it possible for Woolf to highlight the characters' thoughts through parataxis without pushing the degree of control of her narrator to the point of omniscience which would allow presentation of thoughts as precise wordings. Of the two 'free' forms, free direct report in particular is often used for verbal projections as well. For example, in *To the Lighthouse* almost half of the free direct reports are verbal. In *Mrs. Dalloway*, the 'free' projections are 74% mental. In *A Room of One's Own*, free indirect projection is very scarce, yet the free direct projection is so prominent as to give the high overall percentage we can observe in Figure 5.3. Most often the projecting clause of these free direct projections is *I thought*, or similar mental Processes like *I recollected, I reflected, I wondered*, or else *I* followed by another verb used for sequencing the thoughts in the discourse: e.g. *I added, I continued, I concluded.*

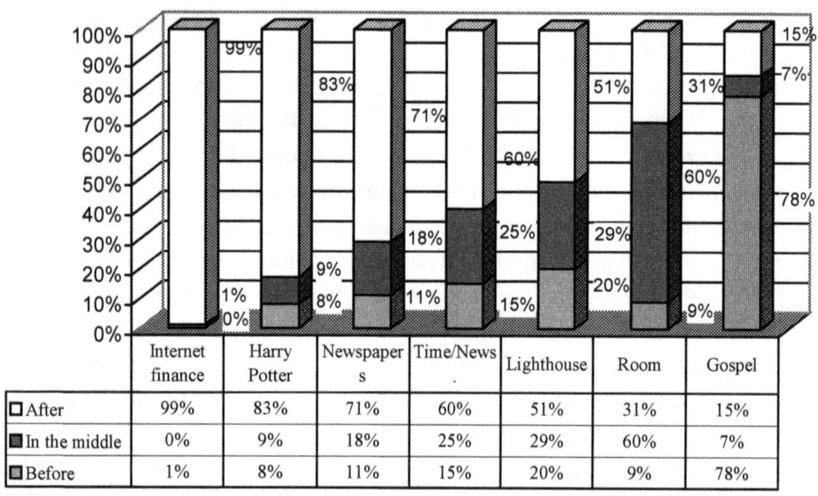

	Internet finance	Harry Potter	Newspapers	Time/News.	Lighthouse	Room	Gospel
☐ After	99%	83%	71%	60%	51%	31%	15%
■ In the middle	0%	9%	18%	25%	29%	60%	7%
▨ Before	1%	8%	11%	15%	20%	9%	78%

Figure 5.4: Position of projecting clause in paratactic projections

Figure 5.4 highlights the position of the projecting clause when the projection is paratactic. The subcorpora considered are Internet economic and financial articles, *Harry Potter*, newspaper articles, *Time* and *Newsweek*, *To the Lighthouse*, *A Room of One's Own*, and *Saint John's Gospel*. Paratactic projection, as was said above, allows freedom in the sequencing of the elements. The position of the projecting clause before the projected clause is, of the three, the one that indicates greatest speaker/writer/narrator control, since what is immediately made evident as the sentence begins is that he or she is reporting someone's speech or thoughts, and whose speech or thought is being reported. Leaving the projecting clause to appear as a 'tail' at the end of the quote is a way of downtoning that control.[12] It is almost as if the characters or sources were allowed to speak out for themselves. In informative texts, the information is foregrounded when it is given front position, and the source is only mentioned in the 'tail' at the end. On the other hand, the final position of the projecting clause gives it end focus and allows it to be elaborated, expanded or extended with extra information about the Sayer or Senser (particularly when there is Subject-Verb inversion – see Example 11 above) or about something that is going on at the same time as, or immediately following, the saying or thinking (see Examples 20, 21, 22 and 23 above). Middle position of the projecting clause hides it away where it is probably least prominent (Hartnett, 1995), giving both the importance of Theme and the focus of New information to the projected clause.

Figure 5.4 shows how the few paratactic projections in the Internet financial articles foreground the information and leave the source in a tail at the end. Rowling's novel, where parataxis prevails, also prefers end position for the projecting clause, since this at once foregrounds the characters' speech and allows her to carry the story forward by elaborating, extending and expanding the projecting clause. The preference both in the newspaper articles and in the magazine articles is for end position, followed by middle. In these informative texts, as in the Internet subcorpus, the information given is foregrounded rather than the sources. In *To the Lighthouse*, end position also prevails, but both middle and front position are also frequent. *A Room of One's Own* is where Woolf makes the greatest use of middle position, so as to tuck her projecting *I thought* away where it is least noticeable. The Gospel gives the prominence of thematic position to the main Sayer, Jesus.

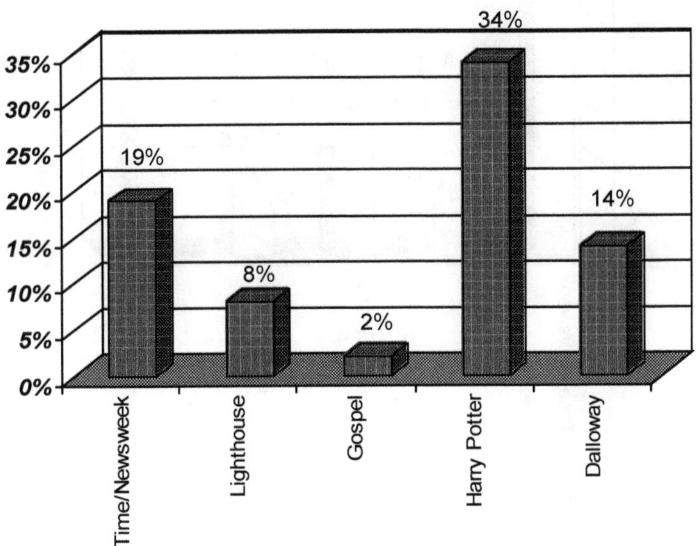

Figure 5.5a: Overall percentage of projecting clauses with VS

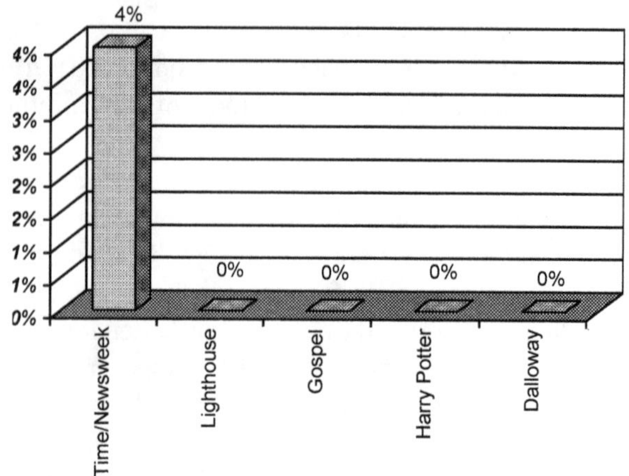

Figure 5.5b: Overall percentage of projecting clauses before with VS

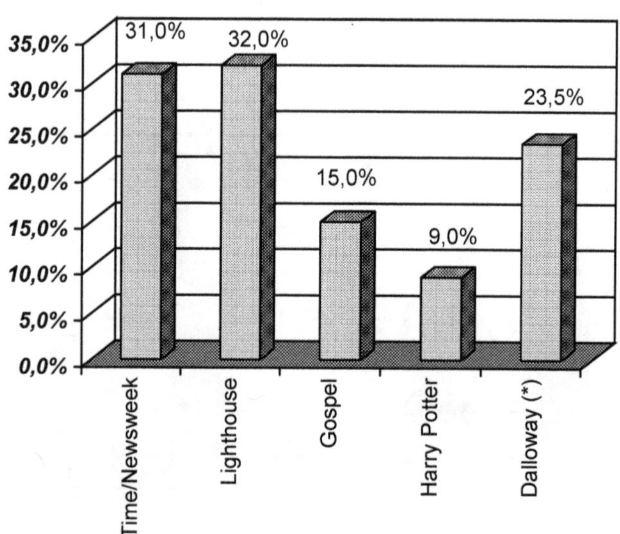

Figure 5.5c: Overall percentage of projecting clauses in the middle with VS

(*) This percentage is based on the first half of the book only.

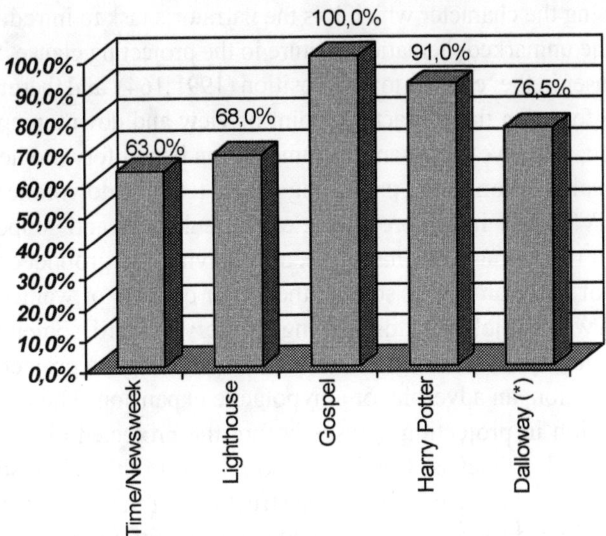

Figure 5.5d: Overall percentage of projecting clauses after with VS

(*) This percentage is based on the first half of the book only.

Figures 5.5 (a–d) are devoted to the phenomenon of Subject-Verb inversion in the projecting clause in five of the subcorpora studied: *Time* and *Newsweek* articles, *To the Lighthouse, Saint John's Gospel, Harry Potter and the Philosopher's Stone*, and *Mrs. Dalloway*. Figure 5.5a gives the overall percentages of Subject-Verb inversion in these subcorpora. It is immediately clear that Harry Potter is the one with the highest percentage of VS order. Figures 5.5b, 5.5c, and 5.5d show what percent of the projecting clauses in each of the three possible positions displays Subject-Verb inversion. Clearly, the main environment for this phenomenon is after the projected clause, since all five of the subcorpora in this position present the VS structure more than 60% of the time. Saint John in his Gospel always opts for VS in this environment, and Rowling in *Harry Potter and the Philosopher's Stone* chooses it 91% of the time. On the basis of our data, it seems that in most genres the option of VS in a fronted projecting clause is hardly available. Of the five subcorpora compared in Figure 5.5b, only the articles in *Time* and *Newsweek* provide examples of this option.[13] Middle-position projecting clauses do present Subject-Verb inversion, but the percentage is never very high: the maximums are *Time* and *Newsweek* articles with 31%, and *To the Lighthouse* with 32%.

In an analysis of point of view in *To the Lighthouse* (Taylor Torsello, 1991: 161) I posited that Subject-Verb inversion in the projecting clause makes the verbal or mental Process its marked Theme, that is to say, the narrator's emphasised starting point in organising the message contained in the projecting clause, what is closest to him as narrator. The name of the Sayer or Senser, then, becomes the Rheme, expressing the character which it is the narrator's task to introduce. I also posited that the unmarked thematic structure in the projecting clause, SV, put the Sayer or Senser in the 'control-tower' position (1991:164), and therefore could be related to focus on the character's point of view and downtoning of narrator intervention. I believe these same arguments can be put forward here.

Whereas the final position of the projecting clause tends to downtone the narrating role, the VS order in the projecting clause enhances and supports it. It is as though, at that point in the narrative, after having foregrounded the words or thoughts of the character or source, the writer or narrator wanted to take over and go on with the job at hand, carrying the story forward, something that is done quite often by elaborating, extending or expanding the projecting clause with an apposition, an adverbial or a hypotactic expansion. The use of Subject-Verb inversion in projecting clauses before the projected clause in the *Time* and *Newsweek* articles is, I believe, also related to the informative function of these texts, and to their information structure. Of the 11 examples in the subcorpus, six introduce a new source, and add some information about that source in an apposition. The other five do not, and may simply foreground the journalist's role as introducer of the quote and its source.

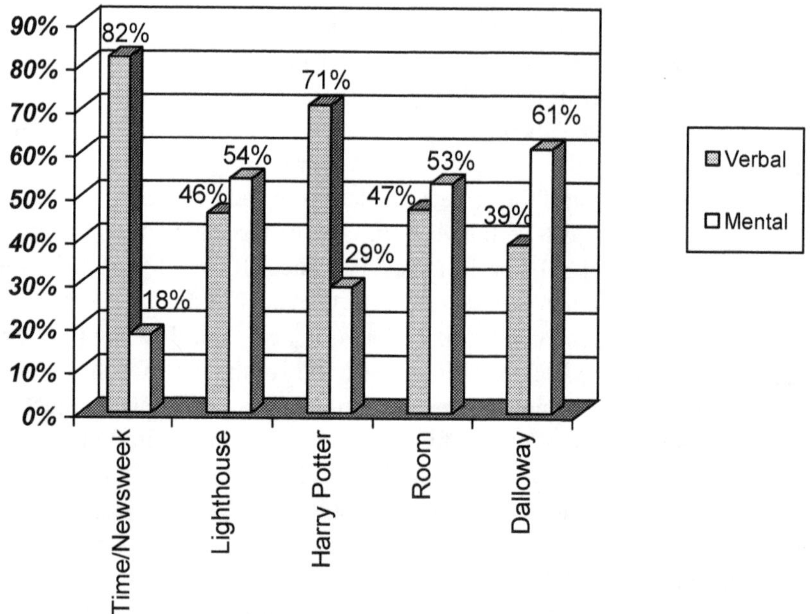

Figure 5.6: Verbal and mental projections

Figure 5.6 represents the percentages of verbal and mental projections in *Time* and *Newsweek* articles, *To the Lighthouse, Harry Potter, A Room of One's Own, and Mrs. Dalloway*. Paratactic and hypotactic projection is the grammatical structure which allows us to '[…] set up [one clause] as the representation of the linguistic "content" of another – either the content of a "verbal" clause of saying or the content of a "mental" clause of sensing' (Halliday, 2004: 443). Of the five subcorpora represented in the Figure, the most verbal are clearly magazine articles and Rowling's novel. All three of the works by Woolf, on the other hand, use projection structures more often for thoughts than for locutions. Woolf's way of bringing her narrative forward is, to a large extent, through the representation of the thoughts of her characters.

I believe that, despite some gaps and uncertainties in the data, this study can help us understand how projection is used in a range of different text types, and in a few literary texts. As always, what is special about the language of literary texts can only really be understood by comparison with the language of non-literary texts, and the data presented here provides some elements for this comparison. It also allows us to compare three works by Woolf, and to compare these with two very different works by Rowling and Saint John. The results definitely confirm what Halliday (2004: 447) says about the significance of projection as a discourse variable: 'Since the amount and type of explicit projection is a significant discourse variable, it is important to show exactly where and in what form it occurs'.

Notes

1   The page numbers given here for the examples are those of the following publications: J. R. Rowling (1997 [2000]) *Harry Potter and the Philosopher's Stone.* London: Bloomsbury; V. Woolf (1945 [2000]) *A Room of One's Own.* London: Penguin; *Mrs. Dalloway* (1992 [2000]). London: Penguin; *To the Lighthouse* (1992 [2000]). London: Penguin. Digital versions made use of include *Major Authors on CD-Rom*: *V. Woolf To the Lighthouse* (1981) San Diego: Harvest/ Harourt Brace Javanovich, Inc., and Hussey, M. (general editor), *Major Authors on CD-Rom – Virginia Woolf* (1997) Woodbridge CT: Primary Source Media, as well as *The Bible in English*. (1966) Cambridge: Chadwyck-Healey.

2   The first study on newspapers was done by hand, but all the others were done on the computer with the help of Wordsmith Tools 3. The tagging systems evolved and were adapted for each project, and the information highlighted in the various analyses was not always the same.

3   The phenomenon referred to here with the term 'free indirect report', is not the same as Leech and Short (1981: 325) refer to as 'free indirect speech', which is not a paratactic structure (e.g. *He would return to see her the following day*). In the discussion of free indirect speech, Leech and Short (1981: 330) also apply this same term to hypotactic structures which here (and in Halliday's description) are classified as indirect report. At the end of their presentation of free indirect speech, Leech and Short (1981: 333–334) also extend the same term to cover the type of paratactic structures which in Halliday's description, and in my use here, are free indirect report.

4   Leech and Short (1981: 322–323) use the term 'free direct speech' for various phenomena of which the one I am referring to here is only one. Leech and Short (1981: 342–348) also describe 'free indirect thought' and 'free direct thought'.

5   *International Herald Tribune*, July 1, 1993, *USA Today*, July 29, 1993, *Los Angeles Times*, July 28, 1993, *The Wall Street Journal Europe*, July 16 and 17, 1993, *The Independent*, June 30, 1993, *The Guardian International*, June 30, 1993, *The Daily Telegraph*, June 30, 1993, *Today*, September 9, 1993.

6   Some errors in the presentation of the data in the 1996 publication were found in this respect and the material has been reanalysed.

7   The articles appeared at Bloomberg.com, Nasdaq.com, and CNNfn.com (now CNNmoney.com) between March and June 2001.

8   The version used for the corpus belongs to the *Good News Bible. The Bible in Today's English Version* (1976) extracted from *The Bible in English.* (CD-Rom) (1996) Cambridge: Chadwyck-Healey.

9   The last sentence of Example 24 is an example of free indirect thought, whereas if it were free direct thought it would be *She looks pale, mysterious, like a lily, drowned, under water, he thought.* The two types of free report are not distinguished here in the analysis of *Mrs. Dalloway*, but they are distinguished in the study on *To the Lighthouse* presented below.

10   Leech and Short (1981: 344–345) say that, although indirect thought is the norm for presentation of thought, '[…] in the twentieth century novel at least, it is arguable that FIT [free indirect thought] is the more common mode'. Remember, however, that their use of the 'free indirect' category contains various forms which here are not calculated as free indirect report (see notes 3 and 4 above).

11   It is of interest here to consider Leech and Short's (1981: 324) proposed 'cline of 'interference'' in report, although it must be kept in mind that their terms cover different categories than the ones used here (see notes 3, 4 and 10 above).

12   'In spoken English, the projecting clause is phonologically less prominent than the projected: if it comes first, it is often proclitic (non-salient and pre-rhythmic […]) while if it follows all or part of the projected, instead of occupying a separate tone group, it appears as a 'tail', a post-tonic appendage that continues the pitch movement of the preceding projected material […]' (Halliday, 2004: 446).

13   Complete comparable data was not available on the other works treated above, but *A Room of One's Own* does present a couple of cases of Subject-Verb inversion in projecting clauses before the projected clause, one in Chapter 1 (page 21) and another in Chapter 2 (page 33).

References

Aló, F. (2000) *Proverbs in English: A Corpus-based Linguistic Analysis.* Unpublished thesis for the 'Laurea in Lingue e Letterature Straniere', University of Padua.

Barbato Ferrisio, A. (2003) *Grammatical Mood in a Parallel Italian-English Corpus of Instruction Manuals.* Unpublished thesis for the 'Laurea in Lingue e Letterature Straniere', University of Padua.

Baretta, M. (2004) *Projection in Virginia Woolf's 'To the Lighthouse'*: *A Corpus Analysis*. Unpublished thesis for the 'Laurea in Lingue e Letterature Straniere', University of Padua.

Bettio, G. (2000) *A Linguistic Study of Virginia Woolf's 'A Room of One's Own'*. Unpublished thesis for the 'Laurea in Lingue e Letterature Straniere', University of Padua.

Chatman, S. (1978) *Story and Discourse*: *Narrative Structure in Fiction and Film*. Ithaca: Cornell University Press.

Coulmas, F. (ed.) (1986) *Direct and Indirect Speech*. Berlin: Mouton.

Halliday, M. A. K. (1979) Modes of meaning and modes of expression: types of grammatical structure, and their determination by different semantic functions. In D. J. Allerton, E. Carney and D. Holcroft (eds) *Function and Context in Linguistic Analysis*: *A Festschrift for William Haas* 57–79. Cambridge: Cambridge University Press.

Halliday, M. A. K. (2004) *An Introduction to Functional Grammar*, 3rd edition (revised by C. M. I. M. Matthiessen). London: Arnold.

Hartnett, C. (1995) The pit after the theme. In M. Ghadessy (ed.) *Thematic Development in English Texts* 198–212. London and New York: Pinter.

Janssen, A. J. M. and van der Wurff, W. (eds) (1996) *Reported Speech*: *Forms and Functions of the Verb*. Philadelphia and Amsterdam: Benjamins.

Leaska, M. A. (1970) *Virginia Woolf's 'Lighthouse'*: *A study in Critical Method*. London: The Hogarth Press.

Leech, G. N. and Short, M. H. (1981) *Style in Fiction*: *A Linguistic Introduction to English Fictional Prose*. London and New York: Longman.

Longacre, R. E. (1985) Sentences as combinations of clauses. In T. Shopen (ed.) *Language Typology and Syntactic Description* Volume 2: *Complex Constructions* 235–298. Cambridge: Cambridge University Press.

Lucy, J. A. (ed.) (1993) *Reflexive Language*: *Reported Speech and Metapragmatics*. Cambridge: Cambridge University Press.

Marcon, E. (2002) *Economic-Financial News Articles on the Internet*: *A Corpus-based Analysis*. Unpublished thesis for the 'Laurea in Lingue e Letterature Straniere', University of Padua.

Martin, J. R. (1988) Hypotactic recursive systems in English: toward a functional interpretation. In J. D. Benson and W. S. Greaves (eds) *Systemic Functional Approaches to Discourse*: *Selected Papers from the 12th International Systemic Workshop* 240–270. Norwood, N. J.: Ablex.

McGregor, W. (1990) The metafunctional hypothesis and syntagmatic relations. *Occasional Papers in Systemic Linguistics* 4: 5–50.

Munro, P. (1982) On the transitivity of 'say' verbs. In P. Hopper and S. Thompson (eds) *Syntax and Semantics*, Volume 15: *Studies in Transitivity* 301–318. New York: Academic Press.

Partee, B. H. (1973) The syntax and semantics of quotation. In S. Anderson and P. Kiparsky (eds) *A Festschrift for Morris Halle* 410–418. New York: Holt, Rinehart & Winston.

Pegoraro, M. (2004) *Projection in Rowling's 'Harry Potter and the Philosopher's Stone'*. Unpublished thesis for the 'Laurea in Lingue e Letterature Straniere', University of Padua.

Peraro, V. (2005) *Projection in a Small Corpus of Articles from 'The Economist'*. Unpublished dissertation for the 'Laurea in Mediazione Linguistica e Culturale', University of Padua.

Pesaresi, R. (2005) *Projection in Virginia Woolf's 'Mrs. Dalloway': A Corpus Study of the Second Half of the Novel*. Unpublished dissertation for the 'Laurea in Mediazione Linguistica e Culturale', University of Padua.

Petronio, F. (2004) *Projection in Virginia Woolf's 'Mrs. Dalloway'*. Unpublished dissertation for the 'Laurea in Mediazione Linguistica e Culturale', University of Padua.

Rosenbaum, P. (1967) *The Grammar of English Predicate Complement Constructions*. Cambridge, Mass: MIT Press.

Rosenberg, B. C. (1995) *Virginia Woolf and Samuel Johnson: Common Readers*. New York: St. Martin's Press.

Rossetto, E. (2003) *Projection in Magazine Articles*. Unpublished dissertation for the 'Laurea in Mediazione Linguistica e Culturale', University of Padua.

Rowling, J. R. (1997 [2000]) *Harry Potter and the Philosopher's Stone*. London: Bloomsbury.

Scarso, M. (1998) *Projection in the Gospel of St. John: A Corpus-based Study*. Unpublished thesis for the 'Laurea in Lingue e Letterature Straniere', University of Padua.

Simpson, P. (1993) *Language, Ideology and Point of View*. London and New York: Routledge.

Stockwell, R. (1977) *Foundations of Syntactic Theory*. Englewood Cliffs: Prentice Hall.

Taylor Torsello, C. (1991) How Woolf creates point of view in *To the Lighthouse*: an application of systemic-functional grammar to a literary text. *Occasional Papers in Systemic Functional Linguistics* 5: 159–174.

Taylor Torsello, C. (1996a) On the logical metafunction. *Functions of Language* 3.2: 151–183.

Taylor Torsello, C. (1996b) Reporting speech: evidence from newspapers for grammatical description. In E. Siciliani, A. Cecere, V. Intonti and A. Sportelli (eds) *Le Trasformazioni del Narrare: Atti del XVI Convegno Nazionale dell'Associazione Italiana di Anglistica* 623–645. Fasano: Schena Editore.

Taylor Torsello, C. (2000) Il genere discorsivo. *Rassegna Italiana di Linguistica Applicata* 32. 3: 49–66.

Thompson, G. (1994) *English Guides 5: Reporting*. London: Harper Collins.

Woolf, V. (1945 [2000]) *A Room of One's Own*. London: Penguin.

Woolf, V. (1992 [2000]) *Mrs. Dalloway*. London: Penguin.

Woolf, V. (1992 [2000]) *To the Lighthouse*. London: Penguin.

Zampiron, E. (2005) *Projection in Virginia Woolf's 'Mrs. Dalloway': Analysis of the Middle Part*. Unpublished dissertation for the 'Laurea in Mediazione Linguistica e Culturale', University of Padua.

Zwicky, A.M. (1971) On reported speech. In C. J. Fillmore and D. T. Langendoen (eds) *Studies in Linguistic Semantics* 73–77. New York: Holt, Rinehart & Winston.

6 Collocation as the determinant of verbal art

Bill Louw

University of Zimbabwe

Editors' Introduction

Bill Louw is Senior Lecturer in Modern English Language at the University of Zimbabwe, where he also teaches courses in Communication and Negotiating Skills on the MBA, using data-assisted methods. He has published widely in stylistics, classroom concordancing, data-assisted literary criticism, semantic prosodies and contextual prosodic theory (CPT).

Following closely in the footsteps of John Sinclair's work on corpus linguistics and also stylistics, Louw's challenging and provoking paper gives us another exploration of the possibilities of collocations as a way of analysing verbal art. It too is valuable for scholars and students interested in combining stylistics with the latest developments in corpus linguistics. For Louw, however, it is actually the task of corpus stylistics to make the act of reading poetry, prose and drama *data-assisted*, if not *data-driven*, within the verbal art of individuals and the literary movements with which their work has become associated. He holds that for critics of literature, digital instrumentation for language offers, on the one hand, verification of their insights, and, on the other, the stimulus of rendering vulnerable *all* critical statements which are merely the intuitively derived products of 'normal' reading. Hence his suggestion that ordinary reading may now be inadequate for the determination of verbal art. The suggestion is essentially much like Hasan's own, but the confident belief in the interpretative powers of the nine-word collocational window is distinctively his own.

The initial section of Louw's paper illustrates the theoretical premises of his analysis and focuses on the figures of Jakobson and Firth. Louw writes that Jakobson's article entitled 'Poetry of grammar and grammar of poetry' (1968) shows that his investigative technique was very close to that of Firthian stylistics. At the same time, however, he also argues that Jakobson's work managed only a glimpse into the possibilities offered by the notion of 'context of situation' as theorised by Malinowski and Firth, and that, as a consequence, his theory of poetry is marred by this serious limitation. For Louw, Jakobson's work left his readers with the problem of finding a level of language other than syntax as the basis for proving the existence and power of his 'poetic function'. He proposes collocation as the solution to this problem, noting that Firth suggested that collocation should be considered at a superordinate level, one much closer to context of situation than to syntax or grammar. In other words, poetical potential is not to be found in lexical and grammatical relations, so much as in the 'trope', that is to say, in that '[…] phenomenon which […] twists words away from their usual meanings […]' (Wales, 2001: 398). The modern and contemporary literature texts that Louw addresses include Erza Pound, George Orwell, and contemporary Singaporean poet, Edwin Thumboo. His collocation analysis, however, makes use of concordance data from a vast array of machine-readable corpora which has been gathered from texts spanning a long period of time.

Scholars could argue that Louw's theoretical position is at times too uncompromising and overly absolute in stating what *is* valuable in the analysis of verbal art (i.e. Malinowskian and Firthian context of situation plus collocation), and what is *not* (pretty much all the rest). Notwithstanding the feasibility and perhaps even fairness of such criticism, there is no doubt that his analysis is not only original, but also effective, in showing that collocation in literature texts can be usefully compared to collocation in large corpora, in order to draw the readers' attention to instances of delexicalisation and relexicalisation that would otherwise pass unnoticed. The powers of our intuitions are, of course, limited. In this article, the linguistic phenomena of delexicalisation and relexicalisation are also shown to play a covert role in the manipulation of language to serve dubious ideological purposes. Particularly intriguing is his treatment of the way in which literature texts exemplify Malinowskian institutional meanings seen as 'modes of action', rather than as 'countersigns of thought'.

1 Introduction

It is now almost *de rigeur* within the discipline of stylistics for anyone making an opening statement to refer to the now famous 'closing statement' delivered by Roman Jakobson at the conclusion of a conference on style at Indiana University in 1959 (Sebeok, 1960: 350–377, and in Weber, 1996: 12–35). Jakobson's paper was published in the same year that John Rupert Firth, who first propounded the power of collocation and who taught John Sinclair, died. The subject of Jakobson's address was not very far from the concerns of a recent conference on the subject of verbal art in Bologna 44 years later. [1] In his address, Jakobson attempted to demonstrate the basis of what he called the 'poetic function' of language: a project which he had been refining for much of his career within at least two 'schools' of literary theory and in at least three different countries. He offered, with some elucidation but with insufficient literary exemplification, the following terse, if slightly obscure statement of the principle behind it:

> The poetic function projects the principle of equivalence from the axis of selection into the axis of combination. (Jakobson, 1960: 358)

Intuitively, the poetic function and the manner proposed for its operation commend themselves to stylisticians and even to some literary critics. The literary writer, instead of confining him/herself to *single acts of choice* at the level of paradigm, contrives to find some aesthetically pleasing way of propelling into the syntagmatic fabric of the work of art *one of several* of the forms which might have presented themselves as candidates for selection at a *single* point of choice. Whether this is meant to operate cumulatively within the work of art is left unelaborated. The theory is fairly readily attested *intuitively* by both literary critic and stylistician, as it purports to explain the richness of literary diction.

In fairness to Jakobson, it must be stated that he clearly appreciated the power of collocation without having had the benefit of studying or researching it. Ironically, Firth attended the same conference at which Jakobson's closing statement was delivered, but John Sinclair (personal communication) believes that there is little evidence to support any suggestion that they had met at length previously or that they ever discussed collocation. Jakobson refers to meetings with Firth '[…] in a New York tavern toward the end of the 1940s and our last heart-to-heart talk of June 1960 in his enchanting Lindfield home […]' (in Bazell, 1966: 242). Sinclair is probably correct in his judgement. In spite of the suggestion at the beginning of Jakobson's article, published in the volume entitled *In Memory of J. R. Firth*, that he and Firth were colleagues who collaborated closely, Jakobson's short article is basically dedicated to an account of the phonemic studies of Henry Sweet. All further reference to Firth is abandoned after the introductory paragraph.

However, Jakobson's references to 'tropes' throughout his work prove that he could be said to have been 'thinking' collocationally. Tropes are described by Katie Wales as a phenomenon which '[...] twists words away from their usual meanings or *collocations* [...]' (2001: 398, emphasis added).

Freeman (1970: 12) offers an extended example from Thomas Hardy's *The Mayor of Casterbridge* in support of Jakobson's idea of the projection of equivalence and does so as if it were also likely to suffice as an example of the poetic function. Jakobson, however, does not produce an example of the poetic function at this stage in the closing statement. Here he offers only an example of the principle of equivalence. The fact of the matter is that the poetic function is concerned with grammatical parallelism (see Miller in this volume) and, although Jakobson offers some brief examples of this powerful principle in the closing statement, it is altogether better elaborated in his paper entitled 'Poetry of grammar and grammar of poetry' (1968). It is in that paper that we find proof that Jakobson's investigative technique in stylistics was very close indeed to the manner in which Neo-Firthian stylisticians began to proceed, and that 'context of situation' may well have offered him a better line of fit for interpreting the patterns uncovered by the exhaustive procedures required for the investigation of the poetic function.

We begin with Jakobson's superb manifesto which is as current today in the thinking of stylisticians as it was novel when he wrote it eight years after Firth's death.

> Any unbiased, attentive, exhaustive, total description of the selection, distribution and interrelation of diverse morphological classes and syntactic constructions in a given poem surprises the examiner himself by unexpected, striking symmetries and anti-symmetries, balanced structures, efficient accumulation of equivalent forms and salient contrasts [...] (1968: 603)

If we turn to Culler's (1975: 59) commentary upon Jakobson's analysis of Baudelaire's 'Spleen' poems, we realise what a superb integration might have been possible between Jakobson's structural analysis and Firth's contextual analysis as the latter has now been further elaborated in semantic prosody (Louw, 1993, 2000).[2] Space permits us to refer to one stanza only of Spleen LXXVIII. The italicised third line becomes the subject of Culler's commentary below.

> Des cloches tout à coup sautent avec furie
> Et lancent vers le ciel un affreux hurlement,
> *Ainsi que des esprits errants et sans patrie*
> Qui se mettent à geindre opiniâtrement.

Baudelaire's use of personification does nothing to alter the pervasive negative semantic prosody within the stanza, or to assuage the pessimism of the entire passage. Culler, however, suggests that the poem might even have to be altered in translation in order to bring it in line with Jakobson's analysis of its patterning. He proposes that the line *Ainsi que des espirits errants et sans patrie* be altered thus: *Like wandering and homeless spirits*. The alteration,

> […] changing the non-transitory adjective *errants* to a participle with an appropriate complement (e.g. *errant sans compagnie* for *errants et sans patrie*) introduces two new transitory forms and makes the poem adhere more closely to the pattern of organisation that Jakobson would see in it. (Culler, 1975: 61)

Firth would have been quick to point out that the sudden introduction of the form *compagnie* would alter the context of situation by introducing into a literary world bereft of human comfort the notion of men and the breaking of bread. Its introduction would counteract the poet's semantic prosody by adding human beings to the context of situation only to negate them through the application of *sans*. Those who would argue that *sans* would maintain the negative prosody are referred to Sinclair's marvellous line! (1970: 141)

> Her smile was not in the least like the grin of a decomposing vampire.

Indeed, if we move to the projection of equivalence, we find that it is dominated by purely mechanistic considerations. However, we also begin to appreciate that Jakobson's beautifully concise principle may need more space to work itself out than that often available within a poem (especially a short poem such as a *haiku*). It is likely that Jakobson would not have followed the principle slavishly, but the very crispness with which it is stated as a compositional formula renders it vulnerable in considering very short poems.

His definition of the principle of equivalence is falsifiable for several reasons, all of which are related to the power of collocation, especially during what might now be termed its *digital* rather than its *analogue* phase.[3] Collocation's analogue phase was characterised not so much by the failure of human intuition to retrieve collocates accurately as by the total failure of anyone to *notice* at the time that this was the case!

The main reason for the failure of Jakobson's definition of the poetic function is entirely logical, and is perhaps best illustrated by means of a brief elaboration of the way in which he saw the principle of equivalence being 'projected'. Jakobson suggests that several *potential* choices are possible at any single point of choice from the vertical axis. The poet selects only one of these for inclusion at any particular point in the work of art. However, Jakobson's theory is attractive because it suggests that those choices which *might* have been made somehow remain 'in play' and may be expected to be propelled *later* into the syntagmatic fabric of the same work of art. This process further purports to render a piece of writing more recognisably poetic. However, we need to ask whether it would be true to assert that if this phenomenon were found *not* to occur within a poem, the artistic work in question would then demonstrably fall short of acceptable poetic norms, or be perceived by consensus as prosaic or aesthetically inadequate.

Jakobson would presumably have answered this question in the affirmative. However, an affirmative answer is likely to mean that very short poems *must then* be regarded as inferior pieces of work, because there is simply too little syntactic *space* within them for his theory to work itself out. As it is risible to suggest that Jakobson would have rejected short poems in order to save his theory (and many an academic is less than scrupulous in this regard), we are left with the alternative of finding a *level* of language other than syntax as the basis for proving the existence and power of the poetic function. This paper proposes collocation as the solution to this problem. It also takes Firth's position that if *collocation* is to be considered a level of language it will at the very least have to be a superordinate level and one much closer to *context of situation* than to grammar and syntax (in Palmer, 1957 [1968]: 161).

It is important to point the reader in the direction of a short poem which bears out the argument so far. If we examine the first line of Ezra Pound's poem 'In a Station of the Metro' (1913), we find that it is, by design,[4] only 14 words long (and only its first line, containing eight words, needs to be quoted below). The reader may wish to refer to a detailed critical analysis of this poem provided by Rodger (1983). Rodger was a colleague of Sinclair's at the University of Edinburgh and was one of the first academics to make stylistics accessible in second language study. His analysis demonstrates something of the power of the *haiku* in affording compression of expression.

The first line of Pound's verbless 14 word poem follows below. If the projection of equivalence is to work itself out, it has, at the end of this line, only six words left in which to do so!

The apparition of these faces in the crowd [...]

If Jakobson's definition were followed slavishly as part of the process of composition, we might well have expected the poet to assemble equivalences in readiness for their projection from the paradigmatic axis into the syntagmatic axis. In the pre-computational era, one might have sought to mirror this process by referring to Roget's *Thesaurus*.

> apparition 1. appearance, manifestation, materialization, presence, vision, visitation. 2. chimera, ghost, phantom, revenant, shade (Literary), spectre, spirit, spook (Inf.), visitant, wraith. (*Roget's Thesaurus* in the Collins English Dictionary on CD-Rom)

In Pound's poem, this particular fairly prosaic way of developing alternative choices for projection mercifully does not occur. If it had, it would have reduced the poem to mere doggerel. The *faces* are, within six words of verbless syntax, implicitly compared to *petals*, with the implication that they have been sundered from their flowers by a storm (they are on a wet, black bough rather than attached to a *flower*). *Apparition*, *faces* and *petals* offer not only a poor grammatical and categorial fit to the left and right of *of*, but are on their own fairly powerless to explain either the poem's deeper significances or its verbal art beyond fairly simplistic levels. Jakobson would certainly have seen the course of the poem as a trope and would have alluded also to the undeniable beauty of its rhythm. His analysis would undoubtedly have been sophisticated. This leaves us with a question that is difficult to answer: *why* does he offer us in his 'closing statement' a prosaic example of the projection of equivalence (referring to options among *child*, *kid* and *tot*)? Even if Jakobson had had some exposure to collocation during its analogue period, he would (at the time at which he was writing) have experienced the limitations of human intuition in recognising collocation profiles. The digital phase of collocation is only now sufficiently well equipped and ready to bring the poetic function to fruition, albeit with some alterations to Jakobson's theory as it was first envisioned.

Poetic potential is *not* to be found in synonyms and syntax so much as it is in the trope and, as we have seen, *that* involves collocation, a phenomenon unknown to Jakobson. A practical criticism class would doubtless have invoked entirely putative notions such as 'connotation' in order to offer an explanation. It is easily demonstrated that *connotations*, if they exist at all, may well be the product of *collocations*. However, if our discipline is expected to advance *scientifically* to the point where it, and especially collocation, are recognised as providing *instrumentation* for language, the putative ought never to be preferred to the empirically recoverable. For the sake of convenience and experimental rigour, it is perhaps better to deny the existence of connotation altogether, except within the conventions of polite conversation. We shall return to the *haiku* by Ezra Pound in due course.

If recourse to *Roget* on the matter of the term *apparition* is likely to give rise to poor poetry, how are we to access collocation instead of synonyms? The answer lies in corpora rather than in dictionaries. Although dictionaries of collocation exist, they are less valuable than corpora for the reason that dictionaries often concern themselves with providing collocates for words rather than for phrases. A material aspect of the poem we are considering is the fact that we are *not* dealing with *an* apparition so much as *the* apparition. *An* apparition is a scary apparition. *The* apparition is an apparition well known, if you like, a delexical one, 'washed out' through the frequency of its appearance (to use Sinclair's analogy which suggests that delexicalisation is akin to the washing of blue jeans! The more blue jeans are washed the more they fade. The more frequently an expression in the language is used, the more its meanings will, progressively, be 'washed out').

Once our investigation is unfettered by the 'dictionary mentality', collocates of the forms which appear in literary works of art become fully recoverable. Such collocates may be recovered from large corpora of natural language, and *replicably* so, as each investigator effectively finds the same collocates independently, both within the literary work itself and across a range of corpora. Replicability means that meaning may be objectively verified both within the literary work under consideration, as this is held in a machine-readable form, and across a range of corpora against which the features of that particular literary work are being 'read'. The test of replicability also acts as a safeguard against the alteration or homogenisation of corpora. Tampering with the construction of a corpus might, for example, be prompted by attempts to keep 'spin', or other institutional meanings, opaque in the perception of the ordinary reader (Louw, 2003).

A good example of a concordance follows in the next section of this paper. The request behind it was for the computer to co-select *dark* in the environment of *night*. The results of the search will be similar from one corpus to another. The reason for this is that once the reader begins to select more than one word the result will be powerfully *contextualising*, both textually and situationally.

What we then have is the evidence that constitutes a data-assisted reading. This type of reading has not always been possible by means of the ordinary or conventional reading process, and for at least two reasons. Firstly, because there will always be vast relative discrepancies within the reading background of different individuals and hence within their prior knowledge as individual readers. The second reason is more compelling. Human intuition is largely blind to collocation patterns in delexical phrases. Larger corpora are to be preferred to smaller ones, but cross-correlation will always occur between corpora that have been properly sampled as part of corpus development. Corpus development refers to the content of corpora and the way in which that content is selected in order to offer us an objective sample of authentic language in the real world. The technique of reading by data-assisted means will advance as corpora improve and assume the status of living documents. Sinclair puts this latter point more succinctly and elegantly: 'It is now possible to create a new kind of corpus, one which has no final extent because, like the language itself, it keeps on developing' (Sinclair, 1991: 25).

2   Collocation and delexicalisation

At this stage, it is worth repeating Firth's view of what is involved when we are dealing with collocation:

> Meaning by collocation is an abstraction at the syntagmatic level and is not directly concerned with the conceptual or idea approach to the meaning of words. One of the meanings of *night* is its collocability with *dark* [...] (in Palmer, 1957 [1968]: 197)

If we test Firth's own example of *night's* collocability with *dark*, we find that our intuition was capable of predicting fairly well only *some* of the syntactic correlation which surrounds these two collocates. As said above, this is because there is a point beyond which intuitive prediction does not work. The forms of language which we could *not* predict and which are uncovered by the corpus-based search are especially revealing. They involve the recovery of *delexical phrases*. The collocates involved in such phrases are often entirely opaque to human intuition, the frequent and vociferous claims of '20:20 hindsight' notwithstanding (Louw, 2003, 2004).

```
MicroConcord search SW: night CW: dark

80   Characters per entry

Sort : 1R/SW unshifted.

1   ition along Glen Road. It was a dark night and  there was no lighting.  The sol
2   to the naked eye on a dark, moonless night at only about 1,000. Objects as faint
3   ool nearby. "You could not go out at night, because after dark they just killed
4   with musketry, opened upon us.  The night being extremely dark, it was only the
5   dier being confronted in the dark of night by a moving vehicle. That is a differ
6    Brighton was. Dark pier (OK, it was night), dark arcades, dark flats there must
7    hut, an eerie murmur filled the dark night. "Don't worry about that, it's just t
8   om behind and spoke to you on a dark night. His would be the voice that was comi
9    we would not care to meet on a dark night; I still cannot understand the Golden
10  r'. They are there for you on a dark night in January, not just in the sunshine
11  y back to 1978, just before the dark night of Thatcherism fell upon Tory occupie
12  itian people have awoken from a dark night of fear to a new dawn of hope," he sa
13  e broody and moody. In the real dark night of his soul, it can always be three o
14  augham as "a sudden hope in the dark night of the soul", the pagoda is the most
15   a starry sky for Mr WW's final dark night of the soul before our redeemed hero
16  tter (duly trotted out are "the dark night of the soul", "let there be light", "
17  d to keep hope alive during the dark night of dictatorship. For this he is honou
18  aitian people have moved from a dark night of fear to a new dawn of hope."  Des
19   had personally experienced the dark night of the soul.      </Group>    </Story>
20  nd started laughing loudly. The dark night outside the glass walls and room was
```

```
21 ct the Earth wants to meet on a dark night. Several hundred thousand more are mo
22  drivers to "see" in the dark, using night sights like those used on RAF fighter
23 llop   On a dark, miserable winter's night stuck on a lonely road miles from any
24 ertising the extremely dark 'Arabian Night'. The density of the blackness of thi
25 on its two hour, half dark midsummer night, the inhabitants don't go to bed at a
26 ts frame. There is the dark world of night thoughts, the ardent landscape of the
27  a flash of lightning on a pitch dark night; the scene it illuminated was lurid b
28 nsible.   Wharton Tigar chose a dark night to make a personal reconnaissance and
29 e, of course, referring to that dark night two years ago when the Portuguese sco
30 ed through the government lobby that night wearing dark glasses and holding thei
31 .   Anderson's orchestral piece Dark Night, which won the Royal Philharmonic Soc
```

(Source: *The Times* Newspaper for the year 1995)

Where *dark* and *night* are followed by *of,* we find that, between them, they are capable of attracting the largely unexpected collocate: *soul.* Some readers, especially those of the Roman Catholic faith, may find that they are better able to predict this form than other readers.

However, there may be an argument for reading the quotation from Firth differently and with the benefit of access to data, which Firth did not have in 1957. The question we would need to ask of the quotation is this: if a single word is 'abstracted' (Latin *ab+trahere*, '*drawn away from*') at the syntagmatic level, what evidence remains that it was ever part of that level? Surely abstraction at the syntagmatic level would, in 1957, have involved at the very least *two* adjacent words or *two* intuitively recognisable collocates. The latter, in the terminology of modern corpus linguistics, would be referred to as two 'skip-searched' words, or 'co-selected' words. However, unless strenuous efforts are made to recover the co-text from which forms are said to be 'abstracted', the whole exercise can degenerate into an intuitive investigation of a word offered from the mind of the investigator on its own as a *citation* form. It is likely that Firth saw this process of abstraction as one which would inevitably lead to the creation of a new and separate *level* of language for collocation. This becomes clear in Firth's writing *after* his association with the anthropologist, Bronislaw Malinowski, which led to the fully-acknowledged adoption on Firth's part of 'context of situation'. In a paper in which he sets out the contribution of Malinowski, Firth reserves for collocation a level of the highest abstractness:

> Linguistic analysis I reserve for statements about language data in terms of phonetics, phonology, grammar, stylistics, lexicography and textual analysis in a background of *statements of collocation and of contexts of situation* as I understand these terms. (1957 [1968]: 161, emphasis added)

The attempt to work with *The apparition* rather than simply *apparition* marks a departure from normal intuitively-based critical practice. The concordancer allows us to search for two words by means of co-selection, but it is more natural for collocates to be found *near* one another than in an inflexible relationship of rigid contiguity. With terms that *must* follow one another, we are dealing with a special form of collocation, although for Kjellmer (1984), collocation is regarded as syntactically bound.

Sinclair, in the OSTI Report, alludes to how easy it is to overlook the fact that collocation '[…] restricts the meaning of the words involved, it does not enhance it' and that collocation has a 'focusing' function rather than a 'selective' function. Sinclair says '[…] it took a long time to give up the traditional concept of the word as the unit of meaning' (Sinclair et al., 2004: xxi). In doing so, he postulates collocation *as* the very basis of the unit of meaning. This means that stylistics needs to make room for it. This adjustment needs to be made, notwithstanding the huge contribution to date of all stylisticians, and especially Jakobson's work, on the grammatical basis of the poetic function. Sinclair acknowledges the possibility for a different vision.

In his recent book, entitled *Trust the Text* (2004), Sinclair refers to this focusing function by way of explaining its use in what might perhaps be termed 'verbal art'.

> W. E. Louw (personal communication) argues that 'literal' and 'figurative' are points close to the extremities of a continuum of *delexicalization*. Words can gradually lose their full lexical meaning, and become available for use in contexts where some of that full meaning would be inappropriate; this is the so-called figurative extension. Louw points out that a writer, especially a literary writer, must exercise vigilance so that the meaning of each word is interpreted at the intended point on the continuum. Such features as collocation are part of the *control mechanism* available to the writer. (Sinclair, 2004: 198, emphasis added)

One consequence of this stance on the role of collocation in literary texts is that much of its impact will be experienced as *relexicalisation*. Sinclair (1991: 175) has always made it plain that collocative power is concentrated within a nine word window, four words to the right and four words to the left of the node. The phenomenon offers a potential device for the production of verbal art, even from the delexical scraps and detritus of the language, such as idiomatic phrases. Either way, the control mechanism of collocation is powerless once we move beyond the nine word window. For this reason, any notion of literary worlds needs to focus on the *microstructures* involved in the process of reading, rather than the purported *macrostructures* of its product. We can see something of this in the opening line of the novel *Tropic of Capricorn* by Henry Miller.

> Once you have given up the ghost, everything follows with dead certainty, even in the midst of chaos. (1966: 9)

By placing *dead* within four words of *ghost*, the author produces a 'zombie effect' which causes the dead bodies of these totally delexical expressions (i.e. 'give up the ghost' and 'dead certainty') to twitch within the perception of the reader as they are suddenly, and only briefly, relexicalised. Proof of the power of this phenomenon in Miller is easily furnished from the BNC, if *ghost* and *dead* are co-selected.

```
MicroConcord search SW: ghost CW: dead
80 characters per entry
Sort : 1R/SW unshifted.
1 through a footbridge. Every new-dead ghost Comes to that worn-out blood for its
2 ected from an old singer in 1906 the ghost of the dead lover returns after a yea
3 hrough the woods who was chasing the ghost of his dead father, Bradley neverthel
4 sts! By using magic he can order the ghost of any dead person to be his servant
5 ed himself to be in contact with the ghost of the dead king, were complications
6 re had introduced - contact with the ghost of the dead king - was not only the o
7 apparition? An earth-bound soul? The ghost of the dead Lady Eleanor? </p> <p> Fa
8 p> Yes, but you're talking about the ghost of a dead person, aren't you? This ma
9 <p>  The Romans called the spirit or GHOST of a dead person his manes or mares,
10 like one returning from the dead, a ghost (the allusion is to the drowning of P
11 and distaste. Surely the dead man's ghost would object to this? Was his soul st
```

A second consequence of viewing verbal art as collocation may be more compelling. Particular forms are dominated *within the corpus* by collocates which the reader cannot retrieve, either in the text that is being read, or intuitively from past experience. It may induce a sense of shock when the corpus reveals that these collocates are not only massively frequent but are simultaneously of immense ideological importance. This fact alone is capable of demonstrating the inadequacy of Schema Theory in cognitive approaches to literature (Louw, 2004), which propose that readers are capable of creating a literary world from a single prompt. This gives us denotations (attributes of pubs such as *food, drinks, bar* etc., Stockwell, 2002: 77), and connotations (smoke and stink), but cannot assess the *frequency* of collocates which surround the term *pub* in corpora: the terms *groups, chains* and *operations* Louw (2004). Hence, it may be argued that schemata, which Wales (2001: 351) defines as '[…] skeletal organisations of conceptual knowledge', flatter our mental ability for dealing with the obvious and the personal, whilst simultaneously leaving *ideologies* untrammelled. Landlords and the drinking habits of pubs' patrons are subject to unwitting and lucrative forms of control. The landlord-owners of pubs are an endangered species.

'Reference corpora' will become a natural and indispensable part of all corpus stylistic work.[5] This confirms Sinclair's argument that collocation '[…] restricts the meaning of the words involved, it does not enhance it'. We need perhaps to add the words, 'especially where delexical phrases which are opaque to human intuition may be recovered computationally by means of co-selection'. *Dark night of the soul* and *pub + groups, chains, operations* demonstrates the existence of *latent* institutional meaning. The computer exposes *both* it *and* the hidden ideologies that lurk behind it. Delexical phraseology is the hitherto largely unnoticed 'sleeping giant' of semantic prosodies (Louw, 1993: 173).

To demonstrate just how much detail escapes Systemic Functional (SF) distinctions, such as grammatical metaphor (see Louw, 2000b), we might cite Coffin et al. (eds) (2004: 1), where they offer the following sentences:

(a)   Traditionally, fishermen used to catch 100,000 tons of fish per year in the North Sea.

(b)   The North Sea used to provide 100,000 tons of fish per year.

The authors correctly point out that the second sentence obfuscates and glosses over the problems faced by fishermen. It is commendable that SF approaches provide some insight into this. However, collocation (which SF practitioners downplay in favour of grammatical approaches) produces a much more powerful Firthian/Malinowskian analysis. If we extend the view that one of the meanings of *night* is its collocability with *dark*, we find, in the British National Corpus (BNC), that one of the meanings of *fishermen* is its collocability with *their*. If we search for *their* in the co-selected environment of *fishermen*, we produce the following concordance.

```
MicroConcord search SW: their CW: fishermen

80 characters per entry

Sort : 1R/SW unshifted.

1  facing fishermen, slowly destroying their ability to make a living and support

2 n coastline of Japan on both legs of their annual migration. Fishermen of the Ki

3 hought as the other fishermen nodded their approval of sound advice. </p> <p> An

4 alk of revolt by Shetland fishermen. Their association has described the early c

5 e following day the 11 fishermen and their boat returned to Xiamen, Fujian provi

6  on human prey. Fishermen sleeping in their boats anchored several hundred yards

7  to the cove where the fishermen kept their boats, while curlew, disturbed by my

8  an sheep-ranch, fishermen hauling in their catch off the Faroe Islands, a ceremo

9  is used by local fishermen to unload their catches and berth their boats. </p> <
```

10 survive. </p> <p> The fishermen and their children have a habit of holding fish
11 cy, and the two young fishermen told their crews that they had found nothing but
12 t sort after by the fishermen and by their customers. Now if this contaminated f
13 rt of lime. The local fishermen keep their equipment in the arched openings nowa
14 social position of the fishermen and their families means that they are scared t
15   stamped on their pass fishermen and their families won't be able to emigrate or
16 study concentrating on fishermen and their families. </p> <PS000:> </p> <PS2S7:>
17 simply need to provide fish bait for their fishermen. Other countries could boyc
18 been possible to assess the state of their health, but fishermen have advised ma
19 ll, actually a net, the knitting, so their husbands were fishermen and that's a
20   floor as the fishermen laboured for their livelihood. </p> <p> Joe Harries woul
21 fishermen, they'd been fishermen all their lives, their fathers had been fisherm
22 e's surface and its fishermen propel their long narrow boats with a unique leg-r
23 rest in the way that this relates to their membership of fishermen's organisatio
24 he next tide. Nearby, fishermen sort their nets before hanging them up to dry in
25 ary, when commercial fishermen bring their nets closer to shore, following the b
26 a, an area where the fishermen dried their nets and the inhabitants dumped their
27 ndrew watched over fishermen mending their nets, holding the mesh taut between t
28 ire coast. Local fishermen pulled in their nets, seagulls hovered elegantly over
29 the turtles do not become trapped in their nets. The fishermen will have to use
30 cluded episodes of fishermen mending their nets. Having to use existing music, J
31 while watching the fishermen mending their nets. </p> <p> The fact that Limone i
32 dissimilar to the way fishermen make their nets. It produces a slight herringbon
33 ing houses and the fishermen started their night's work. In the morning the visi
34 anges susu are hunted and killed for their oil. Indian fishermen use dolphin oil
35 here we painted fishermen working on their outrigger boats, extraordinary craft
36 Fishing: Keen fishermen should bring their own tackle as the Wolfgangsee is reno
37 Fishing: Keen fishermen should bring their own tackle, the fishing in the lake i
38 interest groups. Fishermen, who had their own local unions, defied national org
39   whiting, which they can't get from their own fishermen. </p> <p> The potential
40 criminal records will be stamped on their pass fishermen and their families won
41 ly to intensify as fishermen step up their protests against the imports they bla
42   ,they had always been fishermen and their quarry had always been herring and ee
43   oggers and fishermen fiercely defend their rights to pollute or exploit resource
44   outlaw many part-time fishermen and their small boats from traditional grounds
45   eeding grounds by fishermen reduced their stocks during the eighteenth and nine
46 ural policy; her fishermen have lost their stocks to the Common Fisheries Policy
47 uest on three fishermen drowned when their vessel foundered in the Irish Sea in
48 café at Tersane Local fishermen show their wares Under cruising chute in the Kek

This concordance restores something which SFL has gradually taken away in the 44 years since Firth's death: the primacy of *context of situation*. Concordance lines 24–32 might very easily have been drawn from the New Testament or from Malinowski's *corpus inscriptionum kiriwiniensium*, written in 1922 and produced as part of his ethnographic studies in the Trobriand Islands. The primary institutional meaning of modern fishermen of the North Sea is *not* that they use or mend nets, but that their livelihood is threatened.

Neither ought we to look to *nature* and *grammar* for meaning, as Goatly (2004: 198–201) does, but to context of situation. Goatly is primarily concerned with the Newtonian principle '[…] that nature is passive and controllable and that human observers and actors are separate from what they observe and act on'. He deplores the fact that the fish are an inert or passive goal and agonises over the problems of labelling of his own making (such as *animation* or *personification*), as he feels these are involved in the grammar of reporting that *a boulder tops the hill* or *the bed is crawling with ants*.

Such reasoning confirms that the Firthian tradition is now completely lost. Firth is concerned with *outcomes which flow from contexts of situation*. If there has been over-fishing, the plight of fishermen is better disclosed by the outcomes pointed to by the collocate *their* than by the invention of a plethora of labels which are applied to the surface of grammar in ways that are akin to false tagging.

Collocation takes us to the meaning of the *outcome*. It is a form of reading or writing and *not* a form of *labelling*, which leads in cumbersome ways to a fractured and only partial interpretation, which is skewed both by the author's grammatical choices and the 'dead' metaphorical *appearance* of idiomatic English. A more compelling grasp of hidden meanings is to be obtained by looking to collocation instead and to Firth's 1957 taxonomy for context of situation, as he established it together with Malinowski (Firth, 1957 [1968]: 155), and as it has now been partially automated by Louw (2003). It is only in this way that we are likely to discover what exactly gets 'disappeared' by the assertion that the North Sea 'used to provide 100,000 tons of fish'. Speculation about the interface between grammar and nature is finally less important than an outcome in the real world. Outcomes are traceable through collocation and the problems they identify are finally cured by human intervention. Nothing is to be gained by demonstrating that linguistic forms are metaphors we die by. No material help flows from showing that we are victims of grammatical happenstance.

With the above preparation in mind, it is now time to return to the single line of poetry in Pound's *haiku*: 'The apparition of these faces in the crowd […]'. If we apply the principles of delexicalisation and collocation to the first two words of our poem, we find exactly the same phenomenon that we experienced earlier. As said, the grammar offers only a small prompt: we are dealing with *the apparition* and not *an apparition*. The shock induced by the apparition is one to which we are becoming accustomed. The appearances of Our Blessed Lady both in the world and in a collocation search are welcome. The daily apparition of the faces of workers on the *Metro* bound for factories is unwelcome, but it holds no great surprise for us, especially in our modern world stricken as it is by globalisation. Our response to this particular apparition will be measured, rather than be likely to precipitate a heart attack.

The heart attack is likely to be brought on gradually, as we begin to feel *guilty* about having connived with an *ideology*. This ideology manufactures our consent to the idea that breaking up communities and forcing their members into factories as a form of cheap labour and for profit is acceptable and inevitable. It is difficult to prove that the ideology stated in the poem reflects Pound's own political position rather than part of his polemic to prove the power of the *haiku*. The latter seems more likely, even though Pound's opposition to American policy is well documented. The delexical collocates of *the apparition* (from The Bank of English) are identified by their frequency. They embody something of the poet's delexical intention. Readers who are determined to find *connotations* may wish to refer to the long tail two occurrences, or of *hapaces*, or single occurrences in the list below:

of	48	5.588986
the	57	4.915268
virgin	9	2.996542
an	9	2.609823
mary	5	2.224156
blessed	3	1.730057
saw	3	1.690318
shrine	2	1.413003
startled	2	1.412777
holy	2	1.407435
sudden	2	1.406625
friend	2	1.379340
mother	2	1.356143
seen	2	1.345831

children	2	1.297025
exorcize	1	0.999982
scrooge	1	0.999759
scowling	1	0.999758
exclamation	1	0.999624
spectral	1	0.999600
fatima	1	0.999555
wondrous	1	0.999384
forlorn	1	0.999296

(Source: *The Bank of English*)

The subject of the *haiku* is the *recurrent* apparition-like appearance on the underground railway in Paris of those who leave their communities in order to travel to work every day. The event is as frequent as the working day itself and hence inevitably *delexical*, but this does not operate to the detriment of the poem, as it so easily might have done. As Sinclair correctly states it (2004: 198), the 'control mechanism is collocation'. The delexical *apparition* reaches forward to equate itself with the equally delexical *faces in the crowd*. It becomes plain that the *petals* are no longer on the flower, but moribund, shattered by what may be inferred as a 'storm', perhaps of the Industrial Revolution. This 'storm' has broken up the 'flowers' of families and carts off their members ('petals') daily on underground railways to their places of work, possibly in factories.

At last we begin to appreciate the *now verifiable* power of meronymy. Wales defines it as '[…] a term to describe a 'part-whole' relation of meaning […] dictionaries for foreign learners of English often rely on *meronymy* as a substitute for definition: providing *pictures* of cars or the human body and labelling their distinctive parts' (2001: 247, emphasis added). As we see from the collocation frequency list for *petals* below, collocation in the digital age is capable of providing a linguistic rival to those pictures.

This is a most exciting development within the connotative rather than the denotative medium of language. Its impact on verbal art is at last demonstrable. Note that if the frequency scores for *flower* and *flowers* are added together, they place this *content* or *lexical word* form well within the envelope of structural or 'grammar words'. This offers us some measure of the power of Halliday and Hasan's (1976) research on lexical cohesion. It is a great pity that it was not carried forward into collocation's digital period.

Collocation list

Collocates: 3 to left and 3 to right of 'petals'

the	207	of	114	and	89	a	58
with	58	p	49	in	44	rose	38
to	33	flower	29	on	27	white	24
like	23	are	22	as	22	or	21
their	18	from	16	which	16	flowers	15
leaves	15	its	14	they	14	heart-shap*	13
four	13	that	13	i	13	five	13
at	12	for	11	so	11	all	11
it	10	into	10	her	10	were	10
pink	9	have	8	can	8	by	8
faded	8	dried	8	one	7	you	7

(List of collocates and frequencies obtained from all occurrences of the form *petals* in The British National Corpus)

3 Collocation as the control mechanism for verbal art

We now examine in greater detail how collocation as the control mechanism of delexicalisation allows poetry to work, in spite of the fact that most of a particular poem's linguistic fabric is statistically and recoverably *swamped* by the delexical forms of everyday language. Edwin Thumboo is a friend and colleague of Sinclair's. He is a renowned Singaporean poet and academic. David Birch (1996: 208) quotes one of Thumboo's most famous poems, 'Steel', whose theme is political resistance to colonial domination. In the poem, Thumboo's persona wishes to create a sense that colonial settlers might eventually encounter armed resistance. However, he wishes to make this suggestion without appearing to be fomenting a revolution. He creates an image in which the poem's very syntax is simultaneously both a line of poetry and a line of battle.

Steel
They gave me subterraneous thoughts
How to work effects with words; for sauce
I gamed with alphabet,
Marshalling sense into the line
Till cunning showed beneath the verbs, cunningly.

Till mind, my mind, grew slanting
With habitations of the past.
Bowels of the soul congested, cough
In a current of fixed sounds.

How can others know my tongue-fire
Agony deprived of action?

O Abel, Rima's chords are lost:
The serpent bites,
Green Mansions, a scarecrow of steel
To hang our automatic greetings.

Edwin Thumboo (1956)

Only collocation can account for achieving this delicate balance between warning and incitement because the term *marshalling* (line 4) is totally surrounded by delexical forms *in the corpus and hence in the readers' prior knowledge* which are likely to defeat the poet's intentions.

In the first place, as can be seen in the collocation list below, there are semantically unrelated forms, such as *marshalling yards*, *railways* and *harbors*. These could cause distractions of provenance.

Secondly, some of the delexicalisation present has become associated with *ameliorative semantic change* (Ullmann, 1962: 231) during the history of the language: a frequent collocate of *marshalling* is the conciliatory word *support* rather than an aggressive word. This meaning would be quite the opposite of the poet's intention! The problem is easily rectified by the inclusion of an appropriate collocate within the window of acknowledged collocational power.

The poet needed to move a collocate to within *four* words of *marshalling* which would have the effect of *relexicalising* it *into* a form of verbal art by reinstating its primary meaning of resistance. This collocate is *line*, both 'line' of protest poetry and 'line' of battle, or of soldiers on parade. The nine word window of collocational power (Sinclair, 1991: 175) is the determinant of verbal art here. It allows the delexical threat to become entirely *invisible* at the level of the reader's intuition. This is precisely where cognitive stylisticians go astray. They see metaphors everywhere and aver that we live by them (Lakoff and Johnson, 1980). The fact is that the metaphors they see are the washed out *dead* metaphors of which *all* language is comprised. I would propose that *'real'* poetic power consists in collocation's ability to conceal the unwanted common core of the language whilst simultaneously bringing to prominence, through *relexicalisation*, those, and only those, meanings which the poet's purpose requires at the time.

Collocation list (data from a sample of 200 citations from The Bank of English)
Collocates: 3 to left and 3 to right of 'marshalling'

the	83	and	43	of	40	in	28
his	26	for	26	a	22	yards	22
to	18	is	16	was	14	by	13
with	12	support	12	p	12	at	11
yard	10	as	10	from	9	on	9
defence	9	but	7	its	7	he	7
troops	7	be	6	area	6	forces	6
this	6	more	6	into	6	railway	62
it	6	are	6	that	5	marshallin*	5
all	5	them	5	himself	4	him	4
resources	4	evidence	4	will	4	when	4
also	4	their	4	about	4	has	4
game	3	well	3	facts	3	which	3
we	3	an	3	city	3	internatio*	3
after	3	large	3	i	3	rail	3
been	3	have	3	her	3		

There is a deeper reason why this example ought deservedly to bring increased levels of anxiety into the lives and work of cognitive stylisticians. It is a falsehood, which is nonetheless central to cognitive linguistics, to use intuition to relexicalise the delexical and then to *reify* it as a respectable subject for investigation. More recently, members of this school of linguists have purported to use corpora to 'verify' their science. Let us be clear. Metaphors cannot be created by the process of intuitive labelling of the type we find in so much cognitive work on metaphor, such as

[...] COMMERCIAL-ACTIVITY-AS-PATH;
COMMERCIAL-ACTIVITY-AS-CONTAINER;
COMMERCIAL-ACTIVITY-AS-WAR [...]

(Martin, 2006)

Metaphor involves transference of meaning. In the case of 'dead' metaphors no transference occurs. It only *appears* to occur if instances are presented as single made up examples and as citation forms in single sentences (cf. Bruner et al., 1956: 54). Collocation is capable of providing *relexicalising transference of meaning* uniquely within the nine-word window, but the examples must be authentic and labels such as those of Martin above, offered from intuition alone, would destroy the process by attempting to control it. Furthermore the labels provided in so doing would mislead investigators who attempted to replicate the research years later. Readers' intuition runs riot when prompted by examples of relexicalisation within the nine word window of collocative power, like the single line from the Bank of English below. The writing is reminiscent of the powerful innuendo achieved by Philip Roth (2000) in his book entitled *The Human Stain*. Only collocation has the power to re-allocate and re-categorise a mere grammatical object such as *resolve*:

> The hidden hand stiffened the President's resolve.

4 Collocation and context of situation as literary worlds

When it comes to considering language and context, very few linguists have taken the trouble to settle the question of *primacy*. In an address at Sophia University in Japan in 1980, Michael Halliday states the issue at the beginning of his talk:

> Let me begin, then, by trying to explain both these notions: what do we mean by text and what do we mean by context? I am going to do this in the opposite order: that is to say, I am going to talk about context first, for the reason that, in *real life, contexts precede texts*. The situation is *prior* to the discourse that relates to it. Also – and perhaps for this reason – there was a theory of context before there was a theory of text. I have in mind here the work of Malinowski, and in particular his theory of context of situation [....] (in Halliday and Hasan, 1980: 6, emphasis added)

For his audience in Japan, Halliday explains exactly how Firth, in an article written in 1935, adopted and adapted Malinowski's taxonomy.

> [...] The context of situation for Malinowski is an ordered series of events considered *in rebus*.

> My view was, and still is, that 'context of situation' is best used as a suitable schematic construct to apply to language events, and that it is a group of related categories at a different level from grammatical categories, but rather of the

same abstract nature. A context of situation for linguistic work brings into relation the following categories:

A. The relevant features of participants: persons, personalities.
(i) The verbal action of the participants.
(ii) The non-verbal action of the participants.
B. The relevant objects.
C. The effect of the verbal action.

(Firth, 1957: 182)

The taxonomy set out above operates in fairly predictable ways in real life; the classic applied example is probably still T. F. Mitchell's 'The language of buying and selling in Cyrenaica' (1975). However, once we enter the world of fiction, the Malinowski-Firth classification assumes an entirely different complexion. The question of the primacy of context of situation becomes more difficult to assert within a fictional environment. Halliday and Hasan would argue that literary works of fiction establish their own contexts (see Halliday, 1978: 146, and Hasan, 1996: 50–54). Firth seems to offer no scope for this. Sinclair (personal communication) attended Firth's inaugural lecture delivered at the University of London. There Firth used the taxonomy agreed with Malinowski as the basis for providing detailed stylistic analyses of Shakespeare's plays. The lecture elicited rousing applause and a standing ovation. Sadly, all copies of this lecture are lost and it was apparently never published.

One of the first semantic prosodies uncovered by Sinclair operates around the term *happen* and its related collocates such as *something*. In the hands of a skilled writer like Scott Fitzgerald they operate, often in concert, across vast tracts of text in order to establish an increasingly febrile sense of suspense (Louw, 2000a). A good example is line 13 below, in which the guests who know that Tom is having an affair try to eavesdrop on his conversation. The terms almost disappear once the atmosphere has been created. The novelist contrives to make them collocate climactically with the *name* of the protagonist himself in line 31. After this line, there are no further occurrences of *happen* in the novel. The reader is thereafter left with very few indications as to the manner and the time of Gatsby's demise: 'Even Gatsby could happen without any apparent wonder' (line 31).

```
MicroConcord search SW: happen*
80 characters per entry
Sort : 1R/SW unshifted.
1  ppened to us together, and what had happened afterward to me, and she lay perfec
2  ~c Grcat Gatsby next to nothing. It happened, and that's all I know.' 'Well, if
3  t to go back a little and tell what happened at the garage after we left there t
4  surprising thing was that it hadn't happened before. They were a party of three
5   ichaelis tried to find out what had happened, but Wilson wouldn't say a word - i
6  he said decisively. 'But how did it happen? Did you run into the wall?' 'Don't a
7  exploded. 'I can't speak about what happened five years ago, because I didn't kn
8   that afternoon; so everything that happened has a dim, hazy cast over it, altho
9  tron of Gatsby's library. 'How'd it happen?' He shrugged his shoulders. 'I know
10 y with dejection or sleep. 'Nothing happened,' he said wanly. 'I waited, and abo
11 o hear what happens.' 'Is something happening?' I inquired innocently. 'You mean
12 a car corning the other way. It all happened in a minute, but it seemed to me th
13 n. 'Don't talk. I want to hear what happens.' 'Is something happening?' I inquir
14 lling her back inside? V\~hat would happen now in the dim, incalculable hours? P
15 s in haughty rivalry. 'Anything can happen now that we've slid over this bridge,
16 ecoverable football game. And so it happened that on a warm windy evening I drov
17 lder. 'What you want, fella?' 'What happened? - that's what I want to know.' 'Au
18 ttle in the wind, and whenever this happened the red, white, and blue banners in
19 ~ic Grcat Gatsby thing that merely happened, the end of some inevitable chain.
20 ow?' demanded Tom of me. 'How'd you happen to come up this far to eat?' 'I've be
21        lf-  shiem  - that much I happen to know. I've made a little investiga
22 ured her. 'It's a bona-fide deal. I happen to know about it.' Tom flung open the
23 burglar blowing a safe. 'How did he happen to do that?' I asked after a minute.
24 and talked over and around what had happened to us together, and what had happen
25 orget some- thing very sad that had happened to me long ago.' With an effort I m
26 trying to forget the sad thing that happened to me.' He hesitated. 'You'll hear
27 'At lunch?' 'No, this afternoon. I happened to find out that you're taking Miss
28 ght pick up a nice bit of money. It happens to be a rather confidential sort of
29  man telling over and over what had happened, until it became less and less real
30  a series of invisible but alarming happenings were taking place outside. Finall
31 thing at all ...' Even Gatsby could happen, without any particular wonder. Roari
```

But note the effect that this suspense has on the taxonomy of situational context. Once Gatsby and 'happen' are caused to collocate, Scott Fitzgerald creates the potential for things to happen to Gatsby, as well as for Gatsby to *cause* things to happen. Collocation as contextual prosodic theory is capable of re-assigning the subject within mere grammar (Louw, 2000a). Firth offers us the potential for cruel mismatches between appearance and reality: the *persons* (already a '*mask*' within its etymology), or author-created characters, are afforded the possibility of a Janus-faced relationship with their own personalities. Dr Jekyll can be, and is, Mr Hyde. Hamlet is heir apparent, son, ditherer and, through the assumption of an 'antic disposition', a madman. Gatsby is 'Oxford man', reveller and Daisy's lover, but in his case the list is left incomplete. His other personalities have demonstrably created *enemies* for him. To re-phrase Firth, 'You shall know a fractured context of situation or literary world by the collocates it keeps'.

Louw (2000a) makes the point that negative semantic prosodies are the product of fractured contexts of situation. It is for this reason that they are associated with suspense. Louw offers the example (repeated in Louw, 2000b) of the word *footsteps* in literary contexts. Where the 'owner' of the footsteps is known, there is no suspense. Where this is *not* the case, the context is immediately perceived to have been invaded by an interloper and all of the stylistic markers of a negative semantic prosody begin to appear. At the far end of the delexical cline we have fixed expressions such as *follow in his mother's footsteps* which are totally free of any sense of suspense or situational fracture.

Of course, we cannot expect the novel, play or poem to fit the taxonomies in the form in which Malinowski and Firth provide them. However, the classification is sufficiently generalisable for adjustments to be easily made. For example, in Michael Frayn's recent novel (2003), *Spies*, the Firthian section on 'relevant objects' is realised by the dominant presence in the novel of an odoriferous plant with pheromonal properties which are borne upon the air. The air is also simultaneously the medium which facilitates attacks during the war and against which air raid shelters need to be sought. In the early part of the book the *air* is filled with the smells of spring (citations 1, 3, 13) and is redolent with sexuality. Unanswered questions are also delexically left in the air (citations 2, 4, 12). Note how we get the same form of words *h*ng*+3air* (*or would, if we were skip searching*) to refer to unanswered questions (citation 4), and to the mysterious smell which keeps on haunting the narrator (citation 21). However, once war breaks out, the same air becomes the vector of the enemy's planes and bombs. These are all too visible. Citations 14 and 15 appear to prepare for the physical manifestation of the bombing raids and the need for shelters and wardens. The concordance allows us to appreciate the way in which the writer has created this powerful sense of ambivalence.

```
MicroConcord search SW: air
80 characters per entry
Sort : 1R/SW unshifted.
1 that I know what it was, scenting the air all around us. Then the laughter's gon
2 solved, that some secret thing in the air around me is still waiting to be disco
3  time. I catch it on the warm evening air as I walk past the well-ordered garden
4  unanswered ques-tions hanging in the air at the Haywards' house than there are
5 I know represents not grey at all but air-force blue, and that belongs to a brid
6 ent of fast-growing evergreens in the air. But of that wild, indecent smell that
7  ond stretches away through the golden air, empty all the way to the letter box a
8  's just while Mr Tracey's away in the Air Force. Deirdre says lots of ladies hav
9  mmer sun and making our famously good air fresh and exhilarating. There's nothin
10  getation standing head-high, and the air's heavy with the buzzing of flies and
11 ands and the cone chill ml thc ois;1U air. I can see the candles flickering, mid
12 le, disturbing presence in the summer air? If only I knew what the magic blossom
13  the feel of a weekday morning in the air; it's unmistakable, even if the season
14 re somehow rematerialising out of the air itself. It takes me a moment to locate
15 ut my hand inside. The texture of the air seems to change and thicken around my
16  into the high mountain passes of the air-raid shelter, where spectacular bridge
17 e'll get some more candles out of the air-raid shelter.' I shiver. Already I can
18 I think the thought, a cool breath of air stirs, and the moon sails behind a clo
19 a snap of him in Mummy's bag. He's an air-raid warden.' 'Barbara! I'm not going
20  ti-aircraft defences, probably - the air-raid wardens' post on the corner of th
21 . A characteris-tic scent hung in the air. What was it? Sawdust, certainly, and
```

5　Conclusion

Not all of the verbal art expressed through collocation is 'primal' in this way, but the fractured situations which writers delineate by means of verbal art will themselves become marked forms within the very fabric of the writing itself. Fractured situations will always be at the heart of literary works. A single line such as 'Nellie, I *am* Heathcliff' is enough to cause chaos both within Firth's section on 'persons, personalities' and on a larger scale within the section entitled 'effect of the verbal action'. Those shocking words become the sub-text of a whole work: the characters act them out in *Wuthering Heights* by Emily Bronte. They even induce so strong a sense of shock in the narrator, Nellie Dean, that she declares that she may not remain silent on the subject.

Collocation is in the process of becoming instrumentation for language in general and literary language in particular. Language may well be the last science to receive instrumentation. The process of bringing it about will have its enemies and opponents because literary fiction is not terribly far away from the domain of all other untruths (Sinclair, 1987). This does not mean that all stylistics conducted hitherto has been wasted. All it means is that there have been imbalances that require correction. Even Jakobson, without knowing it, was very slightly looking in the wrong place because the right place is only now becoming recognisable. Others, like Halliday, worked in the right place for a number of years and then drifted away from it, inexplicably.

As the future of collocation will always be computational, this means that reading itself will become at the very least a partially computational act in the future. The computer is no longer an optional accessory. As reading becomes more of a science, criticism is likely to lead that process rather than drag its feet as it has in the past. Our young scholars have justifiably become impatient. They no longer wish to defend structuralist or mentalist schools of thought that are now so easily falsified by collocation studies.

I close with a concordance for *brother* from George Orwell's novel *1984*. Note that the last line of this concordance (Appendix A) contains the only reference to a natural sibling for the term in the entire book and even then this single context for it is a violent one. Only in the world of fiction are we likely to find such powerful examples of Malinowskian institutional meaning as 'modes of action', rather than as the 'countersign of thought' (Firth, 1957 [1968]: 148). The *brothers* of the secret societies have swamped and neutralised natural *brothers* who have sisters.

> Winston raised his hands above his head, but with an uneasy feeling, so vicious was the boy's demeanour, that it was not altogether a game.
>
> 'You're a traitor!' yelled the boy. 'You're a thought-criminal! You're a Eurasian spy! I'll shoot you, I'll vaporize you, I'll send you to the salt mines!'
>
> Suddenly they were both leaping round him, shouting 'Traitor!' and 'Thought-criminal!', the little girl imitating her brother in every movement. It was somehow frightening, like the gambolling of tiger cubs which will soon grow up into man eaters. (Orwell, 1949: 24)

The collocate missing from this single account of a sibling *brother* in the book is, of course, the word *big*! The reader supplies it almost as a slip of the tongue.

Appendix A

```
MicroConcord search SW: brother
80 characters per entry
Sort : 1L/SW unshifted.
1  uption or incompetence. Perhaps Big Brother was merely getting rid of a too-popu
2  nces. There were occasions when Big Brother devoted his Order for the Day to com
3   away on rival versions of what Big Brother had actually said. And presently som
4  plate without feelings of envy. Big Brother added a few remarks on the purity an
5   the pyramid comes Big Brother. Big Brother is infallible and all-powerful. Ever
6  le system of thought, as though Big Brother and the Party and the Thought Police
7  the Party histories, of course, Big Brother figured as the leader and guardian o
8  o importance. He exists.' 'Will Big Brother ever die?' 'Of course not. How could
9  rtainty as to when he was born. Big Brother is the guise in which the Party choo
10 n toward an organization. Below Big Brother comes the Inner Party, its numbers l
11 s ultimately on the belief that Big Brother is omnipotent and that the Party is
12 nfallible. But since in reality Big Brother is not omnipotent and the Party is n
13 ltaneously. In that sense, does Big Brother exist?' 'It is of no importance. He
14 'Next question,' he said. 'Does Big Brother exist?' 'Of course he exists. The Pa
15 se he exists. The Party exists. Big Brother is the embodiment of the Party.' 'Do
16 n possible, for example, to say Big Brother is ungood. But this statement, which
17 hy should you get excited about Big Brother and the Three-Year Plans and the Two
18  to spit out again. The face of Big Brother swam into his mind, displacing that
19 e Party, almost on a level with Big Brother himself, and then had engaged in cou
20 sian army, he might be praising Big Brother or the heroes on the Malabar frontit
21 ners voicing their gratitude to Big Brother for the new, happy life which his wi
22 k and looked at the portrait of Big Brother which formed its frontispiece. The h
23 0 none of them was left, except Big Brother himself. All the rest had by that ti
24 igues against the leadership of Big Brother which had started long before the Re
25 en been demonstrations to thank Big Brother for raising the chocolate ration to
26 DOWN WITH BIG BROTHER DOWN WITH BIG BROTHER DOWN WITH BIG BROTHER over and over
27 DOWN WITH BIG BROTHER DOWN WITH BIG BROTHER over and over again, filling half a
28 DOWN WITH BIG BROTHER DOWN WITH BIG BROTHER DOWN WITH BIG BROTHER DOWN WITH BIG
29  the neck i dont care down with big brother He sat back in his chair, slightly a
30 ry open on the table. DOWN WITH BIG BROTHER was written all over it, in letters
31  the neck i dont care down with big brother they always shoot you in the back o
32  moments his secret loathing of Big Brother changed into adoration, and Big Brot
33 her changed into adoration, and Big Brother seemed to tower up, an invincible, f
34 p the screen. Nobody heard what Big Brother was saying. It was merely a few word
35 DOWN WITH BIG BROTHER DOWN WITH BIG BROTHER DOWN WITH BIG BROTHER DOWN WITH BIG
36 CE IS STRENGTH. But the face of Big Brother seemed to persist for several second
37 large neat capitals-- DOWN WITH BIG BROTHER DOWN WITH BIG BROTHER DOWN WITH BIG
```

38 being spoken. Then the face of Big Brother faded away again, and instead the th
39 mply to reverse the tendency of Big Brother's speech. It was better to make it d
40 ward him and began dictating in Big Brother's familiar style: a style at once mi
41   through the offending article. Big Brother's ()rder for the Day, it seemed, had
42 ssary to rewrite a paragraph of Big Brother's speech in such a way as to make hi
43 t be rendered: The reporting of Big Brother's Order for the Day in the Times of
44 ic about a papiermAche model of Big Brother's head, two meters wide, which was b
45 ted column, at the top of which Big Brother's statue gazed southward toward the
46 despatches and all-an end, said Big Brother, which it was impossible to contempl
47 o f solitude, from the age o f Big Brother, from the age o f doublethinkgreetin
48   mistaken prophecies uttered by Big Brother, have been rewritten a dozen times s
49 f the seventeenth of March that Big Brother, in his speech of the previous day,
50 o him in the name of Ingsoe and Big Brother, and ask him sorrowfully whether eve
51   taken in by it. He was abusing Big Brother, he was denouncing the dictatorship
52   taken in by it. He was abusing Big Brother, he was denouncing the dictatorship
53 nciples of Ingsoc, he venerated Big Brother, he rejoiced over victories, he hate
54 ess. Whether he wrote DOWN WITH BIG BROTHER, or whether he refrained from writin
55 , but, on the contrary, against Big Brother, the Party, and the Thought Police;
56   figure melted into the face of Big Brother, black-haired, black mustachio'd, fu
57 mn to the wisdom and majesty of Big Brother, but still more it was an act of sel
58 ling of slogans, the worship of Big Brother-it was all a sort of glorious game t
59 t the apex of the pyramid comes Big Brother. Big Brother is infallible and all-p
60   r he had first heard mention of Big Brother. He thought it must have been at som
61 er face of the coin the head of Big Brother. Even from the coin the eyes pursued
62   be no love, except the love of Big Brother. There will be no laughter, except t
63 ing thing of all? He thought of Big Brother. The enormous face (because of const
64 on looked up at the portrait of Big Brother. White always mates, he thought with
65 ked up again at the portrait of Big Brother. The colossus that bestrode the worl
66   victory over himself. He loved Big Brother. THE END EWSPEAK was the official la
67 ke the last step. You must love Big Brother. It is not enough to obey him; you m
68 spiration. Nobody has ever seen Big Brother. He is a face on the hoardings, a vo
69 what they had done, and love of Big·Brother. It was touching to see how they lov
70 n outnumbering the portraits of Big Brother. The proles, normally apathetic abou
71 inston's face at the mention of Big Brother. Nevertheless Syme immediately detec
72 rlier than he had known that of Big Brother. But also they were outlaws, enemies
73 ies, and a full-sized poster of Big Brother. There was the usual boiled-cabbage
74 t were his true feelings toward Big Brother? There was a heavy tramp of boots in
75 Thought Police? To the death of Big Brother? To humanity? To the future?' 'To th
76 t are your true feelings toward Big Brother?' 'I hate him:' 'You hate him. Good.
77 al!', the little girl imitating her brother in every movement. It was somehow sl

Notes

1   The September 2004 conference, organised by the Centre for Linguistic-Cultural Studies (CeSLiC, see http://www.lingue.unibo.it/ceslic/bologna2004.htm) of the University of Bologna in Italy, was entitled: 'Towards a linguistic approach to verbal art: theory and practice'.

2   The label *semantic prosody* was jointly agreed upon between Sinclair, who discovered the phenomenon (1991: 112), and the author of this paper, in Harare, Zimbabwe during a visit by Sinclair to the University of Zimbabwe as external examiner. Louw (1993) demonstrated the involvement of the phenomenon in the creation (literary or otherwise) of *irony* or *insincerity*, as a result of the reversal of a semantic prosody. The factor which determines *which* form occurs, irony or insincerity, is *advertancy* or *inadvertancy* of use by the speaker/writer. The strength of the theory is to be found within this *binarity* of choice. The theory was further elaborated in Louw (2000a), in which the distinction of *primal* prosodies is elaborated as *fractured contexts of situation*. Even the absence from a poem of the form *a* is stylistically significant as *a* always introduces something *new* into a literary world. This approach is pursued into prosodies of insincerity which dominate delexical fixed expressions (Louw, 2003), and beyond that into Louw's current research which seeks to 'automate' Malinowski's view of *context of situation* as a *mode of action* rather than the *countersign of thought* (Malinowski, 1923). As a result of detailed research on phraseology in corpora begun in 1996, Sinclair in his recent volume *Trust the Text* (2004) has created a gradation within lexis which identifies a specific and verifiable place for semantic prosody.

3   It is appropriate to record that the work of Ruqaiya Hasan on texture and lexical cohesion (Halliday and Hasan, 1976, 1980) involved what is arguably the most sophisticated pre-computational treatment of collocation to be found anywhere. In particular, the power of her (and Michael Halliday's) category of meronymy is fully borne out through corpus-based computational verification as will become apparent later in this paper. This acknowledgement is made notwithstanding her public disavowal (to a group of colleagues which included Sinclair) at the Bologna Conference on Verbal Art of either the existence, or power, of collocation. Her words were: 'I do not believe in collocation. Colligation, yes, but not collocation'.

4   Pound wrote in *Gaudier-Brzeska: A Memoir* that the haiku provided a model of compression in verse, a 'one-image poem' which recreates '[...] the precise instant when a thing outward and objective transforms itself, or darts into a thing inward and subjective' (cf. Gottesman et al., 1979: 1028). Pound clearly believed that such compression enhanced and refined rather than restricted the power of poetic composition. The power and popularity of the poem referred to bears this out.

5   The author has used this technique to demonstrate, from its title alone, that the South African Truth and Reconciliation Commission (TRC) is a fake institution invented fraudulently in order to extract from the victims of apartheid waiver of their claims against those who conspired against and murdered members of their families. The monograph appears as an Occasional Paper in the online *Quaderni*

del CeSLiC at http://www.lingue.unibo.it/ceslic/e_occ_papers.htm. Copies may also be obtained from the author Bill Louw, Box A746, Avondale, Zimbabwe (louw@mango.zw). It is currently being considered by John Benjamins Publishers, Amsterdam for publication and possible inclusion in the series *Studies in Corpus Linguistics*.

6   The author is indebted to Ms Bettina Starcke (personal communication) of the University of Trier. She believes that the inclusion of a reference corpus in the experimental design for corpus stylistic research may now be shown to be mandatory rather than optional for any investigation involving the study of collocation. The exhaustive pursuit of stylistic work without corpus access is no longer possible.

References

Bazell, C. E., Catford J. C., Halliday, M. A. K. and Robins, R. (eds) (1966) *In Memory of J. R. Firth*. London: Longman.

Birch, D. (1996) Working effects with words – whose words?: stylistics and reader intertextuality. In J. J. Weber (ed.) *The Stylistics Reader: From Roman Jakobson to the Present* 206–221. London: Arnold.

Bruner, J. S., Goodnow, J. J., Austin, G. A. (1956) *A Study of Thinking*. New York: John Wiley.

Coffin, C., Hewings, A. and O'Halloran, K. (eds) (2004) *Applying English Grammar: Functional and Corpus Approaches*. London: Arnold.

Culler, J. (1975) *Structuralist Poetics: Structuralism, Linguistics and the Study of Literature*. London: Routledge & Kegan Paul.

Firth, J. R. (1957) Modes of meaning. In *Papers in Linguistics 1934–1951* 190–215. London: Oxford University Press.

Firth, J. R. (1957 [1968]) Enthnographic analysis and language. In F. R. Palmer (ed.) *Selected Papers of J. R. Firth, 1952–1959* 137–167. Bloomington and London: Indiana University Press.

Frayn, M. (2003) *Spies*. London: Faber and Faber.

Freeman, D. C. (ed.) (1970) *Linguistics and Literary Style*. New York: Holt, Rinehart and Winston.

Goatly, A. (2004) Nature and grammar. In C. Coffin, A. Hewings and K. O'Halloran (eds) *Applying English Grammar: Functional and Corpus Approaches* 197–215. London: Arnold.

Gottesman, R., Holland, L. B., Kalstone, D., Murphy, F., Parker, H. and Pritchard, W. H. (eds) (1979) *The Norton Anthology of American Literature*. New York and London: W. W. Norton.

Halliday, M. A. K. (1978) *Language as Social Semiotic. The Social Interpretation of Language and Meaning*. London: Edward Arnold.

Halliday, M. A. K. and Hasan, R. (1976) *Cohesion in English*. London: Longman.

Halliday, M. A. K. and Hasan, R. (1980) *Text and Context*. Sophia Linguistica VI: 4–15. Tokyo: Sophia University.

Hasan, R. (1996) On teaching literature across cultural distances. In E. James
(ed.) *The Language-Culture Connection*. Anthology Series 37, 34–63.
Singapore: SEAMEO Regional Language Centre.

Jakobson, R. (1960) Closing statement: linguistics and poetics. In T. A. Sebeok
(ed.) 350–377.

Jakobson, R. (1968) Poetry of grammar and grammar of poetry. *Lingua* 21:
597–609.

Kjellmer, G. (1984) Some thoughts on collocational distinctiveness. In J. Aarts
and W. Meijs (eds) *Corpus Linguistics* 163–171. Amsterdam: Rodopi.

Lakoff, G. and Johnson, M. (1980) *Metaphors We Live By*. Chicago: Chicago
University Press.

Louw, B. (1993) Irony in the text or insincerity in the writer? The diagnostic
potential of semantic prosodies. In M. Baker, G. Francis and E. Tognini-
Bonelli (eds) *Text and Technology: In Honour of John Sinclair* 157–176.
Amsterdam: John Benjamins.

Louw, W. E. (2000a) Contextual prosodic theory: bringing semantic prosodies to
life. In C. Heffer and H. Sauntson (eds) *Words in Context: A Tribute to John
Sinclair on his Retirement* 49–94. Birmingham: ELR.

Louw, W. E. (2000b) Some implications of progressive delexicalization and
semantic prosodies for Hallidayan metaphorical modes of expression and
Lakoffian 'Metaphors we Live By'. *Functions of Language* 4: 1–35.

Louw, W. E. (2003) Dressing up waiver: a stochastic-collocational reading of
'The Truth and Reconciliation Commission (TRA)'. Harare: mimeo; also
available in the *Occasional Papers dei Quaderni del CeSLiC* at http://www.
lingue.unibo.it/ceslic/e_occ_papers.htm.

Louw, W. E. (2004) Truth, literary worlds and devices as collocation. Keynote
address presented at the sixth Teaching and Language Corpora (TALC)
Conference, Granada, Spain, July 2004. Harare: mimeo.

Malinowski, B. (1923) The problem of meaning in primitive languages, supplement 1. In C. K. Ogden and I. A. Richards (eds) *The Meaning of Meaning*
451–510. London: Kegan Paul.

Martin, J. H. (2006) A corpus-based analysis of context effects on metaphor
comprehension. In S. Gries and A. Stefanowitsch (eds) *Corpus-based
Approaches to Metaphor and Metonymy*. Berlin and New York: Mouton de
Gruyter.

Miller, H. (1966) *Tropic of Capricorn*. London: Panther Books.

Mitchell, T. F. (1975) The language of buying and selling in Cyrenaica. In T. F.
Mitchell (ed.) *Principles of Firthian Linguistics* 167–199. London: Longman.

Orwell, G. (1949) *1984*. New York: Harcourt Brace Jovanovich.

Palmer, F. R. (ed.) (1957 [1968]) *Selected Papers of J. R. Firth, 1952–1959*.
Bloomington and London: Indiana University Press.

Rodger, A. (1983) Language for literature. In C. J. Brumfit (ed.) *Teaching
Literature Overseas: Language-Based Approaches*. British Council ELT
Documents 11, 537–565. Oxford: Pergamon.

Roth, P. (2000) *The Human Stain*. London: Vintage.

Sebeok, T. A. (1960) *Style in Language*. Cambridge, MA: MIT Press.

Sinclair, J. M. (1970) Taking a poem to pieces. In D. C. Freeman (ed.) *Linguistics and Literary Style* 129–142. New York: Holt, Rinehart and Winston.

Sinclair, J. M. (1987) Fictional worlds. In M. Coulthard (ed.) *Talking about Text* 43–60. Birmingham: ELR.

Sinclair, J. M. (1991) *Corpus, Concordance, Collocation*. Oxford: Oxford University Press.

Sinclair, J. M. (2004) *Trust the Text*: *Language, Corpus, Discourse*. London: Routledge.

Sinclair, J. M., Jones, S. and Daley, R. (2004) *English Collocation Studies*: *The OSTI Report*. Birmingham: University of Birmingham Press.

Stockwell, P. (2002) *Cognitive Poetics*: *An Introduction*. London: Routledge.

Thumboo, E. (1956) *Rib of Earth*. Singapore: privately published.

Ullmann, S. (1962) *Semantics*: *An Introduction to the Science of Meaning*. Oxford: Blackwell.

Wales, K. (2001) *A Dictionary of Stylistics*, 2nd edition. London: Longman.

Weber, J. J. (1996) *The Stylistics Reader*: *From Roman Jakobson to the Present*. London: Arnold.

7 Text linguistics and comparative literature: towards an interdisciplinary approach to written tales. Angela Carter's translations of Perrault

Ute Heidmann and Jean-Michel Adam

University of Lausanne, Switzerland

Editors' Introduction

Ute Heidmann is Full Professor of Comparative Literature and Director of a postgraduate program in Comparative European Languages and Literatures at the University of Lausanne. She also founded, together with J.-M. Adam, C. Calame and M. Hennard Dutheil, an interdisciplinary research group working on textual and comparative discourse analysis (see the website http://www.unil. ch/lleuc). Jean-Michel Adam is Full Professor of French Linguistics at the University of Lausanne. He has published widely in the fields of discourse analysis and genre, rhetoric and politics, speech act theory, French linguistics and stylistics.

Heidmann and Adam's article proposes the use of both the tools of linguistics and a comparative literary analysis in order to fashion and illustrate an interdisciplinary and analytical method that combines textual and discourse analysis. Micro-analysis in this case is used towards an investigation of macro-concerns. The first part of their article sketches the theoretical precursors of their approach, which include Bakhtin and his Circle, Jakobson and Benveniste, all scholars who, like the authors, advocate a linguistics that goes beyond the sentence to stress the importance of the textual dimension. Indeed, Heidmann and Adam call their theory of discourse 'Textual Discourse Analysis', a critical approach that is characterised, however, not only by text-internal dynamics, but also by the aim of tracing those intertextual relations that they believe dialogically link any text to other texts and their socio-discursive contexts. This intertextual dimension is at the centre of the authors' attention and it can be said that they make an original contribution to its re-elaboration. According to Heidmann and Adam, intertextuality as a concept cannot stand alone. It needs to be investigated together with elements of paratextuality (i.e. those elements that play an important role in directing and controlling the reception of texts by their readers), together with co-textuality (i.e. the specific ways in which authors and/or editors compose a volume), and *genericity* (which focuses on the complex *process* by which a text *relates* to generic categories as well as allowing for literary texts to relate, not only to *one*, but simultaneously to *several* existing genres). These are the several ingredients of what they call *intertextual dynamics*, a complex notion that comprises textual dimensions, as well as stylistic, narrative and discursive ones.

All these elements are taken into consideration and applied to the authors' in-depth and innovative comparative analysis of Angela Carter's translations of Charles Perrault's *Histoires ou contes du temps passé. Avec des Moralités* (1697), first published in her *The Fairy Tales of Charles Perrault* (1977), and later on, in *Sleeping Beauty and Other Favourite Fairy Tales* (1982). Heidmann and Adam's comparative and (trans)textual discourse analysis is ultimately meant to reveal the complexity and the semantic density of the dialogue between languages, literatures and cultures that such translation enacts. This too is a clearly interdisciplinary paper which brings together stylistics, genre theory, the history of literature and last, but certainly in no way least, the field of literary translation theory. To these areas of study, Heidmann and Adam contribute an exciting theory which sees translation as the epistemological enactment of different utterances, produced in different socio-cultural contexts.

---

1   Introduction

The present essay combines the tools of linguistic and comparative literary analysis to propose a method of *comparative and textual discourse analysis*. This method was originally developed to analyse rewritings of Greek myths and tales (Heidmann, 2003, Adam and Heidmann, 2002, 2003, 2004). Here we suggest applying it to Angela Carter's translations of Charles Perrault's *Histoires ou contes du temps passé. Avec des Moralités* (1697), first published in *The Fairy Tales of Charles Perrault* (1977) and later in *Sleeping Beauty and Other Favourite Fairy Tales* (1982). The main focus is on two tales: *Bluebeard* (*La Barbe Bleue*) and *The Fairies* (*Les Fées*). The essay will show the French and the English texts as referring to different linguistic, literary and cultural contexts. The linguistic and cultural specificity of the French *Histoires ou contes du temps passé*, addressed to a court audience in seventeenth century France, becomes more evident when compared to the English texts. Comparative textual analysis will make clear how Angela Carter transforms the French *Histoires et contes du temps passé* into English *Favourite Fairy Tales* for modern children by introducing subtle stylistic, generic and narrative changes.[1]

2 Discourse as common object for linguistic and literary studies

The traditional disciplinary separation of linguistic and literary studies confines linguistic expertise to the sign, with the sentence as its broadest unit. In the same way, the study of literary works is often considered the exclusive domain of literary scholars. This division has serious consequences. If the literary scholar renounces the study of micro-linguistic units, s/he eventually neglects the verbal dimension of the text. As for the linguist, positing the sentence as a limit is tantamount to forsaking the study of the textual dimension that is important for any kind of discourse, but particularly for literary discourse. The works of the Bakhtin Circle criticise this limitation and the arbitrary division between linguistics and stylistics, as the following excerpt from an early study by Bakhtin demonstrates:

> [In linguistics] [...] nothing has been worked out yet in the department concerned with the study of large verbal entities – long utterances from everyday life, dialogue, speech, treatise, novel, and so on – for these utterances as well can be and must be defined and studied in purely linguistic terms, as verbal phenomena. [...] The syntax of large verbal wholes [...] still awaits its foundation and validation: scientifically, linguistics has still not moved beyond the complex sentence. The complex sentence is the most extended phenomenon of language that has been scientifically examined [...]. (1924 [1990]: 293)

Bakhtin advocates the development of a metalinguistics informed by the dialogical principle, whose aim is to stress the importance of the textual dimension of discourse and underline the importance of speech genres. In 1973, Roman Jakobson comments on the idea of discourse as an object for linguistic studies in the following terms; '[...] The idea that linguistic studies are confined within the narrow limits of the sentence [...] is contradicted by the fact that discourse analysis, nowadays, is one of the objectives placed at the forefront of linguistics' (1973: 485–486, *our translation*).

In one of his last articles, Emile Benveniste sketches a very interesting theoretical framework for linguistic work on discourse:

> In conclusion, we must go beyond Saussure's concept of sign as a unique principle, on which depend both the structure and the function of language. This transcendence is achieved through two channels:
>
> > in *intra*linguistic analysis, through the opening of a new dimension of meaning, that of discourse, which we call semantic, henceforth distinct from that which is connected to the sign, which we call semiotic;
> >
> > in *trans*linguistic analysis of texts and literary works, through the elaboration of a metasemantics founded on the semantics of utterance.
>
> The instruments and methodology of this 'second generation' semiology shall in turn contribute to the development of other branches of general semiology. (1981: 21; our revised translation)

If we consider discourse as an object of study common to linguists and literary scholars, the two disciplines become complementary fields which, taken together, allow a better understanding of the complexity of discourse in general, and of literary discourse in particular. Tzvetan Todorov explains this very clearly:

> A coherent field of study, for the time being parcelled out among semanticists and literary critics, sociolinguists and ethnolinguists, philosophers of language and psychologists, thus demands imperiously to be recognized; in it, poetics will give way to the theory of discourse and to the analysis of its genres. (1990: 12)

Seen from this perspective, *discourse*, and in particular *literary discourse*, can be considered as privileged objects for interdisciplinary research. By combining the tools and methods of textual linguistics and comparative literary analysis, we mean to contribute to such interdisciplinary discourse analysis.

3 Textual and transtextual dimensions

We think that this theory of discourse requires a coherent concept of the text and a corresponding method of analysis. We suggest calling this method *textual discourse analysis* in order to signal the importance of the textual dimension of discourse (Adam, 2003: 248). According to Bakhtin, the main centripetal forces that ensure the cohesion of any text are the *thematic-semantic configuration*, the *textual composition* and the *micro-linguistic texture*.[2] We consider them as the main aspects of *textual dynamics* and propose to analyse their complex interactions (Adam and Heidmann, 2003: 36–40).

However, a text considered as discourse cannot be reduced to the dynamics of *internal* textual relations. Each text is shaped by the act of utterance and its dialogic nature, as Bakhtin points out: 'In reality […] any utterance, in addition to its own theme, always responds (in the broad sense of the word) in one form or another to others' utterances that precede it' (1986: 93). This means that every text opens up to the *intertextual relationships* that dialogically link it to other texts and to the languages and speech genres used within a given socio-discursive context. Todorov, in his book on Bakhtin's *dialogic principle*, clearly states that 'The most important feature of the utterance, or at least the most neglected, is its *dialogism*, that is, its intertextual dimension' (1984, as quoted by Allen, 2000: 28).

The complex ways in which a text refers to other texts, languages and speech genres can be considered as *transtextual* dimensions. We use the word *transtextual* in reference to Genette's works on textual *transcendence* (1997a, 1997b), but prefer the notion of *transtextual dynamics* to his more static term of *transtextuality*. We indeed consider the transtextual dimensions as *dynamic* forces rather than structural features.[3] The concept of language which underpins our method of textual discourse analysis is based on the idea that every text (considered as discourse) results from socio-discursive activity. It is, therefore, oriented in time and space and, as such, an ongoing process, rather than a system.[4]

3.1 Intertextual and generic dimensions

There are, of course, multiple ways for a text to transcend its internal textual dynamics. One of them is *intertextuality*, defined by Genette as '[…] the actual presence of one text within another' (1997a: 1–2). We suggest, here again, to emphasise the dynamic aspect of this phenomenon. Rather than merely affirming the *presence* of one text within another, we propose to examine and compare the complex *ways* in which a text relates to others.

Another important form of textual transcendence closely linked to intertextuality is the inscription of the utterance into a given genre of discourse, either by conforming to it or subverting it. Todorov has convincingly described this generic inscription as being a socio-cognitive necessity for every speaker (1990: 13–25). To refer to this phenomenon, we suggest using the term *genericity* rather than *genre* (Adam and Heidmann, 2004) which is commonly used as a category label, for instance, *fairy tale*, *novel*, *short story*. As a generic label, it suggests that literary texts essentially *belong* to an established generic category. The more dynamic notion of *genericity* lays focus on the complex *process* by which a text *relates* to generic categories. It also allows us to take into account the fact that many literary texts relate not only to *one*, but simultaneously to *several* existing genres.

A comparative transtextual analysis of Perrault's *La Barbe Bleue* and the Grimms' *Blaubart*, for instance, shows that the French text, which is included in a collection of histories or tales of the past time, borrows characteristics from another popular genre in seventeenth century France, namely the *histoire tragique*, also called *canard sanglant*, while *Blaubart* integrates elements from the German popular *Volkslied* into the *Kinder- und Hausmärchen* (Adam and Heidmann, 2003: 41, 46).

In the case of our written tales, *genericity* is a complex process which involves not only the stages of production, but also of edition and reception-interpretation of texts. A comparison of Perrault's and Grimms' tales shows that it is useful to distinguish the author's conception of genre (*généricité auctoriale*) from the reader's perception (*généricité lectoriale*), which often differs, and then further distinguish these from the editor's generic classification (*généricité éditoriale*) of a literary text (Adam and Heidmann, 2004: 62–63). Considering *genericity* as a dynamic and complex aspect of writing, reading and editing tales enables us to perceive important linguistic, social, historical and cultural *differences* in every corpus of written tales, as the following study of Perrault's and Carter's texts aims to demonstrate.

3.2 Paratextual and coextual dimensions

Genericity also closely interacts with other transtextual dimensions, such as *paratextuality*. According to Genette (1997b), the *paratext* '[…] marks those elements which lie on the threshold of the text and which help to direct and control the reception of a text by its readers' (Allen, 2000: 103). As Graham Allen explains, the paratext is the sum of the *peritext* (titles, prefaces, notes on the threshold of the text etc.), and the *epitext* (interviews, letters etc. outside the text in question). Perrault's *Histoires ou contes du temps passé.*

Avec des Moralités and Grimms' *Kinder- und Hausmärchen* give crucial information concerning their complex genericity and meaning of the tales through the choice of titles, prefaces and notes and other paratextual elements (Adam and Heidmann, 2003: 42–44). Carter's choice of *The Fairy Tales of Charles Perrault* as the title for her first collection, and *Sleeping Beauty and Other Favourite Fairy Tales* for her second collection, must be understood as signalling an important generic transformation of Perrault's *Histoires ou contes du temps passé*, which were called *Contes de fées* in later editions only by the editors (Adam and Heidmann, 2004: 64–65). Interesting information on both texts' complex *genericity* could also be gleaned by the comparative analysis of Perrault's dedicatory preface and Carter's comments in 'About the Stories' (1982: 125–128).

Another transtextual dimension (not mentioned by Genette) plays an important role in the *genericity* of written tales, although it is rarely taken into account, namely their particular position in the collection of tales, or in the book we read them in. We suggest calling this dimension *cotextual* (Adam and Heidmann, 2004: 69). The way the author or the editor composes a volume of tales, selects some of them or changes the order in which they are presented, has an impact on the idea of the genre conveyed to the reader and determines the meaning given to the tales themselves. In Carter's *Sleeping Beauty and Other Favourite Fairy Tales*, 'Bluebeard' is the fourth and 'The Fairies' the seventh in a series of twelve tales. Two of them, 'The Foolish Wishes' and 'Donkey-Skin' are taken from the collection containing a *nouvelle* inspired by Boccaccio ('Griselidis') and two *contes* written in verse and published by Perrault in 1695. The different cotextuality of this earlier volume, as well as its different paratexts, convey a quite different idea of the *conte* as a literary genre rather than the collection of prose tales published under his son's name in 1697. Two other tales in Carter's collection, 'Sweetheart' and 'Beauty and the Beast', are translated from Madame Le Prince de Beaumont's *Magasin des enfans, ou dialogues entre une sage Gouvernante et plusieurs de ses Elèves*, published in London in 1756, which reflect still other generic conventions of the fairy tale in the eighteenth century. Angela Carter's juxtaposition of Perrault's and de Beaumont's tales in her own new collection of *Favourite Fairy Tales*, addressed to modern children, thus creates another and different kind of *genericity*, as the close reading of her translations from Perrault will illustrate. Figure 7.1 below illustrates the various kinds of dynamic transtextual dimensions which have been discussed.

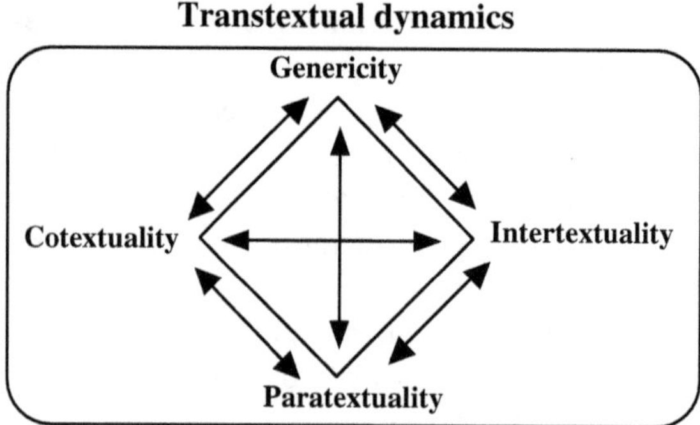

Figure 7.1: Dynamic and interacting transtextual dimensions

4 The meaning of written tales

So then, according to our discursive concept of text, the meaning of written tales is generated by this complex interaction of textual forces such as thematic-semantic configuration, textual composition and micro-linguistic texture, with text-*transcending* forces such as genericity, intertextuality, paratextuality and cotextuality. The literature of written tales informed by folklorists' research on oral tales tends to neglect the textual and transtextual dimensions, precisely what we see as crucial for their meaning and interpretation. Folklore studies put the main focus on the examination of motifs and themes, i.e. on the thematic contents of the tales, but fail to take into account the specific context of their utterance, let alone their textual and transtextual strategies. We argue that the complex meaning of a written tale is produced by the specific linguistic, textual and discursive *articulation* of the chosen motifs and themes, while folklore studies often assume that the meaning of a tale is simply inherent in a universal grammar of motifs and symbols.

Important research on the socio-historical and ideological context of written tales in Europe and America has been carried out in the last three decades by Jack Zipes (1979, 1983, 2000), Marina Warner (1995), Maria Tatar (1987, 1992), Donald Haase (1993), and other scholars. We entirely share their idea that the motifs and themes of tales need to be analysed in relation to the historical and ideological context of their production and reception. However, our approach puts a stronger focus on the linguistic, textual and transtextual dimensions of the written tale. Indeed, we think that micro-linguistic and (trans)textual discourse analysis can reveal complex discursive strategies and implicit meanings that cannot be perceived through the analysis of themes alone.

4.1 Differential comparison and translation

Before exemplifying the method as outlined above, we still need to consider some epistemological principles of comparison as a specific heuristic tool for textual discourse analysis. It is crucial not only for the process but also for the results of comparative and (trans)textual discourse analysis to recognise the importance of *difference* (Heidmann, 2003, 2005). Most comparative studies on myths and fairy tales tend to neglect differences, as they privilege thematic similarities in order to establish a supposedly universal meaning for the tale or myth in question. It is certainly interesting to discover that narratives from all over the world use similar motifs and themes, and this phenomenon was extensively studied in the nineteenth and twentieth centuries. However, we propose to show instead that, *in spite of* thematic similarities, each narrative is fundamentally different, and also to discuss the significance and implications of these differences. From the heuristic point of view, *differential* comparison is productive, insofar as differentiation is an important principle in the development of languages, literatures and cultures (Heidmann, 2005).

The following comparative analysis mainly explores questions of *genericity* and *intertextual dynamics* in Angela Carter's translations of Perrault's *La Barbe Bleue* (*Bluebeard*) and *Les Fées* (*The Fairies*). As we shall see, comparative analysis of generic and intertextual aspects involve textual dimensions, such as the configuration of motifs, as well as stylistic and narrative aspects. From the discursive point of view, a text and its translation can be considered as two different utterances, produced in different contexts. As each text is significantly linked to its own specific linguistic, social and cultural context, the original text and the translation necessarily produce different meanings. In her book on theory and interpretation, Silvana Borutti highlights the epistemological importance of translation. She points out (referring to Maurice Blanchot), that translation is enactment of *difference* ('la traduction est mise en œuvre de la différence', 2001: 69) and *symbolic displacement* ('déplacement symbolique', 2001: 71). The following analysis will, we believe, entirely confirm her arguments.

4.2 From 'La Barbe Bleue' to 'Bluebeard'

Perrault inscribes the story of Bluebeard into the system of genres current in the socio-cultural context of the late seventeenth century (Adam and Heidmann, 2003) and does this through a complex operation on its genericity. When Angela Carter translates Perrault's book, she does something similar. She adapts the French *Histoires ou conte du temps passé* to the late twentieth century English context by subtly modifying its generic orientations and thus transforming it into a *fairy tale* for modern readers. Carter carries out this generic reorientation by means of specific choices in translation. She creates a homogeneous voice and a fluent narration which clearly differs from Perrault's narrator, who is known to interrupt the flow of narration by commenting on it, as the following passage shows:

> D'abord elle ne vit rien, parce que les fenêtres étaient fermées; après quelques moments elle commença à voir que le plancher était couvert de sang caillé, et que dans ce sang se miraient les corps de plusieurs femmes mortes et attachées le long des murs (c'étaient toutes les femmes que la Barbe bleue avait épousées et qu'il avait égorgées l'une après l'autre). (Perrault, 1967: 125)

> *Our literal translation*: At first she did not see anything, because the windows were shut; after some moments she began to perceive that the floor was covered with clotted blood and that in this blood were reflected the bodies of several dead women, ranged against the wall (these were all the wives whom Blue Beard had married and murdered, one after the other).

Angela Carter translates the first sentence by re-establishing the chronological order of the narrated facts: 'The windows were shuttered, and at first she could see nothing; but, after a few moments, her eyes grew accustomed to the gloom, and she saw that the floor was covered with clotted blood' (Carter, 1991: 35). Instead of Perrault's explanatory parentheses, Carter's narrator simply integrates the explanation directly into the description of what the young woman sees: 'In the blood lay the corpses of all the women whom Bluebeard had married and then murdered, one after the other' (1991: 35). Perrault's extra-diegetic comment becomes a descriptive piece of information integrated into the narrative and the temporality of the action. While the narrative voice and the fictional universe are distinct in Perrault, in Carter's translation these are conflated.

It is striking that Carter suppresses the macabre image of the bloody mirror in her translation. This is surely not an oversight, as she uses every potentially macabre motif when, two years later, she rewrites Perrault's *La Barbe Bleue* as *The Bloody Chamber* (1979), reworking it as a typically Anglo-Saxon genre: the Gothic tale. The omission of the mirror of blood in this one of her *Favourite Fairy Tales* could, therefore, be understood as a deliberate generic choice.

The same applies to the famous phrase 'car la clé était Fée'. In Perrault's text, the explanation is not put in parentheses, but inserted in a similar way between two commas in a long sentence: '[…] il y demeura toujours du sang, car la clé était Fée, et il n'y avait pas moyen de la nettoyer tout à fait […]' (1967: 125). Trying to get as close as possible to the original text, we translate:

'[…] the blood still remained, for the key was magic, and there was no means to clean it entirely.'

Carter's narrator again turns the information contained in the explanatory comment into a descriptive statement: 'It was a magic key and nothing could clean it' (1991: 36). This casual observation suggests that the magic element is in no way surprising and extraordinary in a *fairy tale*.

We find a similar simplification in her translation of the following passage:

> Lorsqu'elle fut seule, elle appela sa sœur, et lui dit: Ma sœur Anne (car elle s'appelait ainsi), monte, je te prie, sur le haut de la Tour, pour voir si mes frères ne viennent point; […] (1967: 126).

> *Our literal translation*: When she was alone she called out to her sister, and said to her: 'Sister Anne' (for that was her name) 'go up, I beg you, upon the top of the tower, to see if my brothers are not coming;' […]

Perrault's almost comic insistence on the name of Bluebeard's wife's sister, repeated altogether ten times, can be read as alluding to Virgil's description of *Anna soror* in the fourth book of the *Eneid*. This unexpected intertextual reference to Virgil in the book of one of the main defenders of the Moderns can be understood as being parodic when re-placed in the historical context of the quarrel between the *Anciens* and the *Modernes* (Adam and Heidmann, 2003: 44–45). Carter suppresses, here again, the parenthetical explanation and simply translates: 'As soon as she was alone, she called to her sister, Anne, and said: "Sister Anne, climb to the top of the tower and see if my brothers are coming; […]"'(1991: 37). This matter-of-fact introduction of the character of Anne draws attention to the strangeness of the device used by Perrault at this point and thus exemplifies the role of the stylistic variation involved in the translation process. By simplifying the sentence, Carter also suppresses the scholarly intertextual reference inaccessible to the young readers of this favourite fairy tale.

4.3 From 'Les Fées to 'The Fairies': the treatment of magical action

Angela Carter makes similar choices in her translation of *Les Fées*. The comparison between the French and English texts clearly shows that Perrault foregrounds the social and human action of the tale, while Carter highlights magic as she transforms it into a *favourite fairy tale*.

In Perrault's *Les Fées*, the narrator clearly focuses on the discrimination of the youngest daughter, who is repeatedly referred to as 'cette pauvre enfant' (*this poor girl*) or 'cette belle fille' (*this beautiful girl*). The young daughter is abused by the widow, whom Perrault's narrator insistently designates by 'cette mère' (*this mother*). Carter omits the anaphoric repetition of the deictic. She translates 'cette mère' by *the widow*, 'cette pauvre enfant' by the simple pronoun *she*, and 'cette belle fille' by *the lovely girl*. However, she significantly chooses to use the deictic when the magic event takes place, namely when the fairy appears. Moreover, she puts added emphasis on the magical action by inserting the word *now*, which is absent from Perrault's narrative:

> Now, this old woman was really a fairy who had assumed the form of a poor peasant in order to test the girl's good heart. As soon as she finished her drink, she said: 'You are so beautiful, so good and so kind that I feel I must give you a special present. My fairy gift is this: at each word you say, either a flower or else a precious stone will fall out of your mouth'. (1991: 64)

Now is surely used here as a marker of orality, but it may also signal a strong shift in the diegesis: the precise moment when the old woman becomes a fairy. It is noteworthy that the translator goes so far as to invert the order of the sentences to put more emphasis on the magical action. She introduces the speech of the fairy by insisting on the fact that she was *really* a fairy, whereas Perrault gives this explanation only afterwards, by inserting it into one of those parenthetical comments he also uses in *La Barbe Bleue*, as we have seen before:

> La bonne femme, ayant bu, lui dit: 'Vous êtes si belle, si bonne, et si honnête, que je ne puis m'empêcher de vous faire un don (car c'était une Fée qui avait pris la forme d'une pauvre femme de village, pour voir jusqu'ou irait l'honnêteté de cette jeune fille.) Je vous donne pour don, poursuivit la Fée, qu'à chaque parole que vous direz il vous sortira de la bouche ou une Fleur, ou une Pierre précieuse'. (1967: 148)

> *Our literal translation* : You are so beautiful, so good and so honest, that I cannot help giving you a gift (for this was a Fairy, who had taken the form of a poor country-woman, to see how far the good manners of this young girl would go.) I will give you for gift, continued the Fairy, that at every word you speak, there shall come out of your mouth either a Flower or a Jewel.

As Carter shifts the narrative focus onto the magical action, she subtly changes the genre of Perrault's texts. Her reworking of the motifs strengthens this generic transposition. In Perrault's *Moralités*, whose order Carter inverts, she translates 'les Diamants et les Pistoles, Peuvent beaucoup sur les Esprits' (1967: 149) with 'Diamonds and pearls make powerful impressions' (1991: 68). She thus replaces Perrault's explicit allusion to the exchange value of coins (*pistoles*) by the more fairy-tale-like and historically unmarked element of the 'pearls'.

4.4 Carter's intertextual dialogue with Perrault

The intentional modification of certain motifs in the process of translation leads us to the question of the intertextual relations between the two texts. Carter translates Perrault's repeatedly used word 'don' (*gift*) in various ways. She translates 'je ne puis m'empêcher de vous faire un don' (1967: 147) (*I cannot help giving you a gift*) with 'I feel I must give you a special present' (1991: 64). Having strengthened Perrault's *don* with the adjective *special*, she changes Perrault's 'Je vous donne pour don' (1967: 148) (*I give you as a gift*) into 'My fairy gift is this' (1991: 64). Through the addition of *fairy* she makes explicit that the gift is special *because* it is magical (*fairy gift*), while this is not specified by Perrault, who repeats once again the same word *don*.

In another passage, the mother asks her favourite daughter: 'ne seriez-vous pas bien aise d'avoir le même *don*?' (1967: 148) (*wouldn't you be pleased to have the same gift?*). Carter again takes a significant liberty as she translates: 'Wouldn't you like to be the same?' (1991: 65). She thus transforms the object into a personal and inner moral quality, a process that becomes even more explicit in the rest of the text.

In the next-to-last sentence, and with a particular insistence on that same word, Perrault writes:

> Le fils du Roi en devint amoureux, et considérant qu'un tel don valait mieux que tout ce qu'on pouvait donner en mariage à un autre, l'emmena au Palais du Roi son père, où il l'épousa. (1967: 149)

> *Our literal translation*: The King's son fell in love with her, and considering that such a gift was worth more than any dowry one could give to someone, conducted her to the Palace of the King his father, where he married her.

Carter translates the sentence with 'The prince was charmed with her and decided that her remarkable talent was worth more than the dowry of any princess in the world; he took her to the palace of the king, his father, and married her' (1991: 68). This transformation of the magical gift into a personal quality contrasts with Perrault's text, which ironically underlines, in the sentence quoted above, the *monetary* value of the gift that eventually earns the poor, victimised maiden a princely wedding. This shift from the gift of fortune into a *talent* reflects the modern narrator's cultural standpoint. Indeed, it is difficult to write today that a girl should purchase a prince by means of a dowry, or be rewarded for her obedience. Here, this idea is replaced by one which is more consistent with Carter's feminism, namely that her talents, which a fairy has made more conspicuous to the eyes of others, will help a maiden to be loved.

5   In closing

Comparative analysis thus shows that literary translation takes the form of an intertextual dialogue. As her reworking of the motif of the gift demonstrates, Angela Carter initiates a critical-creative dialogue with Perrault's text by disclosing and questioning the monetary value of the gift of speech (already ironised by Perrault). In an important essay, where she reflects on her relationships with her literary predecessors, Carter encapsulates the nature of her dialogue with Perrault in a metaphor that gives the measure of her temperament:

> Reading is just as creative an activity as writing and most intellectual development depends upon new readings of old texts. I am all for putting new wine in old bottles, especially if the pressure of the new wine makes the old bottles explode. (1983: 37)

From the discursive and comparative perspective, *intertextuality* can thus be considered as an *intertextual dialogue*, as the dialogic phenomenon is identified and studied by the members of the Bakhtin circle. The terms *dialogue* or *dialogism* emphasise, as does *genericity*, in opposition to *genre*, the dynamic role played by this process in the construction and understanding of meaning. This term also suggests, and this is very important for comparison, the *non-*hierarchical relationship between two utterances, and therefore a relationship between two speakers in which neither dominates, but where both communicate, dialogically.

The dialogic nature of literary translation confirms the idea of the dialogic nature of all literature, as pointed out by Bakhtin. Comparative and (trans)textual discourse analysis is ultimately meant to reveal the complexity and the semantic density of this dialogue between languages, literatures and cultures.

Notes

1   Some of the issues presented here are developed in more detail in an essay on the use of close reading and differential comparison for Comparative Literature as a discipline (Heidmann, 2005). We dearly thank our friend and colleague Martine Hennard Dutheil de la Rochère for her comments and corrections of this essay.

2   These notions are presented in Aucouturier's French translation, as 'contenu thematique, style et construction compositionnelle' (Bakhtin, 1984: 265).

3   For a precise description of the terms used by Genette, see Graham Allen's very informed book on intertextuality (2000: 97–115), where he describes how the idea of intertextuality has been taken up in different theoretical movements by Kristeva, Barthes, Riffaterre and others. In Adam and Heidmann (2003: 40–48), we discuss the use of Genette's terms for comparative

discourse analysis, relinquishing his category of *architextualité*, while high-lighting *para- and péritextualité.*

4   For a more detailed discussion of the concept of language that underlies the definition of discourse, see Heidmann (2005).

5   Concerning the history and term of the 'fairy tale', see Gillian Avery's excellent article on British and Irish Fairy Tales in *The Oxford Companion to Fairy Tales* (in Zipes, 2000: 66–78.)

References

Adam, J.-M. (2003) Postface. In U. Heidmann (ed.) *Poétiques comparées des mythes. De l'Antiquité à la Modernité* 243–256. Lausanne: Payot.

Adam, J.-M. and Heidmann, U. (2002) Réarranger des motifs, c'est changer le sens. Princesses et petits pois chez Andersen et Grimm. In A. Petitat (ed.) *Contes: l'universel et le singulier* 155–174. Lausanne: Payot.

Adam, J.-M. and Heidmann, U. (2003) Discursivité et (trans)textualité: la comparaison pour méthode. L'exemple du conte. In R. Amossy and D. Maingueneau (eds) *L'analyse du discours dans les études littéraires* 29–49. Toulouse: Presses Universitaires du Mirail.

Adam, J.-M. and Heidmann, U. (2004) Des genres à la généricité. L'exemple des contes (Perrault et Grimm). *Langages* 153: 62–72.

Allen, G. (2000) *Intertextuality.* London and New York: Routledge.

Bakhtin, M. M. (1924 [1990]) Supplement: the problem of content, material, and form in verbal art. In M. Holquist and V. Liapunov (eds) *Art and Answerability. Early Philosophical Essays by M. M. Bakhtin* 257–325. Austin: University of Texas Press.

Bakhtin, M. M. (1984) *Esthétique de la création verbale.* Paris: Gallimard.

Bakhtin, M. M. (1986) *Speech Genres & Other Late Essays.* C. Emerson and M. Holquist (eds) V. W. McGee (trans.). Austin: University of Texas Press.

Benveniste, E. (1981) The semiology of language. *Semiotica: Special Supplement* 5–23.

Borutti, S. (2001) *Théorie et interprétation. Pour une épistémologie des sciences humaines.* Lausanne: Payot.

Carter, A. (trans. and foreword) (1977) *The Fairy Tales of Charles Perrault.* M. Ware (illustrations). London: Victor Gollancz Limited.

Carter, A. (1979 [1995]) *The Bloody Chamber and Other Stories.* London: Vintage.

Carter, A. (trans.) (1982 [1991]) *Sleeping Beauty and Other Favourite Fairy Tales.* M. Foreman (illustrations). London: Victor Gollancz Limited.

Carter, A. (1983) Notes from the front line. In A. Carter *Shaking a Leg: Collected Journalism and Writings* 36–43. London: Vintage.

Genette, G. (1997a) *Palimpsests: Literature in the Second Degree.* C. Newman and C. Doubinsky (trans.). Lincoln, Ne. and London: University of Nebraska Press.

Genette, G. (1997b) *Paratexts*: *Thresholds of Interpretation*. J. E. Lewin (trans.). Cambridge: Cambridge University Press.

Haase, D. (1993) Yours, mine, or ours? Perrault, the Brothers Grimm and the ownership of fairy tales. In M. Tatar (ed.) *The Classic Fairy Tales. Texts and Criticism* 353–364. New York and London: Norton & Company.

Heidmann, U. (2003) Préface; and (Ré)écritures anciennes et modernes des mythes: la comparaison pour méthode. L'exemple d'Orphée. In U. Heidmann (ed.) *Poétiques comparées des mythes. De l'Antiquité à la Modernité* 5–13; 47–65. Lausanne: Payot.

Heidmann, U. (2005) Comparatisme et analyse de discours. La comparaison différentielle comme méthode. In J.-M. Adam and U. Heidmann (eds) *Sciences du texte et analyse des discours. Enjeux d'une interdisciplinarité* 99–118. Geneva: Slatkine.

Jakobson, R. (1973) *Questions de poétique*. Paris: Seuil.

Perrault, C. (1967) *Contes de Perrault*. G. Rouger (ed.) Paris: Garnier Frères.

Tatar, M. (1987) *The Hard Facts of the Grimms' Fairy Tales*. Princeton: Princeton University Press.

Tatar, M. (1992) *Off with Their Heads. Fairy Tales and the Culture of Childhood*. Princeton: Princeton University Press.

Todorov, T. (1984) *Mikhail Bakhtin: The Dialogical Principle*. W. Godzich (trans.). Manchester and New York: Manchester University Press.

Todorov, T. (1990) *Genres in Discourse*. C. Porter (trans.). Cambridge: Cambridge University Press.

Warner, M. (1995) *From the Beast to the Blonde*: *On Fairy Tales and Their Tellers*. New York: Ferrar, Straus and Giroux.

Zipes, J. (1979) *Breaking the Magic Spell*: *Radical Theories of Folk and Fairy Tales*. Austin: University of Texas Press.

Zipes, J. (1983) *Fairy Tales and the Art of Subversion*: *The Classical Genre for Children and the Process of Civilisation*. London: Heinemann.

Zipes, J. (ed.) (2000) *The Oxford Companion to Fairy Tales*. Oxford: Oxford University Press.

8 Translation teaching and methodology: a linguistic analysis of a literary text

Mirella Agorni

Catholic University of the Sacred Heart of Milan

Editors' Introduction

Mirella Agorni has a PhD in Translation Studies from the University of Warwick, UK, and has published widely in the field. Her research concentrates predominantly on literary translation, and focuses on translation theory and both the history and teaching of translation. In this paper, she manages to bring together these diverse strands into one coherent and convincing whole.

Like the preceding, her paper is also about the translation of verbal art. It is also about, however, the teaching of such translation. It should be said that the position Agorni takes towards the status of literature vis-à-vis that of any other text type is very much an 'on the one hand, and on the other' one. In short, on one hand she would underwrite Hatim and Mason's opinion concerning the dangers of '[…] creating artificial boundaries amongst translation activities'. As they do, she would stress what it is that diverse acts of communication have in common and see literature as being simply another one of these. On the other hand, however, she readily admits that the relationship between text producer and receiver in the case of the literary text is often much more intricate, especially when there is not simply linguistic and cultural distance between these, but also a temporal distance that makes the translator's task of mediation an exceedingly challenging one. This is not to say that Agorni wants things both ways, as much as to point out the complexities of the issue itself.

Complexity, of course, is also inherent in the issues surrounding the question of which methodology is best for both translating, and teaching translation. Agorni makes it clear from the start that she sees an inextricable interrelationship between theory and practice, recognising the role that research on translation, but also research on translation teaching and training, is playing today in the modelling of theory. That is to say, that the models being generated within the 'applied' area can actually be seen to be dialoguing with, and even exerting a specific influence on, the theoretical and descriptive branches of the discipline. This is an innovation that she does not limit herself to acknowledging, but also quite clearly applauds.

As far as her own methodological preference is concerned, she argues for what she calls a 'comparative' approach, in place of the 'contrastive' one that, she says, has recently come under scrutiny. The reasons for her choice are also interconnected. In the first place, she argues that the method is better able to collaborate with an interest in the reception of translated texts and a belief in translation as more properly belonging to the target (rather than to the source) culture. Secondly, this comparative method pairs more satisfactorily with a conception of the translation as being at least a partially autonomous text, and the translator as playing a fundamental mediating role in its making. Hence, her refusal to see divergences between Source Text (ST) and Target Text (TT) as 'losses' which could somehow have been avoided with a 'better' translation. Indeed, the method seems to be particularly useful to the translation of literary texts and the vital mediation performed by their translators. It achieves an even-handed emphasis, on one side, on the degree of freedom they enjoy, as well as, on the other, the responsibility they are called to.

But what does the comparative method more precisely consist in, and how does it differ from the contrastive method? The comparative analysis Agorni illustrates here is based mainly on Toury's descriptive methodology (1995). This focuses on the 'problems' encountered in the process of translating, but also on the *relationship* between the ST choices and strategies which analysis identifies and those which may best function in the TT. It stresses the translator-analyst's *linguistic and cultural mediation between* the two texts, rather than merely privileging the ST, and the, as Agorni puts it, '[…] problems which may (or may not) turn up in the process of translating' it. In this way, students are made aware that translation is a decision-*making* process, and that their role as translators needs to be a very active one indeed.

1   The role of a comparative methodology in translation teaching

Research in the field of translation teaching has grown enormously in the last ten years, although the importance of this area within the discipline of Translation Studies as a whole is still a matter for debate for many scholars (Toury, 1995; Venuti, 1998).

Indeed, recent approaches, particularly those belonging to the linguistic area of translation, have emphasised the mutual dependence, rather than the autonomy, of the three branches of translation initially described by James Holmes (1988), that is, the theoretical, descriptive *and* applied areas (see, e.g., Baker, 1992; Hatim and Mason, 1997; House, 1997).[1] This development has even influenced approaches which do not focus specifically on translation teaching. Gideon Toury, for example, has been shaping the descriptive perspective of the field for more than ten years. His recent publications have developed the concept of 'norms' and investigated the ways in which they are acquired in translation, recognising the fundamental role that research on translation teaching and translator training is playing in this respect. This is evidence of the fact that the models generated within the 'applied' area are not only closely connected to the theoretical and descriptive branches of the discipline, but have also grown and spread widely, to the point of being able to exert a specific influence on them.

The analysis of translation, which is a basic component of most translation classes, particularly when students are asked to work into what is the students' second language, is a clear example of the way in which translation teaching is taking an active part in the dialogue with the theoretical and descriptive areas. As a matter of fact, traditional *contrastive* analysis of the Source Text (i.e. a detailed discursive, pragmatic and linguistic examination of ST features, usually followed by individual or group translation into the Target language) has come under close scrutiny in recent years. This new development, in fact, is part of a general trend towards considering translation as a phenomenon more properly belonging to the Target culture, a trend which has created a new interest in the reception of translated texts. Both scholars who adopt a linguistics-oriented approach (Hatim and Mason, 1997; Baker, 1992; House, 1997; Snell-Hornby, 1988) *and* those opting for a more literary or cultural-oriented perspective (Toury, 1980, 1995; Bassnett, 1980, 1997; Bassnett and Lefevere, 1998; Hermans, 1985) are involved in this tendency. The tendency is not restricted to the field of Translation Studies. For example, Linguistics has for years been registering a shift away from the analysis of abstract non-authentic structures, in order to focus on the distinctive functional features of contextualised communicative events. However, questions of evaluation, reception and the effects of texts on readers in the real world are of interest to Translation Studies as well as Linguistics.[2]

Traditional contrastive analysis has given way to a new model in recent years, one which I will define here as a *comparative* analysis, also often adopted by those translation teachers who are not deliberately working within a specific theoretical perspective. Rather than focus only on the ST, and examine the abstract problems which may (or may not) turn up in the process of translating (as *contrastive* analysis does), this new framework emphasises the importance of the relationship between the ST and TT, in order to work on the concrete, specific problems which have emerged in the doing of a given translation. The detailed comparison between the ST and TT brings to the fore not only the 'unique' difficulties involved in a particular translation, but also an array of choices, strategies and alternative solutions. In this way, students are made aware that translation is *de facto* a decision-making process, and that their role as translators must be a very active one.

The role of the translator has indeed become a central issue in Translation Studies. However, long before Lawrence Venuti's campaign for translators' 'visibility' (1995, 1998), Susan Bassnett had worked on the notion of 'gain' as opposed to 'loss' in the process of translating (1980). In her opinion, translators have the possibility of improving the ST, for example by 'activating' meanings which were only, so to speak, 'between-the-lines' in the original. Bassnett's approach is a radical move against the traditional concept of translation as a faithful reproduction of the original: given the impossibility for a TT to be a flawless copy of its ST, differences have traditionally been interpreted as 'losses', and often as somehow due to the shortcomings of the translator. On the other hand, if a translation is conceived of as a (partially) autonomous text, belonging to a specific cultural context and aimed at a readership which does not correspond to that of the original, the fundamental mediating role of translators logically comes to the fore.

The comparative analysis I would like to introduce and illustrate here is based mainly on Toury's descriptive methodology (1995). Such an approach focuses on the 'problems' encountered in the process of translating; these are reconstructed retrospectively by the analyst, who works comparatively on the ST and TT. Toury's definition of the 'coupled pair of replacing + replaced segments' (1995: 87–89) is applied to the TT and ST segments representing, respectively, a specific 'problem' and its 'solution', which are exemplified by a particular translation. Toury makes clear that '[…] the two should be conceived of as determining each other in a mutual way' (1995: 77), the only principle for their definition being that '[…] beyond the boundaries of a target textual segment no leftovers of the 'solution' to a certain 'problem', posed by a corresponding segment of the source text, will be present' (1995: 89). This means that the translation has to be mapped methodically onto the ST, examining in its entirety any solution to a translation problem raised by a segment of the ST (according to Toury's 'no leftovers'). Rather than being based on a *prospective* analysis of the ST alone, coupled segments are identified in a close, *retrospective* comparative reading of the ST and TT, which brings to light the specific strategies and solutions adopted in a given translation.

This type of comparative analysis can of course be applied to a large variety of texts, but here, given the theme of this volume, I shall apply it to the translation of a literary text. Many scholars have dealt with the specificity of literary translation (Bassnett, 1980, 1997; Boase-Beier and Holman, 1999; Bush and Malmkjær, 1998). According to Hatim and Mason, however, this is one of those concerns which run the risk of creating artificial boundaries amongst translation activities. Rather than 'splitting' translation into clear-cut compartments, they prefer working on common features and concerns, as can be inferred from their definition of translation as '[…] an act of communication which attempts to relay, across cultural and linguistic boundaries, another act of communication (which may have been intended for different purposes and different readers/hearers)' (1997: 1). Literature too can be considered a communicative act, as a text producer and a text receiver are brought together through the act of reading. This relationship, admittedly, is more complex in the case of a translation of a literary text, as the greater linguistic and cultural (and oftentimes temporal) distance between the ST and TT entails the risk of creating a fracture in the communicative process. The task of the translator is to provide the necessary mediation, so as to bring the process to a successful conclusion.

Discourse analysis has amply demonstrated that both literary and non-literary texts share a large variety of linguistic devices (Fowler, 1986): the specificity of the literary text appears to be a question of degree, rather than of kind. Be that as it may, and allowing for the 'distance' mentioned above, I support Hatim and Mason's position on the issue, as it pays special attention to the ways in which language is creatively bent to the service of translation, to ways which cut across discourse genres, or text types. In other words, as they say:

> We are interested in the signals that text producers send to text receivers about the way they view the world, in the way meaning is inferred beyond the words-on-the-page, so to say, and how the resources of language users for doing this kind of thing transcend any artificial boundaries between different fields of translating. (1997: 7)

2   The texts

At this point, I will introduce an example of comparative analysis applied to a literary text.

2.1 The ST: 'Mary takes the better part'

This is an extract from a collection of short stories by Marina Warner, *The Mermaids in the Basement* (1993: 21–23). The authors of the translation are Dr Loredana Polezzi (Department of Italian, Warwick University, UK) and myself.

> I found the broken plate in the cupboard. I was stacking too many dishes on top of it and I heard the crack. It was a clean break and the plate was porcelain, always easier to mend than earthenware – its grain is so fine. There was a little heap of other things, a teacup handle, a brooch with its clip off. So I gathered up these bits and pieces, and, spreading a newspaper on a chair in the kitchen, began mending.

> I like glue. I usually use quick-drying, but the last time I was in the ironmonger's the young man told me slow-dry was more reliable, and I took his advice. The tubes and their tops were colour-coded, so that I shouldn't stick the wrong tops on the wrong tubes after using them the first time. His fingers were like spanners, flat and square; his arms were as strong as jemmies, with the sleeves of his overalls pushed up and a name bracelet 'Darrell' showing.

> I squeezed out equal amounts of the white and then the yellow, and mixed them with a match. The glue coated the end of the little stick immediately in a viscous cocoon. The plate was a pretty, scalloped one my father had given me. It's painted a beautiful cobalt, with birds of paradise in the centre in rose and green and freely decorated in gold around the edge. It had broken in three pieces, cracking from the centre where the dishes had weighed on it. I smeared the edges and brought the two larger pieces together. They made contact, but there was a rift; I pushed the opposite way; the rift became a hairline. The glue oozed up under pressure.

> The way china fits, even after a break, is so satisfying. It's a surprise to me, too, each time that it does so, that there hasn't been any loss of chips or powder, that even while breaking, the integrity of the object somehow remains, undiminished. And that's not something that you can fake, I thought as I squeezed the plate. (With the slow glue, I soon realized, you need patience; the tackiness that makes mending with rapid epoxy a race against time takes longer to develop.) I sat holding the pieces as tightly together as possible, waiting.

2.2 The TT: 'Maria si prende la parte migliore'

Trovai il piatto rotto nella credenza. Stavo accatastandovi sopra troppe stoviglie, e sentii lo schiocco. Era una spaccatura netta ed il piatto era di porcellana, sempre più semplice da aggiustare della terracotta – la grana è così fine. C'era un mucchietto di altri oggetti da rincollare, il manico di una tazza, una spilla da cui si era staccata la chiusura. Così presi pezzi e pezzettini e, con un giornale steso su una sedia da cucina, iniziai ad aggiustarli.

Mi piace la colla. Di solito uso quella a pronta presa, ma l'ultima volta che sono stata dal ferramenta il ragazzo mi ha detto che quella lenta è più sicura, e mi sono fidata del consiglio. I tubetti ed i tappi erano tutti coordinati per colore, mi ha fatto notare il ragazzo, in modo che non infilassi i tappi sbagliati sui tubetti sbagliati dopo averli usati per la prima volta. Aveva dita come chiavi inglesi, piatte e quadrate; le braccia erano forti come piedi di porco, con le maniche della tuta arrotolate ed un braccialetto col nome 'Darrell' in bella vista.

Spremetti quantità uguali di colla bianca e poi gialla e mescolai con un fiammifero. La colla subito ricoprì la punta dello stecchino con un bozzolo vischioso. Era un bel piatto, smerlato, che mi aveva dato mio padre. E' dipinto in un bellissimo blu cobalto con al centro degli uccelli del paradiso rosa e verde e un'abbondante decorazione in oro sul bordo. Si era rotto in tre pezzi, spaccandosi dal centro, dove si era concentrato il peso delle stoviglie. Cosparsi i bordi di colla e misi insieme i due pezzi più grossi. Si toccavano, ma c'era uno spiraglio. Feci pressione nella direzione opposta, e lo spiraglio divenne un'incrinatura sottile. La colla trasudò lentamente sotto la pressione.

Il modo in cui la porcellana combacia, anche dopo essersi rotta, è particolarmente gratificante. E mi sorprende anche, ogni volta che accade, che non ci sia alcuna perdita di schegge o di polvere, e che, anche rompendosi in qualche modo, l'integrità dell'oggetto si conservi, intatta. E questa non è una cosa che si possa fingere, pensai mentre stringevo il piatto. (Con la colla a presa lenta mi sono presto resa conto, ci vuole pazienza; la viscosità che trasforma l'aggiustare qualcosa con un collante rapido in una corsa contro il tempo, ci mette di più a formarsi.) Mi sedetti tenendo i pezzi il più possibile stretti l'uno contro l'altro, in attesa.

3   Macro-textual analysis

I shall concentrate mainly on syntactic problems in this analysis, although a more detailed examination of lexis would also be extremely productive in the case of this text, i.e. closely investigating the rich texture of this extract, which challenges the ability of the translators to deal with idioms, collocations, 'false friends', parallel structures, etc.

The extract is a detailed description of a sequence of actions, interspersed by the thoughts of the narrator in a stream of consciousness mode. The narrator describes a series of everyday events and actions: she finds a broken plate in the kitchen and depicts the process of mending it. Flash-backs and loosely related thoughts break into the narration and create a lack of coherence which could frustrate readers' expectations. In all likelihood these will be centred on the events of the story. The distinctive presence of cataphoric reference patterns creates a certain amount of suspense, paradoxically counterbalanced by the ordinary, familiar setting in which the events take place.

> Ex. **Par. 1**: 'the broken plate'/'il piatto rotto'. This is an example of a marked use of the definite article in the opening paragraph of the narrative in the ST, in the absence of any co-textual or contextual information which may have helped the reader to clarify the meaning of this referent. It would have been more typical, e.g. to have the indefinite article appear first. Moreover, the plate will be described only in the third paragraph. In this case, the TT aims at reproducing the ST author's choice.

> Ex. **Par. 2**: 'the young man'/'il ragazzo'. The same strategy is used to introduce the young man at the ironmonger's. As can be noticed, once again this cataphoric use of the definite article has been retained in the TT, although the character is being mentioned for the first time. Significantly, his physical characteristics are described in some detail before the reader is even given his name, which appears only at the very end of the sentence.

Generally speaking, this translation attempts wherever possible to reproduce most of the characteristics of the ST from a linguistic point of view. The main difficulty is related to verbal choices. The translator has to create a coherent time-sequence by selecting a tense and aspect that is consistent with a rather complex narrative, characterised by the presence of two different narrative threads: the central story and the flash-backs, or 'loose' thoughts. Obviously, verbs are used in a very different way in the two languages. Translators are usually very sensitive to this kind of problem, and I would like to draw attention to the different strategies adopted in the TT reproduced above.

The actions and events of the story can be narrated either by using the simple past or the present perfect in Italian. Although the simple past is the customary tense of narration, the use of the present perfect can be justified in all those cases in which events are perceived as being closely related to the present. As there are no textual indications of this kind (i.e. no reference to the here-and-now present is to be found in this segment of the story), translators are free to make their own choices.

The text displays what is often thought of as an 'elevated' tone, as it is characterised by a high degree of grammatical parallelism, almost reminiscent of the Bible, but also of orality (see Miller, this volume), which may paradoxically appear to be in contrast with the everyday events being described. Such a tone is the only aspect which links back to the title, 'Mary takes the better part', an allusion to the parable of Martha and Mary. The Italian simple past (which is perceived as a rather formal option in many areas of the North of Italy) appears to be the most suitable choice for such an atypical tone. Translators, however, have to handle the problem of verbs very carefully; they must be aware of the constraints represented by the *consecutio temporum* (sequence of tenses) norms in Italian, so as not to compromise the logic of temporal sequences. Flash-backs are a real challenge in this respect, as they are signalled by a shift in time in the ST. Had the translators opted in this case for using the same verbal tense both in the body of the story and in the flash-backs, they would have been left with no way of stressing that temporal ambiguity which is a fundamental characteristic of the stream of consciousness here. The solution adopted in the TT is to use the simple past for the central story, and the present perfect, together with certain other tenses (present tense, past continuous) to indicate different narrative threads.

4 Micro-textual analysis

4.1 Sentence structure

In the ST, clauses tend to be short and are generally paratactically linked. Instances of coordination among clauses within the sentences are indeed quite frequent. However, this structure is found mainly in those text segments related to the principal plot line, as flash-backs and 'loose' thoughts feature more hypotactic structures (cf. **Par. 1** and **Par. 4**, for example). Such a differentiation allows the author to express the shift of perspective associated with the 'interruptions' of the main narrative thread.

Sentence structure is faithfully reproduced in the TT, which seeks, as said above, to stay with the intention of the original author, by reproducing the characteristics of the ST, clearly only whenever this is acceptable in the Target language. The translators even go so far as to preserve the use of the dash, although this kind of punctuation is not at all typical in Italian (cf. **Par. 1**).

The frequent occurrence of the first person 'I' in thematic position in the ST should also be noted. Obviously, placing the subject at the beginning of the clause is typical of unmarked sentence construction in English. The reiterated Theme here, however, seems to be a strategy to strengthen textual coherence, adding to an illusive simplicity pervading the whole story, and at various levels, i.e. syntax, lexis, but also contents. The flexible syntax of Italian shapes the TT in a considerably different way: it allows for more variety of what in English would be marked thematic elements (as the subject can be, and typically is, omitted).

Some examples of this are:

Par. 1: 'I found', 'I was stacking', 'I heard the crack'/'Trovai', 'Stavo accatastandovi', 'sentii lo schiocco'. Such translators' choices reflect their intention of strengthening TT cohesion, which is obviously different from that of the ST. For example, a small number of verbs have been deliberately moved into thematic position, as below:

Par. 2: 'His fingers were like spanners'/'Aveva dita come chiavi inglesi'. 'Le sue dita erano come chiavi inglesi' would have been another acceptable solution). By beginning this sentence with a verb, the translators succeed in strengthening TT cohesion, as the principal consequence of the frequent omission of the subject in Italian is a high occurrence of verbs in thematic position (cf. especially **Par. 1**). Such a structure conveys the same illusive simplicity as the reiteration of the Theme 'I' does in the ST.

4.2 Verbs

As I have already pointed out, the simple past tense has been used for the narration of the principal events, whereas the present perfect and a number of other tenses (present, past continuous) have been adopted to distinguish the different threads of the narrative.

Par. 1: 'I found'; 'I was stacking'/'Trovai'; 'Stavo accatastandovi'. In the TT, the simple past has been used to follow the thread of the principal events.

'It was a clean break'/'Era una spaccatura netta'. This is an obligatory choice: according to Italian syntactic rules, it is also necessary to use the imperfect tense to describe a state in the past.

'its grain is so fine'/'la grana è così fine'. This is a case of a general, 'timeless' statement, and the present tense is typically used in both languages to construe these.

Par. 2: 'the last time I was'/'l'ultima volta che sono stata'. The introduction of the present perfect in the TT here signals a flash-back and the radical shift of perspective this brings. In this case, verbal tenses are not employed to classify events according to a logical sequencing, but rather to mark an 'interruption' of the main story line.

'after using'/'dopo averli usati'. The TT once again follows the Italian rules for sequence of tenses and constructs the same hypothetical environment within a shift back in time as in the ST.

'His fingers were'; 'his arms were'/'Aveva dita'; 'le braccia erano forti'. The imperfect tense has been used in the TT for the description of the young man's physical features, just as in the English.

Par. 3: 'The plate was pretty'/'era un bel piatto'. As in the previous example, the imperfect tense has been employed in the TT to describe the plate's characteristics.

'It's painted'/'E' dipinto'. The narrative suddenly shifts back to the present to focus on the details of the plate, as these were, and still are. Possibly the Italian translators would have been more consistent if they had used the imperfect tense here, following the strategy adopted in the previous sentence. However, in this case it seemed that a close adherence to the present tense of the ST was the most important criterion, so as to reproduce the choice of the ST author, without violating Italian lexical and grammatical rules, as this gets us into the head of the narrative voice, as a way to represent thought.

Par. 4: 'The way china fits'/'Nel modo in cui la porcellana combacia'. The present tense has been chosen in the TT, and most likely also in the ST, in order to mark the introduction of the protagonist's 'stream of consciousness'.

'I thought as I squeezed'/'pensai mentre stringevo'. Here we go back to the time of the main story line, but the imperfect has been used in the TT hypotactic temporal clause in order to convey a sense of duration, as is typical in Italian.

'I soon realized'/'mi sono presto resa conto'. The present perfect in the TT once again marks the presence of a 'stream of consciousness'.

'that makes mending [...] takes longer'/'che trasforma l'aggiustare [...] ci mette di più'. In this case, both texts register a shift back to the present, due to a timeless general statement.

'I sat'/'Mi sedetti'. This sentence is open to two interpretations: either the narrator is describing the action of sitting down (in this case the TT option 'mi sedetti' would be the correct one), or she is describing her position as she waits, and in this case the imperfect in the TT would be a better solution, as it conveys a sense of duration. In the absence of further contextual and co-textual information, translators are free to choose between these alternatives. But the students must be made aware of these two equally acceptable possibilities, which emerge in the comparative process.

4.3 Style

Although the images and the language of the text are rather evocative, traditional rhetorical devices (figurative language, metaphors, parallel structures, etc., to which I am giving the term 'style') are rare. The style of the extract is deliberately plain, this simplicity being reflected at many linguistic levels, as has been pointed out above (see for example the author's preference for simple sentence construction, everyday words, parallel themes, etc.). However, there are two exceptions.

> **Par. 2**:'his fingers were like spanners', 'his arms were strong as jemmies'/ 'dita come chiavi inglesi', 'le braccia erano forti come piedi di porco'. Of course, both these examples are similes, the simplest form of figurative language, as references here are made explicit.

Notwithstanding what may be seen as a lacklustre simplicity, the text manages to keep the interest of the reader by various means, including opaque cataphoric strategies, right from the start of the extract (when the plate, recall, is introduced by using the definite article). A certain amount of suspense is also created at the intertextual level: the title alludes to the Gospel story of Martha and Mary and in particular to Jesus' words to Martha regarding her sister Mary's preference for sitting still to listen to him, rather than dashing about doing for him, but readers' likely expectations are frustrated throughout the story, as there is no explanation or further allusion to the story in the body of the text. The only clue in this direction is the peculiar tone of the extract (a combination, as said, of simplicity and solemnity). This too influences the translators' selection of verbal tenses, as has been pointed out in the course of analysis.

5 Conclusion

The examples from the texts examined in this article are somewhat limited. A more exhaustive account of the options made in translating would need to take into consideration other aspects, such as the author and her idiolect, as well as all those issues connected with the notion of 'tenor' in a Systemic Functional approach, i.e. to interpersonal meanings (Halliday, 1994), and the attitudinal value of much of the lexis mentioned above.

In addition, a systemic approach (e.g. Hermans, 1999), would focus principally on other issues related to textual production and reception. In other words, what position does this text occupy within the Source literary system? Does it belong to the centre or to the margins, of the system? And what happens when the TT is inserted into the Target (in our case, the Italian) literary system? Would the original position be confirmed, in some ways, or radically altered? And again, in what ways would the reception process influence the translation of this text? Questions of this kind would surely take us far beyond where we've been, and bring in analytical considerations of a sociological nature, such as differences concerning publishing or marketing practices in the two systems.

Only a very small number of translation approaches have examined the 'space' of the reader, that is, the effect of translation strategies and choices upon the reader. The positions available for the reader are those of: exclusion, participation, or observation, vis-à-vis the translated text (Pym, 1992). Readers are 'excluded' every time a 'foreignising' strategy is adopted in a radical way (Venuti, 1995, 1998), that is, when the translator aims at a close reproduction of the ST, the most important criterion being the preservation of its specificity. In this case, 'excluded' readers have to make their own way into the text, in order to decipher its meaning. A 'participating' reader is not left by him/herself, since the reading process is facilitated by 'reader-friendly' translation strategies which have been recently described as 'naturalising', or 'domesticating' (Venuti, 1998). The position of the 'observing' reader is in a way somewhere between the two extremes, and this is the option respected in the case we have just analysed, as the aim of the translators was to let the TT readers 'observe' (and learn to appreciate) the specificity of Marina Warner's literary style. The translators decided to preserve the overall effect of the ST, but to do this *not* by reproducing Warner's characteristic choices, as this would have obviously been impossible, due to the structural differences between the two languages. The similarities in terms of effect, however, have been meticulously constructed by using the specific linguistic devices of the Italian language, as is clear in the reproduction of that illusive simplicity pervading the ST. This is accurately re-created in Italian by means of different strategies (see for instance the differences in terms of thematic structures pointed out in the section above on sentence structure).

An analysis which does not take these issues into due consideration betrays its limits, and yet this paper's methodological relevance for translation teaching is not without its significance: by working comparatively on both ST and TT, students are enabled to observe the difficulties and possible solutions which are part of the translating process. Although many translation scholars may express some reservations – in the sense that presenting students with ready-made solutions might be perceived as an act which limits their involvement in a translation exercise – I believe that bringing a translated text to class does *not* necessarily limit scope for discussion. On the contrary, I suggest that analysing a TT through a detailed comparison with a ST has the advantage of making discussion less abstract, less oriented towards general and potential problems, as would be the case in a broader 'contrastive' perspective. A 'comparative' methodology of the type illustrated in this article concentrates on textual/linguistic details, and traces the way in which coherence and cohesion are textually built in a specific translation.

This does not mean, however, that the TT presented to the students should be imposed as a model with no alternatives – quite the opposite. A close comparison between the two texts should allow students to experience translation as a decision-making process, making them aware that alternative solutions are possible at many levels, and that such decisions would produce different texts, with different basic criteria of coherence and cohesion, as classroom activities should be concerned to make clear. Rather than inhibiting students, my experience in class confirms that this methodology stimulates them and, in fact, enables them to evaluate translations with a view to eventually outlining strategies of their own.

Notes

1   Baker and Hatim and Mason concentrate on translation teaching in the volumes mentioned above, while House offers a linguistic model for the assessment of translation quality.

2   The same is true for other relatively recent disciplines such as Cultural Studies, for example.

References

Baker, M. (1992) *In Other Words. A Coursebook on Translation*. London and New York: Routledge.
Bassnett, S. (1980) *Translation Studies*. London and New York: Routledge.
Bassnett, S. (ed.) (1997) *Translating Literature*. Cambridge: D. S. Brewer.

Bassnett, S. and Lefevere, A. (1998) *Constructing Cultures*. Clevedon: Multilingual Matters.

Boase-Beier, J. and Holman, M. (eds) (1999) *The Practices of Literary Translation: Constraints and Creativity*. Manchester: St Jerome.

Bush, P. and Malmkjær, K. (eds) (1998) *Literary Translation in Higher Education*. Amsterdam and Philadelphia: John Benjamins.

Fowler, R. (1986) *Linguistic Criticism*. Oxford: Oxford University Press.

Halliday, M. A. K. (1994) *An Introduction to Functional Grammar*, 2nd edition. London: Arnold.

Hatim, B. and Mason, I. (1997) *The Translator as Communicator*. London and New York: Routledge.

Hermans, T. (ed.) (1985) *The Manipulation of Literature: Studies in Literary Translation*. London and Sydney: Croom Helm.

Hermans, T. (ed.) (1999) *Translation in Systems*. Manchester: St Jerome.

Holmes, J. (1988) The name and nature of translation studies. In J. Holmes, *Translated! Papers on Literary Translation and Translation Studies*. Amsterdam: Rodopi.

House, J. (1997) *Translation Quality Assessment: A Model Revisited*. Tübingen: Narr.

Pym, A. (1992) *Translation and Text Transfer*. Frankfurt am Main: Peter Lang.

Snell-Hornby, M. (1988) *Translation Studies: An Integrated Approach*. Amsterdam and Philadelphia: John Benjamins.

Toury, G. (1980) *In Search of a Theory of Translation*. Tel Aviv: Porter Institute.

Toury, G. (1995) *Descriptive Translation Studies and Beyond*. Amsterdam and Philadelphia: John Benjamins.

Venuti, L. (1995) *The Translator's Invisibility*. London and New York: Routledge.

Venuti, L. (1998) *The Scandals of Translation*. London and New York: Routledge.

Warner, M. (1993) *The Mermaids in the Basement*. London: Chatto and Windus.

9 Deconstructing standard syntax: tendencies in Modern German prose writing

Anne Betten

Universität Salzburg

Editors' Introduction

Anne Betten studied German and Latin philology in Kiel, Berlin and Erlangen, where she got her PhD. Her fields of research include orality, text linguistics and stylistics and she has also published widely on historical syntax, language preservation of German-Jewish emigrants in Israel, and language in historical and modern milieu plays. Her work on language and literature include studies of Friedrich Dürrenmatt, Botho Strauß, and Thomas Bernhard.

In this paper, Betten looks closely at *non-standard* syntax in modern German prose writing, a phenomenon that is all the more worth noting, as it took some hundred years for German literary prose to get to the point where style experimentation became an issue. But even then, in the first half of the twentieth century it was the traditional art of refined normative language use which Thomas Mann's prose style represented once again, though probably for the last time, in its ultimate perfection.

Here, however, Betten focuses on experimental practices, and especially on those of Austrian writers, evaluating Thomas Bernhard, Elfriede Jelinek, and Marlene Streeruwitz, as being paradigmatic of those writers who deconstruct and dislocate language, and each in different, if equally effective, ways. But why concentrate on Austrians? The reason Betten offers is that post-war Austrian literature has always centred on language (in the tradition of Wittgenstein and Karl Kraus), in a way which was not possible in the German Republic. Here, there was a strong demand for a literature that served political purposes, linked to the 1968 counter-cultural movement and any language experimentation there was in Germany, was largely restricted to poetry. In Austria, however, she maintains, things were different and experimentation with language itself, i.e. for its own sake, and not only restricted to narrative perspective and point of view, was widely and readily practised by prose writers too. Betten's argument is that, instead of a change in the concept of literature occurring from the 'outside', as in Germany, in Austria literary transformation occurred from within. And it is on that internal development that she concentrates her attention. Of course, the recent phenomenon of Turkish immigration into Germany, as Moraldo's paper in this volume demonstrates, is working its own changes on the German scene, which is now the site of significant stylistic experimentation with a marked socio-political function as well.

Betten does not make Jelinek a prime subject of her paper, but she does make her the starting point, calling attention to her montage techniques, or the 'co-existence of various language levels' in her work: a veritable morass of language through which her characters are made to struggle. Nonetheless, Betten opts to focus on Bernhard and Streeruwitz. Why? Because Jelinek is not intent on manipulating grammatical forms. If one of her sentences often seems to lack any fit with another, they are still always 'proper' sentences; i.e. her deconstructing means are not syntactical, and it is precisely the deconstruction of syntax that Betten wants to address.

So she guides us firstly through the excessive repetition and accumulation of lexical, syntactic, textual and rhetorical structures that Bernhard is best known for, pointing out special grammatical practices that 'offend', when they don't actually violate, existing grammatical and stylistic 'norms', e.g. his extreme expansion of sentences and their absurdly nested struc-tures, his exaggerated parallelisms and outrageous accumulations of pluperfect forms and subjunctive moods in embedded indirect speech, confusing amounts of *inquit*-formulae, etc. Bernhard's neologisms, we learn, are nominal compounds derived from his contexts, being continu-ously expanded and varied in ever-larger segments of text. It is a delight to see how these are 'built up' and no surprise to be told that Bernhard himself commented on the pleasure he derived from the process. But as Betten is careful to specify, Bernhard's experimentation with grammar and style is not mere 'play'; it is purpose-ful, and always in the service of the themes and argumentation of the text. In addition, however, she argues that it functions to engage even the frustrated and resistant reader, drawing him/her into the text, slowly but surely, and even against his/her will. Style as reader-engagement mechanism is an interesting suggestion indeed.

Betten presents Streeruwitz as having been influenced by Bernhard, at least in the first stages of her career, but even then, as much more than a brilliant imitator. Her own original contribution to style experimentation regards the representation of spontaneous speech mechanisms, including her well-known fragmentation of utterances, achieved by the insertion of multiple full stops representing silences. We are treated to her most recent prose experimentation as well: an endless inner monologue lacking even these full stops and created through the use of other typical features of spoken language, such as redundancies, hesitations and self-corrections, false starts, right and left dislocation, beyond-the-norm ellipsis, and an absence of standard syntactical sequencing. But style is once again serving a purpose beyond that of sheer ornamentation: in Streeruwitz's case, to actually enact the mis-communication that is a constant theme in her work. Betten hypothesises that her fragmentation techniques, and in particular her non-standard use of logical connection, represents the utter futility of logical reasoning, condemned to failure. As Betten informs us, for Streeruwitz, 'the complete sentence is a lie'.

Betten's paper concentrates on just one aspect of literary experiment: the innovative use of language in the syntactic domain. Her paper is far from being a superficial illustration of the stylistic experiments of the two writers she analyses. Indeed, the crucial question of the function of that style is never far from her sight, or ours.

---

1   Austrian consciousness of language use and literary experiments

After World War II, mistrust in the tradition of poetic language, with reference to all forms of aesthetics, but also regarding merely norm-oriented verbosity, became the dominant attitude of some young German writers, like Wolfgang Borchert, Günther Eich and others of their generation. Their reaction was to demand the destruction of language, meaning the deconstruction of grammar, and a use of everyday language in literature in an artificially reduced, lapidary form, which later would be referred to as 'clear cutting literature' ('Kahlschlagliteratur').[1]

In the early 1950s in Austria, however, we find, along with strong conservative, i.e. traditionalist literary tendencies, young poets, e.g. the members of the so-called 'Vienna Group' ('Wiener Gruppe'), who made use of the experimental devices typical of modern European revolutionary movements of the beginning of the twentieth century, like Expressionism and Dadaism. It is almost commonplace to state that Austrian writers in general are very interested in language use, language games, and linguistic experiments: Nestroy, Hofmannsthal, Karl Kraus and others are famous examples from the past. The 'Vienna Group' experimented at all linguistic levels, specifically by using dialect in an innovative ironic, critical, indeed anarchic and subversive way. H. C. Artmann's *med ana schwoazzn dintn* ('with [a] black ink'), from 1958, is exemplary, and probably the best known of this group's publications. Although at that time these experimental groups had not yet been acknowledged as representative of Austrian literature, and some of their members, like the afterwards famous Ernst Jandl, only became successful after publishing in Germany, the German approach (or return) to experimental poetry only came later, in the 1960s, when 'Concrete Poetry' ('Konkrete Poesie') was for a while considered to be the only form of genuine modern writing.[2]

In Germany these language experiments remained mainly restricted to poetry, and, afterwards, the 1968 generation emphatically criticised and even condemned such artistic experiments, considering them illustrations of 'art for art's sake' rather than of a literature which serves political purposes, as they obviously thought it ought to do. In Austria, however, experimenting with language itself, and not only with narrative perspective and point of view, was also practised by prose writers such as: Ingeborg Bachmann in her short stories; Peter Handke – starting with dramatic experiments and then publishing his first novels *Hornissen* (*The Hornets*) and *Der Hausierer* (*The Panhandler*) in 1967 – and Thomas Bernhard, who published exciting new prose almost every year after his 1963 debut novel *Frost*. Ingeborg Bachmann's (1969 [1978]: 363) comment on Bernhard's novel *Verstörung* (*Gargoyles*) (1967) is often quoted: 'In all those years we have been wondering what the new will look like when it comes along. Well, here it is'.[3]

According to Wendelin Schmidt-Dengler, the author of histories of post-war Austrian literature, and of monographs on Ernst Jandl and Thomas Bernhard, among others, and always very alert to all phenomena of language in literature, the 1968 revolution in Austria took place in the aesthetic, literary domain, rather than in the political sphere, as in Germany. Instead of a change in literature and in the concept of literature occurring from the outside, a literary transformation occurred from within (Schmidt-Dengler, 1995: 219). Schmidt-Dengler points out that what the new Austrian approaches in all genres – lyric poetry, drama, and novel – have in common is that they fill predetermined moulds with a new language and, in so doing (deliberately) fail to meet readers' expectations. They decline the demand that '[...] art should create a reality that is of an equal structure to reality' and they single out language as their central theme: 'Language refers to itself'. These artistic approaches are closely connected with the 'contra-positions' the authors embrace: they problematise genres which previously had positive connotations, such as the 'milieu play' ('Volksstück') or the 'homeland novel' ('Heimatroman'), as well as the concept of nature, as in the case of Thomas Bernhard, and later, Elfriede Jelinek, whose entire work is dedicated to the deconstruction of myths. A further characteristic of these positions, which defined the dynamics of literature around 1970 in Austria, is '[...] equating language and society. Criticism of society can only occur through criticism of language' (all quotations from Schmidt-Dengler, 1995: 237–238).

Most of these statements remain valid for Austrian literature today, of course with many variations and modifications as far as literary topics and techniques are concerned. Though some renowned authors, like Peter Handke, have changed their styles and fields of interest considerably in the meantime, most of those who are considered representatives of the peculiarities of Austrian literature can be characterised by their linguistic approach to literature, i.e. by the dominance of language in their work, to such an extent that language itself creates, or even becomes, the actual topic of that work.

Elfriede Jelinek, who is one of the most important Austrian writers since the 1970s and was awarded the Nobel prize in 2004, confirmed that this phenomenon was, and is, the main difference between Austrian and German literature. As she put it:

> In a way, post-war Austrian literature has always been centered on language [...]. This also originates from the linguistic critical tradition of the early Wittgenstein and Karl Kraus. This literature has always attempted to bring everything that is possible out of language; it turned the language over and over, so to speak, to test it from every angle, to see whether anything more could be elicited from it [...]. In contrast, literature in the German Republic was and is primarily content- and narration-dominated [...]. In the latter an entirely different set of traditions asserted itself. (Jelinek, 2002/03: 18–19) [4]

And Jelinek continues by saying that she too, like many others of her generation, is most indebted to the 'Vienna Group'.

Though I will not focus on Jelinek in this paper, at least a few remarks must be made, as all of her work is marked by language. There is almost no serious literature about Jelinek which does not refer to this important role of language, i.e. the analysis and critique of language use we can see in her novels, as well as in her plays. What follows are just a few representative titles by way of illustration:

- *Elfriede Jelinek. Sprach- und Kulturkritik im Erzählwerk* (*Elfriede Jelinek. Criticism of language and culture in her prose*) (Hoffmann, 1999);

- *Sprachspiel als Lebensform. Strukturuntersuchungen zur erzählenden Prosa Elfriede Jelineks* (*Language games as a life form. Structural analyses of Elfriede Jelinek's narrative prose*) (Schestag, 1997);

- *Vom Dialog zur Dialogizität. Die Theaterästhetik von Elfriede Jelinek* (*From dialogue to dialogicity. Elfriede Jelinek's theatre aesthetics*) (Pflüger, 1996);

- *Textherstellungsverfahren bei Elfriede Jelinek* [...] (*Elfriede Jelinek's text creation techniques* [...]) (Sander, 1996);

- *Elfriede Jelinek: framed by language* (Johns and Arens, 1994).

One of Jelinek's main purposes is to present her characters neither psychologically, nor in their development. Her figures are 'types' who pour out language, language they have heard in advertisements, comics, politics and especially in the media. Her technique is montage, characterised by '[...] the co-existence of very different language levels' (Jelinek, 2002/03: 20). The characters, as well as the author herself, struggle through this morass of language, and it's often difficult to distinguish who is speaking or thinking: whether it is one of the characters, or the author, or those authors Jelinek is quoting.

The reason why I won't go any deeper with my analysis here, is that Jelinek intends to deconstruct neither standard syntax nor any other grammatical forms of so-called surface-structure. She just deconstructs language itself, but mostly by means of 'proper' sentences, unless the quotations are elliptic or deviant in themselves. Mainly well-formed sentences collide against each other. One sentence doesn't 'fit' the other, or the situation, but this is not achieved by syntactical means.

In the following part of my paper I intend to concentrate on two other Austrian authors: Thomas Bernhard, born in 1931, extremely productive from the 1960s till his death in 1989, and Marlene Streeruwitz, who was born in 1950 but only started her literary career in the early 1990s. Both of these are, like Jelinek, equally successful as prose writers and dramatists. With Jelinek, they also share a substantial critique of Austrian politics and mentality, and so often, like her, scandalise the public that condemns them for 'dirtying their own nest'. They also share with her the typical Austrian concentration on language, but they do it by exploring how flexible the formal vehicle of their thoughts and intentions is: i.e. by experimenting with syntax at the borders of word and text. But both of them, Bernhard and Streeruwitz do this with different results, as we shall see.

2   Thomas Bernhard's violations of stylistic norms: repetition, exaggeration, sentence extension, and more

Thomas Bernhard started to write when formal experiments in so-called 'Concrete Poetry' were at their peak, which may have influenced him. But, in contrast to the promoters of this movement, he did not attack grammar itself by substituting or transforming elements on the phonetic, morphemic, lexical or syntactic levels, at least not in the same way as, for example, Ernst Jandl did. During a certain period of his poetic and dramatic writing, Jandl used all verbs in the infinitive, deliberately producing a sort of 'guest-worker German', or 'baby talk'. Bernhard, however, focuses the reader/addressee's attention on grammar by using forms which in and of themselves are correct, but whose excessive repetition and accumulation run counter to standard stylistic conventions.

Repetition in all possible forms, in lexical, syntactic and rhetorical constructions and also at the level of text structure, is a, if not *the*, main characteristic of Bernhard's style, combined with modifications and variations of such oft-repeated patterns. Oliver Jahraus (1991) entitled one of his books about Bernhard, *Die Wiederholung als werkkonstitutives Prinzip im Œuvre Thomas Bernhards* (*Repetition as the Constituent Principle of Thomas Bernhard's Œuvre*).

Repetition is also one of the techniques by which exaggeration, another stylistic device of Bernhard's, is achieved. And Bernhard is not exaggerating only a little bit, or a little bit too much, as is often argued by those readers who have *not* understood the constitutive function of exaggeration for Bernhard's way of presenting especially negative aspects of the world. Schmidt-Dengler (1997) entitled a collection of his studies about Bernhard, *Der Übertreibungskünstler* (*The Master of Exaggeration*). And this art of exaggeration is formally achieved by an exuberant use of all of the myriad linguistic means which produce this stylistic effect, hyperbole and repetition being the most important.

While repetition and exaggeration may be regarded as predominantly stylistic devices, a closer look has to be taken at the preferred grammatical forms they emphasise.[5] In the lexical domain, Bernhard is famous for neologisms, most of which are nominal compounds derived, or 'distilled', from the context (cf. Betten, 1987). These ad-hoc-compounds are often 'built up' in several steps, and the author himself has commented on the pleasure of this process. Example (1) presents one such metalinguistic remark:

Example 1
[…] und das immer größere Vergnügen andererseits ist dann die Arbeit.
Das sind die Sätze, Wörter, die man aufbaut. Im Grunde ist es wie ein

Spielzeug, man setzt es übereinander, es ist ein musikalischer Vorgang. Ist eine bestimmte Stufe erreicht nach vier, fünf Stockwerken – man baut das auf – durchschaut man das Ganze und haut alles wie ein Kind wieder zusammen. (Bernhard, *Drei Tage*, 1971: 80–81)

[…] on the other hand work is always the greater pleasure. The sentences and words one constructs. Basically it is like a toy, one stacks it; it is a musical process. When you reach a certain stage, after four or five stories – you build it up – it all becomes transparent, and you knock it down like a child. (*Three Days*)

The next example (2) in the original text is not divided into different lines, as here, but rather presented in run-on lines. It illustrates how a simple constituent can be expanded step by step, adding a first element to the noun in line 2, and extending this again in line 3, by simultaneously using other forms of attribution, like the adjective 'literary' in line 2, and an additional post-modifying prepositional phrase in line 3:

Example 2
urplötzlich zur Pose,
zur literarischen Zweck-Pose,
zur literarischen Mehrzweckpose für gebefreudige Politiker
(Bernhard, *Holzfällen. Eine Erregung*, 1985: 255)

[from …] to a sudden pose,
to a literary purpose pose,
to a literary multipurpose pose for generous politicians
(*Cutting Timber. An Irritation*)

This example illustrates Bernhard's method most instructively, even though in most cases the relations between the continuously expanded and again and again varied compounds extend over much longer stretches of text. Sometimes they encompass several pages or even chapters. Example (3) demonstrates the author's satisfaction with this sort of linguistic game:

Example 3
Der Auersberger, der geile Schriftstellerverschlinger, dachte ich jetzt und ich hätte über diese meine Wortschöpfung im Augenblick auflachen können, wäre ich nicht zu müde gewesen dazu. (Bernhard, *Holzfällen. Eine Erregung*, 1984: 269)

The Auersberger, the horned devourer of authors, I thought then, and I would have laughed about this, my creation, if I had not been too tired to do so. (*Cutting Timber. An Irritation*)

But of course such compounds are not only intended as a source of surprise at and pleasure in witty creativity. Their function is also, and mainly, as in other text-types, the well-known textual function according to which compounds condense preceding portions of the text, rendering them available for further modifications and developments.

In Example (1) above, Bernhard talks not only about word formation but also about constructing sentences in a comparable way. This syntactic technique can mainly be observed in his plays. He only started to write for the theatre in 1970, after having published almost a dozen important prose texts within a mere seven years, years in which he had already experimented with rather different types of syntactic devices.

Formally, his mainly monologic dramatic texts are characterised by verse-like fragmentation, without any punctuation. Starting a new line may indicate rhythmic stops, but need not do so. This arrangement in verse form is considered by some critics as proof of Bernhard's own claims that his writing follows mathematical as well as musical principles. But many of his text constructions can equally be compared with spontaneous dialogues, where utterances are expanded by supplements, modified repetitions etc., in a sort of unsegmented, continuous 'crawling' from one idea to the next. Because of the obscurity of this segmentation, which Bernhard's texts share with spontaneous dialogue, his first critics analysed it as either 'sentence decay' ('Satzzerfall'), or extreme syntactic expansion, which sounds contradictory, but can actually be regarded as two different and contrasting ways of analysing the same text (see Betten 1985: 378ff. and 1998: 170ff.).

Example (4) gives only a very brief impression of this technique. Bernhard's metalinguistic remark comparing his process to stacking and knocking down toys in Example (1) above should also be kept in mind:

Example 4

Sandwiches Frau Frölich	Sandwiches Mrs Frölich
Sandwiches	Sandwiches
nach und nach	one by one
hat er ihm einmal	he stuffed
[*Regieanweisung*]	[*stage direction*]
die zwölf Sandwiches	the twelve sandwiches
die kostbarsten Sandwiches	the most precious sandwiches
die ich jemals gemacht habe	that I ever made
ihm in den Mund gesteckt	into his mouth
ihm	him

<table>
<tr><td>

(*schaut in den leeren Hundekorb*)
ihm
nach und nach
ganz musikalisch Frau Frölich
ganz nach dem musikalischen Gesetz
daß ich gestaunt habe
(Bernhard, *Der Präsident*, 1975:
67–68)

</td><td>

(*looks into the empty dog basket*)
him
one by one
so musical Mrs Frölich
so in tune with the musical law
that I marvelled
(*The President*)

</td></tr>
</table>

When I said above that Bernhard experimented with different prose styles, I should have added that he always does so in close relation to the topics of the work. For example, his early prose text, *Amras*, from 1964, had as a theme the sense of two young men that '[…] everything around us and in us and with us was crumbling' ('[…] in uns und um uns und mit uns zerbröckelt alles', *Amras*, 37) and '[…] that you are nothing but fragments' ('[…] daß du nichts bist als Fragmente', *Amras*, 78). Formally, this is constructed by sentence segments, broken up by three dots, as here in Example (5):

Example 5
…Wir verschoben dann […] unter närrischen, konfusen Zurufen, **Sätzezerbröckelungen** […] immer wieder die Tische und Sessel und Bänke und Kasten im Turm… (Bernhard, *Amras*, 1964: 22)

… amidst crazy, jumbled exclamations, **sentences fragmenting** […] we kept moving the tables and chairs and benches and cupboards in the tower… (*Amras*)

More typical for Bernhard, however, are extremely long sentences. His prose does have punctuation, but a full stop sometimes only shows up after three pages or more! The texts usually have neither chapters nor titles; at times, they have two-part titles, as in Bernhard's famous early novel, *Verstörung* (*Gargoyles*), whose (longer) second part is called, *Der Fürst* (*The Prince*). It consists almost entirely of this protagonist's monologue – a monologue which received much attention in literary criticism, and admiration from literary colleagues such as Handke, who was fascinated by the effect of this 'stream' of monologue (see Handke, 1967 [1970]).

Again, many metalinguistic comments can be found in Bernhard's texts, referring to simple, or fragmented, or highly complicated sentence constructions. From one of these remarks, I took my title for a detailed study into Bernhard's syntax: 'Das ist mir zu blöd, drei Seiten ein Satz' ('This is ridiculous, a three page sentence'):[6]

Example 6

[…] man […] konstruiert eine Prosa, die die Leute langweilt, weil sie sagen:
Das ist mir zu blöd, drei Seiten ein Satz. Und das ist doch der Reiz […],
daß man was macht, was die Leute ablehnen und ihnen Widerstände macht.
(Interview Bernhard von Hofmann, Bernhard, 1988: 43)

[…] one […] constructs prose, that bores people, because they say: **This
is ridiculous, a three page sentence.** And that is what makes it interesting
[…], that one is doing something that people reject and which resists them.
(Interview of Bernhard by Hofmann)

The constructions of these tapeworm-like sentences display a large number of
specific syntactic devices. One of them, consists in his preference for nested
sentences ('Schachtelsätze') and is typical of a certain period of Bernhard's
writing, when he emphasised the isolation or captivity of the individual. This
notorious peculiarity of German syntax is often used by Bernhard in the most
absurd, though grammatically correct ways. An example is (7), where the three
complex predicates of the subordinate clauses nested within one another come
one after the other, a sequence which is not even comprehensible for German
readers and can only be reconstructed clause by clause:

Example 7

[…] und dem diese meine Absicht, wie ich sofort nach den ersten Sätzen,
die Moro in seiner Kanzlei zu <u>mir gesprochen hat</u>, <u>erkannt habe</u>, schon
völlig <u>vertraut war</u> […] (Bernhard, *Ungenach*, 1968: 8–9)

[…] and to whom my aim, as I from the first few sentences, which Moro in
his chambers <u>spoke</u>, <u>have noted</u>, <u>was</u> completely <u>clear</u>. (*Ungenach*)

By accumulating abstruse grammatical structures like these, the author draws
special attention to them and forces the reader to interpret them, or, even should
the reader fail to react consciously, the effects of this language use will still
be most likely to draw him, by and by and even against his/her will, into the
specific mood.

Another typical device is the embeddedness of direct and indirect speech:
often three or four levels of different characters' speeches are embedded in the
main speaker's speech. And, here again, the *inquit*-formulae of the reported
speech ('X said' – 'said Y') deliberately follow each other in clusters, frustrating
the reader's capacity to assign them to the right utterances, as in Example (8),
which is, however, a rather 'restrained' one:

Example 8

Wahrscheinlich, **so Zehetmayer'**, **sagte der Fürst**, 'ist er jetzt, nach
vier Jahren, schon wieder heraus. Ich kenne die Justiz hierzulande, **hat
Zehtmayer gesagt'**, **sagte der Fürst**. (Bernhard, *Verstörung*, 1967: 86)

> Probably, **according to Zehetmayer'**, **said the prince**, 'he is now, after four years, out again. I know the judiciary here, **Zehetmayer said'**, **said the prince**. (*Gargoyles*)

Again, the unusual accumulation of grammatically possible units underlines the author's technique, in this case, of emphasising that his world, or his fictional world, does not consist of facts or actions which can be objectively described, but exists only in a mediated way, refracted through and contained within the points of view of multiple individuals or instances.

Other techniques, despite their intelligible construction, still baffle the reader with grammatical forms which were, at least in the kind of build up we find in Bernhard's texts, formerly excluded from literary and other forms of 'aesthetic' language. The extensive use of the analytic pluperfect is an example of this. It has sometimes been interpreted as an indicator of the *mise-en-scène* of the narration, producing distance and an aura of artificiality, but its mimetic function also has to be considered. In Example (9), it is the 'heavy' analytical verb forms that successfully evoke impressions of hammering – a hammering mimicking the hammering in the brain of the narrator, who is breathlessly talking about being, or not being, mad:

Example 9

[…] **denn wie** der Paul damals wieder einmal in eine seiner Lebenssackgassen <u>geraten war</u>, <u>war</u> auch ich in eine meiner Lebenssackgassen <u>geraten</u> **oder noch besser gesagt**, <u>hineingetrieben worden</u>. **Wie** der Paul, <u>hatte</u> ich, **wie ich sagen muß**, meine Existenz wieder einmal <u>übertrieben</u> **und also** <u>überschätzt</u> **und also** über das Äußerste hinaus <u>ausgenützt gehabt</u>. **Wie** der Paul, <u>hatte</u> ich selbst mich wieder einmal über alle meine Möglichkeiten hinaus <u>ausgenützt gehabt</u>, alles über alle Möglichkeiten hinaus <u>ausgenützt gehabt</u> mit der krankhaften Rücksichtslosigkeit gegen mich und gegen alles […] (Bernhard, *Wittgensteins Neffe*, 1982: 32)

[…] **for as** Paul then <u>had</u> once again <u>entered</u> one of the dead ends of his life, I also <u>had got</u> into one of the dead ends of my life, **or to put it better**, <u>was driven</u> into it. **Like** Paul, **as I must say, I** <u>had</u> once again <u>exaggerated</u> my existence **and thus** <u>overestimated</u> **and thereby** <u>exploited</u> it beyond the utmost limit. **Like** Paul, I <u>had</u> once again <u>exploited</u> myself beyond all my means with this pathological recklessness towards myself and towards everything […] (*Wittgenstein's Nephew*)

Example (9) also shows more favoured techniques, like parallelism, which is here regarded as a form of repetition at sentence level. Moreover, it gives at least a slight impression of the typical argumentative mode of Bernhard's characters, or the anonymous narrator: using lots of argumentative particles, which evoke an impression of logic and precision, whereas the reader, following various, albeit confusing, signals in the text, in most cases only slowly realises that the 'pretended' logic is actually absolutely illogical and that the speaker is either obsessed or already insane (as in the case of *Wittgenstein's Nephew*). (Pseudo-)accuracy is also conveyed by expressions like 'oder noch besser gesagt' ('or to put it better'), or 'wie ich sagen muß' ('as I must say').

In other novels, the author builds up argumentative particles at the beginning of the text, thus leading – and, as it turns out, *mis*leading – the reader's expectations about the seriousness and logic of what is to come. However, this stylistic device should be seen as giving fitting expression to the main topics of all Bernhard's texts. He doesn't want to tell stories; he proudly declares he is a 'Geschichtenzerstörer' ('destroyer of stories'),[7] but rather he portrays characters preoccupied with philosophising, arguing, reasoning, etc. Thus the choice of (pseudo-) scientific and (pseudo-)precise stylistic devices may also be seen as Bernhard's parody of a purely scientific approach to existential questions.

Schmidt-Dengler, in a study entitled, 'Von der Schwierigkeit, Thomas Bernhard zu lesen' ('On the difficulty of reading Thomas Bernhard'), pointed out that Bernhard's reader can '[…] only rarely explain why a text enthralls him/her, especially because it contains many factors which would otherwise be off-putting when reading' (Schmidt-Dengler, 1981: 125). The best analysis of the strange fascination Bernhard can evoke by using often absolutely unpoetic language is by Franz Eyckeler, in his book *Reflexionspoesie* (*The Poetry of Reflection*). He invented the word 'Sprachsog' ('maelstrom of language') to suggest the effect of Bernhard's personal rhetoric, '[…] which is responsible for the reader staying with the text, even though s/he is denied the normal means of making reading more pleasurable' and instead often finds '[…] a considerable amount of redundant and monotonous content and language' (Eyckeler, 1995: 76).[8]

3 Marlene Streeruwitz's fullstops: fragmentation and other stream-of-consciousness stylistics

Bernhard's style has had an enormous influence on young writers in German. Marlene Streeruwitz, who knew him well personally, initially experimented with prose using his sentence style, but soon looked for different, more original ways of writing. Her trademark became the full stop. Having developed her characteristic style in her very successful early dramas, she transferred the technique to her prose, starting with her 1996 novel *Verführungen* (*Seductions*). Literary critic, Reinhard Baumgart, reviewed this book,[9] which recounts '[…]

the bleak love-life, and everyday-life, of a 30-year-old divorced mother of two', as follows:

> She hammers a hard beat, notes short, also torso-like, knocked-together sentences, litters the text with full stops and pauses, eradicating almost all subordinate clauses, sweeping away adjectives, thereby creating breathless yet hefty, mighty prose.

The next example may be regarded as emblematic, but not in any way as an extreme case:

Example 10

Im nächsten Moment dachte sie, keiner nähme sie zur Kenntnis. **Ja.** Blickte weg. Absichtlich. Verächtlich. Als gäbe es sie gar nicht. (Streeruwitz, *Verführungen*, 1996: 142)

The next moment she thought, nobody acknowledged her. **Yes.** Looked away. Deliberately. Scornfully. As though she did not exist. (*Seductions*)

Full stops are used, instead of commas or hyphens, which could also indicate subsequent additions. How calculated this fragmentation by separation with full stops is, is demonstrated by the titles of two of her poetic lecture series talks and a volume of essays and collages:

Example 11

Sein. Und Schein. Und Erscheinen. (Streeruwitz, 1997)
(Being. And seeming. And appearing.)

Können. Mögen. Dürfen. Sollen. Wollen. Müssen. Lassen. (Streeruwitz, 1998)
(Being able to. Liking to. Being allowed to. Having to. Wanting to. Being forced to. Not doing.)

Und. Überhaupt. Stop. (*Collagen. 1996–2000*, Streeruwitz, 2000)
(And. At all. Stop.)

Streeruwitz herself comments on her technique: 'The complete sentence is a lie'; the only adequate expression for those with confused identities is the 'staccato of stammering' (Lohs, 2000).

Some critics have already drawn parallels between Streeruwitz and other authors who in the 1920s and 1930s revitalised and adapted the folk, or 'milieu', play. They have drawn particular comparisons with the Austro-Hungarian writer, Ödön von Horváth – but mainly with respect to his frequent stage direction, 'silence', about which Horváth himself gives the following account:

> Bitte achten Sie genau auf die Pausen im Dialog, die ich mit 'Stille' bezeichne – hier kämpft das Bewußtsein oder Unterbewußtsein miteinander, und das muß sichtbar werden. (Horváth, 1978: 664; cf. Betten, 1985: 209)

> Please pay particular attention to the pauses in the dialogue, which I mark 'silence' – here the conscious and subconscious are in conflict, and this must be visible.

Streeruwitz and her critics claim that her full stops are supposed to have effects similar to this silence. With her, the full stop interrupts the flow of language and, in the pauses between, is '[…] the search to find. oneself. expression.' (Lohs, 2000). But there are more, and more obvious stylistic parallels, as I want to point out with the following considerations.

The so-called 'critical milieu play' of the 1970s (by authors like Rainer Werner Fassbinder and Franz Xaver Kroetz in Germany, or Wolfgang Bauer in Austria, and dozens of other playwrights) rediscovered writers like Horváth and discussed their linguistic techniques in detail. Horváth:

> […] was concerned with showing that the petty bourgeoisie of his time no longer commanded a genuine language of their own, but possessed […] a kind of pseudo-educated jargon (Bildungsjargon), whose false or empty phrases prevented them from recognizing the true state of affairs and hence from bettering their lot. (Betten, 1983: 1077)

The authors of the 1970s argued a lot about who best represented the people of their time, and which alienated language (uneigentliche Sprache) was best to bestow on them. Kroetz and other German authors turned to the underprivileged, representing them with a proletarian 'restricted' code,[10] a language unable to express their situation, and solve their problems, while the Austrian Wolfgang Bauer's plays are set in the student and artist bohemian milieu, perfectly imitating their informal, colloquial tone. The neo-realistic dramatists of this period did not recreate spoken language by means of lexical and phonetic markers alone, as in former times. They also became aware of syntax, and added to the small set of traditionally used devices, like ellipsis and aposiopesis, quite a lot of other phenomena which are found in spontaneous speech, such as redundancies, hesitations and self-corrections, false starts, left- and right-dislocation, attention signals, and so on. But even with this general tendency towards loosening up the sentence structure of standard written language, there always remained – and will always remain – a difference between their representations and the permanent struggles for intelligibility of 'real' speakers, which in literature would distract the reader far too much, and hinder her/his reading. This is at least one of the reasons why authors tend to limit their use of spoken language phenomena to those which can express something relevant to the communicative problems dealt with in their work.

The 'new realism' of the 1970s and its writer-specific ways of stylisation are thoroughly analysed in Betten (1985). In my opinion, Streeruwitz can be included in the tradition of this stylised imitation of spontaneous speaking. And she adds still more phenomena, distilled from spontaneous speech, refining them by incessant, deliberate use, inventing countless variations, so that they penetrate the reader's perception and become, as these did in the 'new realism', an author-specific stylistic device.

One of these devices consists in isolating particles, preferably followed by a full stop, e.g. 'Aber'. ('But'.); 'Und'. ('And'.), and others. Compare Example (11) above, where they are highlighted by being used as book titles. And 'Ja'. ('Yes'.), in Example (10) above, also belongs to this set.

Linguistics has extensively described the phenomenon of isolating argumentative particles, like the German causative 'weil' ('because'), which should grammatically be followed by the verb in second position, which is, if used correctly, the typical position in main clauses only. One of the explanations offered is that the conjunction is not handled like a clause-opening particle, but rather like an independent signal of argumentation, followed by a short pause. Streeruwitz, by using this in written texts with unusual punctuation, transforms it into a mark of her own distinctive stylistic mode. One might hypothesise that it gives her the opportunity to underline the struggle of her female protagonists in their interior monologues for sensible reflection about what's going on, and what they think about what is happening to them. But the fragmentation of these logical signals also leaves space for one to assume the contrary, or it may even indicate that all logical reasoning is in vain, condemned to failure.

My last examples of the several which might be offered are chosen to demonstrate Streeruwitz's technique of elaborating on an utterance, step by step, in presumed imitation of our way of thinking in a kind of 'spontaneous' speech. Example (10) above, and (12), illustrate this proceeding:

Example 12
Im Haus war es warm. Roch nach Krankheit. Desinfektionsmittel und Urin. Stechend. Und süß. (Streeruwitz, *Nachwelt*, 1999: 7)

In the house it was warm. Smelled of illness. Disinfectant and urine. Pungent. And sweet. (*Posterity*)

In the two novels the examples are taken from, *Verführungen* (*Seductions*) (1996) and *Nachwelt* (*Posterity*) (1999), Streeruwitz still represents this process by isolating additions with full stops.

Her last novel, *Jessica, 30.*, came therefore as quite a surprise. Most critics wrote that the author had changed her style completely in this breathless interior monologue without any full stops. This is, however, not quite true. On the contrary, she has made her accumulative style even more intricate, combining it with numerous, slightly varying repetitions (which I have placed in bold below):

Example 13
Scheiße, Scheiße, Scheiße, auf was hast du dich da wieder eingelassen, **allein in der Wohnung, allein mit ihm in der Wohnung**, aber wen hätte man fragen können, niemand lässt sich auf so etwas ein, und es wäre nicht fair, <u>obwohl ihm gegenüber</u>, <u>aber es wäre doch so</u>, und **ich traue es mich nicht, eigentlich traue ich mich nicht**, <u>es wäre eine, eine Komödiensituation wäre das</u>, jemand sitzt im Badezimmer hinter dem Duschvorhang und kommt heraus [...]. (Streeruwitz, *Jessica, 30.*, 2004: 92)

Shit, shit, shit, what have you let yourself in for once again, **alone in the flat, alone with him in the flat**, but who could one have asked, nobody wants to get involved with something like that, and it would not be fair, <u>although towards him</u>, <u>but it would be so</u>, and **I dare not, actually I dare not**, <u>it would be a, a comical situation it would be</u>, someone sits in the bathroom behind the shower curtain and comes out [...]. (*Jessica, 30.*)

Streeruwitz combines this attention-grabbing stylistic device realised by all sorts of repetitions with many other more or less typical phenomena of spontaneity, producing the impression of the breathlessness of this interior monologue. In this example, two fragmentary constructions following each other (underlined above) break off the sentence where the protagonist hesitates, to then become more explicit, although the reader can easily grasp what is being represented as going through her mind. Another construction is also underlined ('it would be a, a comical situation it would be'), an *apokoinu* construction which is also typical of orality, once again reflecting the process of thinking. These signals of discontinuity and disruption are used by the author to indicate the nervousness of the protagonist, who, at that point of the story, is planning a coup against her lover, a so-called 'normal' man: married, with other mistresses besides herself, a high-ranking politician, playing the 'normal' mean political games.

4 Final remarks

Some brief remarks concerning my methodological approach should be added. As may hopefully be deduced from what I have shown here, the foil for these analyses is the normative sentence style as described in our grammars and elaborated over some hundred years of cultivated, norm-oriented prose writing, which reached an apex not only in the classical periods of the eighteenth and nineteenth century, but also in writers of the twentieth century, like Thomas Mann, an example of the ultimate perfection of a refined prose style, operating within grammatical norms. Against these norms, all modern literary revolutions were oriented, deconstructing language in order to bring to, or to go beyond, consciousness what we are doing with, or what is done to us via, language. If the analytical process has to have a name, it may be labelled as a sort of 'deviation stylistics'.

A theory of deviation in literary language/language in literature would usefully distinguish, as Roelcke (2004: 3095) has done, among several types of deviation. He divides literary deviation into what we find in non-poetic language vs. that in poetic language. This latter is, in turn, sub-divided into the kind of deviation close to a non-poetic language use (the principle of realism) and the one marked by new language use (principle of innovation). My analyses have shown that such categorisation can only be regarded as a preliminary and very rough analytical approach. It would of course be possible to characterise Bernhard's poetic language as innovative, and Streeruwitz's as realistic. But it would also be possible to characterise them both as realistic, albeit reaching very different results. And one could also say that Bernhard constructs his poetic language by using non-poetic stylistic means in extraordinary (i.e. innovative) reiterations and combinations, while Streeruwitz could be said to expand poetically traditional means of mimicking orality, reaching novel forms of an already stylised proximity to natural speech.

In my analyses here I concentrated on just one aspect of the literary experiment: the innovative use of language, and this in the syntactic domain especially. According to critics, Roelcke (2004: 2204) points out, there are more varieties of literary experiments, e.g. those examining social and individual groups, or others experimenting with language and communication in more general, pragmatic, but not formal (i.e. grammatical) ways. These kinds of experiments can be found in texts using conventional grammar and style, as well as in texts which innovate. Ideally, it would be necessary to analyse my authors' poetic techniques in as many textual and non-textual dimensions as possible with our current knowledge and interpretative competence. Nevertheless this analysis has allowed me to show that both authors' innovative experiments are essentially grounded in the linguistic material itself, and that

this experimentation involves deconstructing standard syntax, each in his/her
own way.

Notes

1   I have to thank Ben Stephens for translating all special German terms and
quotations from primary and secondary sources, as well as correcting the first
English version of this paper. For help with the final version and a lot of editorial
work I warmly thank Donna Miller. Though many of the texts from the authors
I quote have been translated into English, I preferred to have a new translation
for this paper, one as close to the original as possible. These translations are thus
my own work.

2   Cf. the article of Helmut Heißenbüttel (1980) who himself was one of the main
writers of 'Concrete Poetry'.

3   'In all den Jahren hat man sich gefragt, wie wird es wohl aussehen, das Neue.
Hier ist es, das Neue' (Bachmann, 1969 [1978]: 363). For more on the subject,
see Betten (1998: 169).

4   The original text: 'In gewisser Weise ist die österreichische Literatur der Nach-
kriegszeit (vor allem die der Wiener Gruppe, aber natürlich auch Artmann,
Mayröcker, Jandl) immer schon sprachzentriert gewesen. Das kommt auch
aus der sprachkritischen Tradition eines frühen Wittgenstein oder Karl Kraus.
Diese Literatur hat immer versucht, aus der Sprache alles herauszuholen, was
nur möglich war, sie hat die Sprache um- und umgedreht, um sie sozusagen nach
allen Seiten hin abzuklopfen, ob noch was aus ihr rauszuholen ist. Und wenn
man sie prügeln musste… Während die Literatur der Bundesrepublik Deutsch-
land doch eher inhaltlich, erzählerisch dominiert war und ist (die der DDR ist
wieder eine andre Sache). In der bundesdeutschen Literatur hat sich eben eine
ganz andre Traditionslinie durchgesetzt' (Jelinek, 2002/03: 18–19).

5   Several of the following examples have been systematically analysed in Betten
(1998).

6   The quotation comes from an interview of Bernhard by Kurt Hofmann, in *Zeit-
Magazin* 46, 1988: 40–50. See more on this in Betten (1998: 173). My article,
entitled with this quotation, was published in a special edition on T. Bernhard in
the Austrian literary journal, *Die Rampe*. It is mainly an abbreviated version of
Betten (1998), therefore not included among the references below.

7   Cf. Bernhard in *Drei Tage* (1971: 152): 'Ich bin ein *Geschichtenzerstörer, ich bin
der typische Geschichtenzerstörer*'.

8   For more and different aspects of Bernhard's style in prose and drama, see
Betten (1991, 2004, 2005).

9   Published in *Die Zeit*, here quoted as reported in Lohs (2000). For the function
of Streeruwitz's full stops also see Mangold (2000).

10   The coincidence with Basil Bernstein's much discussed theories at that time is
obvious and not only by chance, but typical for the socio-cultural 'climate' of the
1970s.

References

Bachmann, I. (1969 [1978]) [Thomas Bernhard:] Ein Versuch. *Entwurf.* In I. Bachmann *Werke*, Volume 4. C. Koschel, I. v. Weidenbaum and C. Münster (eds): 361–364. München and Zürich: Piper.

Bernhard, T. (1964) *Amras.* Frankfurt am Main: Suhrkamp.

Bernhard, T. (1967) *Verstörung.* Frankfurt am Main: Suhrkamp. [English (1970): *Gargoyles.* R. and C. Winston (trans.). New York: Alfred A. Knopf].

Bernhard, T. (1968) *Ungenach. Erzählung.* Frankfurt am Main: Suhrkamp.

Bernhard, T. (1971) Drei Tage. In T. Bernhard *Der Italiener* 144–161. Salzburg: Residenz.

Bernhard, T. (1975) *Der Präsident.* Zürich: Suhrkamp.

Bernhard, T. (1982) *Wittgensteins Neffe. Eine Freundschaft.* Frankfurt am Main: Suhrkamp. [English (1986): *Wittgenstein's Nephew.* E. Osers (trans.). London: Quartet Books Ltd.].

Bernhard, T. (1984) *Holzfällen. Eine Erregung.* Frankfurt am Main: Suhrkamp. [English (1988): *Cutting Timber. An Irritation.* E. Osers (trans.). London: Quartet Books Ltd.; and (1989): *Woodcutters.* D. McLintock (trans.). Chicago: University of Chicago Press].

Bernhard, T. (1988) Alles ist grauslich. Interview mit K. Hofmann. *Zeit-Magazin* 46: 40–50.

Betten, A. (1983) Language in modern drama as compared with authentic spoken discourse. In S. Hattori and K. Inoue (eds) *Proceedings of the XIII International Congress of Linguists: August 29 – September 4, 1982, Tokyo* 1077–1081. Tokyo: CIPL.

Betten, A. (1985) *Sprachrealismus im deutschen Drama der siebziger Jahre.* Monographien zur Sprachwissenschaft 14. Heidelberg: Winter.

Betten, A. (1987) Die Bedeutung der Ad-hoc-Komposita im Werk von Thomas Bernhard, anhand ausgewählter Beispiele aus *Holzfällen. Eine Erregung* und *Der Untergeher.* In B. Asbach-Schnitker and J. Roggenhofer (eds) *Neuere Forschungen zur Wortbildung und Historiographie der Linguistik. Festgabe für Herbert E. Brekle zum 50. Geburtstag* 69–90. Tübingen: G. Narr.

Betten, A. (1991) Der Monolog als charakteristische Form des deutschsprachigen Theaters der achtziger Jahre. Anmerkungen zu Thomas Bernhards und Herbert Achternbuschs dramatischer Schreibweise. *Cahiers d'Études Germaniques* 20: 37–48.

Betten, A. (1998) Thomas Bernhards Syntax: keine Wiederholung des immer Gleichen. In K. Donhauser and L. Eichinger (eds) *Deutsche Grammatik – Thema in Variationen. Festschrift für Hans-Werner Eroms zum 60. Geburtstag* 169–190. Heidelberg: Winter.

Betten, A. (2004) Entwicklungen und Formen der deutschen Literatursprache nach 1945. In W. Besch, A. Betten, O. Reichmann and S. Sonderegger (eds) *Sprachgeschichte. Ein Handbuch zur Geschichte der deutschen Sprache und ihrer Erforschung*, 2nd edition Volume 4 3117–3159. Berlin and New York: de Gruyter (HSK [2]2.4).

Betten, A. (2005) Monolog statt Dialog oder Dialog im Monolog? Zur Dialogtechnik Thomas Bernhards. In A. Betten and M. Dannerer (eds) *Dialogue Analysis IX: Dialogue in Literature and the Media. Selected Papers from the 9th IADA Conference, Salzburg 2003*, Part 1: Literature 27–45. Tübingen: Niemeyer.

Eyckeler, F. (1995) *Reflexionspoesie. Sprachskepsis, Rhetorik und Poetik in der Prosa Thomas Bernhards*. Philosophische Studien und Quellen 133. Berlin: E. Schmidt.

Handke, P. (1967 [1970]) Als ich die 'Verstörung' von Thomas Bernhard las. In A. Botond (ed.) *Über Thomas Bernhard* 100–106. Frankfurt am Main: Suhrkamp.

Heißenbüttel, H. (1980) Deutsche Literatursprache der Gegenwart. In H. P. Althaus, H. Henne and H. E. Wiegand (eds) *Lexikon der Germanistischen Linguistik,* 2nd edition 752–756. Tübingen: Niemeyer.

Hoffmann, Y. (1999) *Elfriede Jelinek. Sprach- und Kulturkritik im Erzählwerk.* Kulturwissenschaftliche Studien zur deutschen Literatur. Opladen: Westdeutscher-Verlag.

Horváth, Ö.v. (1978) Gebrauchsanweisung. In Ö.v. Horváth *Gesammelte Werke*, Volume 8. T. Krischke and D. Hildebrandt (eds) *Prosa, Fragmente und Varianten, Exposés, Theoretisches, Briefe, Verse,* 2nd edition 659–665. Frankfurt am Main: Suhrkamp.

Jahraus, O. (1991) *Die Wiederholung als werkkonstitutives Prinzip im Œuvre Thomas Bernhards*. Europäische Hochschulschriften I/1257. Frankfurt: Peter Lang.

Jelinek, E. (2002/03) Was fallen kann, das wird auch fallen. Der Nachkriegsmythos Kaprun und seine unterschwellige Wahrheit. Eine e-mail-Korrespondenz zwischen Elfriede Jelinek und Joachim Lux. In *Das Werk*. Programmheft 77. 9–21. Wien: Burgtheater.

Johns, J. B. and Arens, K. (eds) (1994) *Elfriede Jelinek: framed by language.* Studies in Austrian literature, culture and thought. Riverside, CA: Ariadne Press.

Lohs, L. (2000) Der dominierende Punkt. Über die Autorin und Dramatikerin Marlene Streeruwitz. *Wiener Zeitung*, 10.11.2000.

Mangold, I. (2000) Kurze Sätze, Punkte wie Tretminen. Wie man in Los Angeles seine Verzweiflung los wird. Marlene Streeruwitz' Roman 'Nachwelt'. *Berliner Zeitung*, 22.1.2000.

Pflüger, M. S. (1996) *Vom Dialog zur Dialogizität. Die Theaterästhetik von Elfriede Jelinek.* Tübingen and Basel: Francke.

Roelcke, T. (2004) Sprachgeschichtliche Tendenzen des literarischen Experiments im 19. und 20. Jahrhundert. In W. Besch, A. Betten, O. Reichmann and S. Sonderegger (eds) *Sprachgeschichte. Ein Handbuch zur Geschichte der deutschen Sprache und ihrer Erforschung,* 2nd edition Volume 4 3092–3110. Berlin and New York: de Gruyter (HSK [2]2.4).

Sander, M. (1996) *Textherstellungsverfahren bei Elfriede Jelinek. Das Beispiel 'Totenauberg'*. Epistemata: Literaturwissenschaft 179. Würzburg: Königshausen & Neumann.

Schestag, U. (1997) *Sprachspiel als Lebensform. Strukturuntersuchungen zur erzählenden Prosa Elfriede Jelineks*. Bielefeld: Aisthesis.

Schmidt-Dengler, W. (1981) Von der Schwierigkeit, Thomas Bernhard zu lesen. Zu Thomas Bernhards *Gehen*. In M. Jurgensen (ed.) *Bernhard. Annäherungen*. Queensland Studies in German Language and Literature 8, 123–141. Bern and München: Francke.

Schmidt-Dengler, W. (1995) *Bruchlinien. Vorlesungen zur österreichischen Literatur 1945 bis 1990*. Salzburg and Wien: Residenz.

Schmidt-Dengler, W. (1997) *Der Übertreibungskünstler. Studien zu Thomas Bernhard*, 3rd edition. Wien: Sonderzahl.

Streeruwitz, M. (1996) *Verführungen. 3. Folge Frauenjahre*. Frankfurt am Main: Suhrkamp.

Streeruwitz, M. (1997) *Sein. Und Schein. Und Erscheinen*. Tübinger Poetikvorlesungen. Frankfurt am Main: Suhrkamp.

Streeruwitz, M. (1998) *Können. Mögen. Dürfen. Sollen. Wollen. Müssen. Lassen*. Frankfurter Poetikvorlesungen. Frankfurt am Main: Suhrkamp.

Streeruwitz, M. (1999) *Nachwelt. Ein Reisebericht*. Frankfurt am Main: Suhrkamp.

Streeruwitz, M. (2000) *Und. Überhaupt. Stop. Collagen. 1996–2000*. Wien: Edition Selene.

Streeruwitz, M. (2004) *Jessica, 30*. Frankfurt am Main: Suhrkamp.

10 Kanak sprak: the linguistic features of Turkish migrants' communicative style in Feridun Zaimoğlu's works

Sandro M. Moraldo

University of Bologna

Editors' Introduction

Sandro Moraldo teaches German linguistics at the University of Bologna at Forlì as well as Comparative Literature at the Catholic University of the Sacred Heart in Milan. He was born in Italy, but raised in Germany. He has an MA and PhD from the University of Heidelberg and has published on nineteenth and twentieth German and Italian literature, German linguistics and, more recently, on new tendencies in contemporary German language studies.

Moraldo's article provides a linguistic analysis of the novels of German-Turkish writer Feridun Zaimoğlu, born in Turkey in 1964. Like the characters he portrays in his novels, Zaimoğlu has been living in Germany for most his life and was raised in a multilingual and multicultural environment. His fictional writings challenge the traditional boundaries between documentary and fictional genres and are the result of several years of research on multiethnic migrants' communities. They are creative fictional works based on interviews of young Turkish (wo)men who were born and brought up in Germany. More particularly, Zaimoğlu focuses on the Kanake community. As Moraldo tells us, although 'Kanake' has negative semantic connotations, meaning underprivileged second and third generation migrants, this term has recently been relexicalised and contextualised through its appropriation by the migrants themselves, who use it with pride. The Kanake is a community that, as Moraldo explains, is not ethnically defined, since, besides the Turks, it also includes Italians, Bosnians, Kurds and Albanians. Accordingly, their language can be defined as an ethnolectal variety of the German language, that is to say, a way of speaking that is associated with one or more non-German ethnic groups.

Moraldo's critical approach to Zaimoğlu's novels is firmly grounded in a socio-linguistic perspective, inspired by the theories of scholars such as Rösch, Hinnenkamp and Fix. According to such critical perspectives, the linguistic behaviour of young migrants is closely connected with questions of identity in a social dimension, and has the function of representing a particular social situation. Much of Moraldo's paper focuses on an illustration of the linguistic features of the Kanake language (*kanak sprak*) as it is enacted in Zaimoğlu's works, paying particular attention to this language's phonetic and prosodic elements, graphostylistic aspects, features of orality and phenomena of code-mixing and code-switching from the German language. Besides describing this new variety of German, this detailed analysis serves to explain the way in which the Kanaken articulate their social and political condition. For example, Moraldo points out that, from the lexical point of view, the *kanak sprach* is rich in neologistic compound nouns and phenomena of re-lexicalisation which can be interpreted as the expression of a self-conscious socio-cultural identity that strives to distance itself from that of standard German, as well as from those of other communities of migrants. It is this something new, and 'other', that Moraldo would probe.

The challenging question implicitly posed by Zaimoğlu's docu-fictions is: 'How does a Kanake live in Germany?' Moraldo's socio-linguistic article is written, we believe, with another, albeit similar, challenge in mind: that is, to answer the question: 'How does a Kanake communicate in Germany?' His precise and detailed analysis provides an exhaustive answer to this question, one that interweaves linguistic experimentation with the issues raised by a new migrant literature, meaning that he doesn't leave the question at the descriptive level, as his fundamental concern is the function of the 'how'. The article confronts intricate and highly contemporary matters which link plurilinguistic concerns with the social conditions of the immigrant and his/her identity, as well as cultural diversity and intercultural relations.

1   Introduction

This paper aims at describing from a linguistic point of view communicative style of the second- and third-generation Turkish migrants into Germany through the works of Feridun Zaimoğlu. The expressive forms which characterise this style include, among others, the representation of a particular way of dressing, body language, facial expressions and gestures. This essay, however, will focus on its linguistic features. By using their own distinctive language, the speakers communicate their belonging to a specific group and their desire to be considered as representatives of a hybrid culture. Their language gives expression to their socio-cultural identity. The specific group of Turkish migrants this work intends to study is that of the so-called Kanaken.

In the next sections, I will briefly explain the concept 'Kanake' and I will present the German-Turkish writer Feridun Zaimoğlu and his works. His books represent the socio-linguistic and cultural context which underpins these young people's behaviour. As any effort to describe and/or understand how the language is employed in this specific literary context, without taking into due consideration those extralinguistic factors which clearly influence communication and constitute its social basis, is bound to be futile, I will also consider the ethnic and cultural background of the second- and third-generation Turkish immigrants in Germany. Finally, I will look at the ethnolectal variety of the *kanak sprak*, as well as its stylisation by the media, before concluding by identifying, on the basis of the evolving social conditions which will have been outlined, the linguistic structures, i.e. the pragmatic linguistic features, of the Kanaken's ethnolect in Zaimoğlu's works.[1] I will be attempting to explain them in the light of the socio-linguistic assumptions that characterise multilingualism in the context of migration.

2   The Kanake in the minefield of multiculturalism

The term Kanake has negative semantic connotations which are, however, positively interpreted by the underprivileged second- and third-generations. As Kallmeyer et al. write: '[…] the self-definition 'Kanake' results from the appropriation of the negative definition conceived by others, which is now positively interpreted and used with pride' (2000: 4). The Kanaken are not ethnically defined; in Germany, beside the Turks, also Italians, Bosnians, Kurds and Albanians are counted within this group. The Kanaken's language and their linguistic behaviour is variously defined as *Türkendeutsch* (Turks' German), *Türkenslang* (Turks' slang), *Stadtteilsprache* (district language), *Mischsprache* (mixed language) or simply *Ghetto-Sprache* (ghetto language).

After the publication of Zaimoğlu's works, the definitions *Kanaksprache* or *kanak sprak* have become the most popular.

The linguistic behaviour of the young migrants must be interpreted as an expression of social multiculturalism, which has nothing to do with the development of an ego identity anymore (whether German or Turkish), but rather with questions of identity in a cultural dimension, '[…] which is described through the idea of cultural hybridity in the light of the experiences of people who went through migration and is classified through the concept of multiple identities' (Rösch, 2004: 36). The development of such identity is defined as a permanent and performative process '[…] that takes place in interaction, above all in verbal communication' (Hinnenkamp, 2000: 101). Therefore, with reference to this interactionist notion of identity, the use of a specific style, in this case the *kanak sprak*, must be regarded as a variety that '[…] provides specific behavioural traits […] and whose function is […] to explain a social situation by means of the language' (Fix, 2004: 44).

3   Feridun Zaimoğlu, the Malcolm X of the Turks

Zaimoğlu experienced migration himself and grew up in a multilingual and multicultural environment. Unquestionably, it is his merit to have provided, through his books, a description of this subcultural group from an ethnic perspective, with particular attention to the linguistic and communicative behaviour of its members. Born in Turkey in 1964, Zaimoğlu came to Germany when his parents moved there in search of a job. He defines himself as a political author who '[…] wants to make all the foolishness of a heterogeneous community visible' (Huber, 2002: 26). His works offer a realistic and seemingly unfiltered glance at the world of young migrants in Germany. His commitment to the emarginated Turks, to whom he gives voice, has earned him perhaps superficial titles such as 'the Malcolm X of the Turks' or 'the writing arm of Turkish power' (Persch, 2004: 88). 'As a storyteller', says Zaimoğlu:

> I bear witness to what is happening, then later one will say: 'the story of migrants, their children and the children of their children, is the story of Germans of foreign origin who, in spite of insult and humiliation, in spite of politicians' populism and xenophobia, decided to stay. They stayed, because staying in this country was worth it'. (2001b: 21)

Zaimoğlu has been carrying out his research on multiethnic migrants' communities for years, interviewing young men coming from a Turkish background, most of whom were born and brought up in Germany. 'How does a Kanake live in Germany?' was Zaimoğlu's challenging question. The answer is *24 Mißtöne am Rande der Gesellschaft* (*24 Discordant Voices from the Margins of Society*), the subtitle of his first book, *Kanak Sprak*, which was published in 1995.[2] *Kanak Sprak* is, as has been said, both the literary account of a German-Turkish migrant subculture of the second and third generations and an attempt to show how that subculture is translated into its language. Each single story expresses a powerful self-consciousness in a specific social situation. The biographies are 'confessions' from the private and social lives of this 'league of outcasts' (*KSp*: 84), from the jobless to dustmen, students, mechanics and rappers, to dealers, prostitutes, pimps, transsexuals and Islamic fundamentalists. Everyone has a say. And they say it in their distinctive language: the *kanak sprak*. *Kanak Sprak* is only one of Zaimoğlu's works which has called attention to the social character and ethnic status of the Kanake. The novel *Abschaum* (*Scum*) (1997) tells, in 13 episodes, 'die wahre Geschichte von Ertan Ongun' ('the true story of Ertan Ongun'), the book's subtitle. This is the disheartening tale of a petty criminal and junky who, after years of detention, risks being sent back to Turkey. In 1998, there followed *Koppstoff. Kanaka Sprak vom Rande der Gesellschaft* (*Headstuff. Kanaka Sprak from the Margins of Society*), the female version of *Kanak Sprak*, i.e. 26 accounts of Turkish female migrants of the second and third generations. Most recently, in 2000, *Liebesmale, scharlachrot* (*Lovemarks, Scarlet-red*) was published, a 300 page novel containing letters exchanged between the Kanake, Hakan, and his friend, Serdar.

4   The Kanaken's ethnographic assumptions

The 2.4 million migrants of Turkish origin make up Germany's largest ethnic minority. Most of them moved to Germany in the mid-1950s when many foreign workers were employed. These so-called 'Gastarbeiter' ('Guest-workers') had to satisfy the growing need for manpower resulting from the *Wirtschaftswunder* ('economic miracle'). A few of them went back home. The rest are now an integral part of German society and the second- and third-generation Turkish migrants don't intend to go back home. They feel themselves equally attached to both Germany and Turkey. Their contacts with the German community are stronger than the first generation's. Yet the best word to describe their condition is 'Nahfremdheit', literally 'closed foreignness': they live within the German community but they are strangers to it. Born or brought up in Germany, the Kanaken have, nevertheless, the status of foreigners, due only apparently to ethnic and cultural differences, but, more probably the expression of a political, social and legal difference. Zaimoğlu affirms that:

> Turks are strangers and not integrated and so it will continue to be. Integration
> is actually the wrong word. This has nothing to do with integration, but rather

with putting up with the status of foreigner. In my books, I tell stories about different people with different backgrounds. I think this is much more valuable than the statements about the Turks that have been in fashion for decades: there is the Turk, the Turkish community; the Turks aren't able to adapt themselves. Are they too dumb to adapt themselves?! Are Turks too stupid or…or what? This is the starting point of my work. (Huber, 2002: 6)

In order to critically approach the representation of the social conditions and developments of the Kanaken in Zaimoğlu's work, as I aim to do, I've decided to make use of the model of the *Institut für deutsche Sprache* in Mannheim (see Kallmeyer et al., 2000: 4–5). This allows us to define and differentiate the German-Turkish migrant generations. Such distinctions are also the driving force behind the linguistic-communicative behaviour of the (mostly) young people who inhabit the multiethnic migrant context.

With the model, the condition of the Kanaken can be described as follows: there are almost exclusively ghetto-oriented adolescents, labelled as *the insiders*. The ghetto-oriented usually do poorly in school, unlike the potential 'ghetto-runaways', who aim at being high-achievers, in order to provide the Germans with a positive image of the 'integrated, respectable Turks' (Kallmeyer et al., 2000: 6). Most ghetto-oriented adolescents fail to obtain a school-leaving certificate of any kind, hence they can hardly hope to get any kind of traineeship, and, as a consequence, end up spending their days hanging about in clubs and amusement arcades in their ghettos. Their lives evolve '[…] in the company of a street corner society' (Kallmeyer et al., 2000: 4). And their lifestyle mirrors that of other subcultural groups. As Schlobinski (1996: 229) puts it:

> The style of subcultural groups represents an aspect of group identity. Hence a lifestyle, i.e. a style-ensemble made up of different individual styles including look, music, clothes, accessories, graffiti, sayings and expressions, gives rise to correspondences and so creates a relatively uniform group style. Linguistic features, as well as other characteristics, rooted *inside* the consciousness, imply belonging to a group (solidarity); *outside*, they mark a boundary between them and other social groups (distinction).

Their behaviour is a mixture of coolness and acting tough, like machos. They run their businesses on the margins of legality and are often involved in petty crime. It is important to point out that these ghetto-oriented young people are the true representatives of the *kanak sprak*. Thus they develop, through a complex and life-long process, an inner 'hybrid' identity. In Zaimoğlu's opinion, this is a self-evident truth that, especially today, '[…] no one having a proper regular life-story can boast' (2001b: 8). As Zaimoğlu tells us, although the 'negative self-consciousness' he associates with *Kanak Sprak* below has been partly rectified by research in the field, as mentioned above:

> The image of this community is still associated with a negative self-consciousness, as superficially expressed by the apparent self-definition: Kanake! This word has become the disparaging password that defines their identity, the point of conjunction for this *Lumpenethnier* ('lumpen' ethnic group) [who are now] becoming increasingly conscious of more extensive contexts and issues as happened in the Black Consciousness Movement in the United States. (1995: 17)

The social relevance of this linguistic variety lies mainly '[…] in creating or reinforcing boundaries which unify the members of one speech community while excluding outsiders from intragroup communication' (Saville-Troike, 1987: 662). The Kanaken reject any one-dimensional linguistic and cultural blending, since 'integration' to them means 'nothing but standardization' (Zaimoğlu, 1998: 100).

The difference between the first-generation and the second- and third-generation Turkish migrants can be interpreted linguistically too. The parents, having undergone their primary socialisation (and language learning) in Turkey, speak the so called *Gastarbeiterdeutsch* (Guest-workers' German), which '[…] is characterised by paratactic constructions, poor vocabulary, redundancy, omission of articles, prepositions, conjunctions and proper verb conjugation' (Bußmann, 1983: 157). The Kanaken's communicative style contrasts with this disorderly language, but it is also at odds with the linguistic behaviour of other Turkish groups (politicians, artists, academicians, etc.), who have achieved their linguistic and cultural integration into German society, but whom the Kanaken offensively define as 'Abiturtürken' (Turks who have obtained a higher education certificate) (*AS*: 15), or even 'Assimil-Kümmel' (integrated 'caraway-seeds') (*KS*: 14). Zaimoğlu's opinion, which closes the introduction to his first work, *Kanak Sprak*, is noteworthy:

> Some Turks have learned to behave like the middle-class Germans and have turned into the nice colleague 'Ali' whom one brings to the usual club after work. Others managed to attend the university and frequent the German and international academic circles. For true intellectuals, interculturalism has always been something obvious. They have integrated so well that they have given a definite contribution to German society. They are 'socially tolerable', they possess no socially explosive power. In this book one vainly looks for them. Here the Kanake only has a say.

Such 'socially explosive power' belongs to the *kanak sprak*.

5   Kanak sprak as an ethnolectal variety

The *kanak sprak* is an ethnolectal variety of the German language. An ethnolect in the German context, according to Auer (2003: 256), is a way of speaking '[…] associated with one or more non-German ethnic groups by the language users themselves and/or by other people'. The typical setting of the *kanak sprak* is the inner city, with a high concentration of foreigners, which are perceived as, and called, *ghettos*, even by those who live there. In *Kanak Sprak* for instance: 'wir haben unser ghetto, wir schleppen's überall hin' (1995: 25) (we have our own ghetto, we bring it with us everywhere). In these places '[…] their life is characterised by close relations within their own community and relatively few contacts with the German society which surrounds them' (Kallmeyer et al., 2000: 3).

The ethnolect, *kanak sprak*, which Auer (2003) defines as a primary ethnolect, has been well documented empirically and studied through the analysis of tape-recordings and various other acoustic documents (Füglein, 2000; Keim, 2002 and 2003).

Over the past few years, this ethnic-social slang has been 'discovered' by the mass media; in particular, in communicative contexts such as song lyrics, comics, radio and TV programmes, movies and cabarets, everyday *kanak sprak* is frequently represented in a stylised form. According to Selting and Hinnenkamp (1989: 10), stylisation demands '[…] the active processing of the typical and stylizable core elements of the social model that has to be represented'. Writers, singers, comedians, cabaret artists, film-makers, etc., get inspiration from the primary ethnolect of street Kanaken and imitate it through the effective use of linguistic and semiotic features. This fictitious genre takes the name of secondary ethnolect, since the use of ethnolects by the media always implies the appropriation of the primary ethnolect by people to whom this doesn't 'belong' (Auer, 2003: 256). [3] For example, the cabaret artists of the very successful comedy duo, *Mundstuhl*, are two Germans from South Hessen who represent specific social models typical of the ghetto in their sketches, borrowing the linguistic and behavioural characteristics that play to the audience.

Zaimoğlu's protagonists lie somewhere in the middle. They are the native speakers of the *kanak sprak*, which 'belongs' to them (in Auer's meaning). However, and paradoxically, their language is refracted and recreated through a docu-fictional representation, no matter how realistic that representation aims to be and no matter how praiseworthy it is that this representation has occurred for the first time in his works and apparently encouraged further mediatic interest. Almost at the same time as Zaimoğlu published, the Turkish Hip-Hop band, *Cartel*, with its aggressive *kanak sprak*-like lyrics, also became popular in Germany.

6   The communicative style of the kanak sprak

6.1 Phonetic and prosodic elements

In their everyday communication and audiovisual media representation, phonetic and prosodic elements play a very significant role in the way the Kanaken speak. Zaimoğlu compares their way of speaking to rap: 'They speak in an affected way [...] with an unremitting breathless eclectic stammering, as if there were no full stops or commas, with arbitrarily chosen and improvised idioms' (1995: 13). German is 'distanced' through the use of rhythmic and phonetic features typical of their Turkish mother tongue. Such 'estranging' mechanisms include an overemphasised, monotonous inflection; a rolling /r/ as final sound, the use of the phonetically marked adjectives *konkret* (concrete) and *krass* (gross), used to emphasise or to positively or negatively connote things; an alternation of peaks and lows in the rhythm rather than a sentence-based intonation, where accented syllables mark what is significant in the statement; a voiced articulation of typically voiceless fricative sounds (for instance, *swei* instead of *zwei* (two) or *su weisch* instead of *zu weich* (too soft)); the shifting of palatal fricatives (*isch* instead of *ich*) (cf. Kallmeyer et al., 2000; Keim and Androutsopoulos, 2000; Keim, 2002, 2003; Kallmeyer and Keim, 2004).

Yet Zaimoğlu's works have to deal with the impossibility of representing first hand phonetic and prosodic elements, as well as the facial expressions and gestures. The author rejects any use of metaphonological markers that could make up for this restraint, using, however, targeted graphostylistic and linguistic elements, in order to represent at least some relevant features. It is now time to analyse more thoroughly the *kanak sprak's* style and the way it is realised in writing in Zaimoğlu's works.

6.2 Graphostylistic aspects

In *Kanak Sprak* the use of small letters, instead of the standard German capitalisation of nouns and proper names, is a formal characteristic that immediately attracts the reader's attention. Zaimoğlu seems to use this device, at least as far as the proper names go, much like Faulkner may be doing in his *The Sound and the Fury*, to give expression to his characters' self-alienation towards an existence they are at odds with. Furthermore, among the orthographic, rule-breaking stylistic elements used by Zaimoğlu, there are interventions in the codified association between phonemes and letters, such as the phonetic spelling of German. Spellings such as *Akzion* (instead of *Aktion*) and *erwaxen* (instead of *erwachsen* (grown up)) have a stylistic value, since they visually highlight oral elements. This happens especially with foreign words (mainly Anglicisms, but also Gallicisms) such as *Polis* → [instead of] Police, *taff* → tough; *Äktschen* → action, *Türkenrestoran* → Türkenrestaurant, *Schampanja* → Champagner. Further examples are: *Bisiness* → business, *Fasson* → façon, *Buké* → bouquet, *Niwo* → niveau, *schose* → chose. Since in German, as in many other written languages, there are strict rules concerning the phoneme-grapheme link, these stylistic variants represents a clash with the written conventions in force, i.e. a '[…] longing for autonomy, typical of adolescents, a creative linguistic play realized with standard forms' (Pohl, 1995: 250). Since the written form purposely mirrors the pronunciation, foreign graphemes are avoided.[4]

6.3 Linguistic aspects of an emulated orality

Besides changing the spelling of lexemes deriving from different foreign languages, what is most striking in Zaimoğlu is the fact that his young migrants have a wide range of linguistic repertoires at their disposal, such as everyday German, their original language and a mix of the two. In the introduction to *Kanak Sprak*, the German-Turkish writer himself points out the peculiarity of this style and defines it as '[…] a free translation of an authentic linguistic picture' (1995: 15). This is very important, since it is the first attempt to give a written rendering of the genuine everyday oral communication.

As said above, given that Zaimoğlu avoids representing other relevant non-linguistic expressive forms of the *kanak sprak*, the language is the only distinctive mark which contributes to the development of the identity both of the social group as a whole and of the individual's self-image. The way linguistic strategies are used to translate the process of identity development is, then, decisive. As Zaimoğlu says, 'It is the language that determines the existence: one gives a completely private description of it in words' (1995: 13).

The colloquial tone of everyday conversation used in these self-portrayals also creates an aspect of the tenor in Zaimoğlu's texts. This linguistic style, in which dialogic trustworthiness, and the interlocutor's emotiveness and spontaneity are key criteria, is also realised through the use of the Kanaken's typical appellative 'Bruder' (*KSp*: 47, 62 et passim). In *Kanak Sprak* it is also used to refer to Zaimoğlu as Interviewer: 'Ich sag dir, bruder. In diesem land läuft's zum teil stinkig' (I tell you, brother, in this country things sometimes stink) (*KSp*: 21). This is reminiscent of the African-American model, but not only. This expression marks not only the intimacy between conversation partners, but also the difference from the communicative habits of the rest of the linguistic community. This style is not simply a superficial appropriation of African-American language practice, but also stresses the similarity between the Kanaken ethnic minority's context and political orientation with those of the

Black Consciousness Movement. With 'Bruder', the word's implicit meaning has in fact a significant pragmatic and social function.

The Kanaken talk, in a very spontaneous way, about their attitude towards Germany, their existence as German-Turks and related problems. Most of them live on the fringe of legality. In fact, *kanak sprak* is used for representing such contexts and weaving 'subcultural narratives': i.e. stories of '[…] young characters from the ghetto, who are involved in crimes and drug abuse' (Androutsopoulos, 2001: 327). Semantically, *kanak sprak* also focuses on certain ideas and things that are repeatedly re-lexicalised, such as their status as foreigners and the words for drugs, money, police, sex and racism. As a reaction against discriminating experiences, the Kanake, also called Kanakster due to their young age (from *Kanake* and *youngster*), like providing an aggressive, combative and fiery image of themselves. Their vocabulary is thus mostly obscene, crude, sarcastic, sometimes definitely subversive, and pays no attention to 'political correctness'. It is characterised by numerous rude and offensive words and typically racist expressions such as *Nigger:* 'Ich, Musa, Necdet und Milka, das war n Nigger' (I, Musa, Necdet and Milka, a nigger) (*AS*: 84), or 'alemannenkacker' (Alemannian arsehole) (*KSp*: 81), meant to shock the mainstream reader. The language can get extremely vulgar and taboo: 'Ich kuck an mir runter, mein Schwanz is pervers hochgegangen und voll prall das Teil' (I look at myself down there, my cock is as straight as a post, it's swelling) (*AS*: 34).

The self-conscious socio-cultural identity that marks this subculture is undoubtedly the ideal basis for linguistic creativity and lexical innovation, demonstrated by a complex word-building procedure involving the formation of neologistic compound nouns: *mürbekoppverhalten* (spineless-slacker behaviour), *looserkanake* (kanake loser), *schlimmansteckung* (appalling infection), *arschkrükenhandlung* (idiot behaviour) (*KSp*: 52, 67, 97, 133); *Insgesichtspucker* (face-spitter), *Radieschenvonuntenriecher* (those who sniff the roots from the bottom) (*KS*: 32, 33); and ad-hoc constructions for hyphenated sentences: 'deutsch-ist-nummer-eins-was-gibt' (German is number one) (*KSp*: 85); 'Gibt-solche-und-solche' (There are people and people) (*KS*: 35); 'Lern-lieben-oder-geh' (Learn to love or get out) (*KS*: 35). When in *Kanak Sprak* Zaimoğlu states that 'The Kanaken's language is made up of largely incomprehensible jargonised words and expressions, which do not exist either in German or Turkish' (1995: 13), he surely also refers to these new idioms: single sporadic expressions and neologisms, i.e. original and peculiar new constructions, which highlight the Kanaken's penchant for weighty and meaningfully packed expressions. They articulate their situation artfully, thanks to their exploitation of the effectiveness of clichés and catchwords. The Kanaken take advantage of possibilities which are not employed in normal word formation and which are then used as a model to create new constructions by analogy. Moreover, their new way of calling things mirrors their new way of interpreting and evaluating things. Hyphenated sentences concisely and precisely give expression to everyday events as well. These clash with the common use of language, '[…] hence creating an eloquent novel effect' (Fleischer et al., 1993: 136). The *kanak sprak*'s neologisms and hyphenated sentences, far from playing a cryptic role, are basic elements of the group's language dynamics.

Thanks to the spontaneous dimension of its expressions, the *kanak sprak* in Zaimoğlu is very similar to the spoken language. This free, impulsive, spontaneous language used in natural linguistic contexts mirrors the original spoken form and is realised in various ways:

- the use of the indefinite article and allomorph abbreviations: e.g. *ner* (instead of *einer*), *ne* (instead of *eine*), *nem* (instead of *einem*). Examples within sentences are: 'mausetot und mit *ner* (instead of *einer*) erbärmlichen visage' (stone dead and peaky) (*KSp*: 60); 'So *ne* (instead of *eine*) Scheiße, weißt du, amina koyum' (So shitty, you know, fuck you) (*AS*: 63); 'hört sich so amerikanisch an, inner Gruppe, *nem* (instead of *einem*) Stamm oder was weiß ich' (feels so American, in a group, in a gang or whatever) (*AS*: 62);

- lexical enclisis, e.g. *anne*[*r*] (instead of *an einer*); *inner* (instead of *in einer*), *is'n* (instead of *ist ein*); *da'n* (instead of *da ein*). Further illustrative examples are: 'Der Typ is völlig fertig, sieht aus *wien* (instead of *wie ein*) Crack-Monster oder *wien* Junkie' (The guy is totally stoned, he looks like a Crack-Monster or a Junkie) (*AS*: 26); 'Es gibt nur eine Lösung, die is sicherer als *n* (instead of *ein*) Messerglanz *inner* (instead of *in einer*) Nacht und genauso gut' (There's only one solution which is safer than a blade that gleams in the dark and as good as that) (*KS*: 72); 'Die hatten *nen* (instead of *einen*) Imbiß *inner* (instead of *in der*) Stadt' (they had a snack bar somewhere in town) (*AS*: 52);[5]

- the coordinating use of *weil* with the verb in second position, very frequently used in spoken language, instead of its standard subordinative use with the verb at the end of the sentence, typical of the written language: e.g. 'weil du kriegst futter' ('cause you get fed) (*KSp*: 39); 'weil die Zeit is anders' ('cause time's different) (*KS*: 133). Further examples are: 'weil, bruder, für die is'n haus gipfel der gefühle' ('cause their high point, brother, is having a house) (*KSp*: 74); 'weil die Kieler

Woche dauert ne Woche' ('cause the Kiel week lasts a week) (*AS*: 64);[6]

- the use of the verb *tun* (to do) + infinitive, as a marker of a colloquial register: 'der tut dir ins haus einbrechen' (he gets into your house and cleans it out) (*KSp*: 62). More examples are: 'damit denn nicht'n kanake wie ich kommen tut' (so a kanake like me doesn't come) (*KSp*: 83); 'All das, was so n Liberalpisser vorgeben tut' (all a liberal pisser expects you to do) (*KS*: 11);

- the generalised use of the verb *machen* (to make): 'Auch kein Problem, machen wir Ratenzahlung' (no problem, we'll make a deferred payment) (*AS*: 94); 'Wir haben natürlich ne Biege gemacht' (Of course we took off like a shot) (*AS*: 21);

- patterns typical of adolescent language, at both lexical and phraseological level, e.g. 'Bruder, ich klopf hier kein spruch, aber da draußen tobt ne fehde' (I don't wanna push things too far, brother, but out there a fight's starting) (*KSp*: 47); 'törnt die voll an' (this makes them totally crazy) (*KSp*: 69); 'dann zuckel man hier schwer ab' (shove off from here!) (*KS*: 43); 'und da willst du ums verrecken nich hin' (you wouldn't get there for any reason) (*KS*: 45).

Proximity to the spoken language is clearly increased the higher the incidence of linguistic oral elements. Additional stereotypical features of the *kanak sprak* in Zaimoğlu's works are discourse markers. Beside the expression 'ich schwör' (I swear), as in 'Ich schwör dir' (*AS*: 86), which may open or close speech segments and be used in conversations to point out the truthfulness of the speaker's statements, we have particles functioning as key elements of Kanaken speech which mimic adolescent language. These include: *korrekt* (correct), a common expression used by the Kanaken, e.g. as in 'Brauchst du weich, geb ich dir Kissen, brauchst du hart, geb ich dir korrekt!' (If you need it soft, I'll give you some cushions, if you need it hard, I'll give you what you deserve!) (*LS*: 56); *krass* ('ich will nicht, daß es offiziell bekannt wird, daß er mein Neffe is; so krass!' (I don't want people to officially know that he's my nephew, it's too gross) (*AS*: 8). Both of these are pronounced with a rolling /r/. A final example of such particles is *fett*: 'wo da'n ganz fettes versagen […]' (it's been a complete flop) (*KSp*: 68–69); 'vonner Araberkolonne fett gelinkt worden' (got totally swindled by a bunch of Arabs) (*LM*: 97). Semantically, they are seen as intensifiers and consequently are used in conversations to stress and/or to positively/negatively evaluate things and events. *Korrekt*, *krass* and *fett* are adjectives/adverbs which come from German standard language, but they are used in a completely different way (Volmert, 2004: 142–143). Their use as attributive adjectives or as intensifying verbs is evidence of the Kanaken's tendency to exaggerate and overstate.

From the way oral narrative style is realised in written form, it should be evident by now that the *kanak sprak* is a language of 'proximity'. The above-illustrated examples of diverse linguistic aspects are noteworthy. Along with the informal nature of the situations comes greater spontaneity, which usually implies greater expressiveness and affective participation. Self-portrayals and random topic development are further aspects making up the *kanak sprak*'s communicative style: 'Scheiß drauf! Erste sorge: wo bin ich und wie bring ich meine haut in'n sicheren Hafen?' (Shit! First worry: where am I and how can I save my skin?) (*KSp*: 45); 'Du hörst das von mir, bruder, vergiß das nich, du hörst die gute alte wahrheit von einem ollen kanaken.' (Take it from me, brother, don't forget it, you get god's own truth from a kanake) (*KSp*: 96).

6.4 'Defective' German, code-mixing and code-switching

The linguistic picture portrayed above must not lead us to think that the Kanaken have deliberately manipulated German to their purposes, since, owing to their low educational level, they do not speak perfect German.

There are several proofs of this:

- the elimination of case-morphemes and lack of gender concordance. Examples: 'die allerwahrhaftigste sorge im mensch[en]' (everyone's real worries) (*KSp*: 61); 'das kostet sein[en] Preis' (that's got its price) (*AS*: 111);

- the use of the incorrect relative conjunction *wo*, instead of the relative pronouns *der*, *die*, *das*. Examples: 'Dass du ureigene tarife hast, wo (instead of *die*) nur auf deinem mist wachsen' ('cause you have your own old rates, that only you could think of) (*KSp*: 121); 'und verpassen sich'n saft, wo (instead of *der*) sie schön kaltstellt' (and they give themselves a fix, which makes them harmless) (*KSp*: 122); 'Hab auch den Tag mitbekommen, wo (instead of *an dem*) er die Strafe bekommen hat' (I remember the day he got punished) (*AS*: 119);

- the elimination of definite and indefinite articles. Examples: 'in [die] dunkle nacht wagen?' (do you dare go out into the pitch dark night?) (*KSp*: 62); 'Er is [eine] Leiche' (He's a corpse) (*AS*: 11); '[Der] Mensch is'n hund, der nach'm unsterblichen jault' (Men are like dogs that never stop howling) (*AS*: 63); 'ein kleiner Riß in [der] Haut reißt groß rein' (a small crack on the skin eats a lot inside) (*KS*: 81);

- case and concordance mistakes. Examples: 'in der ungläubigen land' (in the unbelievable country) (*KSp*: 138); 'Wird kein schöner[es] Land daraus' (you won't get a nicer country outside of here) (*KS*: 117).

Judging by native speaker standards, all these examples show an inadequate linguistic behaviour, which is, of course, not perceived as such by those foreign adolescents who live and grow up in inner city ghettos with a high concentration of foreigners, where infringements of linguistic rules are everyday occurrences. The 'ghetto-oriented' Kanaken, those who are interested in neither school nor job training, contribute to this improper way of speaking because of their lack of education.

Moreover, the migration process also results in the natural linguistic code-blending of German and Turkish, especially in those contexts where Turkish migrants' children and second- and third-generation youths socialise together. In this case, they switch from one language to another, or bring expressions of their native language into German.

In Zaimoğlu, there are often entire sentences that are almost incomprehensible for a German reader and passages full of Turkish loan words including interjections, labels and swear-words, which are used with an expressive-emphatic function. A translation is not always provided, as in this example taken from *Koppstoff* (1998: 111): 'Pah! Und dann: shinanay yavrum schinanay nay!' (Pah! And then: shallalla baby shallala!); and *Abschaum* (1997: 110): 'ulan gökte ararken yerde buldum, anima koyduğumun çocuğu' (Hey you, I looked for the sky and found the earth, fuck you baby). A typical loan from Turkish is the interjection *aminá koyúm*, which can be translated into German with *verdammter Mist, verdammte Scheiße* (bloody shit) or *gottverdammich* (god damn) (*KSp*: 52). It expresses both speaker emotion and an informal situation and is placed most often at the beginning or at the end of a sentence, as in e.g. 'Aminá koyúm, die ganze Scheiße hab ich durchgemacht, Alter, ich komm hier draußen nicht klar' (Fuck you, I put up with all this shit, mate, I can't cope with it out there) (*AS*: 179); e.g. 'Das war nicht viel, aber ich brauchte Geld, scheißegal, ich hatte kein Bock zu arbeiten, amina koyum' (It wasn't that much, but I needed money, I don't give a damn, I didn't want to work, fuck off) (*AS*: 108). The exclamation is a socially marked form, since it is not used by all members of the discourse community but only by speakers in the interaction, belonging to a specific social group. Moreover, the diacritical sign of the *Umlaut*, typical of Turkish as well as of German, is applied to the German lexicon but in a Turkish way, thereby breaking the German writing rules. *Leitkultur* (dominant culture) and *Subkultur* (subculture) suddenly become *Leitkültur* and *Süppkültür* (*KS*: 16); *Volk* (people) turns into *Völk* (*AS*: 17), *Professor* into *Professör* (*LM*:

53) and so on. Other examples are: *Haikü-Baracke* (haiku-hut), *gängsteröse Lippen- und Kinnbärtchen* (moustache and pointed beard like a gangster), *süpergeschmeidiger* (mega-flexible) (*LM*: 62, 74, 109).

Zaimoğlu's tendency to conflate the two codes is used to signal that young Turks feel they don't really belong to either one or the other culture. And yet, as Zaimoğlu tells us, the Kanaken '[…] seek no cultural anchorage' (1995: 12). When Turkish expressions are syntactically mixed with German ones, an explicit fractured self-portrayal is being provided: they have grown out of their Turkish culture because of their western socialisation. On one hand, they speak their mother tongue with difficulty, so that in Turkey they are considered Germans, or *Deutschländer* (German foreigners); on the other, because of their 'scrubby' German, they are not seen as true Germans in their current home country. In this minefield, characterised by the combination of two different linguistic systems, code-switching shouldn't be interpreted solely as an expression of a dissociated, torn identity, but also as a sign of a very specific identity of the second- and third-generation Turkish migrants which, for Hinnenkamp, could best be defined as a 'transitional social identity'. This means that '[…] a person hasn't only one identity, but plays and interacts with different ones which continuously clash with one another and with the environment' (2000: 101). The Kanaken distance themselves from the linguistic behaviour both of most Germans and also of their fathers' generation. This means that they find themselves '[…] preserved in linguistic acts, in which a linguistic repertoire that aims at defining and shielding them against an extraneous typification and attempts to underline their belonging to a specific group is employed' (Hinnenkamp, 2000: 101).

7 Conclusion

In this paper I have attempted to describe the language, i.e. the linguistic features, of the communicative style of the second- and third-generation Turkish migrant in Germany and to delineate the social context of the particular subculture that expresses it. I've tried to show that a specific Turkish migrant group, the so-called Kanaken, due to their multicultural and multilingual socialisation, as well as their 'ghetto-oriented' attitude, develop a particular communicative style, which distinguishes them from other internal (Turkish) or external (German) groups and sets them up as an independent socio-cultural unit. Although acoustic (phonetics and prosody), as well as visual (dress, facial expressions, gestures and body language) elements add to the highlighting of this migrant group's cultural identity, I have focused my attention on linguistic features and the way these are stylised in the works of the German-Turkish writer Feridun Zaimoğlu. Zaimoğlu's works are above all characterised by a very colloquial narrative style. The mainly informal conversations between Zaimoğlu and his interviewees (in *Kanak Sprak* and *Headstuff*), Ertan and his friends (*Scum*), Hakan and Serdar (*Lovemarks, Scarlet-red*) are rich in linguistic structures taken from present-day German, as well as from the Turkish language. This type of language contact leads to code-blending, as well as to code-switching during communication. *Kanak sprak* is an ethnically-rooted group language, realised on various levels; *kanak sprak*'s communicative style becomes for these Turkish youths an important means for developing their identity and for tackling the society's attribution of roles and status that they don't readily accept. The *kanak sprak* is the linguistic expression of a transitional social identity that '[…] at the same time both adjusts their allotted identity (as German or Turkish, but also as declared members of an ethnic minority)', whether this has been requested by the core society or not, and also '[…] dismantles and creatively develops it, i.e. adds to it, providing a new independent identity' (Hinnenkamp, 2000: 102).

Notes

1   In order to avoid any misunderstandings, I write *Kanak Sprak* in capital letters when I mention Zaimoğlu's first work and *kanak sprak* in small letters when I refer to the ethnolect.

2   Unless otherwise specified, all translations provided in this paper are my own. To facilitate understanding, the translation is given in brackets next to the German original. The following abbreviations of Zaimoğlu's books will be used: *Kanak Sprak (KSp)*; *Abschaum (AS)*, *Koppstoff (KS)*, *Liebesmale, scharlachrot (LM)*.

3   Auer's scheme of ethnolectal speech is completed by the tertiary ethnolect, in which the 'media input' of the secondary ethnolect gets 'transformed' by the German youths (2003: 256).

4   In the literature of German-speaking countries, Oskar Panizza (1853–1921) had already tried to change the written language through the use of phonetic writing. See Moraldo (2001).

5   These show that linguistic expressive means can be associated with the 'konzeptionelle Mündlichkeit', which is a concept derived from Koch and Oesterreicher in their study on *Schriftlichkeit und Sprache* (1994) (*Writing and Language*), in which they use both terms *mündlich/schriftlich* (oral/written) with a twofold meaning. On the one hand, they refer to the means by which the linguistic expression is realised (*mündlich* = phonetically and *schriftlich* = graphically); on the other hand, to the *ductus* and modality of expression. The latter aspect is summed up in the concept of *konzeptionelle Mündlichkeit/Schriftlichkeit* (conceptual orality/writing). The difference between 'conceptual' oral and written expression lies in their respective 'proximity' (*konzeptionell mündlich*) or 'distance' (*konzeptionell schriftlich*) from either extreme.

6   On the discrepancy in the use of connectors between written language rules in
     grammars and text-books and the actual spoken German, see Küper (1991) and
     Günthner (1993, 2000 and 2002).

References

Androutsopoulos, J. K. (2001) Ultra korregd Alder! Zur medialen Stilisierung
     und Aneignung von 'Türkendeutsch'. *Deutsche Sprache* 29: 321–339.

Auer, P. (2003) 'Türkenslang': Ein jugendlicher Ethnolekt des Deutschen und
     seine Transformationen. In A. Häcki Buhofer (ed.) *Spracherwerb und
     Lebensalter* 255–264. Tübingen and Basel: Francke.

Bußmann, H. (1983) *Lexikon der Sprachwissenschaft.* Stuttgart: Kröner.

Fix, U. (2004) Stil gibt immer etwas zu verstehen. Sprachstile aus pragmatischer
     Perspektive. *Der Deutschunterricht* 51.1: 41–150.

Fleischer W., Michel G. and Starke G. (1993) *Stilistik der deutschen
     Gegenwartssprache.* Frankfurt am Main: Peter Lang.

Füglein, R. (2000) *Kanak Sprak. Eine ethnolinguistische Untersuchung eines
     Sprachphänomens im Deutschen.* Otto-Friedrich-Universität Bamberg:
     Diplomarbeit im Studiengang Germanistik.

Günthner, S. (1993) '… weil – man kann es ja wissenschaftlich untersuchen'.
     Diskurspragmatische Aspekte der Wortstellung in *weil*-Sätzen. *Linguistische
     Berichte* 143: 137–159.

Günthner, S. (2000) Grammatik der gesprochenen Sprache – eine
     Herausforderung für Deutsch als Fremdsprache? *Info DaF* 4: 352–366.

Günthner, S. (2002) Konnektoren im gesprochenen Deutsch – Normverstoß oder
     funktionale Differenzierung? *Deutsch als Fremdsprache* 39: 67–74.

Hinnenkamp, V. (2000) 'Gemischt sprechen' von Migrantenjugendlichen als
     Ausdruck ihrer Identität. *Der Deutschunterricht* 52. 5: 96–107.

Huber, J. (2002) 'Öder Betroffenheitsblödsinn'. *Audimax* 7/8: 26.

Kallmeyer, W. and Keim, I. (2004) Deutsch-türkische Kontaktvarietäten.
     Am Beispiel der Sprache von deutsch-türkischen Jugendlichen. In
     S. M. Moraldo and M. Soffritti (eds) *Deutsch aktuell. Einführung in die
     Tendenzen der deutschen Gegenwartssprache* 49–59. Roma: Carocci.

Kallmeyer, W., Keim, I. and Tandogan-Weidenhammer, D. (2000) Deutsch-
     Türkisches. Sprache und kommunikativer Stil von Migranten. *Sprachreport*
     3: 2–8.

Keim, I. (2002) Sprachvariation und sozialer Stil. Am Beispiel jugendlicher
     MigrantInnen türkischer Herkunft in Mannheim. *Deutsche Sprache* 30:
     97–123.

Keim, I. (2003) Die Verwendung medialer Stilisierungen von Kanaksprak durch
     Migrantenjugendliche. *Kodikas. Ars Semeiotica* 26: 95–111.

Keim, I. and Androutsopoulos, J. (2000) 'Hey Lan, isch geb dir konkret
     Handy'. Deutsch-türkische Mischsprache und Deutsch mit ausländischem

Akzent: Wie Sprechweisen der Straße durch die Medien populär werden. *Frankfurter Allgemeine Zeitung*, 26 Januar.

Koch, P. and Oesterreicher, W. (1994) Schriftlichkeit und Sprache. In H. Günther and O. Ludwig (eds) *Schrift und Schriftlichkeit: ein interdisziplinäres Handbuch internationaler Forschung* 587–604. Berlin and New York: de Gruyter.

Küper, C. (1991) Geht die Nebensatzstellung im Deutschen verloren? Zur pragmatischen Funktion der Wortstellung in Haupt- und Nebensätzen. *Deutsche Sprache* 19: 133–158.

Moraldo, S. M. (2001) L'estrosità linguistica di Oskar Panizza. In O. Panizza *La fabbrica di uomini* 139–145 and 151–154. Milano: Tranchida.

Moraldo, S. M. and Soffritti, M. (eds) (2004) *Deutsch aktuell. Einführung in die Tendenzen der deutschen Gegenwartssprache*. Roma: Carocci.

Persch, P. (2004) 'Identität ist Tofu für Lemminge'. Interview mit dem Kieler Schriftsteller Feridun Zaimoğlu. *Der Deutschunterricht* 51. 5: 87–89.

Pohl, I. (1995) Semantik und Stilwert graphischer Mittel. In P. Ewald and K.-E. Sommerfeldt (eds) *Beiträge zur Schriftlinguistik. Festschrift zum 60. Geburtstag von Prof. Dr. phil. habil. Dieter Nerius* 245–256. Frankfurt am Main: Peter Lang.

Rösch, H. (2004) Literatur interkulturell lesen. *Deutschunterricht* 4: 36–41.

Saville-Troike, M. (1987) The ethnography of speaking. In U. Ammon, N. Dittmar and K. H. Mattheier (eds) *Sociolinguistics. An International Handbook of the Science of Language and Society* 660–671. Berlin and New York: de Gruyter.

Schlobinski, P. (1996) *Empirische Sprachwissenschaft*. Opladen: Westdeutscher Verlag.

Selting, M. and Hinnenkamp V. (1989) Einleitung: Stil und Stilisierung in der Interpretativen Soziolinguistik. In V. Hinnenkamp and M. Selting (eds) *Stil und Stilisierung* 1–23. Tübingen: Niemeyer.

Volmert, J. (2004) Jugendsprachen – Szenesprachen. In S. M. Moraldo and M. Soffritti (eds) *Deutsch aktuell. Einführung in die Tendenzen der deutschen Gegenwartssprache* 134–158. Roma: Carocci.

Zaimoğlu, F. (1995) *Kanak Sprak. 24 Mißtöne vom Rande der Gesellschaft*. Hamburg: Rotbuch.

Zaimoğlu, F. (1997) *Abschaum. Die wahre Geschichte von Ertan Ongun*. Hamburg: Rotbuch.

Zaimoğlu, F. (1998) *Koppstoff. Kanaka Sprak vom Rande der Gesellschaft*. Hamburg: Rotbuch.

Zaimoğlu, F. (2000) *Liebesmale, scharlachrot*. Hamburg: Rotbuch.

Zaimoğlu, F. (2001a) *Kopf und Kragen. Kanak-Kultur-Kompendium*. Frankfurt am Main: S. Fischer.

Zaimoğlu, F. (2001b) Kanak Attack: Rebellion der Minderheiten. In F. Zaimoğlu (2001a) *Kopf und Kragen. Kanak-Kultur-Kompendium* 8–21. Frankfurt am Main: S. Fischer.

11 Debating the function of language in poetry: meta-textual musings in the Spanish 50s generation

María José Rodrigo Mora

University of Bologna

Editors' Introduction

María José Rodrigo Mora is a scholar whose research concentrates on applied linguistics, the history of the Spanish language, discourse analysis, translation and literary language. In her paper, she lucidly combines the first and last of these interests by inquiring into how the poetic practice of the poets of the Spanish 1950s' generation was accompanied by, indeed inextricably mingled with, profound reflections upon their use of language and its very role in their art. These compelling 'meta-textual musings', as she calls them, are clearly much more than that: they are authentic and insightful theoretical meditations – genuine 'poetics', which were often appended to their artistic publications and which critics have actually often considered more interesting than that artistic production itself!

From Rodrigo Mora's study, these Spanish poet-philosophers emerge as intense and enthusiastic in their inquisitive search for, and avid absorption, or rejection, of ideas coming from a vast array of sources. In part, their reflections concentrate on problems explicitly related to, and highlighted by, the contemporary and sometimes remarkable developments going on in various branches of linguistics. These became fundamental issues for these poets' craftsmanship, not least because they were convinced that continuous experimentation with language was a compelling and absolutely necessary task. They also saw it as the main means they had of enhancing the creative and seductive power of their poetry. Through these 'poetics of poetry', Rodrigo Mora traces the path of the Spanish poets' linguistic concerns: not only in the 1950s, during which a common theoretical interest lay in the notion of poetry-as-communication, or in the competing cognitive concept of poetry-as-knowledge, but also in the 1960s and the 1970s, when there were obvious structuralist/formalist/generativist influences on their writings, and right up to the 1980s, when this new generation of poets can be seen to be attempting to apply certain principles of pragmatics to their texts.

It is in fact intriguing to see how these Spanish writers take on Saussure, the Russian Formalists, Sartre, Eliot, Chomsky etc., and to see how these authorities are understood, and perhaps at least in part also misunderstood, but always seriously and even passionately engaged with. These 'musings', though hardly unique, touch upon the most weighty questions that the philosophy of language, in general, and of literary language, in particular, can broach. In just what does the language of poetry consist? How does it relate to the 'norm'? Is it somehow deviant? Or does its peculiarity lie in what it *does*? Can it be said to translate, or give shape to, a prior psychic state? Or does that state, or an understanding of it, only come into being through the creative process itself? And what about the reader? What is the nature of the relationship between the poet and the latter? And how is it mediated by the created artifact, and by the cultural context of its creation? Or is the work of art perhaps not, in itself, 'autonomous'?

Rodrigo Mora dedicates much space to the poetry-as-knowledge vs. poetry-as-communication conflict, which was obviously a heatedly debated topic, one which apparently obsessed some of the most important scholars of language of the times in Spain. Is the poem a vehicle of a previously-intuited truth that is then re-lived by both writer and reader? Or is the poet actually unaware of what the poem would say, prior to the existence of the poem itself? And what is the nature of such intuition? Is it synthetic and unique, or analytic and replicable? Does the poetic text aim at communication, or is communication but a by-product of poetry-making? Should the accent, in any case, be placed on its product, or rather on the *process* itself? Mightn't the very word 'communication' be a misnomer? Can the experience the poet aims at representing ever be genuinely reproduced? And, if not, does it matter? Hefty questions indeed, the conflicting opinions on which are carefully marshalled and set forth. Yet, neither is the question as to what these musings may ultimately be said to have been 'unto' lacking. The author appears to agree with Segre (1985: 300) that:

> Whoever operates within a poetic produces innovations, especially formal ones, but without a belief that these will undermine the prevailing world view. It will then be time itself that will tell if, at some point, quantitative innovation produces a qualitative leap: i.e. if it expresses and validates modifications of that world view.

In the case of the Spanish generation of the 1950s, Rodrigo Mora's study is a first step, we believe, towards being able to say.

---

1   Introduction: the crisis of theory

In a collection of essays published not long ago in Spain, Pozuelo Yvancos (1999: 177–201) drew attention to the scarcity and/or dispersal of theoretical research in Spain on lyric poetry, from the 1950s through the 1970s. He noted that, although studies were numerous, they limited themselves to the analysis of compositional structures, whether metrical, syntactic-positional, or those of *ornatus*. This is quite the opposite of what happened in other disciplines, such as narratology and the semiotics of theatre, which received much in-depth scrutiny during this period. The marginal role that the lyric played in the field of fiction, perhaps because of the die-hard Romantic concept of the lyric as subjective expression, could well have been responsible. This lack of theoretical attention is, however, paradoxical, given that, for twentieth century critical movements in Spain, poetry was where investigation into poetic function and degrees of 'literality' in general took place.

Nonetheless, interaction between the theory of lyric poetry and its practice was not unduly hindered by this general absence of theory on poetic discourse. In fact, intercommunication between theory and creation '[…] has assumed that the lyric is the genre whose theory owes most to creation' (Pozuelo Yvancos, 1999: 180).[1]

Similarly to what happened in Italy with the *Gruppo 63*, neither the members of the 1950s' Spanish generation nor those of the 1970s, or even later generations ever drew up manifestos or joint programs articulating their ideas about poetry writing, although they did attempt to distance themselves both from the innovative poetic circles of the first half of the century as well as from the post-war, more socially committed poets. Neither, during the second half of the century in Spain, did any founding congress ever take place, at least not with the enormity or the ballyhoo that characterised the one that *Gruppo 63* organised in Palermo in 1963, where that celebrated Italian Neo avant-garde group fashioned its identity and objectives. Despite all this, Spain produced many self-reflective theoretical texts in which poets articulated their own, often insightful, meta-linguistic awareness of their art, as seems to have become conventional for the contemporary lyric elsewhere as well. In his introduction to two volumes containing an outstanding selection of Spanish poetry from the 1950s and 1970s, Pedro Provencio remarks the widespread editorial practice of including substantial theoretical material in the anthologies of the times, typically in the form of a *poética* or *cuestionario*:

> It is hard to doubt that these poets take the theorization of their poetry seriously. […] The transformations that the generation of the 50s were bringing about in Spanish poetry during the second half of the 60s, and the first part of the next decade, are in point of fact analyzed in the theoretical pages of their authors. These texts, which make up the bulk of this anthology, are a corpus with sufficient internal coherence to be able to, as indeed they ought to, shed light on developments in recent Spanish poetry. (1988 [1996]: 11)

I cite Provencio's collection of texts, not only because the editor makes access to what were scattered texts finally possible, but also because of his commentaries, incredibly articulate if one thinks of the inherent difficulty of his task, especially as far as the 1970s generation was concerned. Indeed, they lacked any common theoretical position, understandably, as the group was made up of poets with sometimes diametrically opposing views (Provencio, 1988 [1996]: 15).[2]

So then, even if there are obvious difficulties in dating its beginning, the rise of a new generation of lyric poets was formally recognised in 1963, with the publication of the anthology *Poesía Última* (*Last Poems*), edited by Francisco Ribes. Further evidence came in 1968 with the *Antología de la Nueva Poesía Española* (*Anthology of New Spanish Poetry*), edited by Luis Batlló. This included the most important poets of the second post-war generation, namely Ángel González, Carlos Sahagún, Claudio Rodríguez, José Ángel Valente, Jaime Gil de Biedma, Carlos Barral and Francisco Brines.

What do all these poets have in common, apart, that is, from the fact that they belong to the same generation and all critique the social poetry of the previous one? The response of most critics would be that their chief common theoretical interest lies in the notion of poetry-as-communication, which cannot fail to be of special interest to linguistic poetics. There are many texts on this subject, but the most useful for understanding the heated debate around the concept is the one published by Carlos Barral in *Laye*, in 1953, with the decidedly provocative title, *Poesía no es comunicación* (*Poetry is not Communication*), and *Conocimiento y comunicación* (*Knowledge and Communication*), by José Ángel Valente, published for the first time in Ribes's anthology in 1963.

2   Poetry-as-knowledge vs. Poetry-as-communication

In *Poesía no es comunicación*, Barral openly criticises Carlos Bousoño's (1952 [1976]) *Teoría de la expresión poética* (*Theory of Poetic Expression*), going so far as to denounce it for suggesting what he sees as a dangerous simplification of the creative process (Provencio, 1988 [1996]: 67). This is only the first in a series of proclamations that fast turned into a poetics of the 'text-as-knowledge' (Debicki, 1994 [1997]: 148), in clear opposition to that of 'text-as-communication'.

The knowledge-communication conflict received quite a lot of attention in the reflections of some of the most important linguists of the time in Spain. To begin with, Eugenio Coseriu, in 1966, in his collection of essays entitled *El hombre y su lenguaje* (*Man and his Language*), voices the opinion that language, even if 'autonomous', is only one type of knowledge of extralinguistic reality, and adds that:

> Language as such does not tell us much about specific objects, it can only represent them. Linguistic structuring is already knowledge, but no more than the first stage of it, a discriminating form of understanding in which something is being apprehended. (1966 [1977]: 45)

The most frequent opinion among critics is that the controversy which was stirred up by this debate was intellectually vacuous.[3] In my opinion, however, the debate may have simply begun too early, at least from the point of view of linguistic theory. In fact, it was only in the 1950s and 1960s that most theories about poetic language, and thus about artistic communication, were being developed within structuralism. It was only then that the assumptions of its linchpin, Russian Formalism, actually began to receive widespread attention in Spain.

In fact, Girón Alconchel (2000: 87), outlining the development of Spanish schools of grammar, confirms that structuralism arrived in Spain during the 1950s and that it met no resistance, was accepted immediately, and had enduring effects.[4] At the same time, however, a rather unorthodox attempt was undeniably made to mingle structuralism with the strong grammatical tradition of Spanish. One concrete example is Salvador Fernández Ramírez's *Gramática española*, published in 1951, with the clear aim of integrating modern linguistic tendencies into the description of Spanish, which is why it is considered not just one of the best Spanish grammars but also a linguistics treatise in its own right. Indeed, the text re-proposes concepts such as Bühler's deixis, Jespersen's theory of the three ranks, Harris's formal methods of distributionalism and Danish glossematics (López García, 2000: 13).

In *Teoría de la expresión poética*, published in 1952 as noted above, Bousoño begins by revising some of the key points of Saussure's theory. He agrees that language is a system of signs having relations among them, since he sees speakers giving the same meaning to them. However, he interprets Saussure as having affirmed that language is but a *reservoir* of signs, never an *act*, while Bousoño maintains that it is necessary to see it as both *reservoir* and *act* (1952 [1976]: 1, 98).[5]

Starting from his idea of language as communicative act – a notion that today might be better expressed with the term *discourse* (in the pragmatic sense, i.e. as both spoken and written language) – Bousoño goes on to identify *language* with *norm*, in order to make the key claim of his essay, i.e. that:

> [...] poetic work consists in modifying the *language*, in breaking away from the *norm*. The poet's task is to transform the meaning of the signs, or of the relation among the signs, i.e. of the *language* (as *norm*), as such a transformation defines poetry. (1952 [1976]: 1, 98–99, original emphasis)

In short, for Bousoño language as norm cannot be poetry, and so, to turn it into a tool for *making* poetry, it is necessary to transform it, using a series of procedures that he terms *substitutions* (1952 [1976]: 1, 103–104). Essentially, however, all that he's actually doing here is re-proposing the idea of the centrality of the rhetorical figure in poetic language.

In this way, Bousoño engages with the 'immanent theories' of literary language and, in particular, the key notion of 'deviation', observing (1952 [1976]: 1, 103–104, n. 7) that in *Art as Technique*, Shklovsky also talks about 'deviation from the linguistic norm', even if in different terms: those of 'defamiliarisation'. In this seminal essay (1965, 1968: 93), which was published in Moscow in 1929 but began to be accessible to Western Europe only in 1965, Shklovsky rejects all symbolic interpretations of verbal art and attempts to explain in technical terms how this is constructed, since for him the most important thing about verbal art is that it is *made*.[6]

Nevertheless, Bousoño insists that he had formulated his idea about 'substitutions' in 1952, when the first edition of his book was published, while Russian Formalism only became accessible in Europe in 1955, with the translation into English of Victor Erlich's work, *Russian Formalism*. In short, he claims the autonomy of his work, adding that there are additional important differences from a theoretical point of view, since the Russian theorist had no notion comparable to his 'individualisation'.

The immediate negative reaction in Spain to Bousoño's theoretical position is hardly surprising, as it touched upon the very notion of poetic 'creation', about which many of his contemporaries felt very differently. For instance, in *Poesía no es comunicación* (1953; see *Carlos Barral* in Provencio, 1988

[1996]: 61–72), Barral sketches an essentially negative picture of post-war Spanish lyric poetry and its theory, denouncing the predominance of what he calls a series of 'theoretical phantoms', like the notions of 'message', 'communication' or the 'accessibility' of the text to all readers. What is hidden beneath such labels, he objects, is the authors' utter subjection to a not very demanding poetic addressee.

As far as the term *communication* is concerned, Barral recognises it as a common term used by one of Spain's greatest poets, and his own mentor, Vicente Aleixandre, but suggests that its meaning had been distorted as a result of having been injected with a pseudo-scientific sense by Bousoño, who he also accuses of seeing poetry as simply some sort of higher degree of linguistic expressiveness. So it is that Barral rejects the notion of poetry as the communication of ideas, in the well-known tradition of the Anglo-American New Critics (see García Barrientos, 1996: 69).

One obviously has to take into account that the Spanish poets' use of the term 'communication' in this early 1950s' debate is an exceedingly broad one. They never took it upon themselves to formulate the concept scientifically, as they felt that this was the domain of the linguists, one which indeed would be dealt with by structuralists and functionalists some years later.

In the first edition of his essay (see Provencio, 1988 [1996]: 66), Barral strongly criticises Bousoño's definition of the poetic act: i.e. '[...] the verbal transmission of a complex psychic reality, previously known by the soul in its entirety, a synthesis to which a certain measure of enjoyment is later added'. Barral is hostile to what he sees as three premises implicit in this characterisation: firstly, he denies the pre-existence of a psychic content, calling it a Romantic notion antedating Symbolism. Secondly, he refutes such an oversimplification of the communicative process; and, finally, he criticises what he feels is a neglect of the problem of poetic understanding. For Barral:

> Lyric poetry does not consist in the translation, by way of some superior linguistic process, of a prior intuition of a psychic state that is then identified and re-lived by the reader, owing solely to the language construing the poem. [...] The poet is unaware of the lyric content of the poem before the existence of the poem itself. (Provencio, 1988 [1996]: 67)

Two years later, Gil de Biedma tried to refine the terms of the concept of poetry-as-communication in his Prologue to T. S. Eliot's, *The Use of Poetry and The Use of Criticism* (1933), published in Spain in 1955 with the title, *Función de la poesía y función de la crítica* (see *Jaime Gil de Biedma* in Provencio, 1988 [1996]: 113–131). The less radical Biedma also completely rejected the idea that poetry has essentially but one communicative function, and hypothesises four different kinds of artistic communication. It is worth taking a moment to consider the ideas of this poet, who was unanimously recognised as the 'master' of the new generation.

Biedma firstly considers the most straightforward concept of communication, which, he says, he derives from Tolstoy. This consists in evoking a feeling that has been experienced by the author and then transmitting it in a way that allows others to experience the same feeling. He raises the objection that the phases following the initial experience of that particular feeling, i.e. evocation and transmission, cannot be seen as 'communication' in the strict sense of the word. Rather, they consist only in the transmission of the representation of this complex psychic reality, since the feeling actually experienced by the poet cannot ever be truly reproduced.

Secondly, Biedma tackles the idea of communication, and associates it with Surrealist poetry. Such communication expresses psychic states which have been modified linguistically and formally, in, as it were, some sort of 'magma', through what he terms the automatic writing procedure. The original so-called 'magma' is seen as containing a clear emotional sign that translates into poetry through the rhythm of the creative process.

Biedma believes that his third concept – poetry-as-knowledge-in-itself – is the most genuine kind of communication. If the poem is being written to delineate and direct emotion, then it will also help the author to communicate with him/herself. It is in this way that poetry can be considered a kind of knowledge, or understanding. The idea may seem to us to be overly subjective, but Biedma elsewhere states the view that art is objective, especially if considered from the reader's point of view, since to read means to experience an emotional state that has nothing to do with one's individual, everyday feelings.

Finally, the author and the reader are seen as approaching the poem and communicating with it independently. Consequently, what is needed first of all is the author's will to write the poem, and then the reader's willingness to read it. This then would be a sort of 'aesthetic' communication.

Biedma reaches the conclusion that communication is only one element of poetry and that it cannot, in any case, be the main one. However, he asks himself:

> If poetry is neither communication nor knowledge, then what is it? I don't know and I'm not even sure that it would be useful to know […]. All art is the work of human beings and thus it is basically impure, i.e. complex; and poetry, because of the material it works with, is the most impure of all. (Provencio, 1988 [1996]: 125)

In the 1950s, however, it was José Ángel Valente (see *José Ángel Valente* in Provencio, 1988 [1996]: 91–111) who was to most radically reject the concept of poetry-as-communication. This he did in *Conocimiento y comunicación*, published for the first time in Ribes's anthology in 1963 and reprinted as the cornerstone of Valente's critical work, *Las palabras de la tribu* (1971) (*The Words of the Tribe*). In this essay, Valente sees communication as the *end product* of poetic creation, leaving intact the nature of the creative process itself, which, for him, should be the cornerstone of verbal art. He would put a similar focus on linguistic process. For him, the methodological inflation of the 1950s, including structural taxonomies, the principles of behaviourist psychology and of the mathematical theory of communication, had all wrongly privileged the utilitarian and goal-oriented aspects of language.

Nevertheless, in Valente's perhaps less than well-versed view, Generativism leaves room for the most creative aspects, and linguistics, as Chomsky proposes, should indeed be seen as one branch of the psychology of knowledge. [7] Thus Valente sees Mentalism as a positive theoretical innovation, one which, as we know, sparked off a fierce debate in linguistics at the time (Formigari, 2004: 252).

Valente's tacit adhesion to a rational-based, mentalist conception of language led him to make connections between science and poetry. He saw the age-old opposition between these as having been attenuated, since Mentalism recognised that both were vast symbolic systems that acted on reality in similar ways, despite inherent dissimilarities. On the one hand, scientific knowledge is analytic and subject to laws derived from experimentation and verification; these laws are established thanks to the possibility of replicating a well-designed experiment and, as a result, certain consequences can be foreseen. Conversely, poetic knowledge is synthetic and characterised by its uniqueness; it is neither replicable nor controllable. Thus language can be seen as a continuum, with scientific prose located at one end, as one kind of 'norm', and poetic language at the opposite end, as another (Alarcón Castañer, 1998: 44).

The alliance and/or opposition between poetry and science, with only tangential reference to the issue of knowledge, is a topic Brines also comes to consider many years later, in 1984, though his reflections lead him to conclusions quite the opposite from Valente's. In fact, in Brines's opinion (see *Francisco Brines* in Provencio, 1988 [1996]: 141–163), poetry's inherent ambiguity is anathema to scientific truth. In his view, the poet always explores his own inner world, even when his subject is all humankind, while a scientist is characteristically at the service of a human community. Even the functions of their languages, in his estimation, clash. The poet can discover 'truth' only through language itself; the scientist can do so only in the service of a scientific truth which has already been recognised. So, Brines ultimately concludes: 'Science must convince, while poetry need only appeal' (Provencio, 1988 [1996]: 158–159).

But to go back to Valente's ideas: despite recognising the ambiguity of poetry, with reference to the question of knowledge or understanding, he theorises 'the law of necessity', according to which some aspects of experience can be known only through poetry. The poet has only ill-defined material to work with; creation will occur by means of the poet's only available tool: language. Yet, this shapeless material cannot be likened to what Gil de Biedma called 'magma' in describing surrealist poetry, where he openly drew parallels with automatic writing. Valente concludes that:

> Thus each poem is an exploration of previously-unknown experience. This is what it deals with. The more or less complete understanding of such experience means that the poem itself will only be more or less complete. That's why the poetic creative process is a process of knowing in progress: a dynamic exploration in which the definition of each single element will have an impact on all others. (Provencio, 1988 [1996]: 98)

Not only did the concept of poetry-as-knowledge act to undermine that of poetry-as-communication,[8] which had previously been predominant in Spain, but it also subverted the traditional modern poetics of literature, since it denied a previously existent stable meaning which one could count on remaining fixed in the text (Debicki, 1994 [1997]:149).[9] In the heat of this controversy, Carlos Bousoño felt obliged to intervene, which is why, in *Teoría de la expresión poética* (1952 [1976]: 1, 26–27), he firstly re-proposed Novalis' denial that poetry 'communicates' anything at all, and then declared that the way he had used the word 'communication' in the first 1952 edition of his book had been incorrectly interpreted by the critics, as he had never meant it to mean 'the authentic communication of the author'. He added that, in the second edition (1956), he had clearly argued the essentially imaginary nature of the work of art.[10]

This debate profoundly marked aesthetic and linguistic thought in Spain during the early part of the second half of the last century and, although the debate seemed to have died down with time, two decades later, Lázaro Carreter (1980 [1987]: 159) still felt the need to express, and strongly, an opinion on the topic. He stated that art is quite probably 'necessary', but that this necessity has nothing to do with knowledge, since the reader doesn't come to literature in an effort at knowing, but rather by chance, or out of affection, and/or curiosity.

3   On poetic reception

The poets of the 1950s, owing to their belief in the autonomy of poetry, emphasised the reader's role in a totally novel way, which was indeed close to the current ideas of the postmodern period. Debicki (1994 [1997]: 150–151), and also US Spanish scholars on the whole, point out that some of the ideas that critics see as fundamental to postmodern theory can, indeed, already be found in this generation of poets. For instance, they put forth the notion of the indeterminacy of the poetic text, reasoning that both writing and reading are creative processes which make the literary work a work-in-progress rather than a finished product, complete and whole in itself. Because of this tension in the creative act, parody and a strongly meta-poetic approach seemed to them essential. This we can take for granted, as we have clear evidence that the so-called *postnovísimos*, the younger poets of the 1960s and 1970s, had unproblematically accepted the fundamentals of the postmodern movement (Ceserani, 1997). On the other hand, due to the influence of French culture in Spain, it is also probable that these poets had read Sartre's famous *Qu'est-ce que la littérature* (*What is Literature?*) published in 1947, in which the French philosopher emphasises that writing and reading are but opposites sides of the same coin, since for him art exists *for* the 'other' and *through* the 'other'. Writing implies a dialectical relationship with reading, not as a mechanical act, but as a creative one (Sartre, 1947 [1969]: 58–62).[11]

Bousoño, in his *Teoria de la expresión poética* (1952 [1976]: 2, 42–43) distances himself from Sartre's claims by asserting the possibility for the writer to be, at one and the same time, both the author and reader of his own work, by virtue of his/her capacity for creative imagination. However, even a superficial comparison of *Qu'est-ce que la littérature* and Barral's article of 1953, *Conocimiento y comunicación*, clearly reveals that he appropriates most of Sartre's general ideas, except for the plainly Marxist ones, e.g. the ones linking literature with the fate of the working class. Barral asserts:

> The poet ignores the lyric content of the poem until the poem *is*. Similarly, the poem being read demands that the reader contribute the whole of his/her lyrical 'baggage', a collaborative effort that engages the whole of his/her own private and poetic experiences. Poetic reading is a true poetic act, similar to the creator's, though in a different relation to the poem. And, sterile reading exists just as much as sterile writing does. (Provencio, 1988 [1996]: 67–68)

Between the lines here one may infer a certain lack of confidence in the reader's fulfilling such high expectations, not unlike Sartre's own (1947 [1969]:

58–62), or something similar to what Carlos Sahagún suggests may be the reader's incapacity to decode the implicit ambiguities of a poem. And yet, there's a new and essential twist in Sahagún's way of seeing things: '[…] the potentially 'bad' reader, who would force his/her narrow idea of meaning on the poet, may also happen to be a good judge, at least of prose' (Provencio, 1988 [1996]: 197).

All in all, the importance that is still being given here to the reading of the author's intended meanings is evident, but we're still very far from Lotman's theory of 'noise', according to which the reader's incompetence, much like temporal distance or some other perturbation of the communication, can somehow be turned into information (Lotman, 1970 [1982]: 101).

A completely different point of view on the subject is expressed by Goytisolo (see *José Agustín Goytisolo* in Provencio, 1988 [1996]: 73–89), who thinks that in order to create his/her own formal language, the poet primarily has to: 1) keep up with the technological developments in mass media; 2) improve and revise his own poetic language, and then 3) adapt it for expression in any and all possible ways. This idea also finds a parallel in Sartre, for whom one of the writer's tasks is to educate the masses, using every kind of media at hand.

For his part, Brines underlines the reader's role, granting him/her a large amount of interpretative freedom. To distinguish between what he dubs 'the public' from the reader, however, he borrows a paradoxical expression from the Andalusian poet, Juan Ramón Jiménez, namely, the *inmensa minoría* ('immense minority'). Indeed, for Brines, one of the greatest advantages of poetry, in comparison with other genres, is its *lack* of a public, or at least of publicity, which happily keeps it from being treated like consumer goods (Provencio, 1988 [1996]: 154–160).

But then there is Valente, who speaks of the hypothetically perfect reader and reckons that, even if the latter could never truly experience a writer's subjective emotions, s/he would have no trouble recognising the particular angle on reality that a poet reveals in a poem. Valente concludes that a poet does not write for any one person in particular, but rather for the multitude, in which s/he too is obviously numbered (Provencio, 1988 [1996]: 100–101).

From a strictly linguistic point of view, the most interesting remarks are Barral's. His position is that a good poem replenishes the linguistic experience of each reader, because in this genre language is used non-conventionally, and such ways of saying create meanings that belong no longer to the poet, but to the reader (Provencio 1988 [1996]: 70).

4 On context

Another important theme of debate in the 1950s generation which should at least be briefly mentioned, concerns context, which is seen by most of these poets, at least until the 1970s, as being largely historical in nature.[12] Yet, because this generation wanted to distinguish itself from the previous militant left-wing one, their definition of context had to be circumscribed. In 1965, Carlos Sahagún stated that 'All poetry that tells the story of wo/man in history is social', although he also expressed what he called the 'liberal' hope that, with time, social poetry would take upon itself the task of 'disclosing the corruption and fundamental failings of bourgeois society' (Provencio, 1988 [1996]: 200). In the same year, González says something not dissimilar (see *Ángel González* in Provencio 1988 [1996]: 19–41), when he asserts his belief in a critical poetry that would position wo/man in the context of the problems of his/her time, although context will always exert its unavoidable pressures on a writer.

And yet, in some extreme cases, poetry is declared to be a sort of *a-history*, or rather, *History* with a capital H, having however indeterminate boundary lines, almost as though the concept of history were a mere abstraction. This idea is expressed by Goytisolo in his poem 'Así son', in *Bajo tolerancia* (1974) (*Low Tolerance*), with these lines: 'His profession you know it's really old/and it's lasted so far without changing/through centuries and civilizations' – ending with the less than flattering observation: 'Such are poets/the old prostitutes of History' (Provencio, 1988 [1996]: 81–82). Brines expresses a similar idea, stressing, however, the historical necessity of poetry, offering the evidence of '[…] its constant presence in all cultures, from the most primitive to the most elaborate, without exception' (Provencio, 1988 [1996]: 160). Barral adds his thoughts on the subject: 'Poetry is and will always be concerned with modes of existence that are not codified by culture' (Provencio, 1988 [1996]: 70). These non-codified ways of being thus become culture by means of their poetic voicing. And so, for both Brines and Barral, poetry is essential to any cultural system, though the former puts the accent on the resulting product, and the latter on the process.

5 Conclusion

Even from this brief excursus into the meta-textual musings of the poets that start publishing in the 1950s in Spain, the paramount importance they give to the linguistic aspects of the lyrical process should be evident. It actually seems that their poetry can only come about after they've succeeded in pin-pointing the connection between a theory of language and their own creative impulses.

Yet, it's equally important to keep in mind that these poets' thoughts were rooted in a philosophical tradition, rather than in a concrete linguistics, but also that some of the arguments put forth in the knowledge-communication debate could be said to be less than firmly rooted ontologically. Witness the concern with whether or not it's possible to obtain a knowledge of 'reality' by means of the creative process, and whether or not it's possible for poetic discourse to ever really represent existential experience. In spite of all this, however, the attraction the concrete moment of the creation of verbal art had for the *Generación del 50*, as well as their fascination with questions such as poetic reception and social function, and thus also with the reader, makes them essential for any understanding of the evolution of Spanish literary language.

As I've already intimated, these poets were far from having any desire to substitute the linguists at their job, but their meta-poetic reflections and their poetics for their times contained, and in part I think still do, an admonishment of the various schools of linguistics. What they ask is that the linguists give, or at least attempt to give, some answers (theoretical to the degree they want, but systematic) to the many questions posed by poetic creation, the raw material of which is always, after all, language.

Notes

1   Pozuelo Yvancos (1999: 180) specifies that this phenomenon has its origin in Romanticism, when many artists were at the same time poets and philosophers (Goethe, Coleridge, Hugo, etc.). Nevertheless, as Segre reminds us (1985: 297–300), from a historic point of view, literary manifestos criticising the existing literary system in a diachronic perspective, while also urging a renewal of existing models, had begun to spread from the sixteenth century on. The manifestos contrasted with the *poetics*, which were more conservative, as well as synchronic, in their description of the literary system. Segre concludes that:

> 'Whoever operates within a poetic produces innovations, especially formal ones, but without believing that these will undermine the prevailing world view. It will then be time itself that will tell if, at some point, quantitative innovation produces a qualitative leap: i.e. if it expresses and validates modifications of that world view'. (1985: 300)

My heartfelt thanks go to Simona Cocco of the University of Sassari and to the editors of this volume for their scrupulous work of translating my paper, and all works cited, from the original Spanish and Italian into English.

2   See Provencio's anthology for bibliographical references to the authors' works mentioned and discussed below (Provencio, 1988).

3   José Olivio Jiménez minimises its importance :

'It is actually absurd that this theme was debated in such a heated manner, since the idea of poetry-as-communication, originally attributed to a *dictum* by Vicente Aleixandre and theoretically developed by Carlos Bousoño, was necessary and appropriate when it was formulated for the first time [...] never was it forgotten that poetry is, in the first place, a way to know reality, a supreme and exceptional tool for acquiring knowledge.' (1998: 23)

Moreover, according to Jiménez, the theoretical foundation for this generation is Enrique Badosa's 1958 essay, 'Primero hablemos de Júpiter. La poesía como medio de conocimiento' ('First we should speak of Jupiter. Poetry as a means of knowing') (1998: 2–27, n. 5).

4   It was Emilio Alarcos Llorach who paved the way for the arrival of structuralism in Spain. He adapted the structuralism of the Prague Linguists in his *Fonología* (1950). He later tried to implement Hjelmslev's glossematics into his *Gramática estructural* (1969). For an updated account of the history of grammar in Spain, see Girón Alconchel (2000).

5   Bousoño (1952 [1976]: 1, 98, n. 2), rightly or wrongly, argues:

'My own distinction is therefore truly different. Saussurian terminology does not help me because I don't take into consideration every individual gesticulation, every individual intonation of words etc., in language; these elements, as I've already said, do not have a role in poetry with "individualization".'

Bousoño believes that it's fundamental to keep the collective linguistic heritage, the whole tradition, in mind, not only as a linguistic patrimony, but also as a poetic one. Félix Martínez Bonati strongly criticises Bousoño's conception of poetry, dedicating to it a whole chapter of his famous, *La estructura de la obra literaria* (*The Structure of the Literary Work*), published for the first time in Chile in 1960. More specifically, he considers the distinction Bousoño draws between himself and Saussure as unnecessary and ambiguous, because it would mean equating *langue* to the *normal use of words* (Martínez Bonati, 1960 [1972]: 192).

6   Included by Todorov in *Théorie de la littérature*, published in Paris in 1965. All quotations are taken from the Italian edition in Todorov (1968: 73–94). One of the popular English translations is from 1965: *Art as Technique*. In L. T. Lemon and M. J. Reis (eds and trans.) *Russian Formalist Criticism: Four Essays* 3–57. Lincoln: University of Nebraska Press. Miller (this volume) also refers to this notion of Shklovsky's with reference to the poetry of D. H. Lawrence.

7   One can't avoid noticing Valente's interest in novelty in linguistic development. It was R. Hadlich who first applied the standard model of Generativism to Spanish in 1971. His work was published in Spain two years later with the title *Gramática transformativa del español* (1973) (*Spanish Transformational Grammar*). The result was undoubtedly so mediocre that some linguists actually blame it for hindering the fortunes of Generativism in Spain (López García, 2000: 17–18).

8   Other opinions on the subject include Claudio Rodríguez's (Provencio, 1988 [1996]: 165–180). In his piece in Ribes's anthology, he describes poetic activity as the '[...] connection the poet sets up, by means of language, between things and his poetic experience of them'. For Carlos Sahagún (Provencio, 1988 [1996]: 193–202), the poet, albeit concerned in some way with communication, is mainly dedicated to acquiring knowledge and self-confidence by means of a no better defined 'search in the dark'.

9   Debicki (1994 [1997]: 149) quotes Badosa, who affirmed the autonomy of the text: 'When I talk about poetic knowledge, I do so without thinking about the poet at all [...] but only of the perception and understanding which occur despite the poet not being able to keep track of them'.

10   On Félix Martínez Bonati's critique in *La estructura de la obra literaria*, Bousoño (1952 [1976]:1, 27, n. 13), says that 'Even if Martínez Bonati's book is dated 1960, it refers to the first edition of my *Teoría de la expresión poética*, i.e. that of 1952, and not to the second, 1956, edition'. In the sixth edition, Bousoño articulates his position even further:

> 'As far as the essence of the 'poetic' is concerned, it cannot be said that there is any real communication, *but only that there seems to be*; *you have the illusion that there is*. One can imagine this communication, and sometimes this is quite enough, *since this is essentially what the poet is aiming for. In fact, the poet tries to truly communicate an imaginary state of mind to others by means of mere words.*' (1952 [1976]: 1, 44, original emphasis)

11   In 1967, when Weinrich argued his reasons for writing a history of reading literature using the predominant textual linguistics approach, he also referred to this essay by Sartre as the first study to initiate twentieth century critical reflection on the reader's reception (1967 [1989]: 27–32).

12   With reference to the extra-linguistic approach to context adopted by the poets of this generation, it may be useful to recall Raffaele Simone's (2003: 76) distinction between utterances that refer to their own linguistic context and those that refer to an external, 'objective' one:

> 'Animal codes seem to be sensitive to context only in the second sense (i.e. they are externally contextual); on the other hand, the mathematical code seems to be sensitive to context only in the first sense (i.e. internally contextual). Only human languages are sensitive to both, and so at the same time, internally and externally contextual (or 'strongly' contextual).'

References

Alarcón Castañer, P. (1998) *Niveles de lengua. Análisis lingüístico-literario en la poesía española*. Málaga: Universidad de Málaga.
Alarcos Llorach, E. (1950) *Fonología*. Madrid: Gredos.
Alarcos Llorach, E. (1969) *Gramática estructural*. Madrid: Gredos.

Alvar, M. (ed.) (2000) *Introducción a la lingüística española*. Barcelona: Ariel.

Badosa, E. (1998) Primero hablemos de Júpiter (La poesía como medio de conocimiento). *Papeles de Son Armadans* 10. 28: 32–46; 29: 135–159.

Batlló, L. (ed.) (1968) *Antología de la Nueva Poesía Española*. Madrid: Ciencia Nueva.

Bousoño, C. (1952 [1976]) *Teoría de la expresión poética*. Vols. 1 & 2. Madrid: Gredos.

Cabo Aseguinolaza, F. (ed.) (1999) *Teorías sobre la lírica*. Madrid: Arco/Libros.

Ceserani, R. (1997) Raccontare il postmoderno. Torino: Bollati Boringhieri.

Coseriu, E. (1966 [1977]) *El hombre y su lenguaje. Estudios de teoría y metodología lingüística*. Madrid: Gredos.

Debicki, A. P. (1994 [1997]) *Historia de la poesía española del siglo XX*. Madrid: Gredos.

Eliot, T. S. (1933) *The Use of Poetry and the Use of Criticism*. London: Faber & Faber; Cambridge, Mass: Harvard University Press.

Erlich, V. (1955 [1974]) *El formalismo ruso*, Barcelona: Seix Barral.

Fernández Ramírez, S. (1951 [1985–1987]) *Gramática española*. J. Polo and I. Bosque (eds) Madrid: Arco/Libros.

Formigari, L. (2004) *Il linguaggio. Storia delle teorie*. Bari: Laterza.

García Barrientos, J. L. (1996) *El lenguaje literario.1. La comunicación literaria*. Madrid: Arco/Libros.

Girón Alconchel, J. L. (2000) Historia de la gramática en España. In M. Alvar (ed.) *Introducción a la lingüística española* 69–91. Barcelona: Ariel.

Hadlich, R. (1973) *Gramática transformativa del español*. Madrid: Gredos.

Holub, R. C. (ed.) (1989) *Teoria della ricezione*. Torino: Einaudi.

Jiménez, J. O. (1998) *Diez años decisivos en la poesía española contemporánea, 1960–1970*. Madrid: Rialp.

Lázaro Carreter, F. (1980 [1987]) La literatura como fenómeno comunicativo. In J. A. Mayoral (ed.) *Pragmática de la comunicación literaria* 151–170. Madrid: Arco/Libros.

López García, Á. (2000) Teoría gramatical. In M. Alvar (ed.) *Introducción a la lingüística española* 7–22. Barcelona: Ariel.

Lotman, Y. M. (1970 [1982]) *Estructura del texto artístico*. Madrid: Istmo.

Martínez Bonati, F. (1960 [1972]) *La estructura de la obra literaria*. Barcelona: Seix Barral.

Mayoral, J. A. (ed.) (1987) *Pragmática de la comunicación literaria*. Madrid: Arco/Libros.

Pozuelo Yvancos, J. M. (1999) Pragmática, poesía e metapoesía en *El poeta* de V. Aleixandre. In F. Cabo Aseguinolaza (ed.) *Teorías sobre la lírica* 177–201. Madrid: Arco/Libros.

Provencio, P. (ed.) (1988 [1996]) *Poéticas españolas contemporáneas* Volume I: *La generación del 50*. Madrid: Hiperión.

Provencio, P. (ed.) (1988) *Poéticas españolas contemporáneas* Volume II: *La generación del 70*. Madrid: Hiperión.

Ribes, F. (1963) *Poesía Última*. Madrid: Taurus.

Sartre, J-P. (1947 [1969]) *Qu'est-ce que la littérature*. Paris: Gallimard.

Segre, C. (1985) *Avviamento all'analisi del testo letterario*. Torino: Einaudi.

Shklovsky, V. (1965) Art as Technique. In L. T. Lemon and M. J. Reis (eds and trans.) *Russian Formalist Criticism*: *Four Essays* 3–57. Lincoln: University of Nebraska Press. [Italian: (1965 [1968]) L'arte come procedimento. In T. Todorov (ed.) 73–94. Torino: Einaudi.]

Simone, R. (2003) *Fondamenti di linguistica*. Bari: Laterza.

Todorov, T. (ed.) (1965 [1968]) *I formalisti russi. Teoria della letteratura e metodo critico*. Torino: Einaudi.

Valente, J. A. (1971) *Las palabras de la tribu*. Madrid: Siglo XXI.

Weinrich, H. (1967 [1989]) Per una storia letteraria del lettore. In R. C. Holub (ed.) *Teoria della ricezione* 27–42. Torino: Einaudi.

Author index

CPSIA information can be obtained
at www.ICGtesting.com
Printed in the USA
BVHW091217170722
642125BV00002B/27